AMERICAN NIGHTMARE

RANDAL O'TOOLE

AMERICAN NIGHTMARE

HOW GOVERNMENT UNDERMINES
THE DREAM OF HOMEOWNERSHIP

CATO
INSTITUTE
WASHINGTON, D.C.

Library of Congress Cataloging-in-Publication Data

O'Toole, Randal.
    American nightmare : how government undermines the dream of home
ownership / by Randal O'Toole.
        p. cm.
    Includes bibliographical references and indexes.
    ISBN 978-1-937184-88-9 (hardback : alk. paper)
    1. Home ownership—United States. 2. Housing policy—United States.
3. House buying—United States. I. Title.

HD7287.82.U6O86 2012
333.33'80973—dc23

                                                                          2012012197

Printed in the United States of America.

                            CATO INSTITUTE
                    100 Massachusetts Ave., N.W.
                        Washington, D.C. 20001
                            www.cato.org

Dedicated to the memory of my friend Chris Walker, whose work on land-use and transportation issues should inspire everyone who supports free markets and freedom of choice.

Contents

Figures

Contents

Introduction

Along with millions of other Americans, I watched in shock and awe as the world's financial markets melted down in September 2008. The knowledge that this was the beginning of a major recession was especially heartbreaking because several of my colleagues and I had been warning people of this imminent collapse, and ways to prevent it, for several years.[1] Most recently, my 2007 Cato Institute book, *The Best-Laid Plans*, argued that "planning-induced housing bubbles . . . are threatening the world economy," and the inevitable collapse of those bubbles would "cause the world to go into a severe recession."[2]

Numerous researchers have shown that government regulation has made American housing unnecessarily expensive and made many regional housing markets prone to bubbles. In recent years, the focus of state and local land-use regulation has been a war on sprawl that, in practice, became a war on single-family homes. Because 84 percent of people living in single-family homes own those homes, compared with just 14 percent of people living in multifamily housing, a war on single-family homes was a war on homeownership.

In 1997, for example, planners in my former hometown of Portland, Oregon, set a target of reducing the share of Portland-area households who lived in single-family detached homes from 68 percent in 1995 to 41 percent by 2040. If they are successful, hundreds of thousands of people who would have preferred single-family homes will be stuck in apartments instead.[3] To achieve this goal, they limited the land available for new single-family homes while they used tax dollars to subsidize construction of multifamily dwellings. Similar plans have been or are being written for cities and metropolitan areas across the nation.

In places with relatively unregulated housing markets, housing is inexpensive, and when demand increases—whether because of population growth, low interest rates, or loosened lending standards— homebuilders build more homes. When new single-family homes

1

are restricted, housing becomes expensive, and increases in demand lead to higher prices rather than more housing, while decreases in demand result in lower prices—in other words, a housing bubble. The lesson I learned from the housing bubble was that the American dream of owning a single-family home is so powerful that many Americans will go to extraordinary lengths to achieve that dream, including dedicating more than half their incomes to 30-year mortgages on those homes. But many other people learned a very different lesson: the mantra they repeated over and over was "As much as they might want to, some people shouldn't try to own their homes."

"Homeownership has let us down," said *Time* magazine. "The dark side of homeownership is now all too apparent: foreclosures and walkaways, neighborhoods plagued by abandoned properties and plummeting home values, a nation in which families have $6 trillion less in housing wealth than they did just three years ago."[4] When the Census Bureau reported American homeownership rates had fallen from 69 percent in 2004 to 65 percent in 2010, housing economist Ryan McMaken responded that "the present rate needs to drop even more."[5] "The poor are better off renting," agreed an op-ed in the *Wall Street Journal*.[6]

"Homeownership is overrated," says urban planner Richard Florida. "Too many people in economically distressed communities are trapped in homes they can't sell, unable to move on to new centers of opportunity." Florida thinks more people should rent and that we should "updat[e] our definition of the American dream."[7]

Is the American dream of homeownership dead? "In my opinion the American Dream as we know it *is* dead," wrote financial adviser Suze Orman. "In many areas of the country, the dream of homeownership has backfired. Real estate values have deflated to such an extent that a record number of people owe more than their homes are worth."[8]

American Nightmare explores the questions raised by the debate over homeownership. What is the "right" homeownership rate? Is "universal homeownership" possible or even desirable? What roles do the mortgage-interest deduction, Federal Housing Administration mortgage insurance, and other government housing programs play in influencing peoples' decisions to buy rather than rent their homes? What are the real lessons of the housing-market crash? To answer these questions, this book looks at the history of homeownership and its role in people's lives and the economy as a whole.

As recently as 250 years ago, it is likely that fewer than 1 percent of the world's families lived in their own homes. Even just 25 years ago, homeownership was a privilege enjoyed by only a small minority of people. Today, at least 60 percent of the world's families own their own homes, and the percentage in many countries is much higher.

The United States was long a leader in this remarkable transformation. Throughout much of the 20th century, high U.S. homeownership rates contributed to the nation's booming economy, encouraging other countries to remove local barriers to homeownership. But homeownership in this country may be little more than an accident of history. At the time the New World was being colonized, nearly everyone in Europe effectively rented their lands from their monarch, and many Dutch, French, and Spanish land grants in North America followed this pattern. But in 1629, King Charles I of England offered Massachusetts colonists "fee simple" land—that is, the opportunity to own land after paying a single fee rather than annual rents. Soon after the American Revolution, this form of land tenure became dominant in the United States, and Europeans, Asians, and others who wanted to own rather than rent land came to America for the opportunity to do so.

As late as the 1960s, America's homeownership rate of more than 60 percent was one of the highest in the world. But at 65 percent today, America is barely in the middle of the pack. In the 60-some countries for which homeownership rates can be accurately determined, more than 75 percent of people live in their own homes. The fact that almost all those countries have lower per capita incomes than those in the United States flies in the face of the idea that American rates should be even lower because some people are too poor to afford a house.

Three different themes weave through *American Nightmare*'s exploration of this history. First, homeownership provides many benefits, particularly for the children in homeowning families. Yet the main benefits of homeownership accrue to the homeowners and their families, so there is little reason for government to subsidize or otherwise promote homeownership. Instead, government should get out of the way and let people decide to buy or rent depending on their personal needs and the real costs of each of the alternatives. If this happens, the United States will likely end up with a higher rate of homeownership even if today's subsidies and political support for homeownership are eliminated.

Second, the recent financial crash did not result, as many believe, from a political effort to increase homeownership. Instead, it would be more accurate to say that the housing bubble and inevitable crash that followed resulted from a tension between federal policies aimed at increasing homeownership and state and local policies aimed at reducing homeownership. It would be even more accurate to say that the policies aimed at reducing homeownership caused the bubble, while some of the policies aimed at increasing it might have made the bubble worse than it otherwise would have been. But without the policies aimed at limiting homeownership, no housing bubble and no financial crisis would have occurred.

Finally, this book reveals that many of the superficially noble debates over housing, homeownership, and land use are really a form of class warfare in which members of the upper and middle classes attempt to shield their privileges, status, and lifestyles from the working and lower classes. One way of doing so is to promote policies that reduce homeownership—policies that were an underlying cause of the recent financial crisis, yet are overlooked by writers and analysts who have looked at that crisis and made recommendations for preventing future crises. Unless states and cities reverse these anti-homeownership policies, more housing bubbles and crashes are inevitable.

In short, homeownership did not let us down; government planners did by trying to discourage single-family homeownership. Their actions led to the housing bubble whose inevitable deflation was the catalyst for the financial crisis of 2008. This consequence suggests that it is both condescending and defeatist to think that some people should spend most or all of their lives as renters.

Why would anyone want to reduce homeownership? Around four out of five Americans own or dream of owning their own homes. But not all are certain they want *you* to own your own home. Many are certain they *don't* want you to own a home near them—or on any land they regard as "theirs," which can include millions of acres they don't own but feel entitled to control to protect the pastoral or other scenic values they gain from that land. Debates over who gets to own a home, and where they can own it, fill a large portion of this book.

The term "American dream" was coined and popularized by an early 20th-century history writer named James Truslow Adams. His 1931 book *The Epic of America* used the phrase "American dream" more than 30 times and defined that phrase as "the belief in the value of the common man, and the hope of opening every avenue of opportunity to him."[9] Adams, in fact, wanted to name his book *The American Dream*, but his editor argued, "No one will pay three dollars for a book about a dream." The editor was soon proved wrong, as the Library of Congress today lists more than 700 books whose titles contain the term "American dream" that were published after 1931 (and none before).[10]

Adams's book did not specifically mention homeownership as a part of the American dream. Instead, he focused on "the belief in the common man and the insistence upon his having, as far as possible, equal opportunity in every way with the rich one." One of those opportunities was the opportunity to own a home and a piece of land—a desire, other writers have shown, that extends far back into the nation's history.

Thanks in part to advertising campaigns by realtors and home-builders, the American dream has become indelibly associated with homeownership in the public mind. But the American dream is more than just an advertising slogan: homeownership was originally an immigrants' dream, as the opportunity to own land and a home attracted people from European and Asian nations where most residents were denied such opportunities through the end of the 19th century. Although Americans were once proud of providing that opportunity, for more than a century cities and states have passed ordinances and laws whose effective result, if not outright purpose, has been to reduce homeownership.

Homeownership did not become a middle-class dream until developers and planners figured out how to protect homes and neighborhoods from unwanted intrusions, such as factories, shops, and—ironically perhaps—working-class homes owned or occupied by immigrants and minorities. Unfortunately, the long-term result was to blanket much of the nation with land-use regulations that ended up making housing far less affordable.

Without this government regulation, anyone who could pay rent and come up with a modest down payment would be able to afford to buy a home if they want one. Not everyone wants to be a homeowner, and the debate over whether homeownership is really worthwhile for families or society at large is endless. But everyone who wants to be a homeowner should have the opportunity to do so. *American Nightmare* proposes a 10-point plan to both end subsidies to housing and remove restrictions from the housing market. I estimate that doing so will increase the American homeownership rate to as much as 75 percent.

To examine these issues in detail, *American Nightmare* first examines six somewhat overlapping periods in history, before the American Revolution through the post–World War II era. Chapters 7 through 10 look at specific postwar issues: the debate over urban sprawl, public housing for low-income people, government land-use policies, and urban renewal. Chapters 11 through 13 focus on the events leading to the recent financial crisis by looking at housing markets, the housing bubble, and the crisis itself. Chapter 14 reviews homeownership policies and housing markets in other parts of the world, while Chapter 15 shows how reforming America's housing markets will increase homeownership and how that will help make America, once again, a land of opportunity.

Definitions and Data

Before exploring the history of homeownership in detail, defining some terms and identifying sources of data are important. Among the terms are "urban" and "rural"; "middle class" and "working class"; "cities" and "suburbs"; and "single-family home" and "multifamily housing." Among the data are sources for homeownership rates, housing prices, and different ways of adjusting past dollars for inflation.

Urban and rural: Until shortly before 1920, the majority of Americans lived in rural areas—which, by Census Bureau definition, include isolated towns with fewer than 2,500 people. The nation's first census revealed that barely 5 percent of Americans lived in communities—not necessarily incorporated cities—of 2,500 people or more. As late as 1900, 52 percent of Americans lived in truly rural areas outside cities or towns of any size at all.[1] Thus, the 18th- and early 19th-century American dream was more about farm ownership than homeownership.

Today, the Census Bureau defines an *urbanized area* as a central city and all its suburbs, incorporated or not, whose population totals 50,000 people or more. The Census Bureau redefines the boundary of each urbanized area at the time of each census. And although the definition has changed over time, in recent censuses it has generally included all land contiguous to the central city whose population density is greater than 1,000 people per square mile. An *urban cluster* is a central city and all its suburbs whose population ranges from 2,500 to 49,999 people. The 2000 census identified more than 400 urbanized areas and more than 3,000 urban clusters. Together, these areas are *urban* and all other lands are *rural.*

Urban areas are quite different from *metropolitan areas,* which are often used in media reports and some analyses. Metropolitan areas are defined by county boundaries, even though large parts of those counties may be rural. The Atlanta urbanized area, for example,

7

covers fewer than 2,000 square miles of land, while the Atlanta metropolitan area extends over more than 6,000 square miles of land. The history of homeownership is quite different for urban and rural areas. In 1890, for example, almost two out of three rural families lived in their own homes, but only about one out of six urban families did so. Data before 1890 are sparse, but this book will attempt to track the history of homeownership in both urban and rural areas to colonial times.

Middle class and working class: For many, owning a home is a sign of belonging to the middle class. A 1975 survey found that three-fourths of the members of the American Federation of Labor and Congress of Industrial Organizations—most of whom were, by definition, working class—owned their own homes, and most of them defined themselves as "middle class."[2] Americans who pretend to be insensitive to class distinctions tend to define classes by income: upper, middle, and lower classes. In fact, however, distinct cultural differences existed and still exist between working-class and middle-class families even if they earn about the same incomes.

Working-class employees, also known as blue-collar workers, have little college education, earn wages, and have occupations that rely more on physical labor or repetitive activities. Middle-class or white-collar employees are more likely to be college graduates, earn salaries, and have jobs focused more on knowledge and analysis than physical labor. Mainly because of differences in education, the middle class and working class have significant differences in tastes.

Most sociologists break these two groups down still further. The upper-middle class might include corporate executives and top doctors and lawyers; the central-middle class would include middle managers and other professionals; the lower-middle class might include clerks and other low-level managers. Working-class employees are often broken into skilled, semiskilled, and unskilled. Outside these groups are the wealthy—sometimes called the leisure class—who don't have to work and the hardcore poor, sometimes called the underclass, who for some reason are unable to work regularly.

Social class is more than about money; it is about status and opportunity as well. Some divide the upper class into two groups: *old money* and *new money*; old money has, at least to some, a higher status. In the latter part of the 20th century, many working-class jobs paid as much or more than some middle-class jobs. Yet as sociologist

Bennett Berger observes, "It is a great mistake to equate an income which permits most of the basic amenities of what the middle class calls 'decency' with becoming middle class."[3]

One way to show off status is to buy better-quality (or at least more-expensive) goods that are highly visible, such as houses and cars. The purchase of a Cadillac or Mercedes is as much, if not more, about status as it is about transportation. But this type of status display is difficult if your income is no greater than the income of those whom you are trying to impress. In that case, people instead try to deny lower-status people access to those status symbols. As Berger says, "Status groups respond to the clamor by money for prestige by tightening their entrance requirements."[4] For example, old-money owners of co-operative apartment buildings in New York and Boston often reject new-money applicants, such as Calvin Klein or Barbra Streisand, who want to move into one of those apartments.[5] Middle-class efforts to deny homeownership status to working-class families forms the deep background behind much of the debate over land use.

An important question for Americans is *social mobility*, that is, how easily people or their children can move into a higher class. America is supposed to be the nation where anyone can grow up to be president. Yet the most recent president who came from what we would today define as a working-class background was James Garfield. Elected in 1880, Garfield was one of only two presidents who were actually born in a log cabin. The Roosevelts, Kennedys, and Bushes were old-money, upper-class families. The fathers of other recent presidents had upper-middle-class or middle-class occupations, including a manufacturer (McKinley); a lawyer (Taft); a medical doctor (Harding); an engineer (Eisenhower); politicians (B. Harrison and L. Johnson); ministers (Arthur, Cleveland, and Wilson); small-business owners (Carter, Coolidge, Hayes, Hoover, Nixon, and Truman); and salesmen who, depending on how successful they were, were at least lower-middle-class (Ford and Reagan). Obama's father was an economist and his mother an anthropologist.

This history suggests that social mobility in the United States is more myth than reality. Many sociologists believe that, although Americans are highly mobile geographically, social mobility is more limited. Historian Stephan Thernstrom found, for example, that only about one out of five working-class employees in the industrial city of Newburyport, Massachusetts, managed to move into the middle class in the 19th century.[6] Looking at Boston in the 20th century, he found that this pace stepped up slightly to one out of four.[7] This book will argue that homeownership can help children of working-class families move into the middle class, and that efforts to restrict homeownership hamper such social mobility.

Cities and suburbs: The distinction between cities and suburbs is confusing because people often mean different things when they use these terms. Demographically, the *central city* is the largest, and usually the oldest, city (or sometimes two cities, such as Minneapolis and St. Paul, Minnesota) in a metropolitan area, while the suburbs are the cities and other developed lands contiguous to the central city. Stereotypically, cities have higher population densities, lower incomes, and lower rates of homeownership than their suburbs.

These stereotypes are not always realistic. The population densities of suburban Los Angeles, Miami, and San Francisco are greater than the densities of most other central cities. The densities of many suburbs, particularly in the Sun Belt, are as great or greater than their central cities. Median family incomes and homeownership rates in many central cities, particularly those in the Sun Belt, are greater than in their suburbs. In fact, of the nation's 50 largest urban areas, about half have higher homeownership rates in their central cities than in their suburbs.[8]

Urban planners often deride low-density suburbs as "sprawl." The Sierra Club once labeled Los Angeles "the Granddaddy of Sprawl."[9] Yet the Los Angeles urban area (which includes Pasadena, Anaheim, and nearby suburbs) is the nation's densest urban area, about 25 percent denser than the New York City urban area (which includes much of northern New Jersey).

One source of confusion is that American cities were built in three eras: the *pedestrian era*, before 1890, when most people walked; the *streetcar era*, between 1890 and about 1920, when many people traveled by urban transit; and the *automobile era*, after 1920 (but mostly after World War II), when most people traveled by car.

Manhattan, Brooklyn, and much of Baltimore, Boston, Chicago, Philadelphia, Providence, San Francisco, and Washington, D.C., were built in the pedestrian era and feature high-density, mid-rise housing (high-rise in the case of Manhattan) mixed with other uses, including retail and offices. Manhattan has about 60,000 people per square mile, while the densities of Boston, Chicago, and Philadelphia are 11,000 to 13,000; San Francisco has more than 16,000, while the densities of Providence and Washington are above 9,000 and

Baltimore's is 8,000.[10] Most other inner cities built in the pedestrian era have been redeveloped and no longer have these characteristics. Much of Los Angeles, Milwaukee, Minneapolis, Portland Oregon, and Seattle were built in the streetcar era, and their residential areas consist largely of moderately high-density single-family housing on small lots. Los Angeles has an average density of nearly 8,000 people per square mile, and its suburbs are close to 7,000 people per square mile. Milwaukee, Minneapolis, and Seattle have 6,000 to 7,000 people per square mile, while Denver and Portland have 3,000 to 4,000. Developments along streetcar lines outside the pedestrian-oriented inner cities are sometimes called *streetcar suburbs*, even though most of those suburbs have since been annexed into their central cities.

Most Sun Belt cities, including Atlanta, Dallas, Houston, and Phoenix, were built almost entirely in the automobile era, so they typically have much lower population densities than the pedestrian or streetcar cities. Atlanta, Dallas, and Houston have 3,000 to 3,500 people per square mile, while Phoenix has only 2,800. The suburbs of streetcar- and automobile-era cities were built mostly in the automobile era and have around 2,000 people per square mile.

In short, densities of 1,500 to 2,500 are typical of auto-era suburbs; densities of 2,500 to 3,500 are typical of auto-era central cities (which may include some streetcar neighborhoods); densities of 3,000 to 6,000 people are typical of streetcar-era cities; and densities of more than 8,000 people are typical of mixed pedestrian-/streetcar-era cities. All these densities are for entire cities or regions, including the commercial, industrial, and open-space portions of those regions. True pedestrian-era neighborhoods will have much higher densities of around 20,000 to 30,000 people per square mile.

Another source of confusion results from the fact that some central cities include a much larger share of their urban areas' population than others. This larger share occurs because some states have granted cities the power to annex suburbs without the permission of the landowners or residents being annexed, while other states require a vote of those being annexed. Cities with strong annexation powers typically have more than half the people in their urban area, while cities with weak annexation powers typically have much less than half.

Indiana, North Carolina, and Texas have all given cities strong annexation powers. Indianapolis has 64 percent of the population of its urban area; Charlotte has 71 percent; Houston has 51 percent; and San Antonio has an amazing 86 percent. By comparison, Los Angeles has 31 percent of the people in its urban area; Orlando just 16 percent; and Portland, Oregon, 33 percent, all in states whose cities can only annex with the permission of the people being annexed.

Some correlation appears to exist between states with weak annexation powers and states that have passed growth-management laws giving regional planners the power to plan all the cities in an urban area. Virtually all the states with growth-management laws have weak annexation authority. Apparently, if cities cannot gain control of their suburbs through annexation, they will attempt to use other means, such as regional growth-management planning, to do so. This correlation suggests that a lot of the debate over urban sprawl, which is covered in detail in Chapters 7 and 9, is really a debate over who gets to control growth and tax revenues.

Land-use regulation and other government actions also have a significant influence on densities and other differences between cities and suburbs. Manhattan's high densities are partly due to high-rise projects built, often with government funding, during the automobile era. The densities of some other cities, such as San Jose, California (6,900 people per square mile), are high more because of land-use policies, such as urban-growth boundaries, than because they were built in the pedestrian or streetcar eras.

Single-family and multifamily: Stereotypically, single-family homes are owned by their occupants while multifamily housing is rented. This is one stereotype that is fairly valid. The 2000 census found that 87 percent of single-family detached homes, and more than 84 percent of all single-family homes, including row houses and mobile homes, were owner occupied. Meanwhile, 86 percent of multifamily homes, from duplexes on up, were rented.[11] In 2000, 216 million Americans lived in some form of single-family housing, while 57 million lived in multifamily homes.

Single-family homes can be divided into *single-family detached* and *single-family attached* homes, the latter of which includes row houses. Nationally, the 2010 census found that more than 61 percent of housing is single-family detached; less than 6 percent is single-family attached; 26 percent is multifamily; and 7 percent is mobile home, boat, recreational vehicle, or van. Around 20 to 30 percent of the housing in the Baltimore, Philadelphia, and Washington, D.C., metropolitan areas is single-family attached, as is a little more than

10 percent of the housing in Miami, Minneapolis, San Jose, and Virginia Beach. Row houses and other attached housing make up less than 10 percent of homes in most other urban areas.[12]

In the early 2000s, many urban planners believed that American housing preferences were changing from single-family to multifamily homes. One planner predicted that the nation would have a huge glut of single-family homes by the year 2020 as empty nesters and young households without children would move to inner-city multifamily housing.[13] Those predictions encouraged developers to build what turned out to be a glut of high-rise condominiums in many cities.[14] Time will tell whether the demand for such housing will increase with the economic recovery.

Homeownership rates and prices: The Census Bureau first asked people whether they owned or rented their homes in 1890, and data became more detailed in each successive census. Beginning in 1960, the census asked for both home values and family incomes, so housing affordability—measured by dividing median home prices by median family incomes—can be gauged by state and urban area. The Federal Housing Finance Agency has published quarterly housing indexes by state and metropolitan area going back to 1975. These reports represent some of the most important data used in this book.

Money today and yesterday: A 1912 dollar is no more equal to a 2012 dollar than a British pound is to an American dollar. Although at any given time the factors for converting international currencies are relatively simple, there are many different ways of converting the value of dollars in one period to those of another. As appropriate, this book will rely on one or more of three standards: the consumer price index (CPI), a gross domestic product (GDP) index, and an unskilled wage index.

The CPI is based on changes in the cost of a number of goods and services, including food, housing, and transportation, regularly purchased by consumers. Of course, the food, housing, and transportation we enjoy today are very different from those of 100 or 150 years ago, and the index fails to account for such quality differences. It also fails to account for differences in personal incomes. Where the CPI focuses on consumer goods, the GDP index takes all goods and services into account, including those used by government and industry. The CPI is best when comparing costs to individuals and families; the GDP index is best when looking at government budgets over time.

To account for differences in housing costs and incomes, this book also uses an unskilled wage index. This index indicates how much work an unskilled worker would have to perform to buy equivalent goods at different points in time.[15] It produces results that are quite different from the CPI or GDP. For example, a working-class home that might have cost $2,000 in 1890 is worth about $50,000 today using the CPI and $47,000 using the GDP index, but nearly $250,000 using the unskilled wage index, indicating that unskilled workers earned far less, relative to middle-class workers, in 1890 than they do today.

1. The Pre-American Dream

Widespread homeownership is a recent phenomenon in world history. Most people who have ever lived did not own the land they lived on. Just a few hundred years ago, only a tiny fraction of people—probably less than 1 percent—lived in homes that they owned. "Property systems open to all citizens are a relatively recent phenomenon—no more than 200 years old," wrote economist Hernando de Soto in 2000.[1]

The Benefits of Homeownership

Advocates of policies aimed at boosting homeownership have long claimed that homeownership benefits not only the families of the homeowners but also society at large. Homeownership "makes for better children," Herbert Hoover once told a convention of realtors.[2] "When individuals and families own their home, they establish roots in their communities and have a greater stake in the growth, safety and development of their towns and cities," said Elizabeth Dole.[3]

Many of these claims have been supported by researchers who have found many benefits of homeownership. In a 2003 lecture sponsored by Habitat for Humanity, Ohio State University economist Donald Haurin listed some of the documented private and social benefits of homeownership. The main private benefits include the following:

1. Homeownership increases personal wealth, partly because it forces people to save money for a down payment and partly because the house itself appreciates in value.[4] (However, as Chapter 11 will show, such appreciation is not guaranteed.)
2. Homeowners have an incentive to maintain their homes (to protect their investment) and thus "have better physical home environments than renters." Moreover, neighborhoods with high rates of homeownership tend to have more stable property values because people maintain their homes and yards.

15

3. Owner-occupied homes are better for children, who do significantly better in school than children living in rental homes. The difference is greatest for children of low-income families and is negligible for wealthy families.
4. Personal self-esteem rises considerably when renters become homeowners, which is probably one reason why the children of homeowners do better in school.
5. Homeowners have a greater stake in the future of their community and so are more likely to get involved in community programs, public affairs, and politics. As another survey notes, this benefit has been confirmed by numerous studies.[5]

On the downside, Haurin notes that homeowners are less mobile than renters, making it more difficult for them to respond to changes in the employment market. However, as Chapter 14 will show, this lack of mobility is mainly a problem where government policies have made housing expensive. Unfortunately, the other downside is that one major effect of homeowners' getting involved in politics is that they work to boost the values of their own homes—but by making housing expensive, they thereby reduce their own long-term mobility.

Other researchers have found that homeownership can provide families a safety net during bad economic times. Nations with high homeownership rates tend to have lower levels of social spending, apparently because the homes act as a form of social insurance and provide a nest egg for emergencies and peoples' retirements.[6]

Naturally, some debate exists about whether homeownership truly does all these things. "There's a pervasive problem in trying to sort out whether there is something intrinsic about homeownership that causes these externalities or whether the people that become homeowners are the kind of people that generate these externalities," says Massachusetts Institute of Technology economist James Poterba.[7] In other words, there may be a self-selection issue: people who are more likely to buy homes may also be more likely to save money, help their children do better in school, and get involved in the community. Haurin thinks his research on the effects of homeownership on children controlled for enough variables to show that homeownership itself was the cause of children's scoring higher on standardized tests, but the economic literature is full of articles on both sides of the question.

For example, Federal Reserve Bank economist Daniel Aaronson examined the issue in 1999 and concluded that at least "some of the homeownership effect [on child schooling] is driven by family characteristics associated with homeownership, especially residential stability."[8] This conclusion suggests that the children of those families would have done as well, or nearly as well, even if those particular families had rented their homes. But in 2001, New York University sociologist Dalton Conley used multigenerational data to show that homeownership makes a major difference to children in African-American homes. Homeownership, says Conley, "matters not only for the immediate well-being of families, but also for the life-chances of the subsequent generation."[9] Similarly, after reviewing a wide range of variables, policy analysts at Johns Hopkins University concluded in 2003 that "homeownership is beneficial to children's outcomes in almost any neighborhood" and that "children of most low-income renters would be better served by programs that help their families become homeowners in their current neighborhoods instead of helping them move to better neighborhoods but remain renters."[10]

What is clear is that most of the benefits of homeownership mentioned by Haurin accrue to the homeowners and their families, not to society in general. This fact suggests that governments have little reason to subsidize homeownership except to the extent that they subsidize other programs, such as education or poverty reduction, that might be more cost-effectively achieved through homeownership programs. Haurin suggests, for example, that increasing homeownership can increase children's test scores at a much lower cost than investing in the educational system.[11]

Haurin left out one major benefit of living in a society with high homeownership rates: a high level of economic growth. Peruvian economist Hernando de Soto believes that nations that make it easy to own homes grow more rapidly because homeowners can easily start small businesses by borrowing against the equity in their homes. "The single most important source of funds for new businesses in the United States," de Soto notes, "is a mortgage on the entrepreneur's house."[12] This fact doesn't necessarily mean governments should promote homeownership, but they shouldn't stand in the way, as many governments of developing nations do by maintaining large areas of land in public or communal ownership.

Homeownership also has a political component: Many believe that homeownership makes people more fiscally and socially conservative, suggesting that Republican or other conservative parties have an interest in boosting homeownership while Democratic or other liberal parties have an interest in boosting renting. "No one who owns his own house and lot can be a Communist," said homebuilder William Levitt. "He has too much to do."[13]

In fact, the relationship between homeownership and social issues is probably imaginary. Researchers at the University of Louisville found no correlation between homeownership and attitudes toward civil rights, women's rights, or gay rights.[14] The relationship between homeownership and fiscal issues may be more realistic: European nations with high rates of homeownership tend to have much lower rates of social spending. However, it isn't clear whether the high homeownership leads to lower social spending or the low social spending leads to high homeownership.[15]

Homeownership and Property Rights

Economists sometimes describe property rights as a "bundle of sticks." One stick represents the right to use the property. Normally, property owners have this right unless they rent or lease the property to someone else, in which case the renter or leaser has this stick. Another stick is the right to sell the property. Although we normally take it for granted that someone who owns a house has the right to sell it, that hasn't always been true. During some periods in the past, some nations have limited the rights of property owners to sell their land in order to keep most property in the hands of a small aristocracy.

Ownership of all possible sticks in the property rights bundle is known as an *allodial title*. Since the government usually reserves to itself the right to tax, regulate, and take property through eminent domain, it is rare for anyone other than a government to hold an allodial title. However, in 1997 the Nevada legislature, which was apparently in a libertarian mood, allowed homeowners without a mortgage on their home to claim an allodial title to their house and land by paying a fee to the state equal to 5 percent of the value of their property. This fee would relieve them from ever paying property taxes on the home and would also protect their home from being taken by creditors or through eminent domain proceedings. If the owner sells the property or bequeaths it to an heir, the buyer or heir must again pay 5 percent to keep the allodial status. Nevada repealed the law in 2005 so it is likely that the number of Nevada properties that have allodial title is limited.[16]

The combination of sticks that we call "homeownership" has evolved over a long period and is still—some would say unfortunately—evolving today. Landownership by anyone other than a chief or sovereign has been rare in human history. Most hunter-gatherer societies had no concept of landownership at all. Early agricultural societies were probably run by chiefs and, eventually, kings who held effective title to all land and granted its use to individuals in exchange for favors or support.

Homeownership in Ancient Times

Ancient Greece was not a nation but a group of city-states, each of which had its own laws and customs. Many of those city-states, including Athens, allowed and encouraged private ownership of farms. Farm ownership was vested with families, not individuals, and lacked one of the sticks we generally associate with private ownership: the right to sell the land. Instead, the land was tied to the family in perpetuity (or, in actual practice, until a foreign invader changed the system of property rights, generally by putting most land in the hands of a few people).[17] This system of private ownership proved to be very productive, and farm productivity notably declined when it was replaced by a system of absentee owners over large areas.[18]

Ancient Rome, too, had a system of private property rights that probably contributed to that empire's success. Unlike the Greek system, owners could sell their property, which may be why the best lands were eventually held by a few powerful families.

Medieval Homeownership

Roman rule of Britannia influenced English property law for several centuries after the fall of Rome. That law, which became known as the Anglo-Saxon common law, gave landowners the right to sell their land and to will it to whomever they wished. When William the Conqueror successfully invaded England in 1066, however, he overturned those laws and declared that all land in the kingdom belonged to him.[19] He thereby introduced the feudal system to Britain in which he as king would grant lands to his lords. They in turn would divide lands among their vassals who would each manage a piece of land known as a fief. The vassals and lords paid rents, promised military service, or provided other services to their lord or king.

Feudal land grants came with reservations, two of which were *primogeniture* and *entail*. Primogeniture required that only the eldest son could inherit the land (in some countries, but not England, the eldest daughter could inherit if there were no sons). Entail prohibited landowners from selling their land. In effect, the land grants were to families, not individuals, and these reservations kept most land in the hands of a few aristocrats.

One alternative to primogeniture is known as *gavelkind*, in which land was equally divided among all the children (or, at least, all the male children). *Gavel* meant "payment" in Middle English, and English land courts typically accompanied a decision about payments by striking a rock. Today, gavel has come to mean the hammer doing the striking. In any case, although gavelkind might seem more just than primogeniture, it also meant that properties became more and more chopped up into smaller pieces. Primogeniture prevailed in England for any estates where the owner died without a will until 1926, whereas Wales relied on gavelkind, which some say is one reason why England was able to conquer Wales in the late 13th century.

The strongest resistance to William's changes came from the county of Kent. To avoid bloodshed, William agreed to allow Kent to keep the Anglo-Saxon rules (leading the county to adopt the motto *invicta*, meaning "undefeated"). Thus, the Anglo-Saxon rules allowing individual ownership are sometimes known as "Kentish tenure." Rather than deal with annual rents or military obligations, the Kentish system allowed vassals to buy land from the king or lord with one "simple fee" (the word *fee* being derived from *fief*), which became known as *fee simple* ownership. Kentish tenure generally relied on gavelkind, but landowners could specify a different division in their will and could also entail land when willing it to their children. In contrast to fee simple land that could be sold, entailed land was known as *fee tail*.

Colonial Homeownership

In 1629, King Charles I granted land to Massachusetts colonists "as of our manor of Eastgreenewich, in the County of Kent, in free and common Socage, and not in Capite, nor by knightes service." Colonists interpreted that to mean they could use Kentish rules rather than feudalistic ("knightes service," meaning military service) rules. "Socage" nominally meant the land recipients would pay rent to the king, but the charter specified that the only rent to be paid was one-fifth of all gold and silver mined from the land—which, since

Massachusetts has insignificant amounts of gold and silver, meant no rent at all.[20]

Later English grants specified that socage meant the land was "to be held forever in fee without any incumbrance forever." "The holding of land in free and common socage implied the retention of all produce," observe historians Michael Doucet and John Weaver. "Ownership by freehold meant the independence to devise and to alienate, and consequently fed a trust in the worth of improving one's land. It also meant living without the practices of deference toward landlords."[21]

In 1618, Virginia offered 50 acres to every family who moved from England to the colony. Other provinces were even more generous: Maryland initially offered 100 acres for every head of family, 100 for his wife, and 50 for every child under the age of 16. In 1663, Carolina Province offered 100 acres for every man plus 50 acres for his male servants and 30 acres for female servants. Pennsylvania offered 50 acres for every servant, and the servant received another 50 acres when his or her term of service expired.[22]

Similar charters were granted for most of the other colonies or provinces, as some were known at the time. As applied by the trustees for each province, primogeniture ruled in seven colonies—Georgia, Maryland, New York, North and South Carolina, Rhode Island, and Virginia—and gavelkind in the rest.[23] However, Pennsylvania and most New England states tended to follow Mosaic law in giving the eldest son twice the land of other sons.[24]

All the provinces allowed landowners to entail their properties in their wills, and many of them required entail in their original land grants to settlers. The trustees for the Province of Georgia, for example, gave land to settlers, but added an entail requirement out of the fear that, if settlers were allowed to sell their land, a few people would accumulate most of the land.[25] Entail discouraged people from borrowing money against the value of their land. Creditors could not take a debtor's land unless the debtor had specifically pledged the land as collateral, and even then only after going through a tedious and costly legal process.

Despite what the Georgia trustees believed, these customs kept much of the land concentrated in a few hands. Although colonists could theoretically circumvent primogeniture by preparing a will, many had no desire to do so and, especially near the end of the colonial period, the cost of doing so was increasingly high.[26] What all these measures meant was that the great majority of colonists did not own their own homes.

Lack of ownership did not prevent thousands of people from simply farming land they found. From Massachusetts to South Carolina,
squatters occupied some 100,000 acres of land as early as 1725. "Both
[German and Scotch-Irish immigrants] sitt frequently down on any
spott of vacant Land they can find, without asking questions,"
learned John Penn—the only son of William Penn born in America—
from his business secretary John Logan in 1727. "They say the Propri-
etor [meaning William Penn] invited People to come and settle his
Country, that they are come for that end and must live; both they and
the Palatines pretend they would buy but not one in twenty has anything to pay with." Two years later, Logan again mentioned that "the
settlement of those vast nos. of poor but presumptuous People who,
without any License, have entered on your Lands, and neither have
nor are likely to have anything to purchase with."[27]

Although the vast majority of colonials were rural farmers, a small
percentage lived in cities. In this preindustrial time, most city
dwellers were middle-class traders, and some scholars believe that
urban homeownership rates were very high during the colonial era.
Most city residents were involved in either trade or politics, giving
them incomes that were well above the subsistence levels experienced by many rural residents. One study found that 72 percent of
New York City taxpayers owned their homes in 1703, but that homeownership rates declined after 1730.[28] In any case, urban residents
were such a small percentage of the nation's population that their
homeownership rates have little influence on the totals.

At the time of the Revolution, it is likely that roughly half of American families owned their homes, the land they farmed, or both—
though this number might be lower if all were asked to provide a legal
title to their lands. Conflicts over squatters and the disposal of large
land grants presaged debates over home- and landownership in
post–Revolutionary America. Although many of the young nation's
leaders had an egalitarian spirit and wished to increase the share of
Americans who owned their own farms and homes, the nation was
slow to make government-owned lands available for such ownership.
The result was homeownership rates that fell below 50 percent soon
after the Revolution and remained there until after World War II.

2. The Agrarian Dream

Thomas Jefferson may have been the first to express what has become known as the American dream of homeownership. "It is not too soon to provide by every possible means that as few as possible shall be without a little portion of land," he wrote to James Madison in 1785. "The small landholders are the most precious part of a state."[1] At that time, Jefferson's ideal was near-universal farm ownership, rather than what we think of as urban homeownership, but the sentiment remains the same.

The Agrarian Myth

Many historians and popular writers make much of the fact that Jefferson, in the 1780s, believed that the United States should be a nation of farmers. They have built this belief up into a mythical "agrarian movement" that somehow stood up against Alexander Hamilton and others who would turn America into a nation of mercenary bankers and filthy industrialists—with an unwritten and sometimes written regret that the agrarians lost.

Jefferson did express a preference for farmers in 1785. "Cultivators of the earth are the most valuable citizens," Jefferson wrote to John Jay in that year. "They are the most vigorous, the most independent, the most virtuous and they are tied to their country and wedded to its liberty and interests by the most lasting bands."[2] Widespread farm ownership, Jefferson thought, would lead to better government. "I think our governments will remain virtuous for many centuries; as long as they are chiefly agricultural," he wrote to Madison in 1787. "When they get piled upon one another in large cities, as in Europe, they will become corrupt as in Europe."[3]

In the 1780s, Jefferson apparently believed that subsistence farmers were more self-sufficient than office or factory workers, and thereby more inclined to liberty. "Those who labor in the earth are the chosen people of God," Jefferson wrote in the early 1780s, while "dependence begets subservience and venality."[4] "Jefferson is saying that it is impossible to corrupt an entire nation so long as the majority of its citizens are small landowners, dispersed across the landscape, dependent on no one but themselves for their livelihood," comments environmental historian Donald Worster.[5]

Jefferson himself was a farmer, but the fact that he romanticized that occupation does not mean that there was a significant anti-industrial, pro-agrarian movement in the late 18th and early 19th centuries. "Jefferson was not an agrarian fundamentalist," says one historian. "He did move with his times."[6] The myth of Jeffersonian agrarianism sprang up around 1943, the bicentennial of Jefferson's birth, and was probably influenced by the Southern Agrarians, a group of writers featured in a 1930 book titled *I'll Take My Stand: The South and the Agrarian Tradition*. Ironically, considering Jefferson's role in eliminating feudal land policies in Virginia, one idea suggested by the Southern Agrarians was to restore feudalism in order to "bind" people to the land and create the small, independent farmers that the Agrarians (and Jefferson, at least in the 1780s) believed were essential to a free country.[7]

After the end of the Revolutionary War in 1783, the United States developed a thriving trade with England, exporting agricultural crops such as tobacco and importing manufactured goods. When Jefferson wrote the quotes above, he had never seen an American factory because the first such factory (which produced spindles of yarn) did not open until 1790.[8] By 1810, New England alone had at least 250 such factories, small and large.[9]

Perhaps exposure to those factories helped soften Jefferson's stance after he became president. "I trust the good sense of our country will see that its greatest prosperity depends on a due balance between agriculture, manufactures and commerce," he wrote in 1809.[10] He doesn't say what that balance is, but no doubt it is less than the 100 percent agriculture he appeared to favor in 1785.

A few years later, the nation went through another war with Britain, and Jefferson realized the country should not rely exclusively on England for manufactured goods. "Experience has taught me that manufactures are now as necessary to our independence as to our comfort," he wrote in a letter in 1816.

"You tell me I am quoted by those who wish to continue our dependence on England for manufactures," the letter notes. "There was a time when I might have been so quoted with more candor, but within the thirty years which have since elapsed, how are circumstances changed! We were then in peace. . . . A commerce which offered the raw material in exchange for the same material after receiving the last touch of industry, was worthy of welcome to all nations."

The War of 1812 completely altered Jefferson's perception of industry. "We have experienced what we did not then believe, that there exists both profligacy and power enough to exclude us from the field of interchange with other nations: that to be independent for the comforts of life we must fabricate them ourselves. We must now place the manufacturer by the side of the agriculturist." The question of the day, Jefferson wrote, was, "Shall we make our own comforts, or go without them, at the will of a foreign nation? He, therefore, who is now against domestic manufacture, must be for reducing us either to dependence on that foreign nation, or to be clothed in skins, and to live like wild beasts in dens and caverns. I am not one of these; experience has taught me that manufactures are now as necessary to our independence as to our comfort."[11]

A Nation of Farmers

If Jefferson changed, it was from emphasizing the self-sufficiency of individuals and their families to emphasizing the self-sufficiency of the nation as a whole. Yet whatever Jefferson and Hamilton wanted, the bulk of the American population remained rural through the end of the 19th century. That circumstance is at odds with our stereotypical view of the nation in, say, 1790, when we might think of Samuel Adams in Boston, Alexander Hamilton in New York, and Benjamin Franklin in Philadelphia. But these examples are atypical of how people lived in the nation's early years. The 1790 census found that the combined populations of Boston, New York, and Philadelphia (including the Northern Liberties and Southwark "suburbs" of Philadelphia) had fewer than 100,000 people, or just 2.4 percent of the nation's population.[12] For comparison, in 2008, when the nation's land area had grown tenfold, the Boston, New York, and Philadelphia urban areas held more than 9 percent of the nation's population.

That census also found only 24 communities—not all of them incorporated as cities—with more than 2,500 people. The combined population of those two dozen communities was just over 200,000, or about 5.1 percent of the nation's 3.9 million residents. Although some people lived in communities with fewer than 2,500 people, the vast majority of the nation's population was rural.

As of 1790, it is likely that the majority of Americans did not own the homes they lived in. The Census Bureau did not record homeownership status until 1890, but scattered data indicate that farm ownership and homeownership rates at the end of the 18th century were low and declining.

Breaking the Feudal Chains

In rural areas, the 1890 census found that 66 percent of farmers owned their homes, but there are several reasons to believe that the share was lower in 1790. Most importantly, farm ownership and homeownership were hampered by the large land grants created in the colonial era combined with the customs of primogeniture and entail that prevailed in most of the colonies before the Revolution. In many of the colonies, those customs kept much of the land in a few large estates. In addition, the 1790 census found that almost 18 percent of American residents were slaves, who obviously did not own their own homes.

The first widespread weakening of primogeniture and entail began in 1737, when the British Parliament passed the "Act for the More Easy Recovery of Debts in His Majesty's Plantations and Colonies in America." This act made land, buildings, and other real property "equivalent to chattel property for the purpose of satisfying debts," making it easier for people to borrow against the value of their land. Although increasing the risk to landowners, the act boosted economic growth. After the Revolution, most states, recognizing "the importance of the expansion of commerce to the creation of an American meritocracy," followed this precedent.[13]

Revolutionary-era Americans clearly considered entail and primogeniture to be inappropriate for an egalitarian nation. To prevent the establishment of a landed aristocracy, they rapidly moved to abolish these customs. Thomas Jefferson persuaded the Virginia legislature to abolish entail in 1776. The preamble to Jefferson's law claimed that entail "tends to deceive fair traders, who give a credit on the visible possession of such estates, discourages the holder thereof from taking care and improving the same, and sometimes does injury to the morals of youth, by rendering them independent of and disobedient to their parents." The law itself immediately changed any "fee taille" land to fee simple land and prevented landowners from entailing their land to their heirs in a will.[14] Years later, Jefferson listed the abolishment of entail as one of the six greatest accomplishments of his life.[15]

South Carolina and Delaware abolished entail shortly before Virginia, and within 10 years after 1776 all the remaining states except Massachusetts and Rhode Island had done so as well.[16] Massachusetts (and by extension Maine, which was formed out of the original Massachusetts colony) and Rhode Island still allow entail today, though in a modified form: Someone may entail a property to his or her heir or heirs, which would mean the heirs cannot sell it. But the entail would disappear on the death of the heir unless the entail was included in his or her will.

Primogeniture soon followed: of the states that observed this custom, Georgia abolished it in 1777; North Carolina in 1784; Virginia (led again by Jefferson) in 1785; Maryland and New York in 1786; South Carolina in 1791; and Rhode Island in 1798.[17] Landowners could still will their land to their eldest sons, but property of people who died without a will was divided equally among their male heirs or, if they had no sons, their female heirs. The abolishment of entail and primogeniture, combined with the adoption of the credit policies in the Act of 1737, led to the gradual breakup of the great landed estates and in turn increased the share of farmers who owned their own land and homes.

Abolishing primogeniture and entail eventually led to a more egalitarian nation. "No sooner was the law of primogeniture abolished than fortunes began to diminish, and all the families of the country were simultaneously reduced to a state in which labor became necessary to procure the means of subsistence," observed Alexis de Tocqueville in the early 1830s. "Several of them have since entirely disappeared, and all of them learned to look forward to the time at which it would be necessary for everyone to provide for his own wants. Wealthy individuals are still to be met with, but they no longer constitute a compact and hereditary body."[18]

The rejection of feudalism turned America into a magnet for European immigrants. As historians Doucet and Weaver note, "Nineteenth-century immigrants to North America identified property ownership with freedom from customary restrictions," meaning feudal traditions that survived in many European nations until the beginning of the 20th century.[19]

One of the largest land grants in America had been Pennsylvania, granted to William Penn by King Charles II in 1681. The Penn family had sold only about one-sixth of the land by 1779, when the Pennsylvania legislature effectively confiscated the rest and sold it to settlers and speculators over the next two decades.[20]

Yet the transition from large estates to small landowners did not always happen overnight. As late as the 1840s, well after Tocqueville wrote, much of the Hudson River Valley remained in a few large estates granted by the Dutch in the 17th century. That land was still managed in a feudal manner, with tenant farmers who paid rents to the owners as well as taxes on their land. Just one estate, owned by the Rensselaer family, covered about three-quarters of a million acres and had some 80,000 tenants.[21]

One indicator of low farm-ownership or homeownership rates is voting data. Rhode Island maintained a property-ownership requirement for voting until 1844.[22] Virginia did the same until 1851.[23] These data make it possible to compare before- and after-voting data in national elections. The first year for which state-by-state polling data are available for most states was 1824, when the presidential election was particularly contentious, with four different candidates in the running. Yet only about 6 percent of white males in Rhode Island and Virginia voted that year.

By 1840, the last year in which Rhode Island enforced a property qualification, 16 percent of males voted for a presidential candidate. After the property qualification was removed, voting males increased to 25 percent in 1856. In Virginia, just 30 percent of white males voted in 1848, increasing to 45 percent in 1856. These data suggest that only a small share of families owned property in 1824, though the share may have increased by the 1840s. During those years, more than 40 percent of Virginians were slaves, which brings down overall homeownership rates still further.

Another source of data for overall property ownership rates is a 1798 survey of all property in America conducted by the Treasury Department for potential tax purposes. An analysis of this survey led historian Lee Soltow to estimate that the nation had about 433,000 different property owners. Since about 877,000 white males were over the age of 21 at the time, Soltow estimates that about 49 percent of households were landowners.[24] Of course, when slaves are counted, that number falls to around 40 percent, and homeownership rates are lower still to the extent that many properties, such as grants to military combatants, were mainly held for speculation by people who did not live on those properties.

The Trans-Appalachian West

Settlement west of the Appalachians should have increased ownership of farms and homes. However, except in grants given to military veterans, the government was very slow to make those lands available to settlers, and even slower to make them available at prices most settlers could afford.

At the end of the French and Indian War in 1763, many American colonists who had fought in the war were granted lands west of the Appalachians. George Washington, who received 20,000 acres in what would become Kentucky, considered the grant "a Lottery only" because the lands were so inaccessible and were largely under Indian domain.[25] Indian treaties in 1768 and 1770 opened much of that land to settlement, but by the time of the Revolution only about 12,000 whites lived west of the mountains.[26]

Just having the land does not mean that the owners lived on it; instead, many held the land for speculative purposes or sold it to speculators. In the meantime, squatters often started farming lands without a title. Squatters occupied some of George Washington's land in western Pennsylvania. He met with them in 1796, the last year of his presidency, and offered to sell the land to them. They preferred to dispute his title in court; the court decided in his favor and they had to leave.[27]

At the time of the Revolution, Virginia offered actual settlers 400 acres and North Carolina offered 640 acres "at the merest nominal price." Settlers in Maine could also get 100 acres merely for clearing 16 within four years. Within three years, Virginia settlers were required to build a house, plant one acre, and keep stock for one year, or they would lose the land.[28]

After the Revolution, the 1783 Treaty of Paris recognized the United States' sovereignty over land as far west as the Mississippi River. The states ceded to the United States their claims to land west of the Appalachians—about 237 million acres of land that eventually became Alabama, Kentucky, Illinois, Indiana, Michigan, Mississippi, Ohio, Tennessee, Wisconsin, and much of Minnesota. That was a huge amount of land, about 60 acres for every resident of the United States in 1790. Rather than give the land to settlers, however, Congress, at the urging of Alexander Hamilton, tried to sell the land to pay off the nation's debt.

In contrast to Hamilton, Jefferson was against selling land to pay the national debt. "The people who will migrate to the Westward whether they form part of the old, or of a new colony will be subject to their proportion of the Continental debt then unpaid," he wrote in 1776. "They ought not to be subject to more." But by 1784, even Jefferson had accepted the idea and his land ordinance of that year provided for sales.[29]

Selling the Federal Domain

In 1785, Congress asked a minimum of $1 an acre in cash for blocks of at least 640 acres. The lands were to be sold at auction, but only after lands had been surveyed. Surveys were slower than antici-pated, and only about 1.5 million acres were sold to private parties, mostly speculators, under this system.[30]

In 1796, Congress raised the price to $2 an acre for a minimum of 640 acres, with half the money paid within 30 days and the other half within a year.[31] That amount may sound inexpensive today, but in the late 18th century those were high prices: based on the consumer price index, $640 dollars in 1785 would be almost $15,000 today. More significantly, in relation to the wages earned by unskilled workers, it would be more than $240,000 today.[32] That amount is far more than an unskilled worker could pay in cash, especially for land that initially at least would have to be worked on a subsistence basis since it was located too far from markets to sell any crops. As a result, sales were slow, averaging only a little more than 500 640-acre parcels per year from 1800 through 1810.[33]

In 1800, Congress reduced the down payment to one-twentieth of the total cost and extended the time allowed for full payment, at 6 percent interest, to four years. The 1800 law also reduced the mini-mum number of acres that could be purchased to 320, which was reduced still further to 160 acres in 1804. The low down payment encourage speculators, while the high cost per acre still led large numbers of settlers to default on their payments, especially after the recession of 1819. As a result, in 1820 Congress once again changed the terms of land sales: purchasers could buy as few as 80 acres for $1.25 an acre. To discourage speculation, all purchases were to be in cash.[34]

One settler who had trouble gaining secure title to land was Thomas Lincoln, the father of the future president. In 1803, he pur-chased a 250-acre farm in Kentucky for 118 English pounds, but lost 38 acres of it because of an erroneous recording of the land survey. Five years later, he made a $200 down payment on a 348-acre farm, but lost the farm and the down payment because of a title dispute. He then bought a third farm that was part of a 10,000-acre grant re-ceived by Thomas Middleton in 1784. Lincoln and nine other farmers who had purchased part of that grant lost their land in a title dispute with Middleton's heirs. As one historian comments, "There were likely no people in America so cursed with land litigation as the pioneer Kentuckians, because of the lack of adequate land regula-tions pertaining to priority of ownership."[35]

Giving up on Kentucky, in 1816 Lincoln moved his family to Indiana. There he claimed 160 acres of federal land in 1817 with a down payment of $16, or one-twentieth of the total cost. Within 40 days, as specified by law, he paid another $64, bringing his total payment to one-fourth of the cost. However, he was unable to make any further payments. In 1821, Congress passed a law extending the payment period to as long as eight years. In 1827, Lincoln gave up some of his land to gain clear title to the rest, but then turned around and sold the land in 1830.[36]

Congress debated the sale of trans-Appalachian lands for more than 70 years. "More than half our time has been taken up with the discussion of propositions connected with the public lands," complained South Carolina Senator Robert Hayne in 1830. "Day after day the charges are rung on this topic, from the grave inquiry into the rights of the new States to the absolute sovereignty and property in the soil, down to the grant of a preemption to a few quarter sections to actual settlers."[37]

Meanwhile, settlers who could not afford to put up $640 were nevertheless moving west of the mountains, staking claims, and claiming squatters' rights to the land. In 1787, the federal government sent troops to burn homes and evict squatters along the Ohio River. But the squatters returned as soon as the troops left.[38] From 1781 through 1788, Massachusetts aggressively tried to remove squatters from Maine.[39] Continuing troubles with squatters contributed to the decision to spin off Maine as a separate state in 1820.

Another obstacle to pioneers' taking title to the land was Indian ownership of some lands. Although the federal government recognized Indian title to much of the trans-Appalachian territory, it did not recognize the right of Indian tribes to sell land to white settlers. This policy and the government's acquisition was based on an 1823 Supreme Court decision, *Johnson v. M'Intosh*, which in turn was based on a long-standing European tradition that only a sovereign nation has the right to extinguish Indians' interests in their land. The British government, for example, proclaimed in 1763 that "no private person do presume to make any purchase from the said Indians of any lands reserved to the said Indians."[40]

Although the federal government did eventually negotiate the purchase of most trans-Appalachian lands from Indian tribes, the government's acquisition further delayed the ability of settlers to take title to land. In 1807, Jefferson ordered troops to expel squatters from lands recently purchased from the Chickasaw and Cherokee Indians as well as from lands still owned by Indians.[41]

Giving Away the Federal Domain

Eventually, Congress gave up on the idea of selling land to repay the Revolutionary War debt and began giving land to various groups. Between Ohio in 1803 and Arizona in 1912, Congress eventually gave new states 218 million acres of federal land (plus another 105 million acres to Alaska in 1959) on statehood with the intention that the states would sell or manage those lands to pay for schools and other public programs.[42] Starting in 1823, Congress eventually granted 140 million acres (some of which were never claimed, were returned, or were revested by Congress) to private companies to promote the construction of canals, wagon roads, railroads, and river improvements.[43]

Congress intended that the states, railroads, and other entities would sell those lands to settlers, but that didn't always happen. Alaska still owns about 90 million acres of the land it received on statehood, and 22 of the 29 other states that received land grants still own about 45 million acres of their grants.[44] Millions of acres of railroad land grants were either retained by the railroads or sold in large blocks to timber companies.

In 1841, Congress allowed squatters to purchase up to 160 acres of land they had lived on for at least 14 months for not less than $1.25 per acre, and $2.50 an acre on alternate sections of railroad land grants.[45] That price was still prohibitive for subsistence farmers, and land sales—which had peaked in 1836—were 70 percent lower in the decade following the act than the decade before.

In 1850, Congress passed the Donation Land Claim Act, which allowed settlers in the Oregon Territory to claim up to 320 acres each (640 for married couples) at no charge provided that they cultivated the land for four years. This act led 7,317 people to claim about 2.8 million acres, mostly in Oregon's Willamette Valley. The law was mainly for the benefit of settlers who started coming over the Oregon Trail in 1841 in an overt effort to claim the Oregon Territory for the United States, which had jointly held the land with Great Britain since 1818.[46] But it was a generous grant, as Willamette Valley farmlands were much more productive than much of the land that was later homesteaded in parcels of just 160 acres.

The debate over whether to sell federal land to help pay the public debt or give it away to settlers to promote economic expansion was finally settled in 1862, when Congress passed the Homestead Act, granting any actual settler 160 acres (320 for married couples) at a nominal fee of $18 provided they lived on the land for five years. Eventually, about 270 million acres of land were distributed to

1.6 million people under this law.[47] Distribution was not immediate, however: homestead claims did not peak until 1910, and actual title transfers peaked in 1913.

Between 1862 and 1900, only 80 million acres of land were granted under the Homestead Act. At 160 acres per claim, they were enough for 500,000 people. But since many claims were filed by married couples, far fewer families were probably represented. Rural populations grew by 20 million people during that period, which (at the then-average family size of 5.5 people) represent about 3.6 million families. The Homestead Act provided land for just 7 to 14 percent of those families.

During the 19th century, the United States acquired vast amounts of land, including the Louisiana Purchase, more than half of Mexico, the Oregon Territory, and Alaska. Yet most of that land remained unavailable or unaffordable to many settlers until the 1862 Homestead Act. Even the Homestead Act was insufficient since the 320 acres of land that could be granted to a married couple was too little to make a living in the arid West, where most of that land was located.

Through the combined effects of the Homestead Act, the Donation Land Claims Act, and other laws, Congress eventually managed to get several hundred million acres of once-federal lands into the hands of settlers with secure titles. Economist de Soto argues that "the result was an integrated property market that fueled the United States' explosive economic growth thereafter."[48] That's probably a stretch. Although those laws gave nearly two out of three farmers secure title to their land by 1890, urban home- and landownership rates remained low through the end of the 19th century. Yet most of the nation's economic growth after 1840 took place in cities, not in agricultural areas. What can be stated with greater certainty is that secure title to farms contributed to agricultural productivity in the late 19th century, while increased urban homeownership contributed to small-business growth in the latter half of the 20th century.

In sum, it appears likely that homeownership and farm-ownership rates were something less than 40 percent in 1800, or no more than the rate recorded by the 1890 census. From there, historians agree that rates declined for at least the first half of the 19th century.[49] That decline occurred both because of the difficulty farmers had in obtaining title to lands acquired by the federal government and because the nation's growing cities increasingly housed low-paid working-class employees who could not initially afford to own their own homes.

3. The Urban Dream

Though a majority of Americans continued to live in rural areas until around World War I, American cities began rapidly growing after 1840. From 1790 to 1840, the urban share of the American population had barely doubled, from slightly less than 5 percent to slightly more than 10 percent. In 1840, New York, Philadelphia, and Boston—still the nation's three largest urban areas when "suburbs" such as North Liberties and Charlestown are included—housed just 4 percent of the population, and only 20 cities had more than 20,000 people. Still, the 1840 census was the first to find more than 100 communities of more than 2,500 people each—there were just 90 in 1830.

After 1840, the urban share of the nation's population began growing by about 5 percent per decade, so that it nearly doubled to 20 percent by 1860, doubled again to 40 percent by 1900, and doubled again to nearly 80 percent by 2000 (see Figure 3.1). This growth increasingly made urban homeownership rates the heart of our story.

New transportation technologies—the steamboat after 1810, the canal after 1820, and most importantly the railroad after 1830—stimulated the explosive growth of the cities. By greatly reducing the costs of moving raw materials to factories and finished goods to consumers, these new forms of transportation increased industrial production and the demand for workers in urban areas.

If transport and industry provided the jobs, immigration provided many of the employees and their families who made up the growing populations of the nation's larger cities. Immigration grew from under 10,000 people per year before 1825 to more than 100,000 people per year in 1842. From 1840 through 1900, immigrants made up 30 percent of the population growth of the United States, and many of those immigrants settled in industrial cities, such as Chicago, Detroit, and Pittsburgh.

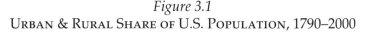

Figure 3.1
URBAN & RURAL SHARE OF U.S. POPULATION, 1790–2000

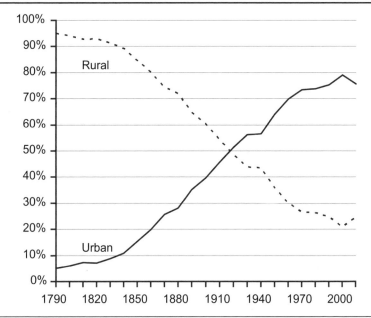

SOURCE: Census Bureau, Washington, D. C.

The Middle-Class/Working-Class Split

The advent of large corporations, such as railroads, textile manufacturers, and steelmakers, created a demand for two types of employees: managers and laborers. Management required special skills and, often, personality traits, so good managers were paid a premium. Laborers were viewed as interchangeable and were generally paid much less. Although management jobs tended to go to native-born Americans with better educations, immigrants mainly took the laborer jobs. The managers became the middle class, while laborers became the working class.

These distinctions were largely unknown before the 19th century. The first recorded use of the term "working class" was in an 1813 book titled *A New View of Society*, which divided people into "poor," "working class without property," "working class with property," and higher classes that employed the working classes.[1]

36

The term "middle class" is older, its earlier meaning referring to traders and merchants who were between the aristocracy and peasants. Its modern usage of referring to professionals and managers has been traced to an English statistician named T. H. C. Stevenson, who worked for the Registrar-General—roughly the British equivalent of the Census Bureau—in his analysis of Britain's 1911 census.[2]

Cultural differences between the middle and working classes go well beyond differences in income, which greatly narrowed in the second half of the 20th century. Qualifying for a management job generally requires more education, and that advanced education helps shape people's tastes in food, recreation, entertainment, and lifestyles in general.

These cultural differences go back many decades. An analysis of 19th-century literature, for example, found that working-class fiction, reflecting the realities of working-class lives, tended to be more violent and more overtly sexual than middle-class fiction.[3] Cultural differences in the 19th century were particularly exacerbated by the high percentage of immigrants—often immigrants from countries culturally much different from the Anglo-Americans who made up most of the native-born population. Irish immigration peaked in the 1840s and 1850s; German immigration came in waves that successively peaked in the early 1850s, early 1870s, and early 1880s; Italian and eastern European immigration became significant in the 1890s and peaked in the 1900s–1910s.[4] These waves of immigration brought in people who were increasingly alien to the Anglo culture that dominated the United States.

Imagine a Sunday summer afternoon in late 19th-century Chicago or Pittsburgh where a working-class family lives next door to a middle-class family. On the front porch, the working-class father plays a banjo and the family sings songs from their native land in their native language, accompanied by clucking chickens and barking dogs. Meanwhile, the middle-class family gathers around the piano indoors. The working-class mother is cooking a meal liberally laced with garlic, strong cheeses, and other odiferous ingredients. The middle-class family eats food that is even blander than English food is noted for today. Boarders come and go in the working-class house along with customers of the in-home sewing business; the only visitors to the middle-class house are as prim as its residents. The potential for conflicts is obvious.

The Immigrant Dream

One of the cultural differences between 19th-century working- and middle-class families was in how they viewed their homes. While middle-class families considered homes to be simply a place to live, working-class families also used their homes as income-producing opportunities. They could raise chickens and vegetables in their yards; take in boarders; and run small businesses, such as sewing, out of their homes.[5] These supplemental sources of income, together with income earned by children and other family members, typically came close to equaling the income earned by the family's principal wage earner.[6]

In addition, working-class families rarely had bank accounts (partly because 19th-century banking hours were so limited— typically from 10:00 a.m. to 3:00 p.m.—that laborers could rarely visit a bank). Instead, they regarded their home as a bank, using their homes as collateral for small loans (from relatives or "real-estate entrepreneurs," not from banks) to start up businesses or tide them over if the leading income producer in the family was temporarily out of work.[7] Realtors of the day said that houses were "better than a bank for a poor man," and "with hindsight," says one historian, "this appears to have been true."[8]

As such, 19th-century working-class families had powerful incentives to own their own homes. "The lure of land ownership served as the single most important magnet for English and European immigrants from the sixteenth century until well into the nineteenth," observes historian William Worley. "In the last third of the nineteenth century, this hunger was transformed into desire for ownership of city and town lots."[9] "The ambition of the immigrant to own property in America is one of his most striking characteristics. For it, he will make almost unbelievable sacrifices both of his own comfort and that of his wife and children," wrote an observer of Chicago working-class living conditions in 1913. "The possession of a house from which one may draw an income is the highest mark of prosperity."[10]

Fortunately for the immigrants, housing was inexpensive. Land in most cities was abundant. Although land within walking distance of factories eventually became scarce, in Chicago, for example, subdividers had created enough lots by 1873 to accommodate a million people, or 2.5 times the city's actual population.[11] Rather than buy a lot, people could save a little money by leasing a lot and building a small, wood-frame home that could be moved when the lease expired.[12]

The cost of erecting a small, wood-frame structure was low and could be made lower if the homeowners did much of the work themselves. Someone could buy a lot and built a small home—suitable for eventual expansion—for $800 to $1,000.[13] Median incomes for late 19th-century or early 20th-century wage earners was $350 to $600 a year, or roughly one-third to one-half the cost of a house.[14]

Early Credit Tools

The financial tools available to 19th-century homebuyers were more primitive than they are today. Until 1886, no one conceived of a contract that would convey a home's title to the buyer only after the buyer had paid off most or all of the house, and sellers were reluctant to give title to someone without a substantial deposit. So most lots and homes were sold with a 50 percent down payment. Working-class homebuyers would have to save this money or, more likely, borrow it from relatives.

The remaining 50 percent would be paid through a nonamortizing loan—which today we would call an interest-only loan—typically at 7 to 9 percent interest, with a balloon payment of the principal after five or six years. A $500 loan would have a monthly payment of less than $4; at each five- or six-year interval, the family would typically refinance the loan. To make monthly payments, families might take children out of school in their mid-teens so they could earn money and contribute to the household budget.[15]

Housing affordability was a major political issue in late 19th-century cities. After the Chicago fire, the city's Common Council considered an ordinance forbidding wood-frame homes and requiring brick or stone instead. That constraint would have easily tripled the cost of home construction. When more than 2,000 people besieged city hall in protest, the council agreed to exclude working-class neighborhoods from the requirement.[16] Even among the middle class, passage of the ordinance slowed home construction. According to a local writer in 1878, the ordinance resulted in "a brisk demand for building lots just outside of the fire limits, and a chronic dullness in the market for moderately choice lots within those limits."[17]

Middle-Class Renters

While working-class families had strong reasons to buy homes, the incentives for middle-class families were quite different. Before zoning, no one could predict what would happen to neighboring properties. Although it was unlikely that anyone would build a factory or

39

dig a gravel pit next to middle-class homes, no one could stop a working-class family from buying a vacant lot and building a small home complete with boarders, in-home businesses, smelly foods, noisy children, and backyard livestock. Unlike today, urban neighborhoods in the 19th century tended not to be divided by income levels.

This lack of security from working-class invaders encouraged the vast majority of middle-class urban families to rent or lease their homes in the late 19th century. Landlords in some cities offered leases for as long as 21 years, blurring the distinction between leasing and renting a home.[18] Since middle-class workers had easier access to banks and other means of saving and investing their money, they did not feel the need to buy a home to use as a savings bank. As a result, working-class homeownership rates, especially among immigrants, were higher than for middle-class families.

The 1890 census found that about 37 percent of nonfarm dwellings were owned by their occupants. However, about 40 percent of "nonfarm" homes were in rural areas; homeownership rates in urban areas, though not specifically recorded by the Census Bureau, appear to have been much lower. An 1890 survey of urbanites by the U.S. commissioner of labor found that just 17.6 percent were homeowners, which would put rural nonfarm homeownership at 62 percent.[19] That figure sounds reasonably accurate since in other decades for which data are available, rural nonfarm and rural farm homeownership rates tend to be similar, and rural farm ownership was 66 percent in 1890.

Homeownership rates for many ethnic groups, who were mainly working class, were much higher. As early as 1870, 27 percent of German families and 20 percent of other immigrant families owned their own homes in Chicago, and homeownership rates among these groups were probably even higher by 1890.[20] Since upper-class homeownership rates were close to 100 percent, middle-class homeownership rates must have been below 10 percent.

Housing Innovations

Several innovations during the late 19th century made it even easier for working-class families to own their own homes. First was the development of new techniques that sped and simplified home construction. Balloon-framed houses held together with nails almost anyone could pound replaced traditional timber-framing methods that required skilled workers to make the mortise-and-tenon joints that held the house together. Sometimes called "Chicago construction" because it was widely used after the 1871 Chicago fire, balloon framing was made possible by the development of machine-made nails and standardized lumber sizes.

The simplification of home construction stimulated another innovation, which was the growth of the home construction industry and the early application of mass production techniques to home building. Traditionally, subdividers would sell lots, and buyers would build or hire someone to build a home. But the 1880s saw the emergence of housing developers who would sell lots *and* build homes on those lots, both to order and on speculation.

One of the largest developers in the country was Samuel E. Gross, a lawyer who began subdividing land and building homes in the Chicago area in the early 1880s. In little more than 10 years, he sold more than 40,000 lots and built more than 7,500 homes—more than any other Chicago homebuilder before or since—in 150 different subdivisions.[21]

Chicago families could buy an S. E. Gross home for as little as $800, and $1,000 to $1,500 would buy a four-room house, the difference in cost depending on whether or not the house had indoor plumbing. Many of Gross's early homes can still be found in Chicago with relatively few modifications other than the addition of indoor plumbing if the home was not originally so built.[22]

In 1886, a Cincinnati subdivider named W. E. Harmon conceived of the idea of a "contract for deed," in which a buyer would not receive the deed to the property until it was completely paid for. Initially, Harmon sold lots with less than a 10 percent down payment; eventually, he reduced that down payment to as little as 1 percent.[23]

Such contracts were quickly adopted by other subdividers and homebuilders. By 1889, Samuel Gross was offering to sell a $950 home with as little as $50 down followed by payments of $8 a month.[24] Though the loans were nonamortizing—meaning buyers faced a balloon payment every five or six years—Gross bragged that he never foreclosed on a loan, instead renegotiating new loans when needed.[25] Like General Motors' encouraging auto buyers to step up from Chevrolet to Buick and Cadillac, Gross helped workers trade up to larger and better homes as their fortunes improved.

Gross has been lauded for having "altruistic motivations" in selling homes to working-class families on such generous terms.[26] Yet he was no altruist, building a fortune estimated in 1895 to be $4 to $5 million.[27] He had merely combined several ideas into a successful business model that focused on a customer base of people who preferred to own, rather than rent, their homes.

Credit Innovations

A third innovation was the growth of building and loan associations (B&Ls, later known as savings and loan associations). Unlike commercial banks, which had owners and customers, the original B&Ls were cooperatives: people who opened accounts and saved money were members. Instead of investing for maximum profits, the associations worked primarily for their members, loaning them money for real estate and other purposes. The first American B&L opened in the Philadelphia area in 1831. By 1893, more than 5,500 such associations across the country had helped more than 300,000 families acquire homes.[28]

Building and loan associations pioneered the use of amortizing loans as early as the 1880s. Amortizing mortgages were less risky for both the buyer and the seller, and they made it possible for many families to become true homeowners instead of mortgagees more rapidly. Before 1913, national banks were not legally allowed to make real-estate loans, and from 1913 to 1934 they could lend only half the appraised value of a property for just five-year terms. Although state banks could make such loans, they relied on non-amortizing loans into the early 20th century. A few developers, such as Boston's Robert Treat Paine, offered amortizing mortgages to homebuyers as early as the 1890s.[29] However, amortizing mortgages from B&Ls were "commonplace by the late nineteenth century," and the vast majority of such mortgages before 1930 were provided by these associations.[30] B&Ls also loaned as much as 70 percent of the appraised value of a home, offered terms as long as 12 years, and generally charged lower interest rates than banks.

Public Health

Even as these innovations made housing more affordable, another innovation made it less affordable: sanitary sewers and water supplies. Clean water delivered to a kitchen or bathroom sink was arguably a private good, and private water supply companies sprang up in many American cities soon after the Revolution. By 1800, Americans had built waterworks in 17 cities, 16 of which were private; by 1830, there were 45 waterworks, 36 of which were private.[31]

If clean water was a private good, polluted water was a public bad. Economically, a *public good* is one that benefits everyone even if only some pay the cost; national defense is the classic example. Conversely, a public bad is one that potentially harms everyone even if only a few are responsible for the problem.

Poor sanitation had been the bane of cities ever since the first cities were built. Before the 19th century, many European cities had higher death rates than birth rates and were able to grow only because of people emigrating from rural areas. These problems were transmitted to the new world as soon as cities grew to a significant size and particularly when world trade expanded the range of microorganisms that were once limited to one or two countries.

One such microorganism is cholera, which one historian called "the classic epidemic disease of the nineteenth century."[32] Before 1800, cholera was largely confined to India, but in 1817 an epidemic affected much of the Old World. An 1832 epidemic reached the New World, killing thousands of people in Chicago, Cincinnati, New York, and many other cities along the Mississippi and Ohio rivers, the Erie Canal, and the Great Lakes. At the time, most people suspected the disease was transmitted through the air; many years, and several more epidemics, were required before public health officials realized that the real problem was contaminated drinking water.

Cholera is a bacterium that infects the human intestines, leading to serious diarrhea. Since many people obtained their water from easily contaminated rivers or wells, the disease could spread rapidly. Cholera was a particularly frightening disease because dehydration killed 50 to 60 percent of infected patients within a few hours; it was not until the 20th century that medical doctors realized that massive rehydration could reduce mortality to 1 percent.

As early as 1842, an English social reformer named Edwin Chadwick called for replacing cesspools and privy vaults with a citywide sewage system consisting of pipes that would use household water to transmit fecal matter and other waste to a single location where it could be composted and sold as fertilizer.[33] Chadwick himself failed to understand the dangers of drinking contaminated water; instead, he believed that cholera, typhoid fever, dysentery, and other waterborne diseases were spread through "foul air," so his goal was to move sources of contagion downwind of the cities.[34]

The first proof that cholera was spread by contaminated drinking water had to wait until 1854, when an English physician named John Snow found that nearly every victim of a cholera epidemic in south London lived near and drank water from a single well. The well was later found to be only three feet from a cesspool that had been contaminated by cholera.[35] Although Snow's report led the city to remove the pump handle from that particular well, Snow's theory of waterborne contamination remained controversial for many years.

Although most American waterworks were eventually taken over by city governments, they could potentially be private and their costs, even when government owned, have largely been paid for out of user fees. From a public health view, however, voluntary user fees might be inadequate to pay for sewers; as long as anyone could refuse to pay the fee and continue to dump their wastes in a cesspool, water supplies could potentially become contaminated. Chadwick's hope that fertilizer sales would cover the costs of a citywide sewage system was unrealistic, and the high cost of sewers combined with debates over the actual causes of diseases kept most American cities from installing universal sewage systems for several decades.

Chicago, for example, built one of the first American municipal sewer systems dealing with human wastes in 1856.[36] Yet 37 years later, a survey found that nearly three out of four Chicago residents still relied on privies rather than indoor plumbing.[37] The reason was Chicago paid for the sewers out of user fees, and the only homes connected to the sewage system were those whose owners could afford to pay for indoor plumbing and hookup fees.[38] It was not until 1902 that Chicago mandated that all new homes be hooked up to sewer systems. This law exempted existing homes, and by increasing the cost of new housing, it made it more difficult for working-class families to buy a home.[39]

The cost of indoor plumbing fixtures and connections to city water and sewer systems could nearly double the price of a small, single-family home.[40] Mandating such hookups would price many working-class families out of the homeownership market.

Boston took a different approach from Chicago's. Though it did not begin to construct an integrated sewer system until after the Civil War, when it did so it paid for the capital costs out of general funds, meaning, mainly, property taxes.[41] This payment method meant that owners of expensive homes effectively subsidized owners of smaller homes. Low-income families who sought to build a home still had to pay for indoor plumbing fixtures and to pay the city for water meters and operating costs.

In the long run, the public sewer model had an even more profound effect on housing costs. The perceived need for publicly owned, centralized sewer systems led to a significant growth in city government. Cities hired sanitary engineers who attempted to forecast future needs and write long-range plans to meet those needs.[42]

These long-range plans set a precedent for later city plans and increasingly specific regulations written to deal with such things as transportation, land uses, parks, historic buildings, watersheds, and trees. Although no one can argue the public health benefits of integrated sewage systems, later policies that, for example, imposed "impact fees" on homebuilders to pay for transportation or created time-consuming permitting processes for the cutting of individual trees significantly increased the costs of homeownership while providing dubious benefits.

Housing for Factory Workers

In the short run, another late 19th-century trend had an even larger effect on housing affordability: the growth of the factory system. The nation's first factory, the Slater Mill in Pawtucket, Rhode Island, employed just nine workers. By 1880, factories remained small enough that close to 90 percent of the families of, say, Detroit could live in individual homes and workers would still be within walking distance of their places of employment.[43]

However, the average number of employees per factory more than doubled between 1869 and 1899 and continued to grow after that.[44] By 1904, 60 percent of all manufacturing employees worked in factories with more than 100 employees, and 12 percent worked in factories with more than 1,000 employees.[45] Moreover, the tendency of many industries, such as Chicago's stockyards, to concentrate in one part of a city created transportation problems for workers.

Although some cities saw the installation of horsecars as early as 1850 and rapid growth of electric streetcar networks after 1890, factory workers earning between $3 and $6 a week could not afford to devote 10 to 20 percent of their incomes to transit fares. The limited amount of land within walking distance of factories, and the resulting high cost of such land, forced many to live in high-density tenements instead of single-family homes.

The word "tenements" brings to mind extremely high-density midrise buildings housing several families per apartment, or even per room, in New York City's Lower East Side. Reformer Jacob Riis photographed residents of these buildings in the late 1880s and early 1890s. His 1889 book *How the Other Half Lives: Studies among the Tenements of New York* included several of these photos and raised public attention about poor housing conditions and influenced the passage of several tenement laws.[46]

Riis's tenements were five to six stories high built on 25-by-100-foot lots, meaning about 16 could fit on a single acre. The front and back of the buildings occupied the full width of the lot with a small airshaft between the buildings in the center. Because they were narrow in the middle to make room for the airshaft, these buildings were often called "dumbbells."[47] Designed to house four families to a floor, or up to 24 per building, they were sometimes packed with far more. The narrow airshafts meant that most rooms had little light, and the odors from the garbage that people inevitably threw to the inaccessible bottoms of the shafts must have been stifling. Many of these tenements had no indoor plumbing; those that did might have only one toilet per floor. Perhaps most scandalous to the middle-class readers of Riis's book was the lack of privacy: children of all ages and both sexes often slept in the same rooms as their parents, other relatives, and unrelated boarders.

New York City tenement conditions were a direct function of the density of inner-city jobs. The Triangle Shirtwaist factory, site of the infamous fire that killed nearly 150 workers, occupied 3 floors of a 10-story building in lower Manhattan and employed 500 workers. The building covered about one-quarter acre out of the nearly 7,000 developed acres in Manhattan. Although pre-1890 factories would have fewer floors, even six-story factories could contain 4,000 workers per acre, most of whom had to live within walking distance of the buildings.

In 1910, the year before the Triangle Shirtwaist fire, Manhattan had about 2.3 million residents at an average population density of about 100,000 people per square mile. (For comparison, the median density of the nation's 50 largest urban areas in 2000 was about 2,800 people per square mile.) Manhattan today has about 2.3 million jobs, and certainly nearly all the pre-1900 residents who had jobs worked in Manhattan. The combination of offices, factories, and residences competing for space made lower Manhattan some of the most valuable real estate in the world. Factory workers who couldn't afford to commute off the island were forced to live in high-density environments, which is why the Lower East Side housed some 334,000 people per square mile in the 1880s.

The problem was compounded by 19th-century construction technology, which made it difficult to build structures taller than about six stories. (The nation's first steel-framed skyscraper, St. Louis's 10-story Wainwright Building, was built in 1891; the tallest commercial masonry building ever built, Chicago's Monadnock Building, is also 10 stories and was also built in 1891.) Residents typically need a lot more space than factory workers; given Manhattan's high land prices, the tenement was the way of packing as many workers and their families as possible into as little land as possible.

Although the conditions in the Lower East Side were truly awful, they were far from "the other half." As historian Robert Barrows observes, "New York City's Lower East Side, the case study most frequently cited because of its immaterial power, was virtually unique, an aberration that, in scale at least was replicated nowhere else in the country."[48] "New York has over 100,000 separate tenement houses, whereas in most American cities that tenement house is the exception rather than the rule," admitted Lawrence Veiller in a 1912 speech. Veiller had worked harder than anyone to promote legislation outlawing the housing conditions pictured in Riis's photographs.[49]

Public concern about urban housing for the poor actually dates back to well before the Civil War. In 1847, a group known as the Association for Improving the Condition of the Poor published a survey showing that New York City tenement housing was "defective in size, arrangement, water supply, warmth, and ventilation, and that rents were disproportionately high." As a result, the poor "suffer from sickness and premature mortality; their ability for self-maintenance is thereby destroyed; social habits and morals are debased, and a vast amount of wretchedness, pauperism, and crime is produced."[50]

This belief in *architectural determinism*—the notion that the built environment shapes human behavior and a poorly built environment leads to debased morals, pauperism, and crime—guided the association's solution, which was government regulation mandating minimum housing standards. Better housing, the association believed, would lead the poor to engage in less crime and more productive work, which would guide them out of poverty. Failing to persuade the New York City Council, the association went to the state legislature, which in 1867 passed a tenement house law requiring builders to provide a 10-foot backyard and a water supply and forbidding the renting of apartments that were totally underground. An 1879 law required a window in every room in a tenement.[51]

Ironically, the result of these laws were the dumbbell tenements that so horrified Jacob Riis: the narrow airshafts that created the dumbbell shape ensured that every room had a window even if the lower-story windows let in almost no light. This experience would be repeated over and over as low-income housing advocates, sometimes called "housers," would propose government programs that, as finally implemented, did little for poor people other than make housing less affordable.

The New York State Tenement House Act of 1901, for example, required builders of new tenements to provide sanitary facilities, outward-facing windows in every room, and a courtyard for garbage removal in place of the airshafts where people tossed garbage. This act was considered a model law, but as historian Gwendolyn Wright observes, "The stipulations proved so strict that few speculative builders would divert their money into this kind of construction any more, and the housing shortage for the poor grew worse."[52]

Wright points out that the housers "brought moralistic middle-class biases to their crusade" and "considered their own taste to be a universal standard of beauty, hygiene, and human sentiment." When Chicago succeeded in condemning a tenement and was evicting its Italian residents, one reformer noted, "It was strange to find people so attached to homes that were lacking in all the attributes of comfort and decency." One housing proposal urged that tenements be given more of those attributes by equipping them with such amenities as doorbells and bay windows.[53] Such requirements, of course, would do nothing to fix the fundamental problem of urban poverty.

Rather than regulate urban housing, some housing reformers dreamed of moving working-class families to the suburbs, where land was cheap and they could live in uncrowded conditions. In the 1870s, Boston Unitarian minister Edward Everett Hale encouraged working-class men to form and join building and loan associations so they could buy suburban homes. Recognizing the transportation problem, Hale urged the railroads to provide "cheap trains for laboring men."[54]

In New York City, Edward Bassett, a one-term member of Congress who later helped write New York City's zoning code, argued that people should move "from crowded centres to the open spaces" where they could have "sunny homes and plenty of air." Overcoming the transportation problem required "low fares, so that the expense might not deter people from moving where life would be pleasanter." The main obstacle, he believed, was "the real estate forces of New York [who] believe in congestion" and who "prevent the opening up of new areas by five-cent rapid transit" for fear it will reduce property values in the urban core.[55]

Unfortunately, even the traditional nickel streetcar fares were beyond the reach of many unskilled workers. As planning historian Peter Hall notes, the development of the mass-produced automobile, not the five-cent streetcar, managed to "dissolve the worst evils of the slum city through the process of mass suburbanization."[56]

Fortunately for working-class families outside New York City, most low-income housing in Chicago and other industrial cities would be considered luxury housing relative to the Lower East Side. Typical was the "two flat," a two-story building with an apartment on each floor.[57] Less common were three flats (or as they were known in Boston, three-deckers) for three families. Many flats were owned by absentee landlords, but often the owners of a two- or three flat would live on the top story (which was generally quieter and had slightly more square footage than lower stories) and rent out the other flats.

Like New York City tenements, two flats were built on 25-foot-wide lots, but most of the houses were only about 20 feet wide so there was room for a walking path between each one. They generally had small backyards, some of which have been filled with garages since they were first built in the late 19th century. Two flats and three flats on narrow lots, with occasional four- to eightplexes, provided enough density for working-class employees to live within walking distance of work in Chicago and other industrial cities. But the multifamily nature of the buildings meant that most workers could not achieve the immigrants' dream of owning their own home.

Although middle-class families were less attached to the idea of homeownership than those from the working class, they enjoyed relatively high housing standards whether they rented or owned. A late 19th-century working-class home, such as the kind built by Samuel Gross in 1890, might have a parlor, a kitchen that doubled as a dining room, and two seven-by-eight-foot bedrooms, usually with a privy in back instead of indoor plumbing.[58] Even more basic was a two-room working-class cottage, with a kitchen that also served as parlor, dining room, and bedroom for the children, and a bedroom that was sometimes shared with boarders.[59]

"A generation later," says historian Joseph Bigott, housers such as Edith Abbott "denied that cottages ever provided decent accommodation." Abbott argued "that the unskilled are a dangerous class; inadequately fed, clothed, and housed, they threaten the health of the community." She wanted the government to build public housing for low-income families, but such government programs would be politically possible only if Abbott could persuade people that the homes workers provided for themselves were unsafe or otherwise inadequate.[60] In attempting to do so, she was imposing her middle-class biases on working-class families.

Middle-class homes had several features not found in a typical working-class house of the 1890s: water, sewer, and (later) electrical hookups; a three-fixture bathroom; a kitchen sink and other new technologies, such as an icebox, washing machine, and, eventually, electrical appliances; a formal dining room; enough bedrooms so that parents and children could have their own rooms; a front porch; and storage closets (since working-class families had "little to store," their basic homes "made almost no provision for built-in, enclosed storage").[61] Although working-class families aspired to add these features to their homes in the 20th century, the fact that their homes did not have them in the late 19th century did not mean they were ignorant or (except in the case of sanitation) dangerous to the community.

As the 19th century came to a close, Riis's revelations about the abominable housing conditions of many low-income families led middle-class intellectuals to ask two important questions. First, how can the poor be assured of safe and decent housing? And second, how can we make sure they don't move next door to us? Not surprisingly, the second question was answered first by government policies such as zoning and public housing, while the answer to the first question would wait for the ingenuity of entrepreneurs such as Henry Ford and William Levitt.

4. The Suburban Dream

After the end of World War I, the National Association of Real Estate Boards started a campaign encouraging people to "own your own home." On the premise that a home construction boom would revive the nation's economy, the Department of Labor joined in the campaign, distributing pamphlets and flyers. In 1921, the campaign received an even bigger boost when the young secretary of commerce, Herbert Hoover, personally lent his support, encouraging the homebuilding industry to reduce costs by standardizing construction practices and distributing hundreds of thousands of copies of a booklet titled *How to Own Your Own Home.*[1]

Considering that the number of owner-occupied homes grew from 10.9 million in 1920 to 14 million in 1930, many would deem this campaign a success. Some have gone so far as to label the campaign a "conspiracy" aimed at deceiving many Americans into buying homes when they would be better off renting.[2]

In fact, the own-your-own-home campaign was one of the least important factors in the rise of homeownership in the early 20th century. The government, in cooperation with various special-interest groups, conducts all sorts of campaigns aimed at changing our behavior, from urging people out of their cars and onto transit to reducing obesity. There is little evidence that these campaigns have a major effect on behavior.

On the other hand, the years between 1890 and 1930 saw several profound changes that transformed American lifestyles and the role of homeownership for both middle- and working-class families. Those changes included an expansion of credit; new transportation technologies, such as streetcars and automobiles; new industrial technologies, such as the moving assembly line; a new class of homebuilders who combined subdivision planning with home construction; and the use of protective covenants and zoning to protect home values—often by protecting middle-class neighborhoods from working-class intrusions.

Figure 4.1
U.S. HOMEOWNERSHIP RATES, 1890–2010

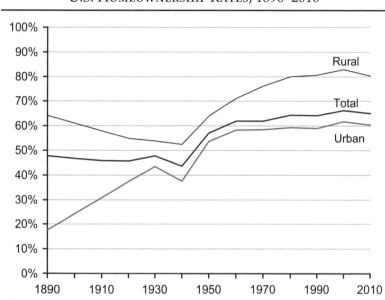

SOURCE: Census Bureau, Washington, D. C.

When combined, those changes dramatically increased urban homeownership rates. Rural homeownership rates were already high in 1890: more than 64 percent of rural families but only 17.6 percent of urban families lived in their own homes (see Figure 4.1). By 1930, the rural rate had declined slightly to 54 percent, but the urban rate increased by 2.5 times to 43.4 percent.[3] Since urban populations more than tripled in that same time period, while average family size declined from 4.76 to 4.01, the number of owned homes in urban areas grew more than 10 times, from about 710,000 in 1890 to 7.4 million in 1930. Most of that increase was before the realtors' own-your-own-home campaign began: in 1920, urban homeownership had already climbed to 37.4 percent, representing 4.7 million homes.[4]

Expansion of Credit

This increase in homeownership was financed by an expansion of credit tools, and especially by the growth of building and loan associations. As previously noted, as of 1893, B&Ls had helped finance about 300,000 homes. By the 1920s, they became the primary source of finance for homebuyers, offering amortizing loans for up to 12 years with as little as 25 percent down. In a decade that saw the construction of 7.03 million new homes, the B&Ls financed 4.35 million homes, lending $15 billion, or nearly $3,500 per home.[5]

Growth of the Suburbs

Between 1890 and 1930, the number of urban homes, rented and owned, more than quadrupled. This rise contributed to the rapid growth of the suburbs: During the 1920s, the first full decade in which urbanites outnumbered ruralites, the suburbs grew twice as fast as the cities.[6] The political reason for suburban growth was the increasingly scarce vacant land inside the cities, and people living outside the cities were increasingly resistant to being annexed at a time when many cities were run by political machines known for their corruption.

The social reason for suburban growth was that it allowed middle-class families to get away from working-class neighbors and settle into communities of people more like themselves. Historians Oliver Zunz and Margaret Garb have shown that, in the 1880s, urban neighborhoods in cities such as Detroit and Chicago were divided along ethnic lines, while by the 1920s, they were divided by income classes.[7] This change hints at a dark side of growing homeownership, which was that it took place mostly or entirely among the middle class, while working-class homeownership rates appear to have stagnated or declined.

Too many, the term "suburbs" evokes images of Levittowns and other post-World War II developments, but people began escaping cities for the suburbs long before that. In the pre-sanitary and public health era—which includes almost all of the 19th century—cities were rightly regarded as unhealthy and unsafe, prime locations for epidemics, not to mention crime and other problems. The ability of those with urban occupations to escape the city for the suburbs depended on their wealth, leisure time, and access to transportation.

New Transportation Technologies

Before the 1830s, the only transportation available to most urbanites was foot or horsepower. Since only wealthy or high-income people could afford to keep horses in cities, most people located within one or two miles of urban job centers. The development of steam-powered trains offered a few people the option of living farther away.

Early steam trains had top speeds of about 30 miles per hour but typically ran much slower. In 1839, Ulysses Grant rode a train on part of his journey to West Point and observed top speeds of about 18 mph and average speeds of 12 mph.[8] These rates still represented a significant advance over walking speeds, and speeds rapidly increased so that, by 1850, trains could achieve 60 mph and typically cruised at 30 to 40 mph. However, commuter train services were available only in the largest cities, and fares were so expensive that only the wealthiest people could use them for commuting.

An alternative to steam-powered trains was the horsecar—a horse-powered vehicle running on rails—which was first offered in New York City in 1832 and was common in many American cities by 1850. San Francisco saw the first cable car system in 1873, and by 1890 cable cars operated in around 30 American cities. However, horsecars and cable cars were both slow and expensive, so although they attracted some middle-class riders, they did not stimulate much suburban growth.

The electric streetcar, which was perfected in the late 1880s, led to the first major suburban boom. Average streetcar speeds of 10 to 15 mph were slow by today's standards, but much faster than any previous form of transport other than the far more expensive steam train. Electric streetcars were so inexpensive to operate that almost all horse- and cable-car lines quickly converted to electrical power, and by 1910 well over 800 American cities had at least one streetcar line. In many cities, developers would build a streetcar line between downtown and their subdivision as a way of attracting homebuyers. Although nickel fares were sufficient to operate the streetcars, the cost of building the lines was actually subsidized by lot and home sales. Later, these streetcar lines often merged and often ended up under the control of the local electric power company.

The streetcar transformed both cities and suburbs. Before the streetcar, wealthy urbanites often built the finest homes on major thoroughfares, where they had easy access to transportation and other services. Wealthy suburbanites tended to live 3 to 10 miles from city centers— close enough to reach by horsepower but too far to walk. But the noise and crowds brought by the streetcar caused the wealthy to retreat from arterial streets, which were soon lined with shops and multifamily housing, and to move as far away as 15 miles from the city center.[9]

Historian Sam Warner estimates that about 5 percent of people in the Boston area of 1900 were wealthy or in the upper-middle class, meaning the owners of large businesses or prosperous lawyers and other professionals. Another 15 percent would be in the central-middle class, including small business owners, teachers, and other professionals. Some 20 to 30 percent were in the lower-middle class, including office workers, shopkeepers, and skilled artisans. The remaining 50 to 60 percent were working class.[10]

The traditional streetcar fare of 5 cents per ride kept working-class commuters out of the suburbs. Warner estimates that about 40 percent of the housing in Boston's streetcar suburbs was multifamily, often two- and three-deckers, and was the home for many lower-middle-class families. These structures tended to be closest to the streetcar stops. Central-middle-class families tended to live in single-family homes on lots that would be considered small by today's suburban standards, typically around 5,000 square feet.[11] The result was that streetcar suburbs tended to be fairly compact, so that commuters would not have to walk long distances between their homes and streetcar stops.

The wealthy and upper-middle class continued to live on large lots, either at the periphery of streetcar suburbs or farther out from the city, and probably relied on forms of transportation other than streetcars. Warner estimates that Boston's streetcar suburbs had a homeownership rate of about 25 percent in 1900—a significant increase over the average urban rate of 17.6 percent in 1890, but well below modern rates.[12]

The first gasoline-powered automobiles were developed at about the same time as the first streetcars. But early automobiles were too expensive for any but the wealthy and upper-middle class to own. That status changed in 1913, when Henry Ford began building Model Ts on a moving assembly line. Ford's system reduced the cost by so much that Ford cut the price of his cars in half even as he doubled workers' pay.

Automobiles were at least twice as fast as streetcars, which meant they could serve four times the land area without increasing commute times. With their door-to-door capability, they were far more convenient than streetcars or any other form of mass transportation. In 1919, Oregon became the first state to approve a gasoline tax dedicated to highways; by 1931 all other states had followed, providing a user-fee-driven source of funds for roads for auto owners to drive on.[13] By 1927, 56 percent of American families owned at least one auto, and 10 percent owned more than one.[14] Those families that owned autos no longer had to live on tiny lots or in multifamily housing to maintain their access to jobs, shops, and other services.

As the streetcar did before, the mass-produced automobile revolutionized the design of cities and suburbs. In the early 1900s, Kansas City developer J. C. Nichols was building homes for what Warner would call the central-middle class. In 1909, Nichols felt that it was essential that the local streetcar company build a line to one of his subdivisions. By 1913, however, Nichols opened a subdivision with no streetcar line and advertised that people could drive to downtown faster than they could get there by streetcar.[15] In 1922, Nichols opened Country Club Plaza, the nation's first suburban shopping mall designed to accommodate auto drivers. Although Kansas City residents initially called it "Nichols' folly," the mall remains a success today.[16]

New Manufacturing Technologies

Henry Ford's moving assembly line also revolutionized the making of everything from soap to railcars. Products built using traditional methods could be manufactured in multistory buildings, but moving assembly lines demanded many acres of horizontal space. This necessity led manufacturers to locate or relocate their plants in the suburbs, where land was less expensive. The oft-heard tale that everyone moved to the suburbs and then created traffic congestion trying to drive to work downtown is a myth: jobs moved to the suburbs along with the people.

Moving assembly lines both enabled and were enabled by widespread auto ownership. Ford's Rouge River plant, for example, covered one and a half square miles and employed 100,000 workers at its peak in the 1930s. Packing all those workers and their families (which averaged 3.5 people in the 1930s) within a one-mile walking distance of the plant would require multifamily housing at a population density nearly as great as Manhattan's is today. Because most employees could drive to work, they could live in much lower densities and many more could afford to own their own homes.

Homebuilders also attempted to adopt assembly-line techniques to make homes at a lower cost. One way was through the sale of kit homes—all the lumber, roofing, flooring, paint, nails, hardware, and other materials needed to build a home, precut and ready to assemble. The manufacturers of these kit homes offered hundreds of different house plans and claimed that homebuyers could save 10 percent or more on the cost of building a home.

In 1906, a Sears, Roebuck manager named Frank Kushel was directed to shut down the catalog company's building materials division because it was losing money. Instead, he proposed to repackage building materials into enough parts to build entire homes. Sears began selling kit homes in 1908 and over the next 32 years sold about 70,000 to 75,000 such homes.

Early Sears catalogs advertised homes ranging from 320 square feet to 2,000 square feet at prices ranging from 50 cents to about $2 a square foot. By 1918, the largest home in the catalog was nearly 3,000 square feet. Buyers had to supply their own labor, bricks, cement, and plaster. Also excluded were plumbing, electrical systems, furnaces, and furniture, though all these things were separately available, of course, from Sears. All the parts in the kit were numbered so assembly was supposed to take as little as a few days to several weeks. At the height of production in the mid-1920s, Sears delivered more than 300 homes per month.

At least eight other companies offered kit homes, including Montgomery Ward, whose homes were made by and were identical to an Iowa kit-home manufacturer named Gordon-Van Tine. But the real center of kit-home manufacturing was Bay City, Michigan, where three companies—Aladdin, Lewis, and Sterling—together sold close to 200,000 kit homes. Aladdin actually preceded Sears slightly by offering a kit boathouse in 1906. Other companies were located in Los Angeles, Portland, Oregon, and upstate New York.

The various manufacturers offered a variety of styles and plans, including Cape Cod, foursquare, Queen Anne, Tudor, Colonial, bungalow, and many other traditional styles of homes. Sears even offered a couple of Prairie School styles and, in the late 1930s, a flat-roofed International home. Buyers could ask that floor plans be reversed or for other custom changes to the basic plans. Duplexes, fourplexes, barns, and other outbuildings were also available.

In 1911, Sears began selling homes with a 25 percent down payment plus a mortgage at 6 percent interest over 5 years or a higher rate for as long as 15 years. Starting in 1917, buyers could even get a mortgage with no money down, though Sears discontinued that after 1921.

Over several decades, kit-home makers sold well over 450,000 homes, most of them between 1908 and 1930. Still, considering that all homebuilders combined built more than 7 million homes during the 1920s alone, kit homes were a small part of the market.

New Development Practices

The other major homebuilding trend in the early 20th century was the growth of planned communities. These communities were subdivisions where the developer either built some if not all the homes or set rigorous architectural standards for any homebuyers or home-builders to follow. The largest planned communities included parks and other common areas, community centers, and other amenities that residents could share.

An example of a minimally planned subdivision is Ford Homes, located in Dearborn, Michigan, near the Rouge River plant. Henry Ford always wanted to show that he could make or do things—from running a railroad to operating a steel mill—less expensively than anyone else, and Ford Homes was an example of that ambition. Ford hired an architect, Albert Wood, to design a site plan for the subdivision. One of Wood's suggestions was to cluster garages in a special service area for each block of the subdivision, forcing residents to walk a block or so to get to their cars. Needless to say, Ford rejected this idea. Wood also designed six basic homes, all in a Colonial style that Ford himself favored, which were used in the neighborhood.[17]

Following his assembly-line methods, Ford had five crews build the houses in stages: one crew dug the basements (using Ford tractors); a second put in foundations; a third framed the building; a fourth did the interiors, including wiring and plumbing; and the last crew did the exteriors, including landscaping. The process was simplified enough that Ford did not need to rely on skilled craftsmen; instead, he simply borrowed workers from his factories, noting that "men ought to spend part of the year working outside factory walls."[18]

Ford offered buyers mortgages at 6 percent interest. The only restrictions Ford put on the homes were that buyers could not resell them for seven years, while the company had the option to buy back the home within seven years if the buyer proved "undesirable" (it isn't clear whether this meant failing to keep up the payments or turning into a labor organizer at a Ford factory).[19]

Ford Homes were not designed to be particularly affordable for working-class families. Ranging from 1,200 to 1,500 square feet, the homes initially sold for $6,750 to $7,750 in 1919 ($85,000 to $98,000 today using the consumer price index; $277,000 to $318,000 today using the unskilled wage index). By comparison, General Motors built several hundred homes near Flint, Michigan, that started at $3,500 and averaged around $5,000. But neither Ford nor GM was trying to build worker housing; instead, they just wanted to show other developers how they could build more efficiently. In fact, many other developers had already adopted and gone well beyond Ford's techniques.[20]

One such developer was J. C. Nichols of Kansas City, who became noted for building one of the largest planned communities in the early 20th century. Although Nichols's Country Club District is sometimes called a master-planned community, a type of community that became popular in the 1960s, the Country Club District was in fact incrementally planned. Nichols started in 1906 with just 10 acres, which he subdivided into about 70 lots. With the profits he earned from that subdivision, he bought more land and subdivided it. Each new subdivision gained from what he learned from previous subdivisions. As mentioned earlier, he also built shopping areas, including the nation's first suburban shopping mall, hotels, apartments, and commercial office space. By 1930, the Country Club District covered 4,000 acres and housed at least 30,000 people in 9,000 homes.[21]

Deed Restrictions

One of the most important features in Nichols's subdivisions was the use of restrictive covenants. These covenants limited what people could do with their land, who they could sell it to, and how common areas would be managed. Nichols also created homeowners associations to manage and enforce the covenants. By prohibiting nonresidential uses in residential areas, Nichols's covenants assured middle-class homebuyers that their neighborhoods would not be invaded by industrial or retail shops. Moreover, by specifying the minimum cost of building a new home or the use of high-cost materials, the covenants assured homebuyers that their neighborhoods would not be invaded by working-class families whose tastes were significantly different from their own.

Nichols was far from the first to use protective covenants. As early as 1749, the Penn family used deed restrictions in some of their land sales requiring buyers to build homes of brick or stone, not wood, within one or two years of purchase.[22] In 1837, homebuyers in a development called Rock Park Estate in Cheshire, England, had to agree to have no fences taller than three feet, to have no businesses other than medicine or teaching, to set homes and other buildings back from streets, and to share in the cost of a community water supply.[23]

In the mid 1850s, a New York City businessman named Llewellyn Haskell put together 350 hilly, wooded acres near West Orange, New Jersey—which at that time would have been a long commute from New York City—and subdivided it into 130 lots of at least 1 acre each. He set aside 50 acres along a creek as a common area and restricted the lots he sold to residential purposes.[24]

Haskell turned out to be ahead of his time, or at least he timed his project badly. He lost control of the project during the recession of 1857, and the Civil War also put a damper on land sales. By 1886, only 38 out of 130 lots had sold.[25]

Nichols was more influenced by Kansas City developer Kersey Coates who, in 1857, put a deed restriction on some of his subdivisions requiring that homes be built of brick, which cost five times as much as wood homes. These subdivisions became known as "Quality Hill." Coates, an abolitionist, also designed subdivisions for working-class families and donated land in one neighborhood to a black Baptist church and a black elementary school. Ironically, Coates's well-intentioned efforts effectively segregated blacks from whites in Kansas City.[26]

In 1868, Frederick Law Olmstead helped design Riverside, a suburb of Chicago whose restrictive covenants required minimum lot sizes of one-half acre and homes costing no less than $3,000 (about $50,000 today using the consumer price index and $350,000 using the unskilled wage index). Also influential was Roland Park, a suburb of Baltimore planned in the early 1890s. Roland Park included a small shopping area that today might be called a strip mall. Deed restrictions forbade nonresidential uses in the rest of the subdivision. Depending on the lot, the minimum cost of houses was set at $2,000 to $5,000 ($50,000 to $125,000 today using the consumer price index and $240,000 to $600,000 using the unskilled wage index). Initially, deed restrictions were perpetual, but the developer later changed them to last for 25 years and be renewable after a vote of the homeowners.[27]

As it happened, Roland Park was managed by Edward Bouton, a Kansas City native, and was designed with the help of George Kessler, a Kansas City engineer. Kessler would later work with J. C. Nichols, and Nichols would credit Roland Park as one of his main inspirations.

Nichols's ability to learn from each new subdivision can be seen in the evolution of the deed restrictions he wrote for them. In 1908, the restrictions for one of his first developments were written to last 25 years.[28] Such restrictions were common to many planned communities, but they created a problem at the end of those 25 years. Developers were reluctant to make restrictions perpetual, because no one could foresee what people in the distant future would want. Some developers urged cities to pass zoning ordinances to take control when the deed restrictions expired.

Starting in 1909, deed restrictions written by Nichols lasted 25 years with an optional renewal by the homeowners association. Nichols thought this option still created a problem because the homeowner association would have to take a positive action to renew the restrictions or they would lapse. So he hit on the idea of having the restrictions renew automatically unless the homeowners association voted not to renew them.[29]

By 1922, Nichols had developed what he considered the optimal set of restrictions, and so he went to the homeowners associations of his already-completed subdivisions, as well as some nearby developments done by others, and urged them to adopt his new restrictions. They all agreed to do so, although a minority group at one subdivision protested as far as the Missouri Supreme Court, which agreed with the majority.[30] Nichols also created deed restrictions and a merchants association for Country Club Plaza, his pioneering shopping mall.

Nichols considered deed restrictions to be such a powerful selling tool that all his advertising emphasized that property values would be "protected" by the restrictions. His restrictions did not specify any particular architectural styles, but they did require that his company approve all building designs. He also included minimum costs for homes and various other limits on uses. "Every year we are planning and studying as to how we can impose upon that property more conditions, and more restrictions," he told other developers in 1921, "and it has paid and it is paying."[31] Restrictions cost the developer almost nothing, but they could add considerably to the value of property by assuring buyers that their land values would not be reduced by undesirable intrusions.

Among the other common areas included in Nichols's developments were "interior parks" in the middle of some blocks, with playground equipment and other features accessible only through the back doors of people's homes. Similar parks had previously been included in Roland Park and were later a part of the much-lauded Radburn, a planned development in New Jersey designed by architect Clarence Stein. Stein treated the streets as service areas only and faced the fronts of the homes in Radburn toward the parks, which included walking paths that connected the homes with the outside world. Nichols also oriented his homes toward the side away from the street.

The problem with interior parks, as Country Club District residents found, is that they expose homes to potential intruders on two fronts: the front and back of the homes. If the interior parks are common areas, as at Radburn and in some Country Club subdivisions, as opposed to private backyards as in more conventional suburbs, then no one can tell if someone walking in the common area is a resident or a potential burglar. Because of residents' concerns about vandalism and break-ins, all but one interior park in the Country Club District were resubdivided among homeowners. Many of the Roland Park interior parks were also eliminated.[32]

The solution to this dilemma turned out to be gated communities. Sometimes decried as enclaves for the rich, a gated community is one way homeowners can protect themselves from turning interior common areas into pathways for crime; without such common areas, there would be no need for gated communities. The first planned community with a common area, Llewellyn Park, is a gated community, and no one from outside the community, except guests of the residents, may visit the common areas without written permission from the community association.[33]

One constant in Nichols's deed restrictions was a provision forbidding homeowners to sell to blacks and, in his early developments, Jews. Some writers have challenged the entire idea of protective covenants based on the fact that some of them included such racial restrictions.[34] Although America's racist past is shameful, covenants and deed restrictions can't be blamed for it any more than today's transit agencies can be blamed for the Montgomery, Alabama, bus company that was required by Jim Crow laws to order Rosa Lee Parks to sit in the back of the bus.

Racial restrictions were actually rare to nonexistent in protective covenants before 1908. Instead, developers implicitly assumed that other restrictions, such as minimum-cost requirements for homes, would effectively prevent blacks and other minorities from moving into their subdivisions.

Zoning and Land-Use Restrictions

The City of San Francisco first introduced racism into land-use rules in 1885, when it tried to restrict the mobility of Chinese by banning public laundries from most of the city. Even though the ordinance was overtly race neutral, the Supreme Court ruled that it violated the Fourteenth Amendment to the Constitution.[35]

In 1910, Baltimore wrote a zoning ordinance that excluded blacks from any block on which more than half the residents were white and excluded whites from blocks where half the residents were black. Baltimore's mayor Barry Mahool, a prominent member of the Progressive Party, commented that "Blacks should be quarantined in isolated slums in order to reduce the incidents of civil disturbance, to prevent the spread of communicable disease into the nearby White neighborhoods, and to protect property values among the White majority." Birmingham, Alabama; Richmond, Virginia; St. Louis, Missouri; and other cities wrote similar ordinances.[36] When the ordinance for Louisville, Kentucky, reached the Supreme Court, the Court unanimously ruled in 1917 that such zoning rules were unconstitutional. After that ruling, southern cities practiced "expulsive zoning," which allowed intrusive uses in black neighborhoods that were forbidden in white neighborhoods.[37]

The Supreme Court's ruling against racial zoning spurred developers to add such racial restrictions to the deeds for more planned developments. In 1928, a legal scholar named Helen Monchow reviewed the deed restrictions for 84 different developments and found racial restrictions in 40 of them, none of which dated before 1908.[38] Over time, the percentage probably increased until 1948, when the Supreme Court effectively invalidated such restrictions by ruling that the courts could not enforce them.[39]

Although deed restrictions preceded zoning by hundreds of years, such restrictions only applied to new developments. Zoning was conceived in the early 20th century as a way of providing the same stabilization of property values to existing neighborhoods. Although New York City is credited for passing the first comprehensive zoning ordinance in 1916, Los Angeles actually passed the first zoning ordinance in 1909—the difference being that the New York ordinance included height limits and setback requirements, while Los Angeles's original ordinance only regulated use.

L.A.'s 1909 ordinance designated certain areas residential, light industrial, and heavy industrial, while it left other areas unzoned. By 1915, the city had created as many as 27 different zones. Unlike most modern ordinances, the Los Angeles rule did not include a grandfather clause, so businesses that found themselves in an area zoned residential were forced to move. A 1915 Supreme Court ruling upheld this policy as a way of dealing with nuisances.[40]

While deed restrictions responded to the market, zoning responded to political pressures. Many landowners anticipated that commercial and multifamily zones were more profitable than single-family residential and lobbied to have their properties zoned for the higher-value uses. Such lobbying led to systematic errors in the allocation of land to various uses.[41]

"By the time less than half the city [of Los Angeles] was zoned, it became obvious that three or four times as much property had been zoned for commercial use as could ever be used and that such zoning often blighted the property as owners waited for commercial development that would never come," reports Robert Alexander, an architect who worked with L.A.'s planning agency in the 1940s. This imbalance was never corrected, and in 1989 the 82-year-old Alexander stated that the city still had too much land in commercial and multifamily zones.[42]

Los Angeles is not the only city to have overzoned for multifamily housing. During the 1920s, as cities were passing their first zoning ordinances, realtors used their political muscle to promote the allocation of more land to multifamily zones. For example, Portland, Oregon's first zoning ordinance, enacted in 1920, put most of the city's residential neighborhoods into a single-family-housing zone. Under pressure from realtors, the ordinance was referred to the voters, who narrowly defeated it. Realtors then campaigned for a new ordinance that included far more land in multifamily housing, which was passed in 1924.[43] The city ended up with a surplus of multifamily housing, relative to single-family homes, that lasted at least into the 1990s.[44] Similarly, in 1960, so much of Staten Island was zoned for multifamily housing that it had a capacity for 7.4 million people; its actual 1960 population was about 222,000; by 2010, it still had only about 480,000.[45]

Zoning conferred so much power on public officials that it soon became a major source of corruption. In 1938, Los Angeles recalled Mayor Frank Shaw from office for, among other things, "buying and selling of planning permits, spot zone changes, and variances."[46] Nearly 30 years later, a writer for *Harper's* magazine was doing research on corruption in zoning. A developer told him that, thanks to a history of bribery, "We know where we stand now—$25,000 for zoning for a trailer park in this country. Why upset things by talking about it?"[47]

The deed restrictions of planned communities protected the middle-class residents of many of those communities from intrusions by working-class families by such means as forbidding chickens and other domestic animals other than cats and dogs; prohibiting boarders; and restricting in-home businesses, all things more commonly found in working-class homes than in middle-class homes.[48] Developers who were building communities for working-class families obviously would not include such restrictions in their deeds, and working-class homebuyers could find plenty of neighborhoods that had no restrictions at all.[49]

Zoning changed all that. Zoning boards and planning staffs, dominated by middle-class planning advocates, didn't hesitate to blanket entire cities with residential zones that forbade working-class practices and habits. By 1930, 981 cities and towns, including nearly 2 out of 3 of the 250 largest American cities, had passed zoning ordinances affecting a total of 46 million of the nation's 123 million people.[50] In many cases, these ordinances helped to price many working-class families out of the market for single-family homes.

"The basic purpose of suburban zoning was to keep Them where They belonged—Out," says Rutgers planning professor Frank Popper. "If They had already gotten in, then its purpose was to confine Them to limited areas. The exact identify of Them varied a bit around the country. Blacks, Latinos, and poor people always qualified. Catholics, Jews, and Orientals were targets in many places."[51]

An analysis of land values before and after Chicago passed its comprehensive zoning ordinance in 1923 found that zoning significantly increased property values, and the greatest increases were in residential areas that were zoned exclusively for residential use. Although Chicago's commercial zone allowed either commercial or residential use, giving landowners more options, the exclusivity of the residential zone apparently made it more valuable.[52]

The effect of such zoning made housing more attractive to middle-class buyers and less affordable for working-class buyers. An analysis of mortgages in Paterson, New Jersey, by sociologist Helena Flam found that the share of loans to middle-class homebuyers increased from 39 percent in the early 1890s to 45 percent in the mid-1920s.[53] Although that's not a large difference, it only counts mortgages in the city; if suburban mortgages were included, the difference would likely be much bigger.

The economic argument for zoning and protective covenants was that the value of one family's property depended partly on how nearby landowners used their property. Certain uses of one particular property can conceivably enhance the value of that property but can detract from the values of adjacent properties by more than the enhanced value of the first. Zoning and covenants are designed to protect collective property values, and the popularity of these tools among homebuyers suggests that those homebuyers, at least, believed in the economic argument.

This argument was put to a legal test when the owner of 68 acres of land in the Cleveland suburb of Euclid, Ohio, challenged Euclid's zoning ordinance, saying that it had reduced the value of the land without compensation and therefore was an unconstitutional taking. Prewar zoning ordinances tended to be "cumulative," meaning that single-family zones allowed only single-family housing; multifamily zones allowed either single- or multifamily housing; commercial zones allowed either residential or commercial use; and industrial zones allowed any use at all. Ambler Realty, which owned the 68 acres, wanted its land to be zoned industrial.

The district court agreed with Ambler Realty and ruled that zoning was unconstitutional. Six members of the Supreme Court, however, were sympathetic to the economic argument for zoning. "The development of detached house sections is greatly retarded by the coming of apartment houses," wrote Justice George Sutherland for the majority in 1926, "which has sometimes resulted in destroying the entire section for private house purposes; that, in such sections, very often the apartment house is a mere parasite, constructed in order to take advantage of the open spaces and attractive surroundings created by the residential character of the district." These apartments bring "disturbing noises" and traffic, while they deprive "children of the privilege of quiet and open spaces for play . . . until, finally, the residential character of the neighborhood and its desirability as a place of detached residences are utterly destroyed." As a result, "apartment houses, which in a different environment would be not only entirely unobjectionable but highly desirable, come very near to being nuisances," and thus are subject to the police power of the state.[54]

The Growth of Multifamily Housing

In 1992, a California land-use attorney named Kenneth Baar argued that the *Euclid* decision was the culmination of a "national movement to halt the spread of multifamily housing." The implication was that, thanks to this movement, many urban areas had "inadequate production of multifamily housing."[55] In fact, the reverse is likely to be true: as previously noted, many cities actually overzoned for multifamily, while areas outside city limits tended to be unzoned through the 1960s, leaving plenty of land for multifamily housing if the market demanded it.

Moreover, though the 1920s were prosperous and saw far more housing starts than any previous decade in American history, the real growth over the decade in many cities was in multifamily housing. In the nation's 255 largest cities, the number of single-family homes built in 1928 was just 4.7 percent greater than in 1921, but the number of duplexes was 10.5 percent greater, and the number of multifamily houses (three units or more) was 281 percent greater. At the beginning of the decade, multifamily housing accounted for less than 20 percent of new dwellings; by the end, it was over half.[56]

An economist named Coleman Woodbury, who would later become a distinguished housing scholar at the University of Wisconsin, wondered why multifamily housing had suddenly become so popular. One possibility was that tastes had changed and some people discovered that they preferred to live in multifamily housing. So in 1931, Woodbury surveyed more than 900 homeowners and nearly 800 apartment renters asking, among other things, if they would rather be renters or owners. Only 14 percent of homeowners said they wanted to become renters, while 53 percent of renters said they wanted to become homeowners.[57]

Another possibility was that high-quality urban transit had enticed people to live in higher densities so they could have access to that transit. Comparing transit improvements with the growth of multifamily housing, Woodbury found a weak correlation—but one that largely disappeared when he excluded the nation's three largest (and most transit-intensive) cities, New York, Chicago, and Philadelphia.[58]

Woodbury did find that wealthier cities seemed to have more multifamily construction, which he took to mean that apartments were attracting well-to-do families.[59] But it is also possible that the apartment boom was stimulated by low-income families in those cities who were priced out of the market for single-family homes. This possibility is supported by Woodbury's finding that cities with higher property taxes tended to have more multifamily construction, with the most construction in the poorest neighborhoods of those cities. He also found a "slight degree of association" between high residential land values and multifamily construction.[60]

Woodbury found the strongest correlation between zoning and multifamily construction. "Zoning in almost all cities has, to some extent, stabilized land values. This steadying of values and the assurance of the character of a district on which it is based, according to this line of reasoning, should enhance the desirability of home ownership and act to increase the building of single-family houses." This stabilization suggests "that zoned cities probably have experienced the apartment house growth in less degree than unzoned cities," Woodbury hypothesized. "In fact, the opposite conclusions are clearly indicated," he found. The 88 cities that had no zoning saw less than an 8 percent increase in apartments, while the 167 cities with zoning saw more than a 33 percent increase in multifamily housing.[61]

Cities that had passed new, stricter building codes also saw more multifamily construction.[62]

Sixty years after Woodbury's research, housing historian Gail Radford offered one more explanation for the increase in multifamily construction during the 1920s: mortgage bonds. These bonds were similar to the bonds that played a major role in the 2008 financial crisis, but in the 1920s they were limited to commercial developments, including multifamily housing. Before the introduction of such bonds into the real-estate market in the early 20th century, builders of large housing projects had to finance those projects with short-term, high-interest loans. Only after construction was complete could they get longer-term, lower-interest loans, and then only for about half a building's net worth. Bonds made it possible to get more money up front at lower interest rates, Radford suggests, and thus precipitated a multifamily construction boom.[63]

Radford's argument is superficially persuasive, but it doesn't explain two things. First is timing: Though mortgage bonds were first issued around 1900, only $500 million of such bonds had been issued by 1920. Yet during the 1920s, another $5.5 billion were sold.[64] Why did they become popular during the 1920s? Second is geography: Radford's analysis looked exclusively at Chicago, one of the cities where zoning had increased land and construction costs. Mortgage bonds were available to developers in any city, yet they were most heavily used in the 1920s in cities with zoning.

More easily available credit for multifamily construction may have played a role in the 1920s apartment boom. But the main story was that middle-class planners and zoning boards, using the deed restrictions of developers like J. C. Nichols as models, enacted their biases and preferences for what housing should be like into city zoning ordinances. This action boosted the value of land zoned for single-family residential, especially in cities like Los Angeles and Portland, Oregon, that had overzoned for multifamily at the expense of single-family, effectively pricing working-class families out of the market for single-family homes. Developers then built multifamily housing for working-class and lower-income families.

In 1931, attorney Edward Bassett, known as the "Father of Zoning" for his role in writing New York City's original zoning ordinance, accused city planners of going well beyond the original purposes of zoning, which he said were to preserve "public health, safety, morals, and general welfare" and to "not be discriminatory." He noted that some cities "simply transferred private restrictions relating to cost, peaked roofs, and style of architecture into a zoning ordinance." Others had zoned schools, hospitals, and churches out of single-family areas and forced them into multifamily zones, effectively making these services inaccessible to many residents of single-family neighborhoods. Such exclusions were "unreasonable," Bassett said, because they were "not based on the public health, safety, morals, and general welfare, but upon a desire to employ this new device of zoning to make exclusive districts more exclusive."[65]

At the other extreme from Bassett (at least in 1931), an architect named Charles Cheney argued that zoning boards should have absolute authority over the aesthetic character and architectural design of all new buildings. He estimated that 90 percent of new buildings, whose dollar value was about three-fourths of all new construction, were "so ugly, so badly planned, so inappropriately located, or on such narrow or inconvenient streets as to be a liability instead of an asset." He arrived at this amount from estimates of the number of buildings constructed without the aid of an architect, presuming that any non-architect-designed building would have a net negative effect on the city or neighborhood in which it was built.[66] The fact that his self-serving proposal would significantly increase the cost of that 90 percent of buildings did not seem to bother him a bit, and many cities have since reduced housing affordability by implementing his demand for architecture review boards.

The Early Suburban Backlash

The fact that zoning was a quiet way to shield middle-class families from the vulgarities of working-class culture doesn't mean that no working-class suburbs of single-family homes were built in the 1920s. They were, and while they were not up to the standards of middle-class suburbs, they tended to provide far better housing than working-class families could find in the cities. As in the 19th century, residents often grew vegetables and raised chickens or other livestock in their backyards. But such suburbs were built mainly in areas that did not yet have strict zoning or protective covenants.[67]

It is likely that the working-class suburbs are what first led American intellectuals to begin their campaigns against the suburbs. As historian John Stilgoe notes, until the 1920s, most elites favored moving people out of crowded cities and into the suburbs. But when they saw what those suburbs were like, they were "substantially unnerved." "In the outer suburbs thrived a mindset," says Stilgoe, "that challenged urban intellectuals profoundly smitten with European thinking."

Fascinated with International-style, flat-roofed architecture, architects were upset that Americans chose to live in Cape Cod, Tudor, and other vernacular pitched-roofed homes. Urban planners entranced with the "City Beautiful" movement and its grand boulevards and public parks were upset that Americans focused on prettifying their own private backyards.[68]

Stilgoe argues that the earliest and best-known attack on the suburbs was Sinclair Lewis's 1922 novel *Babbitt*. Lewis's formula—that the suburbs were boring places inhabited by vapid, mindless people—would be repeated over and over, most recently in James Howard Kunstler's 1993 book *The Geography of Nowhere* and Sam Mendes's films *American Beauty* (1999) and *Revolutionary Road* (2008). These attacks would pave the figurative road for revolutionary new forms of zoning in the 1990s that would attempt to force the reconstruction of the suburbs into high-density cities that the intellectuals appreciated even if they themselves did not always live there.

Urban homeownership increased between 1890 and 1930 because protective covenants and zoning made homeownership attractive to middle-class families who, in the 19th century, would have rented or leased their homes. But covenants applied only to individual neighborhoods, while zoning spread across entire cities. This widespread zoning made homeownership in those cities unaffordable to working-class families who, in the 19th century, put a high priority on homeownership. As architecture critic Anthony Jackson put it in 1976, "The grade of dwelling that private enterprise had supplied for the use of nineteenth-century immigrants had been rejected by the rising standards of housing reform, which served the community rather than the poor by preventing private enterprise from reaching down to this level."[69]

5. The New Deal Dream

"To own one's own home is a physical expression of individualism, of enterprise, of independence, and of the freedom of spirit," President Herbert Hoover told an audience of 3,700 leaders of the construction, real estate, and lending industries in December 1931. People sing songs about their homes, "but they never sing songs about a pile of rent receipts."[1] The occasion was a White House Conference on Home Building and Home Ownership in which participants divided into more than 30 committees to discuss specific housing problems and policies.

Hoover's keynote speech boiled those problems down to two: first, "in what manner can we facilitate the ownership of homes and how can we protect the owners of homes," and second, "the standards of tenements and apartment dwellings" and "the question of blighted areas and slums in many of our great cities." Hoover conceded that the tenement problem was important but suggested "that millions of people who dwell in tenements, apartments, and rented rows of solid brick have the aspiration for wider opportunity in ownership of their own homes. To possess one's own home is the hope and ambition of almost every individual in our country."[2]

Conference participants were acutely aware that the real problem was the Depression that had brought the growth of homeownership, along with much of the rest of the economy, to a screeching halt. Annual housing starts fell more than 90 percent from a peak of 937,000 in 1925 to a trough of 93,000 in 1933. Moreover, many of the people who had purchased homes in the 1920s couldn't afford to keep them: foreclosures rates had increased from 75,000 a year before the Depression to more than 230,000 a year by 1932.[3]

Rescuing Homeowners

Other than handing out Hoover's *How to Own Your Own Home* booklets in the 1920s, the federal government had never before taken any major actions regarding housing. But the Depression led Congress to approve two types of programs. First, a series of laws passed between 1932 and 1938 aimed at helping struggling homebuyers repay their mortgages and, it was hoped, spurring an economic recovery by stimulating home construction. Second, the federal government itself engaged in home construction, including housing projects for low-income families, "new towns" and housing for farmers, and after 1940, housing for defense workers.

Though addressing the two great problems raised by Herbert Hoover, these two types of programs were somewhat opposed to each other. Housing reformers, or housers, wanted to see more public housing for low- and even moderate-income families. But the real estate and homebuilding industries feared that public housing would take away their potential customers: why buy a home if the government will subsidize your rent? Whether or not they helped relieve the Depression, financial programs such as the Federal Housing Administration and the Federal National Mortgage Association (Fannie Mae) would play a huge role in the postwar housing boom. But, due largely to opposition from realtors and homebuilders, prewar public housing programs played a trivial role in the nation's housing.

The first problem was the growing default rate on home mortgages. In response to the Depression, building and loan associations (which were slowly refashioning themselves as savings and loan associations [S&Ls]) tried to minimize foreclosures on people's homes. Many allowed debtors to pay just the interest on their loans, which for most home mortgages might be as little as a dollar or two per month. Others would refuse to foreclose as long as patrons showed they were doing their best to work with the lenders. Such lenience naturally stressed the balance sheets of the S&Ls, a number of which closed or were liquidated in 1931.[4]

To help struggling S&Ls, President Hoover persuaded Congress to pass the Federal Home Loan Bank Act in July 1932. This law created 12 federal home loan banks that could lend to S&Ls to carry them through the Depression and, it was hoped, spur an economic recovery. This legislation was the first federal law specifically aimed at helping homebuyers in general, and it set a precedent for the flurry of laws passed when Franklin Roosevelt became president.

Just 70 days after Roosevelt's inauguration, Congress passed the Home Owners' Loan Act, which aimed to rescue nonfarm homebuyers who were in default on their mortgages. The law created the Home Owners' Loan Corporation, which allowed homebuyers to reduce their payments by replacing short-term mortgages with fully amortizing mortgages lasting 15 years (later extended to 25). HOLC would loan up to 80 percent of the appraised value of a home—but since home values had dramatically declined, this loan was sometimes less than the 50 to 75 percent that homebuyers originally borrowed.

About 40 percent of the nation's homeowners had mortgages, and by 1933, nearly half of them were in default.[5] HOLC opened offices in 400 cities and received loan applications for loans from nearly 1.9 million people, or somewhere between 80 and 100 percent of the homeowners who were behind on their payments.[6]

The total value of the requested loans was $6.2 billion, but HOLC had the authority to lend only $3 billion. HOLC rejected almost 870,000 applications; close to 20 percent of the rejections were for "inadequate security," meaning the house wasn't worth enough to support the loan. The next most important reason was "lack of distress," meaning the homebuyers were not really behind in their payments. Poor credit was the reason for fewer than 10 percent of rejections. About 15 percent of applications were withdrawn, either because the applicants realized they didn't qualify or because they successfully negotiated new terms with their original lender.[7]

By 1935, the corporation had refinanced slightly more than a million mortgages, or about 20 percent of all nonfarm residential mortgages in the country. The average loan of just over $3,000 was, on average, 69 percent of the appraised value. HOLC tried to be lenient in administering the loans but ended up having to foreclose on or otherwise acquire nearly 195,000 homes. The highest foreclosure rates of more than 40 percent were in Massachusetts and New York; the lowest of 5 to 15 percent were in the West.[8]

In the end, HOLC helped more than 800,000 families keep their homes. But it isn't clear that all those families would have lost their homes without government aid. Nonfarm home foreclosures had steadily grown from 68,000 in 1926 to more than 250,000 in 1933, the year HOLC began its operations. Foreclosures then fell to around 230,000 in 1934 and 1935.[9] But that decline could be partly due to the rise in personal incomes, which had declined from $705 per capita in 1929 to $374 in 1933, then grew to $474 by 1935. Still, it is likely that the number of foreclosures would have been higher without HOLC.

The Home Owners' Loan Corporation ceased lending in 1935 and continued to collect mortgage payments until 1951 when it sold its remaining assets and shut down. Moreover, payments from homebuyers and other revenues covered all its costs, including losses on foreclosed properties and interest on bonds sold to finance the loan program, with $14 million left over to provide a tiny profit. Few federal agencies can claim that they helped hundreds of thousands of people, sunsetted as scheduled, and earned a profit besides.

Meanwhile, Congress passed the Housing Act of 1934 creating the Federal Savings and Loan Insurance Corporation, which insured S&L deposits. This act was necessary for S&Ls to compete for depositors with banks, whose deposits had been insured by the Banking Act of 1933. The law also contributed to the "bureaucratization of thrift," that is, the transition of S&Ls "from cozy clubs of shareholders" to institutions not much more personalized than commercial banks.[10]

More important, the 1934 Housing Act also created the Federal Housing Administration, which offered to insure home mortgages just as the federal government insured deposits in banks and S&Ls. Like the Home Owners' Loan Corporation, the FHA chose to emphasize long-term amortizing mortgages with relatively low down payments.

Congress created the Federal National Mortgage Association, or Fannie Mae, in 1938. Fannie Mae bought (and buys) mortgage loans from banks and other lenders, effectively increasing the amount of money available for loans. This system works because financial institutions must keep funds in reserve to repay depositors and investors when they lend money. If the reserve requirement is 10 percent, for example, an S&L that receives a deposit of $10,000 can lend only $9,000. But if Fannie Mae buys that mortgage from the S&L, the S&L then has another $9,000 it can lend. Thus, instead of providing the funds for just one loan, the initial deposit can generate the funds for several.

Public Housing

Government intervention in the housing market was small in the United States compared with other countries. Germany and Britain, for example, each built more than 1 million units of publicly assisted housing in the 1920s; one out of five residents of the Netherlands also lived in such housing.[11] American housers, led by a group called the Labor Housing Conference and its executive secretary Catherine Bauer—who had studied but never practiced architecture—looked on these programs with envy.

Like Edith Abbott, who preceded her as a leader of the housing reform movement, Bauer questioned whether homeownership made sense for working-class families. Her 1934 book *Modern Housing* argued that 19th-century cities had failed to provide decent housing and that "modern housing," meaning public housing, could be found only in Europe.[12] But she closed her eyes to the cottages and bungalows that workers built for themselves and then improved, incrementally, over the years between 1900 and 1930. "After 1910," says historian Joseph Bigott, housers such as Abbott and Bauer "seldom went into the field with open minds to confront the built environment. Instead, they become predictable, relying on old assumptions that showed little respect for the modest gains that altered substantially the character of modern society."[13] In promoting public housing, housers were explicitly opposing homeownership. "The home ownership concept," Bauer argued, was "merely a sentimental if persistent survivor, bolstered by speculative building practice."[14]

The federal government had actually gotten into the business of building housing in a small way during World War I, when the nation engaged in its biggest experiment with central planning up to that date. Among other things, the federal government effectively nationalized both the railroads and much of the nation's merchant marine fleet. A frantic effort to build new merchant ships resulted in a housing shortage in coastal shipbuilding cities, so the Emergency Fleet Corporation—a creation of the United States Shipping Board—and Department of Labor each proposed to build worker housing.

Republicans in Congress suspected these proposals were as much about social engineering as they were about worker housing. "Some gentlemen outside of Congress, interested in uplifting the human race, have hit upon this method to work out some scheme of their own," fretted Senator William Calder (R-NY). The Council of National Defense, the central-planning agency guiding the nation's war effort, had "fashioned a plan of Federal housing throughout the country which was one step further toward the Utopia it is aimed at," charged Senator Warren Harding (R-OH). "Idealists" in the Department of Labor had "the idea of building a whole lot of community centers for individual workers throughout the country that are not needed in any way," worried Senator Joseph Frelinghuysen (R-NJ). Housing plans were "an insidious concerted effort being carried on under the plea of war necessity to socialize this Government of ours, to overturn the entire government of the United States," thundered Senator Albert Fall (R-NM).[15]

The notion that "building a whole lot of community centers" could somehow "overturn the entire government of the United States" seems oddly amusing. Yet the fears that public housing projects could turn into social engineering programs proved accurate just two decades later.

Despite Republican opposition, Congress approved the housing plans. The Department of Labor created the United States Housing Corporation, which set a goal of building 25,000 homes in 89 projects. By the time the war ended, it had built just under 6,000 homes in 42 different projects, while the Emergency Fleet Corporation built just under 9,200 homes in 24 different projects. Together, they also built temporary housing for 15,000 single employees. Congress terminated these programs as soon as the war ended, and the homes were sold to private parties.[16] The Department of Labor spent $45 million on its share of the homes, which works out to $7,500 per home.[17] However, some of that money went for temporary housing and some for planning and preliminary construction of 47 uncompleted projects, so the actual amount spent on each completed home is hard to estimate.

After the war, and despite pressure from housers, the federal government remained out of the housing business for nearly 15 years. In 1932, when Hoover was still president, Congress approved the Emergency Relief and Reconstruction Act creating the Reconstruction Finance Corporation. Among many other things, the law allowed the RFC to make loans for "providing housing for families of low income, or for the reconstruction of slum areas."

After Roosevelt became president, and just three days after passing the Home Owners' Loan Act, Congress passed the National Industrial Recovery Act. This law replaced the RFC with the Public Works Administration. In addition to making loans, Section 202 of the law allowed the PWA to directly engage in "construction, reconstruction, alteration, or repair under public regulation or control of low-cost housing and slum clearance projects." Section 208 also authorized up to $25 million "for aiding the redistribution of the overbalance of population in industrial centers" by "making loans for and otherwise aiding in the purchase of subsistence homesteads." The agency in charge of this program became known as the Resettlement Administration, or RA.

Housers' hopes that the RFC and PWA would build millions, or at least hundreds of thousands, of units of new housing for working-class families were soon dashed. The RFC made only two loans for housing: one of $150,000 for rural homes in Kansas and one of about $8 million for Knickerbocker Village, a 1,600-unit apartment complex on the Lower East Side of New York City. Because it was 12 stories tall, Knickerbocker Village actually housed more people per acre than the dumbbell tenements it replaced.[18] Although the housing was supposed to be low in cost, initial rents were more than twice as much as in the tenements it replaced. More than 80 percent of the slum dwellers who moved in soon moved out because of increasing rents, leaving mainly white-collar workers in the complex.[19]

The PWA didn't do much more. It loaned $10.6 million to seven "low-profit" developers for the construction of a little more than 3,100 apartments and row houses. It also directly built just over 21,100 apartments, flats, and row houses in about 50 different projects in 38 cities. The agency spent $129 million on these projects for an average cost of $6,100 per unit, which was high considering the average cost of new private, mostly single-family homes was under $3,600 in 1935.[20] Except for projects in Puerto Rico and the Virgin Islands, the projects were all segregated, and the government spent 18 percent more per unit on housing for whites than for blacks.[21]

Bauer's *Modern Housing* contained several examples supposedly proving that public housing would cost less than private housing.[22] But she failed to account for the Davis-Bacon Act, which required builders to pay "prevailing wages"; to pay for the costs of "slum clearance"—buying and removing existing structures; or to pay for other bureaucratic and political demands.

A major problem with cost was conflicting missions. The housers wanted low-cost housing, which they felt could best be produced by building on vacant lands. The cities wanted slum clearance to eliminate blight and boost property values and taxes. Although Robert Kohn, the first director of PWA's housing division, tended to agree with the housers, PWA Director Harold Ickes considered the housers "disappointed idealists" who just wanted to "experiment with immature or ill-conceived ideas." Ickes also believed that slum clearance was politically popular, so he replaced Kohn in 1934.[23]

At least some slum-clearance projects were significantly more expensive than projects built on vacant land. A slum-clearance project in Detroit cost 29 percent more per housing unit than a similarly sized Detroit project on vacant land. A large slum-clearance project in New York City cost 14 percent more than a somewhat smaller project on vacant land in the same city. Overall, the 26 slum-clearance projects directly built by the PWA cost an average of just 2 percent more per unit than the 23 projects on vacant land, but not all these projects were directly comparable.

Another important mission was job creation. Work rules established by the PWA had a much larger effect on project costs than the cost of clearing slums. The PWA required that workers be paid "prevailing wages," which, as defined by the PWA, were probably higher than the average wages in most metropolitan areas. To create as many jobs as possible, workers were limited to 30 hours a week, which meant higher on-the-job training costs (and, from the workers' viewpoint, somewhat reduced the benefits of the higher wages).[24] These and other work rules had much to do with the high cost of PWA-built housing.

The real problem was that the PWA had limited funds and a nearly unlimited variety of ways to spend those funds. In its short life span, the PWA spent about $6 billion on dams, bridges, highways, railroads, schools, hospitals, government buildings, rural electrification, and sewage systems, as well as the housing projects. The PWA lost all interest in housing projects after a 1935 analysis concluded that housing created fewer jobs per million dollars spent than other types of construction projects.[25]

New Towns

As the PWA was winding down its housing program, the Resettlement Administration was just getting started. Roosevelt created the RA by executive order in April 1935 and appointed Columbia University economist Rexford Tugwell as director. The agency undertook two main types of projects: *suburban resettlement*, in which it built "new towns" on the periphery of existing cities, and *subsistence homesteads* on farmlands far from urban centers.

Tugwell enthusiastically fulfilled Republican nightmares that public housing would become a social engineering program by attempting to turn the communities his agency built into models of collectivism. His original goal of creating new communities for 650,000 people—more than 0.05 percent of the American population—was thwarted by a lack of funding. But the RA's suburban division built three new towns—Greenbelt, Maryland, outside Washington, D.C.; Greendale, outside Milwaukee; and Greenhills, outside Cincinnati—and the homestead division built at least nine subsistence communities.

For all its communities, the RA carefully screened applicants to ensure that they could work cooperatively with their neighbors. Homebuyers received 40-year mortgages, not just to keep payments low but to allow the RA to control each community as long as possible. Prepayment penalties were severe, and both mortgage and rental contracts allowed the RA to "cull" buyers or tenants if they were found to be less than fully cooperative. In fact, several families were evicted from settlements within months of moving in for having the "improper attitude."[26]

Some of the farms were to be collectively operated, with all the members of the community sharing in the work and decisionmaking about crops to plant and investments to make.[27] All farms were to be worked continuously "in accordance with approved organization and management." Houses included gardens, and residents were required to begin gardening as soon as they moved in. Buyers and renters had to maintain their properties and were not allowed to modify the buildings without government approval. Homes and properties were subject to inspection by government officials at any time. Anyone who decided to sell or rent their home would need government approval on the buyers or renters, a restriction that turned communities into something close to feudal fiefs.[28]

Greenbelt and the other suburban communities were initially rental properties. Greenbelt had 885 units; Greenhills, 676; and Greendale, 572.[29] Most Greenbelt buildings were in the latest International style, with flat roofs and plain white walls. That style seemed modern in the 1930s but looks impersonal today. The other communities used more traditional styles. The communities included some single-family homes but many row houses and apartments as well.

Senator Frelinghuysen would be distressed to know that the Greenbelt town came complete with community centers, as well as libraries, recreation areas, and cooperatively owned stores. Residents had to participate in collective decisions about everything from the prices of goods sold in the stores and services such as haircuts to rules about pets and drying laundry in public.[30]

Although Greenbelt included some single-family detached homes, it was mostly row houses and apartments, yet the average construction cost was $5,423 per unit. The total cost of building Greenbelt was more than $14 million, yet initial rents were to be just $60,000 a year, which means a 237-year payback period at 0 percent interest.[31] As with the PWA, high costs were largely due to labor requirements.

"Because in the construction of the communities the first emphasis was on supplying the maximum of employment to relief labor," reported one historian, "hand methods were largely preferred to labor-displacing machinery." Further, "two shifts a month were worked," which means that workers were either limited to 30 hours a week, as in the PWA projects, or allowed to work only two weeks at a time, followed by two weeks off, which was also a policy of the Works Progress Administration.[32] Unsurprisingly, the managers of these agencies rarely volunteered to receive only half to three-quarters pay for the work they did.

Economist Marion Clawson, who conducted a review of several of the homestead projects in 1943, found that "the record on these projects was shockingly bad; far from being a model which should be imitated, they were examples of what should be avoided."[33]

Some of the problems Clawson found included the criteria used to select settlers sometimes failed to find people capable of farming; the farms were "much too small for efficient operation and adequate incomes"; settlers regarded the farm plans and accounts required by the RA as "useless red tape"; and government supervision aroused "considerable resentment" from residents who felt they had surrendered "too much freedom" to be a part of the projects. Clawson noted that RA personnel tended to be ideologues for whom the program "assumed the status of a crusade," which led them to label anyone who questioned their judgment a "reactionary," and they "wholly disregarded" the critics' ideas.[34]

Historian Diane Ghirardo discovered many similarities between RA projects and similar new towns built around the same time in fascist Italy. "Among other shared features," she found, "were the attempts to ruralize urbanites, to stem the movement of the lowest socioeconomic groups, to isolate low-income or welfare tenants in urban and suburban enclaves, to intervene massively in the day-to-day lives of new town residents, to reduce them to the status of sharecroppers for the state, to reinforce traditional patterns of sexual and racial prejudices, to supervise and control the recreational activities of new community residents, and to discourage residents from seizing the initiative in organizing their own communities."[35]

Although the suburban communities are thriving today, even President Roosevelt himself considered the RA as a whole to be a series of "costly failures." The Resettlement Authority managed to spend $450 million in two years, but in 1937, it was folded into the Department of Agriculture, which planned to manage the communities that had been built to date but promised to build no more.[36] In 1949, the government gave renters the right to buy their homes and homebuyers the right to buy without the onerous 40-year mortgages and other restrictions. All RA homes were sold by 1954, with the government recovering only a little more than half of what it spent to build them.[37]

Public Housing, Version 2

The next housing law passed by Congress was the United States Housing Act of 1937, the first federal law devoted exclusively to public housing. The debate over this bill pitted the Labor Housing Conference against realtors and homebuilders. The housers wanted a federal program of housing not just for low-income families but for moderate-income families as well, similar to many European countries. They wanted a centralized system because they didn't trust either the market or local housing authorities to provide sufficient housing. Paradoxically, they also wanted to put housing in the hands of cooperatives so that residents would have control of their futures. The realtors and homebuilders naturally saw this bill as a government takeover of much of their businesses; they didn't mind slum-clearance projects, which they hoped would enhance real-estate values, but they didn't want government competing for their potential customers.[38]

The realtors won more than the housers in the compromise bill, which created the United States Housing Authority and offered state and local public housing agencies loans of up to 90 percent of the cost of public housing projects. Agencies could also get grants for up to 40 percent of the cost of housing projects provided they involved slum clearance and used relief labor.[39] Although 48 public housing agencies existed at the time the law was passed, the prospect of federal money led cities to form nearly 600 new public housing agencies over the next five years.[40]

The bill set cost limits of $5,000 per dwelling and $1,250 per room built—and just $4,000 per unit and $1,000 per room in cities smaller than half a million people. These limits were higher than private construction costs but less than the $1,421 per room average spent by the PWA.[41] To meet these targets, one of the first developments built with Housing Authority money, in Brooklyn's Red Hook neighborhood, left doors off closets and had no elevator stops on even-numbered floors. Architecture critic Lewis Mumford described the project's style as "Leningrad formalism" and said it was "barrackslike and monotonous."[42]

To avoid competition with the private sector, another provision of the law limited the income of tenants of public housing projects to 20 percent less than the minimum income required to obtain decent housing from the private sector. This limitation supposedly left stranded the people whose incomes were too high to be eligible for public housing and too low for decent private housing—a category that would not have existed, of course, without the public housing. Perhaps more important, the rule discouraged residents from getting better-paying jobs for fear that they would have to move to more expensive housing.[43]

Wartime Housing

Debate over low-income housing was cut short by the approaching war, and the emphasis shifted from slum clearance to defense housing. Shortly after the attack on Pearl Harbor, 16 different agencies—including the Farm Security Administration (which had taken over the Resettlement Administration), the Public Buildings Administration, and a number of defense agencies, including the Defense Homes Corporation, the Mutual Ownership Defense Housing Division, and the Division of Defense Housing—were all engaged in housing construction. In 1942, Roosevelt merged most of these agencies, including the United States Housing Authority, into a new National Housing Authority.[44]

At least one of these agencies, the Mutual Ownership Defense Housing Division, was an experiment in collective ownership. This agency built 4,050 units of housing in eight different projects in Indiana, New Jersey, Ohio, Pennsylvania, and Texas. In a system inspired by the Congress of Industrial Organizations, each project was owned by a mutual housing corporation. Residents would earn equity by paying rent to the corporation, which in turn would repay the government-backed loan used to fund construction. Residents whose housing needs changed (for example, because they had babies or because their children grew up and left home) were supposedly able to swap units in each project, though there is no record of whether this ever happened. The projects included parks, community gardens, and cooperatively owned grocery stores.[45] People who left the projects were eligible to be repaid the equity they had built through their rental payments to the corporations.

In 1942, Senator Harry Truman's special committee on waste in the national defense program investigated fraud in a New Jersey project that was supposed to cost $3.2 million but actually cost nearly $4.5 million. Despite the high cost, reported *Time*, "cellars flooded, roofs caved in, floors buckled, porches sagged, and—in some cases—furnaces were so installed that heating pipes blocked basement entrances."[46] One-bedroom apartments in this project cost more than $6,000 to build, and construction was so shoddy that hundreds more were needed to bring them up to Federal Housing Administration standards.[47] All but one of the mutual-ownership projects survive in cooperative ownership today, though the cooperative groceries have not, probably because the few hundred families in each complex are not enough to support a modern supermarket.

After the attack on Pearl Harbor, no more mutual housing projects were built as the National Housing Authority's emphasis shifted to temporary worker housing. The largest project—indeed, the largest housing project in the world at the time—was Vanport, Oregon, built by Henry J. Kaiser to support his Portland and Vancouver, Washington, shipyards. One of the 20th century's leading entrepreneurs, Kaiser started out building roads in the Pacific Northwest. Then he joined with Bechtel, Morrison-Knudson, and several other companies to build Hoover, Bonneville, and Grand Coulee Dams. When the consortium lost the contract to build Shasta Dam, Kaiser obtained a subcontract to provide sand, gravel, and concrete for the dam. When the Southern Pacific Railroad offered to move gravel 10 miles to the dam site for 27 cents a ton, he built a 10-mile conveyor belt that moved the gravel for just 18 cents a ton.

With the onset of war, Kaiser revolutionized the shipbuilding industry, applying assembly-line methods to take first weeks and then just days to build ships that once required months to launch. He recruited tens of thousands of workers to move to the West Coast to work in his shipyards. Among his recruits, Kaiser brought far more blacks into Portland than had previously lived in the entire state of Oregon. When some unions objected to black workers, he got the federal government to overrule them. "We do not ask what their color is," said one of his recruiters.

To house the workers, Kaiser obtained federal loans to quickly build an entire city of more than 10,000 homes, complete with schools, day-care centers, medical clinics, playgrounds, a library, a college, and five shopping areas. At its peak, Vanport had a population of more than 42,000 people—15,000 of them black—making it Oregon's second-largest city. Although some of its residents preferred segregation, Vanport was also Oregon's most integrated city: the housing itself tended to be segregated (at the insistence of the City of Portland), but schools and all other facilities open to everyone regardless of race. In addition to black shipyard workers, Vanport had Oregon's first black schoolteachers and first black police officers. Although designed to be temporary housing, 18,500 people (including 4,000 blacks) still lived in Vanport until May 1948, when a flood destroyed the entire development.[48]

Because of the Depression, the share of urban households who owned their own homes declined from 43.4 percent in 1930 to 37.5 percent in 1940. The actual number of urban homeowners grew slightly from 7.4 million to 7.7 million, while urban renters grew from 9.7 million to 12.9 million. Rural homeownership also saw a slight decline from 53.8 percent to 52.4 percent. The record might have been far worse if not for the Home Loan Bank System and Home Owners' Loan Corporation, which helped hundreds of thousands of homeowners stave off foreclosure, and the Federal Housing Administration, which reduced the risks involved in lending for single-family homes.

Despite the hopes of the housers, federal programs to build housing in the 1930s were mostly inconsequential. Together, the Reconstruction Finance Corporation, the Public Works Administration, and the Resettlement Administration built or financed fewer than 33,000 new homes between 1933 and 1938. That's only about 0.1 percent of homes built in the country during those years. The United States Housing Authority built another 57,000 in 1939, meaning new public housing was 3.3 percent of all housing starts during the 1930s.

These small numbers were partly due to lobbying by realtors and homebuilders, who considered public housing, especially for moderate-income families, a threat to their businesses. An analysis by economists from the University of Arizona concludes that this threat was real: Despite the small number of homes built by the Public Works Administration, the analysis found that PWA housing "lowered the probability of home ownership by 0.36 percent for whites and 0.25 percent for blacks."[49] These calculations are probably overestimated. There were 7.4 million owner-occupied urban homes in 1930, the vast majority of them white households, so that would mean at least 25,000 fewer owned homes. But the PWA built and financed fewer than 25,000 homes, most occupied by people who had no chance of buying a home in the 1930s. As the postwar housing boom would show, few Americans were really interested in the collective housing programs favored by the housers. Still, if the PWA had met the housers' goal of providing homes for a large share of working-class families, it would have significantly reduced the demand for privately built homes.

6. The Postwar Dream

In 1944, the Lee Rubber and Tire Corporation ran an ad in *Fortune* magazine that did not picture a single tire or automobile. Instead, the ad focused on a family of four gazing at a modest, one-and-a-half-story Cape Cod home with a one-car garage. "Helicopters, ultra-streamlined motor cars, household conveniences akin to magic may be highly desirable," read the ad, and "many of them are doubtless attainable. But the pursuit of that happiness which is guaranteed to every citizen by our Constitution rests on simpler, more fundamental things." Those things include "homes and family; practical, efficient schools; church leadership that makes devotion to religion a spiritual inspiration; elimination of class hatred and resumption of confidence and mutual interest in each other; employment for all who want it and independence for everyone who will work for it: these are fundamental for normal and continued prosperity."[1]

The curious message was that "a greater and a permanently prosperous America" depended more on people having decent homes than on people buying Lee tires. Americans apparently agreed, and when the war was over, they bought homes by the millions. Between 1940 and 1950, the number of owned homes grew by more than 10 million, and nearly all of that growth was after the war ended in 1945. Over the next 50 years, homeownership continued to grow by an average of nearly 900,000 homes per year.

The vast majority of this growth took place in the suburbs. Between 1950 and 2000, the number of rural owner-occupied homes grew by about 10 million, but the number of urban ones grew by well over 40 million. As people spread to the suburbs, the average density of urbanized areas fell. The 1950 census found that 69 million people lived in urbanized areas whose average density was more than 5,400 people per square mile.[2] The 2000 census recorded 192 million people in urbanized areas, but the average density had fallen almost in half to 2,670 people per square mile.[3]

The postwar period saw an increase in homeownership that was at least as remarkable as growth in urban homeownership between 1890 and 1930. In the 40 years from 1890 to 1930, the number of owned homes in urban areas grew by 6.7 million. Between 1940 and 2000, the number grew by at least that amount every single decade. The total number of owner-occupied urban homes thus grew from 7.7 million in 1940 to nearly 52 million in 2000, reaching a peak of nearly 55 million in 2006. When rural homes are included, owned homes grew from 15 million in 1940 to 70 million in 2000, peaking at 75.5 million in 2007.

Homebuilders constructed more than 700,000 new homes in 1941, the greatest number since 1928 and actually more than the average during the 1920s. The war suppressed housing starts to as few as 142,000 new homes in 1944. But immediately after the war, starts rose to an average of 1.5 million per year, more than twice the rate in 1941 or the in 1920s. Though varying with the economy from about 1 to 2 million, they have averaged about 1.5 million per year ever since.

Private homebuilders in the 1950s and 1960s accomplished something planners and housers could not do in the 1900s through 1930s: the movement of most working-class families to better housing in low-density neighborhoods that were healthier and safer than the tenements they left. As in the 1920s, the main factors in the suburban explosion were better transportation in the form of the automobile; moving assembly lines and other mass production techniques; improved home production methods; and a continuing expansion of credit.

Increased Wages

The first two factors—automobiles and mass production—significantly increased worker pay. Automobiles increased commuter speeds, giving workers a larger pool of jobs to choose from and employers a larger pool of workers to hire from, thus allowing a better match between job needs and skills. Studies have shown a direct correlation between commuter speeds and worker productivity.[4] Assembly-line production was highly profitable, but also extremely boring, so Henry Ford led other employers in increasing worker pay to keep employees productive. Ford declared that doubling wages to $5 a day and reducing the workday from nine hours to eight was "one of the finest cost-cutting moves we ever made" because it increased morale and reduced employee turnover.[5]

By 1969, high school graduates who never entered college averaged more than 70 percent as much income as people who received a bachelor's degree.[6] Many industrialized urban areas with high percentages of working-class families actually had higher average incomes than regions that were better educated and had predominantly middle-class jobs.[7] Better pay contributed to higher homeownership rates: In 1970, when California housing was still affordable, 60 percent of households in Detroit owned their own homes, but the same was true of only 33 percent of San Francisco households.[8] From 1950 through 1970, the highest rates of homeownership were found in Michigan, largely due to the high pay earned by autoworkers.[9]

The Gini ratio, which measures income inequality, was at its lowest in postwar history in 1968, meaning incomes were much more equally distributed then than they were before or since.[10] Working-class families often lived side by side with middle-class families, driving similar cars to work on the same roads, shopping at the same stores, and enjoying the same food in backyard barbecues. Despite these superficial similarities, they continued to have very different tastes, habits, and aspirations, separated mainly by education.

Lower-Cost Homes

The construction revolution was partly an extension of techniques developed before the war and partly a response to the huge pent-up demand for new housing after the war. Los Angeles developers, such as Fritz Burns and David Bohannon, pioneered assembly-line production of homes in the late 1930s. They precut wood to size in a mill rather than on site and had separate crews lay foundations, frame the houses, and do interior and exterior work.[11]

Born in Minnesota in 1899, Burns moved to Los Angeles in 1921 to work for a Minnesota-based real-estate firm. He was a millionaire by 1926, but lost all his money in the 1929 stock market crash and spent the next five years living in a tent. The discovery of oil on some of the land he owned allowed him to return to the real-estate business, and between 1938 and 1941, Burns built and sold 1,100 900- to 1,500-square-foot homes in Westside Village, a part of the Palms neighborhood, for as low as $4,000 each (about $62,000 today using the consumer price index; $130,000 using the unskilled wage index).[12] Today, extensively modified versions of these Los Angeles houses sell for $600,000 and up.

After the war, Burns partnered with Henry Kaiser who, like Henry Ford, never met an industry he didn't think he could improve. As early as 1942, Kaiser preached to business leaders that they should plan to build new homes, cars, and other consumer products by 1945, and he himself led the way. Though he was already making cars, aluminum, steel, magnesium, and cement, he joined with Burns in 1945 to form Kaiser Community Homes, which prefabricated kitchens, bathrooms, porches, and wall panels complete with doors and windows on six factory assembly lines, ready for installation in new homes.[13] Featuring Kaiser dishwashers and garbage disposals made with Kaiser aluminum, Kaiser and Burns could configure these modules into dozens of different patterns, and they built more than 8,000 homes in Los Angeles, San Jose, and Beaverton, Oregon. Kaiser Community Homes was the nation's biggest homebuilder in 1946 and 1947.[14]

Homes in the San Fernando Valley's Panorama City, for example, had Kaiser aluminum siding and roofing, and no doubt each house came with flyers advertising Kaiser automobiles to park in the two-car garages. With the help of assembly-line methods, Kaiser crews could finish 40 houses per eight-hour day, or one every 12 minutes, and Kaiser offered the homes for prices ranging from $9,150 to $10,500.[15] Kaiser and Burns built 3,000 homes, a shopping mall, office buildings, parks, and a Kaiser hospital in Panorama City. Kaiser would have built more homes, but a 70 percent marginal tax rate on each additional house sold led him to move into commercial development instead.[16]

By 1948, Kaiser and Burns were eclipsed by the Levitt brothers, who became the epitome of postwar builders with their Levittowns: first on Long Island, then in Pennsylvania, and finally in New Jersey. Real estate attorney Abraham Levitt started his sons in the home construction business in the 1930s. Alfred Levitt, an architect who studied with Frank Lloyd Wright, designed the homes, and William Levitt sold them and managed the company.

Ready for sale in 1947, the first homes in the Long Island Levittown were all in the Cape Cod style, similar to the Lee Tire ad but no garage. Five exterior variations all had the same basic, 750-square-foot floor plan.[17] The homes sold for $7,990 each—about $73,000 today using the consumer price index, $118,000 using the unskilled wage index. Some worried that the simple home styles would degenerate into slums, but the design was soon "modified by its owners in a thousand different ways, as the Levitts always intended it should," planning historian Peter Hall observes, adding, "The trees have grown to maturity, softening the harshness of the original townscape as it appears in the old pictures."[18]

To keep costs down, Alfred and Bill Levitt "broke down the building of a house into 26 operations, and hired 80 subcontractors to do the building," reported a 1950 *Time* cover story. One worker might do nothing but paint windowsills; another would bolt washing machines to floors. Appliances and, in later homes, television sets were built right into the houses. In contrast with New Deal public housing projects, Levitt crews used no handsaws and instead relied on precut lumber and other materials. Using these methods, the crews could complete 36 homes per eight-hour day—one every 13 minutes.

One way the Levitts speeded production was by building interiors with drywall, something that became ubiquitous after World War II but was rare before it. Though first marketed by U.S. Gypsum in 1916, drywall did not replace plaster or "wet walls" until its benefits were demonstrated by the need for rapid construction of wartime housing at places like Vanport, Oregon.[19]

The subcontractors were nonunion but were paid union wages. Levitt's own 400 employees were motivated by construction bonuses and a company pension plan. Because they purchased in large quantities, they could save money by buying appliances and other materials directly from manufacturers. They even bought timberland in Oregon and a sawmill to provide their lumber.

In 1950, the Levitts offered a new style they called the Ranch, though it was really just a Cape Cod turned 90 degrees. The interior had a more open floor plan inspired by Frank Lloyd Wright's homes. When completed, the Long Island community covered 4,700 acres and came with 10 swimming pools, five playgrounds, three softball fields, a baseball field, handball and basketball courts, shopping centers, a $250,000 community center, plus land for eight schools, eight churches, and two synagogues.[20] With 17,442 homes housing more than 80,000 people, Levittown eclipsed Vanport as the largest housing development in history, and Levitt and Sons eclipsed Kaiser Community Homes as the world's largest homebuilding firm.

The Long Island Levittown was built piecemeal with land acquired and developed in stages. With the profits they earned there, the Levitts were able to buy 5,000 acres in suburban Philadelphia and build an even more tightly planned community. When the first homes were finished in 1952, they offered three completely different home styles and plans, with prices ranging from $9,900 to $16,900, and eventually added three more. The 12,000-acre Levittown in New Jersey was also a Philadelphia suburb. Later, William Levitt built homes in smaller developments in Florida, Puerto Rico, and even France.

The Levitts were Jewish and sensitive to racial discrimination issues. Initially, the Levittowns were for whites only, but several white homeowners in Long Island sold to black families without any incident. When, in 1957, a black family bought a home from a white homeowner in the Pennsylvania Levittown, however, residents staged several weeks of near-violent protests.[21] Pressured by Jewish groups to integrate the New Jersey Levittown, the Levitts worked with church leaders to stave off any opposition. By 1964, at least 50 black families had moved in without any problems.[22] Bill Levitt later testified in Congress in favor of a fair housing law, saying that most builders could desegregate their communities only when required to do so.[23]

The Postwar New Towns Movement

Because of slow sales in the New Jersey Levittown, Bill Levitt decided that Americans were tired of large developments, so his later developments tended to be smaller. Not everyone agreed, however. In 1957, Clarence Stein, one of the architects who designed Radburn in New Jersey, wrote *Toward New Towns for America*, which advocated building new towns with large amounts of green space. When it first opened to homebuyers in 1928, Radburn was advertised as "the town for the motor age" because every home had a garage, and it separated vehicle from pedestrian traffic. Stein planned Radburn for 25,000 people, but the Depression intervened and only 640 homes were built.[24]

Stein's book helped persuade James Rouse, a shopping mall developer, to build a new town in Howard County, Maryland, approximately midway between Baltimore and Washington, D.C. Built on 15,000 acres, Columbia, Maryland, was designed with the help of a large committee of social scientists to be a self-sufficient community, meaning it had not only homes, parks, schools, and shopping areas but also offices and other sources of jobs. Columbia was also planned as an integrated community, as Rouse figured that supporters of segregation had plenty of other places to live. The first residents moved in during 1967, and sales went well until an economic downturn in 1973 forced Rouse's company to let many employees go.[25] The company survived, however, and about 88,000 people live in Columbia today.

Robert E. Simon, another developer inspired by Radburn, purchased 6,750 acres in Fairfax County, Virginia, in 1964 and hired an architect named James Rossant to design a master plan for what would become Reston (named after Simon's initials). Rossant's plan called for seven villages of 10,000 to 12,000 people, each served by a shopping and community center, a 1,000-acre industrial-and-office center, 1,500 acres of open space, churches, schools, and a downtown area with a hotel, conference center, and hospital. Although Simon hoped to attract 75,000 people to the city by 1980, today Reston's population has only reached about 56,000 spread over a much larger area of 11,000 acres.[26]

A third new town grew out of the Irvine Ranch, which covered more than 90,000 acres of Orange County, California. When the University of California asked the Irvine Company for 1,000 acres for a new university campus in 1959, the company began drawing up plans for a city of 50,000 people. With the initial success of the development in 1970, the company expanded its plans to become the most continuously profitable new town in America.[27] Today, Irvine has more than 200,000 people.

New Communities

These privately planned new towns of the 1960s fit into the social reforms embraced by Lyndon Johnson's Great Society program, and his administration persuaded Congress to pass the New Communities Act in 1968. This law authorized the Department of Housing and Urban Development to guarantee up to $250 million in loans to new-town developers, an amount that Congress later increased to $500 million. The funds could be used for any of four kinds of projects: true new towns; new suburbs of existing cities; "add-ons" to existing small towns; and—to placate urban mayors who wanted a piece of the action—"new-towns-in-town" meaning redevelopments of existing urban neighborhoods.[28]

HUD picked 14 developments in 10 states and provided assistance to the state of New York for two projects there. Only one of the projects was a true new town: Soul City, North Carolina, a planned integrated city being developed by a director of the civil rights group Congress of Racial Equality. Two were new-towns-in-town, while most of the others were satellites of cities ranging from Columbia, South Carolina, to Chicago. HUD initially provided $325.5 million in loan guarantees for developments that would occupy 90,000 acres and were projected to eventually house more than 900,000 people.[29]

The result, as reported in *Time*, was "a disaster."[30] Almost all the developments ran into financial trouble during the same recession that slowed Columbia sales in 1973. Another problem was red tape: Under the National Environmental Policy Act of 1969, every development had to have an environmental impact statement, which took years to write and offered opponents an opportunity to litigate.

Meanwhile, the average developer faced interest payments of around $6,000 per day. HUD at first responded by extending loan periods. But by 1978, all but one of the developers had defaulted. HUD foreclosed and sold the remaining assets, somehow losing $570 million in the process.[31]

One thing government officials failed to allow for was incentives. The developers of Columbia, Irvine, and Reston, who put their own money on the line, built incrementally to protect themselves against economic downturns. But developers who were financed out of guaranteed loans with no personal responsibility to repay them freely spent the money on infrastructure before having any assurance of revenues.

The Woodlands, north of Houston, Texas, is the only development that avoided bankruptcy. Its current population of 94,000 people is less than two-thirds of the 150,000 projected in the early 1970s, though parts of it are still under development. Curiously, the Rouse Company, which originally developed Columbia, bought the Woodland Corporation in 2003.

Only one of the developments—Flower Mound, near Dallas—has anything close to the planned population, and that is the result of actions taken by developers since the original project failed: only 100 homes had been completed when HUD foreclosed on the original developer. Flower Mound's current population of 64,700 is close to the planned population of 64,000 except that the actual city occupies four times as much land as the planned city.

Some of the other developments were partially completed. Riverside Plaza was supposed to be a new-town-in-town, a Radiant City-like mixed-use, high-rise project—more urban renewal than new town—in Minneapolis. Litigation over the adequacy of the project's environmental impact statement delayed the project, and the developer managed to build just 1,303 of the 12,500 planned apartments before defaulting.[32] Today, it is occupied mainly by immigrants and is sometimes called "little Somalia" for the large percentage of Somalians that live there. The other new-town-in-town was Roosevelt Island, one of the New York state–funded projects, took much longer to complete than expected and today has just over half of its projected population.

Like Flower Mound, some of the other projects were partially completed by developers after HUD foreclosed. St. Charles, Maryland, is an "add-on" to the existing town of Waldorf, which is about 24 miles southeast of Washington, D.C. Today, the development is about half completed and has about half of its original population projection of

75,000 people. Fewer than three dozen homes were built in Soul City before HUD foreclosed; today, it is home to a few hundred people, but not enough for the Census Bureau to consider it a "place."[33]

About a third of the projects never amounted to anything and remain nearly vacant today. They include Harbison, near Columbia, South Carolina; Newfields, near Dayton, Ohio; Radisson, a New York state–funded project near Syracuse; Riverton, near Rochester, New York; San Antonio Ranch, near San Antonio, Texas; and Shenandoah, near Atlanta, Georgia. San Antonio Ranch was held up by environmental controversy.[34] Most of the other developments failed because the developers made the wrong guesses about future growth trends: either the communities weren't growing at all—between 1970 and 2000, the Dayton urbanized area grew by only about a third of the projected population of Newfields—or growth was moving in a different direction than the planned community.

Master-Planned Communities

One result of the complete and utter failure of the New Communities Act is that hardly anyone talks about "new towns" anymore. Instead, developers use the term "master-planned communities," of which the Woodlands is considered a prototype. This term, like so many, has been abused: some developers refer to everything they do as a master-planned community even it is just a six-acre condominium project.[35] In general, however, a master-planned community is a planned community on steroids: much larger and often with far more open space and other amenities included in the development.

J. C. Nichols's Country Club District looks like a master-planned community, with single-family homes, apartments, hotels, shopping centers, and parks. But as previously noted, it was incrementally planned and built. Nichols's early homes relied on septic tanks; as his developments grew larger, he installed sewers for his more expensive homes, but the cost of doing so was high. His solution was to have Kansas City annex his development; the city could then create a special benefits district to fund a sewage system and repay the costs through property owner assessments.[36]

Developers of master-planned communities in Texas don't have to wait for a city to annex their property to create a special service district. Instead, with the approval of the Texas Commission of Environmental Quality, they can create a municipal utility district that can sell bonds to pay for the installation of water, sewers, parks, firehouses, and other utilities and infrastructure. Homebuyers and other property owners within the district pay an annual fee to repay the bonds. Generally, the fee declines to an amount needed to maintain the infrastructure after the bonds are paid off.[37]

In 1976, as the new communities fiasco was winding down, Gerald Hines, who had developed Houston's Galleria shopping mall in 1970, began development of First Colony, a 9,700-acre parcel in Fort Bend County, one of the eight counties in the Houston metropolitan area. Not as large as the Woodlands, most of it was eventually annexed by the city of Sugar Land. Yet First Colony could justifiably be considered an add-on new town as it contains most of Sugar Land's population, a 1.4-million-square-foot office-and-shopping complex that has effectively become downtown Sugar Land, and Sugar Land's city hall.[38]

As of November 2010, Fort Bend County had 36 other planned communities under development, not counting developments of fewer than about 300 homes. None would be considered new towns, as they don't include major job centers, but the largest, Sienna Plantation, actually contains more acres than First Colony. Sienna and several others include shopping areas and schools, and all have parks and open spaces. The projected population of these developments ranges from about 1,500 to 22,000 people. When built out, their total population will exceed 250,000.[39]

Whether or not a city or county has zoning—and neither Houston nor the unincorporated portions of the counties around it do—nearly all planned developments today come with homeowners associations and protective covenants. These covenants have received some bad publicity in recent years because of a few extreme cases, such as people being forbidden to fly American flags or an association foreclosing on a soldier's home for failing to pay his annual fees while he was deployed in Iraq.[40] But developers know that homeowners associations provide people what they want: security from nuisances combined with some flexibility in how they use their own property. Covenants cost developers almost nothing yet significantly enhance property values, particularly in places with either no zoning or with zoning boards that freely alter and enforce zoning codes with seeming capriciousness.

Despite controversy, the rapid growth in the number of community associations shows how successful they are. In 1970, about 10,000 community associations represented about 700,000 homes and a little more than 2 million residents. By 2010, this number had grown to more than 300,000 community associations covering nearly 25 million homes housing more than 60 million residents.[41]

Unlike zoning, which can be fairly uniform—an R-10 zone will be the same throughout a city or region—protective covenants can vary greatly from neighborhood to neighborhood. About half the neighborhoods in Houston have no covenants at all, and that seems to satisfy residents. Such variation gives homebuyers a range of choices: no covenants, weak covenants, strong covenants.

In areas without covenants, Houston allows anyone to petition their neighbors to create a property owners association. Forming an association requires the support of the owners of 75 percent of the property in the area. Once the association is created, it can write or amend covenants that apply to all properties in the area with the support of the owners of 60 percent of the property in the area.[42] This process is in many ways more flexible than zoning and yet provides more assurance that the rules governing property owners will not be changed without the support of a supermajority of the neighborhood's owners.

Covenants give individual homeowners a modest say in how their neighbors use their property but no say at all in how people outside their neighborhood use their land. Although zoning began as a way to provide the same safeguards as covenants to neighborhoods that developed before covenants existed, it started local governments down a slippery slope of intrusions into property rights. Zoning hearings made residents feel entitled to have a say in how anyone in their city, or even their entire state, could use their property. Eventually, zoning became much more than just a way of controlling nuisances; it became a way for powerful interest groups and planners to impose their lifestyle choices on others.

The suburbanization of the 1950s accomplished what planners and housers could not: move masses of working-class families out of the tenements and into low-density suburbs. As the working class gained the mobility and housing once enjoyed only by the upper classes, the almost inevitable result was a backlash from those upper classes who resented sharing the suburbs with people whose cultural values differed from their own.

7. Questioning the Dream

"Suburban sprawl destroys habitats and wild areas, threatens endangered species and moves natural areas farther away from where most people live," claimed the Sierra Club in a 1998 report titled "The Dark Side of the American Dream." The report goes on to blame sprawl, which it defines as "low-density development," for everything from floods to unemployment.[1]

In connection with the report, the Sierra Club put up a website in 2001 that defined the "efficient urban density" as 500 households per acre. Since the average urban household has 2.67 people and there are 640 acres per square mile, this works out to an average population density of more than 850,000 people per square mile. This density is 14 times that of Manhattan's 60,000 people per square mile and 320 times the density of the average American urbanized area, which in 2000 had about 2,670 people per square mile. The Sierra Club's efficient urban density is so dense that every American counted in the 2000 census could fit into the Knoxville, Tennessee, urbanized area, and the entire population of the world could fit into the combined New York and Philadelphia urbanized areas.

When demographer Wendell Cox pointed out these facts on his website, the Sierra Club responded by revising its webpage to define "efficient urban density" as 100 households per acre. But this number still produced an average population density of 170,000 people per square mile, or close to three times Manhattan's density. At this density, everyone in the United States could fit into the Los Angeles urbanized area, and everyone in the world could fit into Kentucky.[2] When Cox pointed this out, the Sierra Club took down its webpage.

The War on Homeownership

As the title of the Sierra Club report suggests, attacks on the suburbs are attacks on homeownership. Even if someone doesn't want to buy a home in the suburbs, the availability of low-cost suburban land keeps housing prices down in both suburbs and cities. Those who oppose sprawl must realize there is a tradeoff between low-density suburbs and affordable housing. Sprawl opponents who already own their own homes are effectively denying homeownership to others who don't yet own homes.

As a pejorative against low-density suburban development, the term "sprawl" was first used by the *London Times* in 1919. But complaints against such development go back at least a century further. "Whenever a new class of people has been able to gain some of the privileges once exclusively enjoyed by an entrenched group, the chorus of complaints has suddenly swelled," observes historian Robert Bruegmann. "Predictably, criticism of sprawl has virtually always been aimed at people outside the speaker's or writer's own circle."[3] In essence, the war on sprawl is a war on whatever economic classes are lower than the warrior's.

The debate over urban sprawl goes back at least to the 1920s and 1930s, when two of the world's most famous architects, having nothing better to do—for however great they were, they received few commissions in those years—decided to soothe their massive egos by presenting their visions of what cities should be like in the future. These visions proved to be highly influential and, in the long run, highly embarrassing for architects and planners. Both visions were based on the automobile as the dominant form of transportation, and yet the visions were as different from each other as they could possibly be.

The architects were the American Frank Lloyd Wright and Swiss-French Charles-Édouard Jeanneret, better known as Le Corbusier. Both agreed on one thing: existing cities weren't working. Le Corbusier called them "mighty storms, tornadoes, cataclysms."[4] Wright called the city "obsolete," noting that thanks to such new technologies as electricity, telephones, and autos, "the necessity that chained the individual to city life is dead or dying away."[5]

However, the two differed greatly in the prescriptions they offered to fix the problem. Wright's 1932 book *The Disappearing City* predicted that America would completely decentralize. Every family in his "Broadacre City" would live on an acre of land. Factories and offices would be spotted across the landscape. Some apartments would be available for those who wanted them, along with train stations and rail lines, but most transportation would be by automobile.[6] In 1935, Wright displayed a 12-by-12-foot model representing four square miles of Broadacre City at museums in New York and other major cities.

By 1930, Wright's major contributions to domestic architecture included the Prairie house—long, low but generally two-story homes with gently pitched roofs—and the open floor plan, in which kitchen, dining, and living areas flowed into one another. Most of his clients had been wealthy, but in 1936 he designed the first of what he called *usonian homes*, one-story versions of the Prairie houses that cost a modest $5,500 or so ($88,000 today using the consumer price index and $210,000 using the unskilled wage index). Architect Cliff May designed similar homes on the West Coast and called them Ranch houses.

Le Corbusier's approach was exactly the opposite. Paradoxically, he sought "to decongest the center of the city by increasing the population density in order to diminish internal distances." In other words, if everything were closer together, people wouldn't need to travel as far to get anywhere. This approach would be "made miraculously possible by the advent of the skyscraper."[7] His proposal, which he called Radiant City, was to house everyone and their offices in tall, narrow skyscrapers surrounded by large green spaces. He seriously proposed tearing down large portions of Paris and Manhattan to build his city.

Le Corbusier's first proposal, in 1922, was to house only the elite in high-rises and surround them with mid-rise to low-rise buildings for lower-middle- and working-class families. But in 1935, he decided that everyone should have the "freedom" to live in a high-rise. To strengthen the appeal, Le Corbusier promised that every apartment in his skyscrapers would be filled with sunlight coming through outside walls of double-pane glass.

To achieve the densities he sought, the architect allotted "152.8 square feet of dwelling space per person," plus 108 square feet of office space per worker, which he considered "generous" in 1932. Each skyscraper would be located on one-fourth of a square mile of land (400 meters square). The high-speed roadways separating the buildings would be built 16 feet off the ground, leaving room underneath for streetcars and trucks plus tunnels for pedestrians. Since the high-speed roads would have much higher capacities than city streets, roads would cover only one-tenth of the area found in modern cities. Redundantly, Le Corbusier also proposed connecting the basements of each tower with subway lines.

Though never mentioning each other by name, for nearly four decades, from 1922 to 1959, the two architects traded potshots at each other like massive battleships firing wet ammunition. Wright called Le Corbusier's proposal "feudal towers a little further apart" than existing skyscrapers.[8] Le Corbusier called the suburbs and, by extension, Broadacre City, "a despicable delusion entertained by a society stricken with blindness!"[9]

Although Americans in general love Frank Lloyd Wright, architects and planners mostly preferred Le Corbusier's vision. "We just don't have that kind of land available" to house everyone in Broadacre Cities, said one California architect recently.[10] Actually, outside of a few city-states such as Monaco or Singapore, most places do have that kind of land available. At nearly three times the population density of China, the Netherlands, for example, is one of the most densely populated nations in the developed world. Yet every household in the Netherlands could live on an acre of land and still leave nearly a third of the country in a rural condition.[11]

American population densities are so low that there is no reason to worry about land shortages. The United States has more than 2.2 billion acres of land and 80 million families, about 80 percent of whom live in urban areas. If each urban family had an acre, they would occupy just 2.8 percent of the nation's land area. Urban areas occupy about this much land today, and much of that is residential, so expanding residential lots to cover a full acre would less than double the nation's urbanized land, leaving almost 95 percent rural.

After World War II, Wright's Broadacre City proved to be more of a prediction than an influence as millions of Americans left dense cities to spread out in the suburbs. Meanwhile, architects and planners were strongly influenced by Le Corbusier to encourage European and American governments to build Radiant Cities for the working class. The results proved to be a huge embarrassment for the architects and planners, as the American suburban version of Broadacre City proved to be far more workable, while the Radiant Cities almost uniformly proved to be disasters; many of the ones that remain in both Europe and America are shunned by natives and are mainly occupied by immigrants who do not yet have the incomes to afford better housing.

The Postwar Suburban Backlash

Elitist complaints about the suburbs grew particularly loud in the United States in the 1950s, when the nearly identical Cape Cod homes of Levittown became the symbol for all the suburbs in the country. Two books published in 1956 expressed the elitist view that the new suburbs (as opposed to older, middle-class suburbs) were dreary, cultureless places inhabited by bored and boring people.

The Crack in the Picture Window by writer John Keats claimed that the suburbs were "conceived in error, nurtured by greed, corroding everything they touch." Keats derided the "tiny homes," "lack of true community," and the invasion of once-rural areas by suburban developments.[12] In fact, the homes were generally much larger than the apartments the suburbanites had left, while sociologist Herbert Gans—having lived in both a Levittown and an inner-city neighborhood, concluded that both had—or lacked—about the same sense of community.[13] As for Keat's worries that the suburbs were overrunning the countryside, it is worth noting that he used the money he made from this and later books to buy himself an entire island to live on in Canada.

The other book, William Whyte's *The Organization Man*, portrayed suburbanites as mindless conformists. Some of Whyte's views contrasted sharply with Keats's, who imagined that suburbanites felt "mutual loathing" and "hatred" toward one another and claimed that residents "make enemies of the folks next door with unbelievable speed."[14] Whyte instead portrays the suburbs as "a communal way of life," with people happily sharing tools, watching one another's children, and working together in a variety of community organizations.[15]

The Costs of Sprawl

In 1973, the newly formed Council on Environmental Quality commissioned a study evaluating the costs of urban sprawl. The study compared the costs of building and providing urban services to high-density versus low-density housing. However, rather than actually measure those costs in actual neighborhoods, the study estimated the costs; that is, the authors fabricated the data.[16] When a Duke University researcher compared the actual costs of urban services in communities of various densities, she found that, at any density above 200 people per square mile, higher densities were associated with higher urban service costs.[17]

In 2000, a researcher at Rutgers University took another look at the question, using a combination of real and hypothetical data. He estimated that urban services to low-density development cost about $11,000 more per home than to high-density development.[18] However, a Heritage Foundation study that looked at actual government expenditures in more than 700 cities found almost no differences in expenses per capita. Annual expenditures by the lowest-density cities, for example, were about $1,265 per person, while the highest-density ones spent $1,180 per person.[19] Note that the Heritage Foundation looked at costs per person, whereas Rutgers compared costs per home; households in low-density neighborhoods tend to have more people, on average, than those high-density neighborhoods, so by using costs per household Rutgers exaggerated the differences in costs per person.

Even if urban services to low-density areas do cost $11,000 more per home, local governments should simply make sure residents pay the full cost of the services they use and leave the choice up to homebuyers. Certainly, telephone companies, power companies, and delivery services, such as UPS and FedEx, do not try to dictate lifestyle choices to their customers; they simply ensure that their customers pay the appropriate price.

The Role of Government in Suburban Expansion

For those who object to government subsidies, historian Kenneth Jackson offered a more significant criticism of suburbs, arguing that they resulted from federal policies and subsidies. Jackson claimed that the Home Owners' Loan Corporation, Federal Housing Administration, and Fannie Mae "revolutionize[d] the home finance industry" by introducing amortizing mortgages with long terms and low down payments.[20] After the war, the FHA offered to guarantee loans with as little as a 5 percent down payment—and 0 percent for veterans. With FHA loan guarantees reducing the risk of mortgage loans and Fannie Mae flooding the market with cash by buying up loans, it is easy to see the postwar suburban boom as dependent on government intervention.

Yet the finance industry was already moving in that direction. Although HOLC introduced amortizing mortgages to some buyers, the building and loan associations (B&Ls) had offered such mortgages since at least the 1890s. Although HOLC initially provided mortgages for up to 15 years, B&L mortgage terms were as long as 12 years. Although the B&Ls required a 25 percent down payment, the FHA initially reduced this to just 20 percent.[21] If the housing market had continued to grow as it was doing in the early 1920s, it seems likely that the thrift and banking industries would have introduced these minor improvements without federal intervention.

In 1948, Congress allowed the FHA to insure mortgages for as much as 95 percent of the value of a home. This 5 percent down-payment requirement is significantly better than the B&Ls were offering before the Depression, but large homebuilders such as Samuel Gross came close to that as early as the 1890s. More significant, perhaps, was the 1944 Servicemen's Readjustment Act, also known as the G.I. Bill, which allowed zero-down-payment loans for returning military personnel, an offer few financial institutions would be likely to make without government guarantees. The 2.4 million veterans who took advantage of this law before it expired in 1952 represented about a fifth of the increase in homeowners during those years.[22] Of course, in the growing economy, many of them probably would have been able to buy homes with a 5 or 10 percent down payment as well.

The 1948 housing act also extended the terms of guaranteed home loans to 30 years.[23] "One reason that long-term mortgage arrangements were not typical prior to the 1930s," Jackson says, "was that an 1864 amendment to the 1863 National Bank Act prohibited nationally chartered banks from making direct loans for real estate transactions."[24] But that law was repealed in 1913. Though initially the revised law allowed national banks to make loans only for farmlands, by 1927 they were allowed to make loans on urban homes, and by 1929 they had captured 12 percent of the nonfarm mortgage market.[25] B&Ls also had to compete against insurance companies, mutual savings banks, and a variety of other institutions that were in the mortgage market before the Depression.

Nor was the multiplier effect generated by Fannie Mae's purchases of mortgages revolutionary. When national banks were allowed to make loans for multifamily housing in 1913, they almost immediately began packaging such loans into mortgage bonds, which fueled the apartment boom of the late 1920s. Sooner or later, banks would have developed mortgage bonds for single-family homes. Moreover, investors commonly dealt with bonds that matured in 30 or more years, so the packaging of home mortgages into bonds would likely have produced long-term mortgages without government intervention. As it turned out, the Depression and Fannie Mae reduced the need for such bonds, so banks did not privately develop this tool until the 1980s.

Jackson and other historians have also criticized both HOLC and the FHA for "redlining," that is, refusing to offer mortgages in certain neighborhoods, notably ones housing blacks. Jackson's argument is that redlining forced middle-class homebuyers to move to the suburbs because they couldn't get loans for homes in the cities. There is no doubt that institutionalized racism was pervasive in the 1930s, and the supposedly liberal Democrats in charge of the New Deal were as guilty of it as the most red-necked southerners. But it can also be argued that redlining, to the extent that it existed, was simply recognition that property values were low and declining in blighted areas of cities, and because of racism those blighted areas happened to be the homes of many black families. In other words, redlining may have been a financial response to urban conditions that also reflected a shamefully racist society.

Not all central-city neighborhoods were redlined, giving middle-class homebuyers a choice of living in cities or suburbs. Given the "rent gradient"—the tendency for land costs to be higher closer to the city center—and the fact that jobs were rapidly moving to the suburbs anyway, many homebuyers would have chosen to live in the suburbs even if redlining hadn't exist. Certainly, the suburbs of cities with low populations of blacks grew just as fast as those of cities with high black populations. This fact is not to excuse federal institutionalism of racism but only to argue that it did not significantly alter settlement patterns. As urban economist Edwin Mills says, "It is almost certain that social issues [such as race discrimination] affecting the central cities have had a greater effect on *who* lives and works in suburbs than on *how many* live and work there."[26]

The Mortgage-Interest Deduction

The other major government support of homeownership is the mortgage-interest deduction. When Congress first imposed an income tax in 1913, it allowed a deduction of the interest on all consumer loans. In the 1986 revision of the tax code, Congress eliminated the deduction for credit card and other consumer loans, leaving one only for home mortgages. At the time, President Reagan argued for retaining this deduction specifically as a means of promoting homeownership.[27] Today, the Office of Management and Budget estimates that the deduction saves taxpayers—or costs the government, depending on your point of view—around $100 billion per year.[28] As a "tax expenditure," this deduction is second only to employer deductions of health insurance premiums.[29] Critics of the deduction often point out that it mainly benefits the wealthy, since those with the highest incomes who buy the most expensive homes get the largest deductions.

Despite the large amount of money involved, the deduction probably has little effect on homeownership. Economists Harvey Rosen and Kenneth Rosen estimate that eliminating the deduction would reduce the homeownership rate by about 4 percent. They consider that 4 percent represents a "substantial influence on the decisions of households to own or rent their housing."[30] Other economists consider 4 percent to be "small."[31]

Whether 4 percent is substantial or small, not all economists are convinced that the effect is even that great. Harvard economists Edward Glaeser and Jesse Shapiro note that "the homeownership subsidy moves with inflation and has changed significantly between 1965 and today, but the homeownership rate has been essentially constant." They conclude that the deduction is "irrelevant" in influencing homeownership because "the poorer people who are on the homeownership margin generally don't itemize [which is required to receive the deduction], even if they own." Instead, all the deduction does is lead some people to buy bigger homes or homes with more expensive features, such as hardwood floors and granite countertops.[32]

Economists Martin Gervais and Manish Pundey point out that the deduction doesn't save taxpayers as much as the OMB estimates because the OMB incorrectly assumes that eliminating the deduction would not lead taxpayers to change their behavior. In fact, the economists point out, eliminating the deduction "would lead households to reshuffle their balance sheet, thereby lowering the amount of interest income taxes collected." Taking such reshuffling into account, the deduction saves taxpayers only about one-third to two-thirds as much as the OMB estimates. Moreover, high-income families have more opportunities to reshuffle their balance sheets, so "the distribution effects of mortgage-interest deductibility are much smaller than conventionally believed" and "[do] not benefit richer households any more than the median wealth household."[33]

The most recent economic analysis of the deduction reaches the stunning conclusion that it may actually *reduce* homeownership rates, at least in states with the sort of restrictive land-use regulation that will be discussed in Chapter 9. The study, published by the London School of Economics, found that the deduction helps wealthy homeowners only "in less tightly regulated housing markets," where it may increase homeownership or encourage people to buy more expensive homes, as described by Glaeser and Shapiro. In more restrictive states, the deduction results mainly in higher housing prices, which in turn reduce homeownership. Since nearly half of American housing is in the more restrictive places, the net effect of the deduction on homeownership may be nil. Regardless of regulation, the study's authors agreed with Glaeser and Shapiro that the deduction "has no impact on the homeownership attainment of low-income households."[34]

Federal Infrastructure Subsidies

Suburban critics also claim that federal funding for highways and sewers promoted the expansion of the suburbs. "In 1944, the Federal Highway Program substantially influenced land development patterns in the United States," says growth-management advocate Henry Richmond. Richmond explains that "urban roads became eligible for [federal] assistance in 1944," and that "the low density pattern found in most of the nation's suburban area would never have been possible without the effect of high-speed highways."[35]

In fact, the federal influence on urban highways was insignificant until well after 1956, when Congress approved the Interstate Highway System. That system, along with most highways before it, was paid for out of gasoline taxes that were explicitly created to be highway user fees. Richmond's own home state of Oregon was the first to pass a gasoline tax as a user fee in 1919.[36] By 1930, every other state had followed Oregon's example, and from then on the majority of highway funding came from such user fees, including tolls and truck-weight-per-mile fees.[37]

Although Richmond is correct that Congress authorized the use of federal funds for urban roads in 1944, such funding was miniscule. In 1946, for example, the federal government collected $883 million in gasoline taxes and other highway fees. Unlike the states, Congress did not at that time dedicate those revenues to highways and instead put them in the general fund. That year, Congress appropriated only $180 million of general funds to highways, just 20 percent of collections. Much of that $180 million went for rural, not urban, roads. By comparison, state and local governments spent more than $2 billion on roads, most of which came out of highway user fees. This pattern continued through 1956.[38]

Although the Interstate Highway System connected many cities with their suburbs, the first urban interstates were not completed until the early 1960s, long after the movement of both people and jobs to the suburbs began. In any case, the cost of those roads was paid for by the users, so even if the federal government had not gotten involved, it is likely that state, local, or private providers would have built many of the roads.

Another claim is that the Environmental Protection Agency subsidized suburban expansion by funding sewer lines and sewage treatment plants. Many suburban subdivisions of the 1940s and 1950s were built with septic tanks rather than sewer hookups, saving homebuyers several hundred dollars each. In the 1970s, the EPA began spending billions of dollars funding sewage treatment plants for both cities and suburbs. But those funds were spent long after the suburbs in question had been built and had no influence on people's decisions to locate in the suburbs. Today, most states require large subdivisions to be connected to sewage treatment facilities, but this requirement has not slowed suburban growth.

Anti-Suburb Pseudoscience

In their eagerness to demonize the suburbs, critics sometimes fabricate or misinterpret data. For example, political scientist Robert Putnam, in his 2000 book *Bowling Alone*, estimated that there is a "'sprawl civic penalty' of roughly 20 percent on most measures of community involvement."[39] Yet Putnam's own data showed that suburbanites have higher levels of community participation than residents of central cities.

Putnam compared data for regions of more than 1 million people, 250,000 to 1 million people, and 50,000 to 250,000 people and concluded that larger regions have less involvement than small ones, a result he blamed on sprawl. But large areas tend to be older and denser: urban areas of 1 million or more people averaged nearly 3,500 people per square mile in 2000, while areas of 250,000 to 1 million averaged 2,100 people per square mile, and areas of 50,000 to 250,000 averaged 1,800 people per square mile. In each of these size classes, his data showed that suburbs have more participation than central cities. Thus, if a relationship exists between density and social capital, it is that lower densities are correlated with more civic participation. To restore social capital, Putnam urged urban planners to redesign suburbs to look more like cities—higher densities, mixed uses, public spaces instead of private yards, and gridded streets instead of cul-de-sacs—even though his data would suggest it would be better to redesign cities to look more like suburbs.[40]

While 1950's critics of the suburbs such as John Keats worried about the effects of single-family housing on people's sense of community, environmental groups jumped on the issue out of a fear that the expanding suburbs would soon pave over the nation's forests, farms, and open spaces. Sprawl "chews up the countryside" and "devastates rural areas," says the Sierra Club.[41] Whoever wrote this either wasn't aware or hoped their readers' weren't aware that all of America's cities and suburbs occupy only a small percentage of the country's land area.

107

The 2000 census found that 68 percent of the population lives in about 450 urbanized areas of 50,000 people or more that occupy just 2 percent of the nation's land area. Adding about 3,200 urban clusters—areas of 2,500 to 49,999 people—brings the total to 79 percent of the population but only 2.6 percent of the land area. Only four states—Connecticut, Massachusetts, New Jersey, and Rhode Island—are between 30 and 40 percent urban; Delaware and Maryland are 15 to 20 percent urban; Florida is about 11 percent urban; and no other state is more than 10 percent urban.

The Sierra Club's "Dark Side" report called Los Angeles "the grand-daddy of sprawl." By the Sierra Club's definition of sprawl being "low-density development," exactly the opposite is true: Los Angeles is in fact the nation's densest urbanized area. The city of Los Angeles isn't as dense as Manhattan, of course, but the Los Angeles urbanized area (which includes Burbank, Pasadena, and much of Orange County) had more than 7,000 people per square mile in 2000, while the New York urbanized area (which includes much of Long Island and northern New Jersey) had only 5,300 people per square mile.

Robert Bruegmann points out that, as the baby boom generation matured, household sizes fell by 20 percent between 1964 and 1990. Since most baby boomers nevertheless sought homes that used about the same amount of land as their parents, the land needed to house America grew faster than the population. At the same time, the entry of women into the workforce required a massive expansion of commercial and industrial land. Household sizes have leveled off, and most women who are going to work are already working, so Bruegmann concludes "that the campaign against urban sprawl, which became most strident in the last years of the twentieth century, was reacting to a trend that actually peaked some forty years earlier."[42]

Suburbs and Driving

The other major argument made by sprawl opponents is that the suburbs make people "auto dependent" and force them to drive too much. While Ralph Nader's 1965 book *Unsafe at Any Speed* criticized the auto industry for building dangerous cars, the earliest criticism of automobiles themselves as a form of transportation dates back to around 1968, when consumer advocate A. Q. Mowbray's book *Road to Ruin* warned that highway advocates wanted to "blanket the nation with asphalt."[43] *Road to Ruin* was quickly followed by a spate of anti-automobile books with titles like *The Death of the Automobile, Autokind vs. Mankind,* and *Highways to Nowhere,* the last of which claimed that autos were "the most inefficient mode of transportation ever devised by man."[44]

In fact, the opposite is likely true. University of California planning professor Melvin Webber once wrote that autos and highways were "the most effective surface-transportation system yet devised."[45] Americans spend an average of about 35 cents per vehicle-mile on driving.[46] Since their cars carry an average of about 1.6 people in urban driving and 2.4 people in intercity driving, the cost of auto transportation averages 15 cents per passenger-mile in rural areas to 22 cents per passenger-mile in urban areas.[47] Although highways and streets are subsidized, mostly at the local level, Americans drive so much—more than 4 trillion passenger-miles per year—that the subsidies average less than a penny per passenger-mile.[48]

By comparison, mass transit cost almost a dollar per passenger-mile in 2008, 77 cents of which was subsidized by taxpayers, mostly auto drivers.[49] Nonmotorized modes of travel—walking and bicycling—are less expensive than driving but are not as effective over longer distances or when trying to move large packages or entire families.

Critics of suburbs invariably point out that automobiles use lots of energy, emit pollution, and are involved in thousands of fatal accidents annually. But all these costs are rapidly declining. The average amount of fuel used per mile of driving cars and light trucks (pickups, sport utility vehicles, and full-size vans) has declined by 40 percent since 1975.[50] Moreover, President Obama's latest fuel-economy standards require that new cars go an average of 54.5 miles per gallon in 2025.[51] If manufacturers meet that goal—and they say they can—the fuel used by the average car on the road will decline by at least another 40 percent by 2030.[52]

Reductions in automotive air pollution are even more impressive. Americans drove 178 percent more miles in 2005 than in 1970. But new cars today emit less than 10 percent as much pollution per mile, and some cars emit an amount less than 1 percent as much, as cars in 1970.[53] As a result, total highway emissions of key pollutants, such as carbon monoxide and hydrocarbons (volatile organic compounds), have declined by two-thirds to three-quarters.[54]

Improvements in auto safety are more impressive still. For every billion vehicle-miles of driving, auto fatalities declined from more than 100 in 1945 to just 10 people in 2010. Total auto fatalities declined from a peak of 55,600 in 1972 to fewer than 33,000 in 2010, the lowest level since 1949.[55] On a per-passenger-mile basis, mass transit uses about the same amount of energy, emits about the same amount of air pollution, and has about the same number of accidental fatalities, so efforts to get people out of their cars and onto transit have little environmental benefit.[56]

The Transportation-Land-Use Connection

Although opposition to automobiles extends back to the late 1960s, critics of the suburbs did not focus on a link between automobiles and the suburbs until the 1980s. They call this link the "transportation-land-use connection." Clearly, the introduction of first streetcars and then automobiles led to major changes in land uses, as they allowed more jobs and people to move to suburban areas where land costs were lower. It isn't as clear, however, that increasing population densities and spending money on mass transit instead of highways can reverse this trend, yet that is what many suburban critics now contend.

In 1988, an environmental group called 1000 Friends of Oregon decided to focus on this connection in its effort to oppose construction of a new freeway in the Portland area. The group commissioned a series of reports called LUTRAQ (Land Use, Transportation, Air Quality) that claimed to show that investments in mass transit combined with higher-density development would do more to relieve congestion than building new roads. As the study itself reported, "an integrated land-use/transportation/demand-management alternative was more successful at meeting the transportation needs of the study area than just building highways."[57]

In 1995, however, University of Southern California planning professor Genevieve Giuliano pointed out that a close examination of LUTRAQ results reveals that "land-use policies appear to have little impact on travel outcomes." Instead, "most of the change [in travel behavior reported by LUTRAQ] is due to the TDM [transportation demand management] policies, rather than to the land use and transit policies." In LUTRAQ's case, TDM means giving all commuters free transit passes and charging all auto commuters for parking even in suburban areas where the costs of providing parking are low.[58]

Suburban critics often compare the amount of driving done by people living in suburbs and people living in dense cities, invariably showing that the latter drive less. But this fact does not mean that the suburbs are leading people to drive more. Instead, a large element of self-selection is involved: people who prefer to drive less choose to live in denser, mixed-use neighborhoods with easy access to transit, while people who want or need to drive more tend to live in auto-friendly neighborhoods. Once this self-selection is accounted for, the effects of density and urban design on driving are very small.

University of California (Davis) urban planning professor Susan Davis reviewed the literature on this subject in 2005. She specifically wanted to learn if building more highways led to more sprawl and driving, if building light rail would lead to increased densities, and if increased densities, mixed uses, and more walkable urban designs would reduce driving. In general, she found that the effects of these actions were small to negligible. New highways, for example, would not increase sprawl, though they might influence where that sprawl would take place.[59]

Suburbs and Obesity

When the Centers for Disease Control began reporting that the United States was threatened by an "obesity epidemic," anti-suburb groups jumped on this issue to argue that the epidemic was at least partly caused by the suburbs. The researchers at one such group used the CDC database to compare obesity rates with urban sprawl. In a peer-reviewed journal, they reported "small but significant associations" between sprawl and obesity. "Small" turned out to be very small: although San Francisco is much denser than Atlanta, only about 2 percent more Atlantans are obese than San Franciscans are.[60] Moreover, as every statistics student knows, correlation does not prove causation: maybe there is some other reason for a small but statistically significant correlation between sprawl and obesity.

Despite the weakness of these results, the group whose researchers did the study issued a press release claiming that the study proved "sprawling development has had a hand in the country's obesity crisis." The release argued that this correlation proved "the urgent need to invest in making America's neighborhoods appealing and safe places to walk and bicycle," which is plannerspeak for increasing urban densities and promoting mixed-use developments.[61]

It didn't take long for less-biased researchers to do more thorough studies and find that suburbs do not cause obesity; instead, found one study, the small association between sprawl and obesity was because "individuals who are more likely to be obese choose to live in more sprawling neighborhoods."[62] A second study confirmed that "the association between sprawl and obesity reported in earlier studies is largely due to self selection."[63] As a result, said the first study, any effort to increase population densities or make other changes to "the built environment to counter the rise in obesity is misguided."[64]

111

Suburbs and Climate Change

More recently, suburban critics have jumped on the climate change issue. A 2008 report from the Urban Land Institute titled *Growing Cooler* argued that the United States cannot meet carbon-reduction targets without reducing driving because the predicted growth in driving is greater than predicted reductions in automotive carbon emissions. To reduce driving, the report advocated more "compact development," meaning, among other things, higher densities, "a mix of land uses," and "interconnection of streets" (no cul-de-sacs).[65] Significantly, the lead author of this report was also the lead author of the study that was used to incorrectly claim that suburbs make people fat, and *Growing Cooler*'s other authors are also affiliated with anti-suburb groups.

One of the first problems with the report is the claim that Americans must drive less to meet carbon-reduction targets. A 2008 report from McKinsey and Company found that the most cost-effective ways to reduce carbon emissions involved the electricity and building sectors, not transportation or urban design. McKinsey concluded that the nation could meet targets by investing in programs that reduced carbon emissions at a cost of no more than $50 per ton of carbon dioxide equivalent. The only transportation program that met this test, McKinsey suggested, was using aluminum and other materials to build lighter-weight cars.[66] Although McKinsey did not evaluate compact development, this strategy would likely cost several thousand dollars per ton of reduced emissions.[67]

Economists Edward Glaeser and Matthew Kahn reviewed the issue in 2008 with a paper that purported to show that regions with numerous land-use restrictions, such as California, were successfully reducing auto driving and carbon emissions by increasing urban densities.[68] However, their analysis had many problems. First, they relied on equation-based estimates of the amount of driving people do in various cities when actual numbers measured by the states were available. The two were very different: Glaeser and Kahn estimated, for example, that New Orleans residents drive a third more than New York metro area residents, when in reality they drive 10 to 20 percent less.[69]

Second, they based carbon emissions from household electrical consumption on average emissions from power plants in each of eight regions, even though data are available on a state-by-state basis.[70] Colorado, for example, gets 95 percent of its electricity from burning fossil fuels, while Washington gets 87 percent of its electricity from hydroelectric dams or other sources that generate no carbon dioxide.[71] Yet Colorado and Washington are both in the same region, so Glaeser and Kahn used the same conversion factors for each of them.

These and other problems led Glaeser and Kahn to greatly overstate the differences in carbon emissions due to population densities. All else being equal, to the extent that density has any influence on carbon emissions at all, it would not be cost-effective for cities to impose density increases on residents simply to reduce emissions.

In response to *Growing Cooler* and similar reports, the Transportation Research Board—a part of the private but government-funded National Research Council—convened a dozen experts of varying political views to determine whether changing the "built environment" could reduce driving and, in turn, carbon emissions. The committee commissioned several papers from academic experts on specific parts of this question.

One of those papers, by University of California economist David Brownstone, reviewed the literature on relationships between the built environment and driving. In a finding reminiscent of the obesity study, he concluded that a "statistically significant link" exists between the built environment and driving, but that the available evidence suggests "the size of this link is too small to be useful" in reducing driving or carbon emissions.[72] Another paper suggested that compact development could actually increase emissions by increasing traffic congestion and concluded that increased fuel-economy standards would be more cost-effective at reducing emissions.[73]

The committee convened by the Transportation Research Board was divided on whether compact development was a practical solution and how much it would actually reduce carbon emissions. Its report concluded that doubling population densities combined with mixed uses, pedestrian-friendly design, and "other land-use factors" would reduce driving by anywhere from 3 to 20 percent—a very broad range.[74] Since fewer than 11 percent of carbon emissions come from urban driving of personal vehicles—which is the kind of driving that compact development advocates seek to curtail—reducing that kind of driving by just 3 percent would have an insignificant effect on total carbon emissions, especially considering the high cost of such policies.[75]

The Desire for Single-Family Homes

Sprawl opponents tell themselves that Americans who dream of living in a single-family home with a yard are merely victims of propaganda, such as Herbert Hoover's "own-your-own-home" campaign.

This belief is supported by Kenneth Jackson's popular 1987 book *Crabgrass Frontier*, which one reviewer accurately described as a "polemic against suburbs."[76] "Jackson assumed that social change began at the top of society and later filtered down as the fashions of the rich and powerful became 'popular with ordinary people,'" comments Joseph Bigott.[77] "From this assumption, Jackson argued that upper- and middle-class suburban cultures created the market for modern single-family housing."

"In *Crabgrass*," comments historian James L. Wunsch, "as soon as the privileged cross the threshold into suburbia, the factories and blue-collar settlements, whore houses and road houses somehow disappear, never to appear again, and this despite the fact that in the latter half of the 19th century, industrial growth beyond the city limits accelerated." In fact, Wunsch notes, suburbs had significant numbers of people—many of the working class—as early as 1850, and many if not most of the workers had jobs in the suburbs as well.[78]

Jackson had expressed many of the ideas in his book in journal articles dating to 1980 or earlier.[79] Yet by 1982, historians were beginning to prove Jackson wrong. As described in Chapter 3, Oliver Zunz's 1982 book about Detroit, *The Changing Face of Inequality*; Margaret Garb's 2005 book about Chicago, *City of American Dreams*; and similar work elsewhere have shown that the desire for single-family homeownership really came from working-class immigrants, not "the top of society."

The Real Reason for the War on Sprawl

Opponents of sprawl have many motives: downtown property owners, for example, want to enhance the value of their land, while cities resent taxpayers' moving out of their jurisdictions. Ultimately, however, the war on sprawl is about aesthetics: not just what urban areas should look like but who has the sophistication to appreciate (and therefore the right to live in) suburbs and rural areas.

Sierra Club members, for example, believe they have the aesthetic sensibility to appreciate rural and wild lands, while those who would ride dirt bikes, snowmobiles, or other motorized off-road vehicles do not. Although some anti-suburbanites live in the high-density cities that they advocate for others, many others do not, and their goal is to keep the suburban or rural areas they live in "pristine"—not counting their own home; to effectively close the door after they have gone through. Once again, much of the debate comes down to a middle-class versus working-class view of the world.

By the 1950s, working-class families no longer took in boarders, kept backyard livestock, or, for the most part, maintained in-home businesses. Yet social scientists continue to find numerous differences between the working class and middle class, including the following:

- Members of the middle class have significantly longer life expectancies than members of the working class.[80]
- The middle class is more likely to participate in political campaigns than the working class.[81]
- Middle-class parents spend more time talking to newborn children and interacting with older children than working-class parents.[82]
- Children in working-class families are more likely to grow up obese than children in middle-class families.[83]
- Students in middle-class families are likely to have a smaller gap between male and female educational attainments than students in working-class families.[84]
- Teenagers in working-class families are more likely to experiment with sex with more partners than teenagers in middle-class families.[85]
- The middle class is almost twice as likely to watch "art films" as the working class.[86]
- Middle-class men even have different tastes in "exotic dancers" than working-class men.[87]

They also have distinctly different views about the environment. Middle-class environmentalists are more likely to believe in preservation of wild lands from any use at all other than nonmotorized recreation. Members of the working class are more likely to label themselves "conservationists" who believe in "wise use" of natural resources, including timber cutting, mining, and other consumptive uses. "Early environmentalism was not a social movement but rather an attempt by privileged classes to preserve a place for outdoor recreation," says historian Stacy Silveira. "Working class individuals and ethnic minorities were generally excluded from conservation and preservation organizations."[88]

Having a more refined aesthetic appreciation of nature is one way for people to declare their superiority over others. When "even a semiskilled factory worker" can "own two cars, a Ranch house, a TV set, and clothe his wife in excellent copies of Paris fashions the same year they are designed, it should perhaps be no surprise that higher-status groups (perhaps without considerably greater income) should defend the potential threat posed by widespread material abundance to their 'status-honor' by designating such economic possessions 'vulgar' and asserting the indispensability of a particular style of life—that is, something that cannot be immediately purchased with no down payment," observed sociologist Bennett Berger in 1960.[89] Joining the war on sprawl is one way to assert that status. It doesn't hurt that, just as zoning in the early 1900s made middle-class neighborhoods too expensive for working-class families, the war on sprawl today makes suburbs too expensive for those who do not share middle-class cultural values.

For decades, architects, planners, and environmentalists have demonized the suburbs, effectively attacking the idea of homeownership. These attacks have a strongly elitist flavor, as the attackers are willing to condemn millions of people to live in forms of housing that the attackers themselves often avoided: Le Corbusier, for example, never lived in a high-rise tower though he planned and built them for, supposedly, everyone else.[90] As the next chapter will show, the unintended consequences of Le Corbusier's density dreams would prove far more unfortunate than the supposed costs of sprawl.

8. Low-Income Dreams

World War II ended with a huge pent-up demand for new housing. Between 1930 and 1945, homebuilders had built fewer new homes than the nation gained new households in every year but one. The result, by 1945, was 4 million more new households than new homes. Counting older, dilapidated homes, some estimated the nation needed at least 8 million new homes. Private homebuilders would do their best to meet the demand, but housers were convinced that low-income families, particularly unskilled workers and the "deserving poor"—meaning people who were poor through no fault of their own—would be left behind.

It took four years and the support of "Mr. Republican," Ohio Senator Robert Taft, but in 1949 Congress finally passed a new housing act. The law set a national "goal of a decent home and suitable living environment for every American family." To achieve that goal, Title II of the law allowed the Federal Housing Administration to insure rural as well as urban mortgages and expanded the total amount of insurance coverage the FHA could provide. For the housers, Title III of the law authorized the construction of 810,000 units of new public housing through 1955, a provision that led the National Association of Real Estate Boards to label Senator Taft a "socialist."[1]

The housers would end up being as disappointed with this law as they were with the 1937 law, and for most of the same reasons: Realtors and homebuilders objected to having to compete with the government, and thanks to the Davis-Bacon Act, the costs of constructing public housing were high. By 1959, Congress had appropriated enough money to build just 250,000 units of housing, barely 30 percent of the amount that it had authorized through 1955.[2]

Decent Homes vs. Slum Clearance

Most important, the goal of "a decent home for every American family" was undermined by Title I of the act, which dealt with slum clearance. This title created a federal Urban Redevelopment Agency and gave it the authority to provide up to 80 percent of the financing needed to remove blighted buildings and replace them with new ones, which weren't always low-income housing.

By 1949, it was apparent to urban leaders that trends begun before the Depression were accelerating after the war: namely, that people were moving out of high-density cities and into low-density suburbs. Before the war, millions of mostly working-class families still lived in high-density housing in the inner cities. Few of these families owned automobiles, and instead workers commuted on foot or by streetcar to nearby factories. Greenwich Village, the neighborhood celebrated in Jane Jacobs's *Death and Life of Great American Cities*, was a typical example of such a working-class neighborhood.[3]

Central-city officials were naturally concerned about the declining incomes in and tax revenues from these neighborhoods, which they called "blighted." They worried that property owners had disincentives to replace or "gentrify" the slums because the value of any new buildings would be dragged down by the continuing decline of adjacent structures. Racial segregation played a role in this assumption, as in that era many whites would refuse to live in even luxury housing if it were next door to homes occupied by blacks.

Urban leaders tried to use the power of government to fix this problem. Under Title I of the Housing Act, 992 cities received grants to carry out 2,532 urban renewal projects over the next 25 years.[4] Adjusted for inflation to today's dollars, these grants totaled to more than $50 billion.[5] Title I also encouraged cities to use eminent domain to acquire all the properties on one or more city blocks. Cities would clear all the structures on these properties and then offer them to developers to replace en masse instead of one at a time.

One such neighborhood was in southwest Washington, D.C. Occupied mainly by blacks, planners considered it a slum even though many of the residents earned middle-class incomes and many of the businesses were healthy. In the early 1950s, the District's urban-renewal agency, known as the National Capital Revitalization Corporation, used the power of eminent domain to condemn the entire neighborhood, both middle-class and poor, thriving businesses, and slum apartments lacking electricity and indoor toilets. The owners of a department store in the area argued that their store wasn't blighted and so should be excluded from condemnation and further argued that the taking was unconstitutional because the urban-renewal agency planned to give the land to a private developer, whereas the Constitution only allows takings for "public use."[6] But the Supreme Court concluded, in an 8-0 decision, that because the government had written a plan that found that the benefits of the taking exceeded the costs, the taking was by definition for public use.[7]

Despite Supreme Court approval, the law soon came under intense criticism, partly due to its contradictory goals. The cities that cleared the slums wanted to replace them with residents and businesses that would pay higher taxes. Realtors and builders wanted no more new residences built than were demolished, and cities were happy to comply, usually building both far fewer and pricing many of them higher than the ones that were cleared.

Moreover, the lag time between slum clearance and the completion of whatever developments replaced the slums averaged 12 years. This lag meant that most of the low-income people displaced by slum clearance were forced to find other housing on their own, usually at a higher cost and often no better in quality. By 1961, Title I had destroyed four times as many units of housing as Title III had built.[8] Because so many of the displaced families were black, novelist James Baldwin dubbed urban renewal "Negro removal" in 1963.[9]

When New York City planners decided to redevelop Greenwich Village, they encountered a force apparently stronger than the Supreme Court: Jane Jacobs. Jacobs is a curious figure. Her book *The Death and Life of Great American Cities* is frequently quoted by libertarians who appreciate her attack on "the pseudoscience of city rebuilding and planning."[10] But she is also worshipped by urban planners, who have built her "new principles of city planning and rebuilding" into their current theories of urban design. "There's no question that [Jane Jacobs's] work is the leaping-off point for our whole movement," says the executive director of the Congress for the New Urbanism, a group that promotes today's most popular urban planning fad.[11]

The best review of *Death and Life* came from Herbert Gans, a sociologist who (unlike Jacobs) had studied both inner-city and suburban neighborhoods in detail by actually living in one of each for a year. Gans noted that, because apartments in the inner city tended to be small, people conducted much of their social lives on the streets. This active street life attracted "intellectuals, artists, and bohemian types" such as Jacobs; they added even more to the street life, and the "exotic flavor then draws visitors and tourists."[12]

By contrast, people in relatively large suburban homes with even larger yards conduct most of their social lives in their homes or backyards, leading visitors who only see the front yards and streets to erroneously conclude that the neighborhoods are socially dead. "But visibility is not the only measure of vitality, and areas that are uninteresting to the visitor may be quite vital to the people who live in them," said Gans. "Middle-class people, especially those raising children, do not want working-class—or even bohemian—neighborhoods."[13]

Gans recognized, as Jacobs did not, that the inner-city neighborhoods "were built for a style of life which is going out of fashion with the large majority of Americans who are free to choose their place of residence."[14] Today, there are few of Jacobs's urban villages outside of New York City and, to a much lesser extent, Baltimore, Boston, Philadelphia, and San Francisco. In the decades after the war, the vast majority of families in these neighborhoods moved to single-family homes in suburbs typified by Long Island's Levittown. As detailed in Chapter 4, two things prompted this change. First, in contrast to prewar factories, which could be installed in vertical factory towers, the moving assembly lines pioneered by Henry Ford in production of the Model T were horizontal, requiring large areas of land. As more industries adopted these techniques, they moved to suburban areas where land was less expensive but where few people would live within walking distance of the factories.

Second, working-class wages grew while the cost of driving declined, so working-class families quickly acquired automobiles. In 1930, about half of American families had an automobile, and these were mostly middle-class (white-collar) and upper-class families. By 1960, nearly 80 percent of American households owned one or more automobiles, giving a majority of working-class employees the mobility they needed to live in single-family homes that might be several miles from their jobs.[15]

As working-class families moved out of the cities, rents on tenement housing declined. In many cases, such housing became occupied by blacks who, due to racial discrimination, had some of the lowest incomes in the nation. Landlords often failed to keep this housing in a state of good repair because they could not afford to do so given high vacancy rates and the low rents they collected on occupied units.

Although race may have been a factor in such programs, the real goal, worthy or not, was to increase property values and tax revenues. Some have argued that urban renewal "was a program designed to demolish poor people's housing in the hope that the people would just go away."[16] But the fact is that many of the people were going away anyway, mostly to the suburbs. An inventory of 400,000 housing units cleared or scheduled to be cleared under Title I as of 1966 found that

25 percent of them were vacant, suggesting that a surplus of dense urban housing was a serious problem.[17]

Between 1950 and 2000, the populations of a majority of major central cities, from Albany to Youngstown, declined by 25 to 60 percent even as the urban areas in which those cities are located grew.[18] Critics blame this "hollowing out of American cities" on federal policies. Yet people had good reason to leave. As sociologist Harlan Paul Douglass noted in 1925, most major American cities had more families than homes. If "every house in New York City was occupied by a single family," Douglass pointed out using data from the 1920 census, "71.4 percent of all families would be homeless."[19] Moreover, as University of Chicago historian Robert Bruegmann observed in *Sprawl: A Compact History*, these trends began before Congress passed Title I of the 1949 Housing Act and continued long after Congress repealed it.[20] They resulted from changes in transportation costs, incomes, and tastes.

Radiant City Slums

To make matters worse, too much of the public housing that was built under the law followed the Corbusian model of high-rise housing surrounded by large public spaces. The most infamous example was St. Louis's Pruitt-Igoe apartments. Designed by Minoru Yamasaki, the same architect who would later design the World Trade Center, Pruitt-Igoe included more than 2,800 apartments in 33 identical 11-story buildings. Initial construction bids were so much higher than anticipated that the public housing authority made major cuts.[21] When the project opened in 1955, new residents found that locks broke, doorknobs fell off, windowpanes blew out, and elevators did not elevate—and when the elevators did work, they only stopped on the 1st, 4th, 7th, and 10th floors of the 11-story buildings.[22]

Beyond construction quality, the project suffered from the fact that the large common areas (as opposed to private yards) and multiple entrances to each building (as opposed to a single entrance with a guard, as might be found in an upper-class high-rise residential building) made it impossible for residents to keep criminals and vandals out. Architect Oscar Newman demonstrated that smaller projects built with more private features were much safer, a concept he termed "defensible space."[23]

A further problem was financial: Although the federal government paid most of the capital costs of public housing, it did not fund operating costs, which were supposed to come out of tenant rents.

But Congress also regulated how much rent local housing agencies could charge, and particularly in cases like Pruitt-Igoe, which were poorly constructed in the first place, the rents were never enough to cover operations and maintenance costs. As a result, the local housing authorities ended up becoming the evil slumlords that they had been created to replace, "squeezing, from necessity, an ever-increasing portion of total income from their poverty-stricken tenants until protests and strikes finally led the federal government to limit the portion of income that could be charged for rent," political scientist Eugene Meehan writes in his history of the St. Louis public housing program. He argues that "the fiscal arrangements made by Congress were the most important single factor in the eventual breakdown of the conventional public housing program."[24]

Pruitt-Igoe was never more than 75 percent occupied. In 1965, the city spent $5 million trying to cure its problems, but by 1970 occupancy fell to 35 percent. In 1972, Pruitt-Igoe reached its peak of fame when the city imploded the entire complex.[25] The failure of Pruitt-Igoe and similar developments, such as Cabrini Green and Robert Taylor Homes in Chicago, and similar high-rise projects in Philadelphia, all of which have been demolished well before their intended life span, has led planning historian Peter Hall to dub Le Corbusier "the Rasputin of the tale" of urban planning.[26] Urban critic Theodore Dalrymple is even harsher, saying "Le Corbusier was to architecture what Pol Pot was to social reform."[27]

Houser Catherine Bauer offered more details about what was wrong with Radiant City. She argues that the minimalist design of the International style pioneered by Le Corbusier was a response to the Depression and the "oversimplification" of housing needs as defined by law: "decent, safe, and sanitary." The social aspects of *postwar* housing design turned out to be far more complex . . . even for the poor," she suggested. "What modern technology has done is to increase productivity, raise incomes and the birth rate, enhance mobility, create new demands, and greatly complicate all the issues involved in housing design and city planning. But instead of seriously investigating these fascinating new problems in order to develop rational new criteria, the former pioneers clung to the old principle and turned it into doctrinaire stylism."[28]

To be fair, Le Corbusier didn't design any public housing projects in the United States, but he designed a few and inspired many more in Europe and Asia, and most of the ones he inspired on those continents turned out to be as much failures as the ones in America.

Reflecting the failure of the Radiant City model, local housing authorities outside New York City today almost exclusively emphasize low-rise construction. Although the resulting housing projects have not proved as disastrous as Pruitt-Igoe and the Robert Taylor Homes, many problems still exist. A recent *Washington Post* analysis found hundreds of millions of dollars worth of stalled or abandoned projects. Under a public-private partnership program, the federal government gives money to local housing authorities, which in turn give it to developers to build affordable housing. But the federal agencies that pass out the money make no effort to monitor the results, and in hundreds of cases developers took the money but never finished the projects. In at least 55 cases, developers did not even begin construction.[29]

Beyond the housing issue, critics asked whether government was capable of improving cities at all. In 1961, Jane Jacobs's book *The Death and Life of Great American Cities* argued that many of the so-called slums that cities wanted to clear were, in fact, vibrant neighborhoods, and that the developments that were built to replace them were "truly marvels of dullness and regimentation, sealed against any buoyancy or vitality of city life."[30]

In 1964, economist Martin Anderson's book *The Federal Bulldozer* charged that urban renewal was not even accomplishing its goals of improving cities. Instead, he said, slum clearances merely pushed slums into other parts of the cities while the projects that replaced the slums failed to increase the overall tax revenues collected by cities.[31] In fact, many of the areas cleared were not redeveloped for many years, if ever, thus resulting in permanent, or at least long-term, loss in tax revenues.[32]

Minority Removal

Rather than provide low-income housing, many cities chose to build "urban monuments." A neighborhood south of downtown Portland, Oregon, housed thousands of Jewish and Italian immigrants and their businesses, including grocery stores, delicatessens, and kosher meat markets, as well as numerous churches and synagogues.[33] In 1958, the city declared the area a slum and condemned and cleared 54 blocks, replacing the homes and businesses with a sterile set of concrete high-rise apartments (that now collect very modest rents due to Portland's oversupply of multifamily housing), a concrete civic auditorium whose evening concerts are patronized by Portland's wealthy, and—one thing even hip Portlanders are proud of—a full block dedicated to a concrete imitation of a Cascade mountain waterfall.[34]

Reflecting Idaho's history of mining, downtown Boise had a thriving Chinatown. The city decided it should be turned into a modern shopping mall, so it condemned and cleared the buildings, with most of the Chinese relocating to California. Developers eventually did build a shopping mall—four miles away—while some of the blocks of the former Chinatown remain vacant to this day.[35]

Jane Jacobs's book and other negative reactions to these sorts of projects led Congress to end the Title I slum clearance program in 1974, replacing it with community development block grants that could be used for a variety of purposes, mostly aimed at reducing or alleviating the effects of poverty. This change meant that neighborhoods that were once in the crosshairs of urban-renewal agencies were left to gentrify on their own—something that was supposed to be impossible under the blight theory—and today make up many colorful historic districts of cities across the nation. In fact, according to Purdue historian Jon Teaford, most urban renewal even before 1974 was done by private enterprise without federal assistance.[36]

In retrospect, the public housing and slum clearance programs were both unnecessary and misguided. They were unnecessary because private homebuilders could easily meet the demand for postwar housing. By 1955, private homebuilders had constructed well over 9 million new homes, a million more than were supposedly needed in 1949. Between 1945 and 1955, homebuilders constructed 5.1 million more new homes than there were new households, more than erasing the deficit that built up during the Depression and World War II. This surplus continued every year through 1973, by which time there were 12 million more new homes than new households. The stock of private housing was enough that even unskilled workers could afford a decent home, leading Martin Anderson to ask in 1964, "Are the principles of federal urban renewal, which were established to meet conditions existing before 1950, valid today?"[37]

Public housing was misguided because the housers' fundamental tenet—that the government could build better housing for the poor at a lower cost than the private sector could—proved to be wrong. Not only did public housing cost significantly more to build, per square foot, than private housing, the quality of the work was often far worse than private construction. Faced with funding limits, local housing authorities cut corners and produced unlivable buildings. As historian D. Bradford Hunt notes, within three years of the opening of Chicago's

Robert Taylor Homes—the largest single public housing project in the nation—residents "faced a daily nightmare of broken elevators, erratic heat, excessive vandalism, and escalating violence."[38]

Public housing "not only derails what the private market can do on its own, but more significantly, it has profoundly destructive unintended consequences," says the Manhattan Institute's Howard Husock. By providing low-income families with a cheap, if heavily subsidized, alternative to owning their own homes, public housing subsidies "undermine the efforts of those poor families who work and sacrifice to advance their lot in life" by discouraging them from discovering the benefits of homeownership.[39] Those benefits are the same as they have always been for the working poor: a source of food and potential income (by growing food and running small businesses that are generally not possible or allowed in public housing), an effective savings bank, and eventually a form of collateral for loans that can be used to start small businesses, send children to college, or retire.

In 1965, the leading houser of the 1930s, Catherine Bauer, looked back with regret on the follies of the ambitious public housing agenda she once supported. "The political leadership of the housing and planning movement was largely democratic-socialist in philosophy," she said. "Quite apart from one's political belief, it seemed inevitable to almost every sophisticated person that collective ways of living would result from modern technology. Nobody quite imagined that we would choose to use technology, beginning in the United States, primarily to enhance individual and family independence. It was assumed somehow that utopia would mean good mass-produced meals, in great apartment complexes where all the services were done for us. Mama would not have to cook or clean any more. But of course, rightly or wrongly, we used technology for exactly the opposite purposes. We used it for gadgets to make ourselves freer and more self-sufficient in the house, rather than less. We used it to mass-produce tracts of one-family houses, and above all, automobiles, i.e., auto-mobility. We chose individualism rather than collectivism."[40]

Although Bauer may have been a starry-eyed idealist in the 1930s, public housing projects also had a dark side: they assuaged liberal guilt for imposing land-use policies that made private housing unaffordable to low-income families and particularly to many blacks and other minorities. As long as the government was providing housing for these disadvantaged families, the middle class could enhance its wealth by imposing increasingly stringent zoning and planning rules that drove up the costs of new housing (and, by extension, the value of their existing homes) without having to worry about the effects of those policies on the poor.

The 20th century's successive low-income housing policies—slum clearance, public housing projects, housing vouchers, the Community Reinvestment Act, and local affordable housing mandates (requirements that private builders sell a certain percentage of homes to low-income buyers at below-market rates)—have mostly proved to be failures because they treat symptoms, not causes. Low-income people live in tenements or other inadequate housing because their incomes are low, not because there is any physical shortage of housing or the capacity to build more. Giving a poor person a house without augmenting their income to pay for upkeep and maintenance can add to their financial burden rather than solve their problems. Today's emphasis on vouchers may be less harmful than building Radiant City high-rises, but in regions where land-use regulations restrict housing supplies, the vouchers may simply drive up rents.

In California, where housing prices are extremely high, immigrants whose incomes often start out low can still achieve respectable rates of homeownership. "Asian immigrants achieved extraordinarily high levels of homeownership soon after arrival," found a 1998 analysis, while "Hispanic immigrants demonstrated sustained advancement into homeownership from very low levels."[41] Census data from 2010 found that 72 percent of non-Hispanic white families own their own homes, while only 44 percent of black and 47 percent of Hispanic families are homeowners.[42] But the low average Hispanic rates disguise a trend: Hispanic immigrants tend to have very low rates of homeownership, but by the second generation their homeownership rates are much closer to non-Hispanic whites.

Blacks, however, have not enjoyed this form of generational progress. In fact, black and Hispanic homeownership rates in 2000 were both at 45 percent, which means that over the decade Hispanics gained while blacks lost.[43] The low homeownership rate for black families is one of the continuing legacies of America's shameful history of racism.[44] This means black homeownership reached 45 percent in 1980, and has remained there ever since.[45]

During the first half of the 20th century, discrimination by the Federal Housing Administration, which refused to insure loans in integrated neighborhoods, and local realtors, who considered it unethical to sell a home in a white neighborhood to blacks, confined blacks to ghetto districts. This reduction in housing opportunities allowed landlords to charge blacks up to 15 percent more for comparable housing than whites. A 1972 study of Chicago housing, where 18 percent of blacks were homeowners, estimated that, in the absence of discrimination, 47 percent of them would have been homeowners. One of the economists who did this study, John Kain, argued that, since traditional housing programs don't solve problems of discrimination, "these programs are characterized by a low ratio of benefits to real resource costs, and that they are designed so that a small percentage of poor households obtain large subsidies while the overwhelming majority receives none whatsoever."[46] At least some policies developed since that time, such as affordable housing mandates, are no better.

As noted in Chapter 7, some trace the first systematic federal discrimination against blacks to the Home Owners' Loan Company, the New Deal program that helped distressed homebuyers refinance and keep their homes. HOLC mapped cities, with blue meaning well-to-do white neighborhoods, yellow meaning declining neighborhoods, and red meaning risky—which were often black or integrated neighborhoods—leading to the term "redlining." However, an analysis of HOLC loans has found that it did not explicitly racially discriminate in the loans it made.[47]

The Federal Housing Administration, however, was explicit in its discrimination against blacks: only 2 percent of the loans it insured between 1935 and 1950 were to nonwhite homebuyers.[48] The FHA long refused to insure loans on homes in black or integrated neighborhoods. During the 1940s, developers in Detroit and Miami were required to build walls to separate black neighborhoods from their properties—the Detroit wall was eight feet high and a half-mile long—in order to get FHA financing for their developments.[49]

FHA discrimination against blacks supposedly ended in with a 1948 Supreme Court ruling, but the agency continued to resist desegregation for nearly a decade afterward.[50] Local discrimination continued for many years after that. A review of fair housing audits conducted in the 1980s found that blacks "averaged a 20% chance of experiencing discrimination in the sales market and a 50% chance in the rental market."[51]

Some federal programs designed to remedy historic discrimination left low-income families worse off than before. In 1968, Congress created a "homeownership for the poor" program that insured mortgages for low-income buyers with down payments as low as $200 and reduced effective interest rates to as low as 1 percent. The program turned into a disaster because "the mortgage insurance was structured in a way that actually made it in the interest of lenders to loan money on uninhabitable homes." Families were sold homes that had no heat and whose electrical systems were unsafe to use. By 1970, the program was considered a "national scandal." Though the Department of Housing and Urban Development tried to fix the program, a 1972 report found that it continued to cause "suffering, anguish, and humiliation" to the families who participated. When the Nixon administration suspended the program in 1973, one of the main questions was how to compensate the people who were supposed to have been helped but who turned into victims.[52]

Some analysts argue that racial discrimination in housing has ended.[53] Even if it has—and many blacks claim it has not—black families still suffer from the history of such discrimination. Children who grew up in families that owned homes are much more likely to buy their own homes than children who grew up in rental properties.[54] One reason may be that they understand better the financial and other obligations that come with homeownership.

Some contend that exclusionary zoning practices, such as large lot sizes and minimum home sizes, are aimed primarily against blacks and other minorities.[55] Yet many of these rules, such as prohibitions against small livestock, requirements that all householders be related to the same family, and restrictions on in-home businesses, seem aimed as much if not more against immigrant and working-class families whose values and lifestyles are very different from those of middle-class whites.

In any case, housing policy is a poor tool for trying to solve problems with persistent poverty and discrimination. Although these problems deserve attention, government housing programs are the wrong way to provide that attention, and history shows they are more likely to make the problems worse than they are to solve them.

9. Spoiling the Dream

In 1992, Karen and Kelly Parkman bought a home in a single-family neighborhood of Gresham, Oregon, Portland's largest suburb. But in 1995, planners rezoned their neighborhood, which was not far from Portland's light-rail line, for "transit," meaning mixed-use, multifamily housing. Historically, most zoning set maximum densities, such as four or eight houses per acre. But Gresham's transit zone was a minimum-density zone so strict that, if a house burned down, homeowners would have to replace it with an apartment or mixed-use development.[1]

Within a year, a 92-unit apartment building was under construction across the street from their home. "I didn't want to live across the street from that," said Karen Parkman, so they decided to sell their home and move. Although they received several offers on the house, would-be homebuyers soon learned that banks refused to lend money for houses in this zone, saying that the strict zoning rules effectively meant there was no collateral for the loan. Exasperated, they moved to a new home and turned the old one into a daycare center.[2]

Such minimum-density zoning of single-family neighborhoods has become common in cities that say they want to emphasize transit and curb urban sprawl. So how did zoning, which the Supreme Court ruled was constitutional in 1926 as a way to protect single-family neighborhoods from apartment "parasites," evolve into a tool used to force single-family neighborhoods to accept multifamily housing?

Democracy vs. Property Rights

The impulse to dictate to other people how they should live and use their property has a long history even in the freedom-loving United States. In the 17th century, Puritans required people to live within one and a half miles of a meetinghouse, which may be the earliest sort of urban-growth boundary in North America. "Town records provide numerous cases of people being required to move closer to the town center during the early generations," observes historian

Gwendolyn Wright. "Even private property was, in theory, superseded by public order."[3]

Two centuries later, America's most famous novelist James Fenimore Cooper, having spent seven years in Europe, returned to the United States to find that neighbors in his hometown of Cooperstown (named after his father) believed that living in a democracy gave them the right to tell him how he could use his land. He records his experiences in his 1837 novel *Home as Found*. When the leading character rebuilds his home in a Gothic style, rather than the then-popular "Grecian" or Classical Revival style, a secondary character subtly rebukes the builder's daughter. "I admire the house," says the character, "but then there are many, a majority perhaps, who do not, and these persons think they ought to be consulted about such matters."

The daughter responds that she does not "see what concern a majority, as you term them, can have with a house that does not belong to them," to which the critic replies, "I do not mean that the public has a legal right to control the tastes of the citizen, but in a *republican* government, you undoubtedly understand, it *will* rule in all things."[4]

Cooper wrote this book, his daughter later noted, to relate his perception that Americans had replaced "self-reliance" with "a vapid and sensitive public vanity, fostered by the fulsome flattery of selfish demagogues."[5] In fact, the book was inspired by Cooper's own personal experiences. Not only did the public disapprove of his taste in architectural styles, but it had appropriated a portion of his family's land for use as a public picnic ground, where people had cut trees and vandalized some of the structures on the property. When he protested, he was told (as he relates in *Home as Found*) that "he does not own it. . . . [T]he public has owned it. The public, moreover, says it owns it, and what the public says, in this happy country, is law."[6]

Some 140 years later, the laws of California, Oregon, and other states gave virtually anyone in those states a legal right to have a say in where in that state people could build their homes and what those homes might look like. Moreover, when property owners complain about the loss of their rights, they are told that property rights are "subject to change" to promote the public's "evolving needs."[7] In other words, what you thought you owned yesterday, you may not own today.

"In *Home as Found*, as in all his fiction, Cooper is concerned with social clashes and the barriers that keep one group clean and cast out another," observes an American literature professor.[8] But Natty Bumpo, Cooper's greatest character, represented the genius of the

American commoner oppressed by elites. In contrast, Cooper's assertion of his property rights made him appear to be an elitist repressing the public's use of "their" land. This seeming elitism may be why this book was less popular than his earlier ones.

The Transmogrification of Zoning

The modern transformation of zoning from a way of protecting neighborhoods to forcing change on those neighborhoods began in the 1960s and 1970s when several states began to pass land-use laws in what has been called a "quiet revolution." According to Fred Bosselman and David Callies, the attorneys who coined this term, before the revolution, land use was managed by a "feudal system under which the entire pattern of land development has been controlled by thousands of individual local governments, each seeking to maximize its tax base and minimize its social problems." The revolution sought to replace this system with "some degree of state or regional participation in the major decisions that affect the use of our increasingly limited supply of land."[9]

The use of the term "feudal" to describe mid-20th-century city planning and zoning is inappropriate, as that system was anything but feudal. As described in Chapter 1, a feudal system uses a combination of legal obligations and inheritance laws to immobilize people on the land. Cities, however, are corporations chartered by the state and effectively compete with one another to attract extremely mobile people and businesses to locate within their boundaries. The quiet revolution sought to negate that competition by conforming the land-use rules of all cities in a region or state to the same standard.

Before the revolution, zoning existed mainly to protect the property values of the areas being zoned while planners worked to efficiently distribute water, sewer, and other services to property owners who needed and were willing to pay for them. After the revolution, planners used zoning as a tool to change existing neighborhoods even as they created artificial shortages of land for housing, industry, and other uses, partly by denying urban services to certain areas that they arbitrarily decided should not be developed.

This quiet revolution stemmed from two movements. In the 1960s and early 1970s, zoning rules once lauded for protecting property values were condemned by supporters of the civil rights movement for excluding blacks and other minorities from suburban neighborhoods. The National Association for the Advancement of Colored People urged blacks "to do battle out in the townships and villages to lower zoning barriers and thereby create new opportunities for Negroes seeking housing closer to today's jobs at prices they can afford to pay."[10]

During the 1940s and 1950s, the courts had supported communities that zoned residential areas for large (one- to five-acre) lots or included minimum square footage requirements in zoning codes. But in the 1960s, state supreme courts in Pennsylvania and New Jersey ruled that such zones were "exclusionary" because they effectively prevented low-income families from moving into these communities.[11] State or regional takeover of land-use regulation was supposed to ensure that every community did not zone only for wealthy residents, thus leaving minorities and low-income families nowhere to go.

The second movement was the modern environmental movement, which some say got its start opposing so-called sprawl.[12] People who worried about the "increasingly limited supply of land"—which, in fact, was hardly limited at all in most states—sought various forms of growth controls that would protect farms, forests, and open space. The first such growth control was passed by the city of Ramapo, New York, which in 1969 decided that it would only approve new developments once the infrastructure needed to support such developments was in place—which, in some parts of the city, was not expected to happen for 18 years.[13] Such control is known as a *concurrency* or *adequate public services* requirement, and it can effectively stifle urban growth.

Three years later, Petaluma, California, implemented a different kind of growth control, deciding to issue no more than 500 residential building permits a year.[14] Soon after that Boulder, Colorado, decided to limit its building permits so that it would grow no faster than 2 percent per year.[15] These laws were widely cheered by environmentalists, but they fretted that growth controls in one community didn't do much good if adjacent cities and counties allowed growth to proceed unabated. "Ramapo was trying to control growth by itself," writes one historian, "without any cooperation from surrounding towns."[16] Moreover, economists were easily able to show that growth controls were a form of exclusionary zoning on steroids.[17]

In addition to a slow-growth permitting system, Boulder was the first American city to impose a tax dedicated to open-space preservation. Even though Boulder is physically adjacent to the 1.5-million-acre Arapaho-Roosevelt National Forest, and very close to the 266,000-acre Rocky Mountain National Park, the city decided to purchase a greenbelt around itself to prevent nearby development. Although the city itself occupies just 15,600 acres, it owns nearly three times that much land in the greenbelt.[18]

Boulder's policies have made it one of the least affordable housing markets in the nation, which is particularly striking as it is in a state that has no growth-management law. In 2009, Boulder's median home price was almost $460,000, more than *4.5 times median family incomes*. The ratio would be much higher except that Boulder's high housing prices have pushed low- and moderate-income families to nearby towns, such as Longmont and Broomfield; with 96,800 jobs in a city of 118,500, Boulder has far more jobs than workers.[19] As urban planning professors Steven Schmidt and Kurt Paulsen have shown, such "open-space preservation [is] a form of exclusionary zoning."[20]

Gradually, a consensus developed among urban planners that, instead of municipal growth controls, what was needed was regional or statewide *growth management*. Such growth management would not attempt to limit the rate of growth, but it would control where that growth would take place. Harvard economist Edward Glaeser suggests that, by covering an entire region or state, growth-management planners could overrule the exclusionary efforts of individual cities.[21] To provide affordable housing, growth managers would require all communities in a region to zone for an appropriate level of multifamily housing, since single-family zoning was supposed to be exclusionary.[22] After 1996, this form of growth management became known as *smart growth*, a term coined by then-governor of Maryland Parris Glendening partly so that planners could demonize any critics as being in favor of "dumb growth."[23]

If the growth-management consensus grew out of the civil rights and environmental movements, it was also strongly supported by city officials. Much of the debate over urban sprawl is really a debate over which municipality gets to tax new developments. Central-city officials resent the suburbs for capturing most of the population growth in the 20th century. Officials in established suburbs resent new suburbs, especially if the older suburbs are landlocked by other cities and have little vacant land for growth.

Taxes were not an issue in the 19th century when residents of new suburbs fully expected to be annexed by the central cities, thus giving them access to city utilities, such as water and sewers. At some point, however, suburbanites came to believe that the added tax burden of joining cities was greater than the value of the services those cities could provide. In Boston, for example, the "annexation movement" ended in 1873 when residents of Brookline voted not to be annexed by Boston.[24]

Some states, including Indiana, North Carolina, and Texas, give cities the authority to annex without the approval of the voters or property owners being annexed. It may be a coincidence, but they are among the states that haven't joined the quiet revolution of state or regional control over land uses. In fact, fewer than 20 states have passed growth-management laws, and some of those laws are fairly weak. In addition, metropolitan areas in a few other states have implemented regional growth-management plans for their regions alone.

Can growth management overcome exclusionary zoning and keep housing affordable? One way to answer this question is to compare housing affordability in states with and without growth management. One standard measure of affordability is the median home price divided by median family income, or price-to-income ratio. In markets with abundant land and no restrictions on home construction, this ratio tends to be around 2.0 or a little less.

At a price-to-income ratio of 2.0 and a 5 percent interest rate, a family making a 10 percent down payment and devoting 25 percent of its income to a mortgage can pay it off in less than 10 years. A price-to-income ratio of 3.0 requires a payoff period of more than 15 years. At 4.0, the period is more than 25 years, and at 5.0 it is more than 45 years.

Since 1960, the decennial census has calculated median family incomes and median home values for the year before each census.[25] The Census Bureau's American Community Survey has the same data for the years 2001 through 2010.[26] For other years, median family incomes for metropolitan areas are published by the Department of Housing and Urban Development (which uses them to calculate who is eligible for federal housing subsidies).[27] Median home prices for those years can be calculated using census data adjusted by house price indexes published by the Federal Housing Finance Agency.[28]

Hawaii

"It all began in Hawaii," say the authors of The Quiet Revolution, as the Aloha State passed the nation's first statewide land-use law just two years after achieving statehood in 1961. Although it might make sense that such a small state would be concerned about land uses, Hawaii actually has more than six times as much land as Rhode Island, and in 1960 it had less than three-fourths as many residents. The 1961 law created a state commission that divided the land into four categories: urban, rural, agricultural, and conservation. The rural category, which some other states call rural residential, allowed homes on half-acre lots.[29] But more than 96 percent of the state was in the conservation or agricultural zones, which virtually prohibited any development other than farming. Less than 3 percent was urban and just 1 percent was rural.[30]

Although proponents say the purpose of Hawaii's law was to protect agricultural lands, the actual history is much more sordid. Moreover, to the extent that the goal was to protect the agricultural industry, it failed miserably.

Using median home value divided by median family income, the 1960 census found that Hawaii already had the nation's least affordable housing. Nationwide, median home values were about 2.5 times median family incomes, and even metropolitan areas that are considered highly unaffordable today were in that ballpark, including Santa Barbara (at 2.6 times median family income) and San Francisco-Oakland (at 2.3 times median family income). The least affordable metropolitan area by far was Honolulu, at 3.4 times the median family income.[31]

Hawaii's housing was expensive not because of a natural shortage of land but because most of the state's land was owned by a handful of major property owners. They included the Bishop estate, which controlled former royal lands covering about 9 percent of the state, and the "Big Five" agricultural companies, which mainly grew pineapple and sugar cane on their lands. Together, these six owners controlled more than half the land in the state, with another 35 percent owned by the state or federal governments, resulting in a system that was almost feudal in nature.

In the middle of the 20th century, before the advent of jetliners, tourism played only a tiny role in Hawaii's economy. Fewer than 50,000 tourists entered Hawaii in 1950 compared with close to 7 million in 1990. The big industries were sugar cane and pineapple: Hawaii produced nearly a million tons of sugar in 1950 and grew 80 percent of the world's pineapple crop.[32]

For the first half of the 20th century, the state's political system was controlled by Republicans who were sympathetic to the big landowners. By 1954, however, enough newcomers had moved to the state— and were frustrated by the lack of land available to ordinary citizens—that Democrats won the legislature on promises of land reform. Many of the Democratic leaders had talked about taking land from the Big Five by eminent domain and distributing it to residents for housing, businesses, and small farms. After gaining power, however, Democratic politicians quickly retreated from those promises. Instead, they effectively sold out to landowning interests. Suddenly, legislators became partners in development projects that were once done solely by the Big Five and a few other wealthy interests. Passing the land-use law effectively prevented anyone without the right political connections from developing land.[33]

In the early 1960s, Henry J. Kaiser decided to alleviate Hawaii's housing shortage by building Hawaii Kai, a development that he expected would house 50,000 people on 6,000 acres of Bishop estate land that he was able to lease west of downtown Honolulu.[34] As built, however, the community houses only 30,000 people, partly because before it was completed, incoming residents used Hawaii's land-use laws to "preserve farms and open space" by stopping any further construction.[35]

With only a tiny amount of land available for urban development, the cost of housing soared. By 1979, a median home in Honolulu cost 5.5 times median family incomes. This cost increased to 6.2 in 1989 and 7.3 in 2006. The result was devastating to Hawaii's agricultural industry, as growers could not pay workers enough for them to afford housing and still compete with other Pacific island producers. Workers moved into the tourist and other industries, while pineapple, sugar cane, and other crops declined. Hawaii now produces fewer than 2 percent of the world's pineapples, and sugar cane production has declined by more than 80 percent.

According to one of the authors of *The Quiet Revolution* (who now lives in Hawaii), "Land use in Hawaii continues to be the most regulated of all the fifty states." As restrictive as the 1961 state land-use law is, it is only "the tip of the iceberg," as literally hundreds of permits and an average of close to 10 years are required before someone can begin residential construction.[36] As a result, housing in Hawaii is close to the least affordable in the nation.

California

California is not usually listed among the states that pioneered growth-management planning.[37] Although the state legislature has never formally passed a growth-management law, in 1963 it passed a law that unintentionally encouraged, and to some degree mandated, cities and counties to practice growth management.

The story really begins in 1950, when a man named A. P. Hamann became San Jose's city manager. At the time, San Jose had just 95,000 people, compared with San Francisco's 775,000 and Oakland's 385,000.[38] But Hamann set a goal of making San Jose the largest city in the Bay Area, and he accomplished this goal through aggressive annexation. Over the next two decades, San Jose made nearly 1,400 annexations, growing to cover eight times as much land.[39] The result was a city whose boundaries were highly erratic, with narrow fingers stretching off in several directions, detached parcels, and pockets of unincorporated neighborhoods entirely surrounded by the city. Annexation also raised the ire of other cities in the area whose officials felt that San Jose was annexing land that would more appropriately be included in their cities.

To reduce conflicts over annexations, in 1963 the legislature passed a law requiring every county to create a *local area formation commission* (LAFCo), whose approval was required for all annexations, city incorporations, or formation of special districts, such as sewer or water districts. The commissions would be made up of two representatives of each city council in the county plus two representatives from the county board of supervisors. The city councilors who dominated these commissions viewed the creation of new cities or special districts and even the annexation of land to other cities as threats to the tax base of their own cities. Particularly in coastal counties stretching from north of San Francisco to San Diego, the LAFCos created urban-growth boundaries outside of which development was restricted or forbidden.[40]

The process was complicated still further when the legislature passed the California Environmental Quality Act of 1970, requiring the preparation of a detailed environmental impact report for all state and local projects. In 1976, a state court decided that annexing land into a city required such a report, and eventually such reports were needed for expansions of urban-growth boundaries as well.[41]

In 1969, median housing prices in San Jose and even San Francisco were still quite affordable, being only 2.2 to 2.3 times median family incomes. In that year, "no-growth" candidates took over the San Jose City Council and Hamann resigned in disgust. One of the last annexations made before this takeover was an area south of downtown San Jose known as Coyote Valley. Working with the county and LAFCo, the new city council drew an urban-growth boundary around the city that excluded Coyote Valley. Despite being within the city limits, Coyote Valley was placed in an "urban reserve," off-limits to development until "the City's fiscal condition is stable, predictable and adequate" to support such development—in other words, a concurrency requirement.[42]

Between 1970 and 2000, San Jose's population doubled, but the city council refused to bring Coyote Valley inside the urban-growth boundary. Instead, the city's population density nearly doubled, and median home prices grew to 5.4 times median-family incomes in 1989 and to 8 times in 2006. Ironically, one of the members of the city council that drew the original urban-growth boundary argued that including Coyote Valley would result in "the Los Angelization of San Jose."[43] In fact, it was the anti-growth policies that were making San Jose the third-densest urban area in America after Los Angeles and San Francisco-Oakland.

In 2002, the city finally agreed to bring Coyote Valley inside the growth boundary provided property owners and developers paid the cost of the environmental impact report.[44] When they published a draft report, the Sierra Club demanded that developers donate $100 million to preserve land from development elsewhere as mitigation for the 25,000 homes they planned to build in Coyote Valley.[45] After spending five years and $17 million writing the environmental impact report, the city asked for another $2.5 million for further analysis. Instead, developers gave up, saying the poor economy combined with the risk that they might never actually receive approval to develop the area did not justify any further work.[46]

With an average price-to-income ratio of 8.3 in 2006, the peak of the housing bubble, California housing was the least affordable in the nation. The affordability of individual California markets varied considerably. Where San Jose's price-to-income ratio was 8.0 in 2006, San Francisco-Oakland's was 8.3; Los Angeles's was 9.8; and Santa Barbara had the dubious distinction of being the national champion at 11.2. Housing in interior cities, such as Bakersfield, Fresno, and Sacramento, was more affordable, but with price-to-income ratios of 5.0 to 7.0, they were still less affordable than 85 percent of the metropolitan areas in the United States.

"Smart growth is the new Jim Crow," says Joseph Perkins, an African-American radio talk show host and one-time president of the Home Builders Association of Northern California.[47] Even before the current recession, so many blacks were leaving California cities that the movement has been called "black flight."[48] This exodus is just part of the movement of low- and even middle-income families out of San Francisco and other California cities for more affordable locations.[49]

To be accurate, California's planning under LAFCos is closer to slow growth than smart growth, since it did not include densification of cities and suburbs. Indeed, several San Francisco Bay Area suburbs have passed rules limiting density or requiring a vote of residents before developers could build even a few new homes. Voters in Danville,

California, for example, passed a measure in 2000 requiring voter approval for any permit allowing the construction of 10 or more dwelling units or any development on more than two acres. In the same election, San Jose voters agreed to require voter approval before the city could make a change in its constricting urban-growth boundary.[50]

In 2008, the state legislature addressed densification in a roundabout way when it passed the Sustainable Communities and Climate Protection Act (SB 375), which among other things encourages cities to increase densities on the premise that doing so would lead to less driving. Cities can opt out of minimum-density requirements, but if they do they will lose some state funding.

In response to the unaffordable housing that the cities created, California cities have required homebuilders to sell a certain percentage of all homes built to low- and moderate-income families at below-market, and often below-cost, prices. Such affordable housing mandates actually make housing even less affordable because they lead builders to build fewer homes and to increase the prices of the homes they do build that aren't sold to low-income buyers. "Cities that impose a below-market housing mandate on average end up with 10 percent fewer homes and 20 percent higher prices," say economists at San Jose State University.[51]

Oregon

One problem facing regional planners in the 1960s was that most states did not require, and many did not even allow, counties to zone land. In 1969, the Oregon legislature passed a law requiring all counties to zone. In 1973, the legislature required cities and counties to write comprehensive plans and to conform their zoning codes to those plans. The 1973 law also created a seven-member Land Conservation and Development Commission that would write goals and guidelines for the comprehensive plans. LCDC had the power to review the plans and to require their revision if they failed to meet the commission's goals and guidelines.

The goals required every city in the state to have an urban-growth boundary. Outside the boundaries, a small amount of land could be zoned "rural residential," which meant 5- to 10-acre lot sizes, but most land had to be in farm or forest zones that greatly restricted development.

It took more than a decade for all cities and counties to write plans that met LCDC's approval. When they were done, 93.8 percent of the state was zoned for farms or forest, and another 3.6 percent was zoned for parks, natural resources, or some other restrictive category. And another 1.3 percent was zoned rural residential (5- to 10-acre lot sizes), rural industrial, or another rural zone that allowed some form of very low-density development. This left less than 1.3 percent of the state inside an urban-growth boundary. Even in the Willamette Valley—the agriculturally productive area that includes Portland, Salem, and Eugene and houses two-thirds of the state's population on less than 12 percent of its land area—only 5.9 percent of the land was inside of an urban-growth boundary.[52]

The original farm zones, for example, had 40-acre minimum lot sizes, which was later increased to 80 acres. When this restriction didn't stop nonfarmers from seeking to build homes in rural areas, LCDC required people to farm the land for five years before building on it. When some people planted blueberries—a crop that takes six years to mature—and then claimed they were farmers after five years, LCDC required people to earn $40,000 to $80,000 (depending on soil productivity) per year farming the land before being allowed to build a home on their own land. The rule was needed, said LCDC representatives, to prevent "lawyers, doctors and others not really farming [from] building houses in farm zones." Because of the rule, the number of homes built in farm zones declined by more than 75 percent to about 100 per year.[53]

Inside the boundaries, LCDC required cities and counties to provide enough land to meet the demand for housing and other uses for the next 20 years. Initially, LCDC intended that cities would expand the boundaries when most of the land inside the boundaries had been developed. However, in 1995, 1000 Friends of Oregon joined with some city officials to form a "zero option committee" that lobbied for no expansion to Portland's boundary.[54] As a result, LCDC decided that cities could meet the 20-year housing requirement by rezoning existing neighborhoods to higher densities. To avoid expanding the boundary, said one planning advocate, neighborhoods have "a duty . . . to take as many people as possible."[55]

As of 1992, 68 percent of housing in the Portland area was single-family detached homes, while 32 percent was multifamily. Metro—the regional planning agency for the Portland area—decided that only 41.5 percent of new housing would be single-family detached homes; 38.5 percent would be multifamily; and 20 percent would be row houses, previously not found in the Portland area.[56] To fulfill the plan, Metro gave each of 24 cities and three counties in the region population and housing targets and required them to rezone to meet those targets. This requirement led to the minimum-density zoning that created problems for Karen and Kelly Parkman.

By 1999, planners decided that row houses were "not dense enough" to meet population targets, and instead they focused on multifamily housing, especially mid-rise (four- to six-story) buildings, which were also previously unknown in the Portland area.[57] Although Metro made some modest additions to Portland's urban-growth boundary in 2002, environmental challenges and planning rules place so many obstacles in front of developers that construction of new homes won't begin for more than a decade after the boundary was expanded, if any are built at all.[58] Metro's central planning has condemned large numbers of people who would otherwise prefer to live in single-family homes to live in apartments or row houses.

Because of the densification requirements, Oregon housing is not as unaffordable as California's. Oregon price-to-income ratios were around 3.0 in 1979. Timber cutting was Oregon's largest industry in the 1970s, but when the Federal Reserve imposed high, inflation-fighting interest rates on the economy in the early 1980s, the nation's housing market collapsed and along with it the timber industry. Oregon's population actually declined in 1982 and 1983, and the housing market did not recover until after 1989, when price-to-income ratios were a little more than 2.0.

In the early 1990s, Silicon Valley companies daunted by California's unaffordable housing built large factories in Oregon. By 1997, the National Association of Home Builders ranked Portland housing the second-least-affordable in the nation after San Francisco.[59] The 2000 census, however, reported price-to-income ratios of 3.0, well under those in California and Hawaii. By 2008, they had reached 4.5, making Oregon the fourth-least-affordable state in the nation.

New England

Unusual in the United States, New England states have either weakened or entirely abolished the county level of government, so nearly all land-use regulation is done at either the city or state level. All New England states except Massachusetts have passed growth-management laws with either the states themselves doing much of the planning or providing strict guidelines for cities to follow.

In 1970, Vermont was actually the second state, after Hawaii, to pass a state land-use law that put most control over new development in the hands of a statewide environmental commission and seven district commissions. Although Vermont nominally has 14 counties, except for sheriff's departments, county governments are nearly nonexistent. Vermont's original law was not as strict as either Hawaii's or Oregon's, but the state passed a stricter growth-management law in 1988. This law allowed cities to designate "growth areas," effectively creating urban-growth boundaries. Cities are not required to practice growth management but receive financial incentives for doing so.[60]

Connecticut, which has completely abandoned county government, passed a law in 1971 requiring a state land-use plan. Completed in 1974, the plan divides the state into eight land-use categories, with the urban categories effectively creating urban-growth boundaries.

Maine and Rhode Island both passed Comprehensive Planning and Land Use Regulation Acts in 1988. The laws required all cities to prepare comprehensive plans that met state standards and to zone in accordance with the plans. The Rhode Island plans did not specifically designate urban-growth boundaries, but the Maine plans divided the state into "growth" and "rural" areas.[61]

New Hampshire passed a statewide planning law in 1985 that requires both cities and counties to write comprehensive plans. It encourages, but does not require, counties to use growth-management planning. Overall, New Hampshire probably has the least strict planning process in New England.[62]

Although Massachusetts has not passed a statewide land-use law, the state is divided into 351 municipalities, leaving no unincorporated land in the state. Each municipality has its own zoning rules and regulations, and many of these codes would be considered exclusionary, including large-lot requirements and limits or prohibitions on multifamily housing.[63] These regulations have greatly reduced the approval rate of permits for new homes. Despite the boom in the state's high-tech industry during the late 1980s and early 1990s, permits in the Boston metropolitan area fell from 172,000 during the 1960s to 141,000 in the 1980s and just 84,000 in the 1990s.[64] Massachusetts planning thus resembles California's slow-growth planning, which aims at keeping population densities low; it is not smart growth, but it is still a form of growth-management planning.

New England statewide plans—or, in Massachusetts's case, local plans—caused a significant increase in housing prices in the late 1980s and again in the 2000s. In most New England states and metro areas, including Boston, price-to-income ratios hovered between 2.0 and 2.5 before the 1980s. But in 1989, they reached from 3.0 to 4.0. By 2004, Massachusetts had become the nation's fourth-least-affordable state at 6.0. Vermont was the most affordable New England state at

3.3. Rhode Island was 4.9, while Connecticut and New Hampshire were 3.9 and Maine was 3.4.

Florida

In 1985, Florida passed a growth-management law that gives municipalities incentives to increase densities within cities and discourage development of rural lands. All cities and counties were required to complete comprehensive plans by 1995, and many of these plans explicitly adopted urban-service boundaries outside of which they would not extend sewer, water, and other services. The law also contains a concurrency requirement forbidding local governments from issuing building permits unless they already have the financing for all necessary infrastructure.[65]

Despite being one of the fastest-growing states in the country, Florida housing remained affordable, with price-to-income ratios in most metropolitan areas ranging from 1.5 to 2.5, through 1999. But prices rapidly grew after 2000, and by 2006 price-to-income ratios reached 4.2 statewide and 5.7 in the Miami metropolitan area.

As a part of his economic recovery program, Governor Rick Scott persuaded the Florida legislature to repeal the growth-management law in 2011. Cities and counties are still free to do growth-management planning but are no longer required to do so.[66]

New Jersey

A 1986 growth-management law divided New Jersey into five categories: metropolitan, suburban, fringe, rural, and environmentally sensitive. Urban growth in the last three categories is limited to existing towns or "centers." Development is limited outside these centers. Before the 1980s, New Jersey price-to-income ratios ranged from 1.7 to 2.6; by 1989, they exceeded 4.0 in some areas; and in 2006, the statewide average reached 4.7.

In contrast to New Jersey and Connecticut, New York State has no growth-management law, and most cities in New York maintained very affordable housing even through the height of the housing bubble. The major exceptions are New York City and its immediate suburbs. Hemmed in by Connecticut on the north and New Jersey on the west, development in New York City itself is hampered by a Landmarks Preservation Commission that allows residents to object to new developments that might "change the character" of their neighborhoods.[67] The city has also frequently downzoned neighborhoods, reducing the potential construction of new housing, in response to demands by residents who want to maintain "the existing scale of this neighborhood."[68] As a result, New York metropolitan area price-to-income ratios grew from just 2.6 in 1969 to 5.5 in 1989 and 8.2 in 2006.

Washington

The Washington legislature passed a growth-management law in 1991 that required fast-growing cities and counties (basically, those in the western part of the state) to write growth-management plans, including urban-growth boundaries, while leaving such planning optional for slow-growing areas (basically those in the eastern part of the state). The law also requires plans to include concurrency requirements.[69]

King County (Seattle) had already drawn its own urban-growth boundary in 1985.[70] Washington price-to-income ratios had been around 1.5 to 2.5 for all metro areas through 1980. Seattle's exceeded 3.1 in 1989, while other Washington metro areas remained affordable through 1999. By 2006, however, all western Washington metro areas had price-to-income ratios above 3.0, and most were above 4.0, while Seattle's was 4.8.

Maryland

A 1992 growth-management law requires that growth in rural areas be directed to existing population centers. The law encourages the local governments to use *transferable development rights* to concentrate populations in existing cities. Under this system, when a county restricts the use of a rural landowner's property, it can give the property owner development rights that can be sold to urban landowners, allowing them to build to higher densities than would otherwise be allowed.[71]

Some cities already had urban-growth boundaries before this law was passed. Baltimore County, for example, drew an urban-services boundary around Baltimore in 1967. However, Baltimore County grew less than 0.7 percent per year after that, so the boundary had little effect on housing supply. Before 2000, price-to-income ratios in Maryland metropolitan areas ranged from 1.7 to 2.4. By 2006, price-to-income ratios in most Maryland metropolitan areas exceeded 4.0, with the highest being the Maryland suburbs of Washington, D.C., where the ratio was 4.9.

Nevada

The Silver State is an unusual case. Although Nevada has no growth-management law and does not even require counties to zone, 85 percent of the state—and more than 89 percent of Clark County (Las Vegas)—is owned by the federal government.[72] These lands effectively form an urban-growth boundary around Las Vegas, which since 1970 has been the nation's fastest-growing urban area, in terms of annual percentage growth. In the 1990s and early 2000s, Las Vegas homebuilders were selling around 20,000 homes per year, which required the development of 5,000 to 6,000 acres per year.[73]

In 1998, Congress passed the Southern Nevada Public Land Management Act, supposedly to provide for "orderly disposal of certain federal lands" to accommodate Las Vegas's growth.[74] Initial sales were slowed by an environmental lawsuit. Even after that was resolved, between 1999 and 2020, the federal government sold fewer than 11,000 acres in Clark County.[75] Moreover, the law required that 85 percent of the proceeds from land sales go to preserve other lands from development, meaning developers would potentially have to buy almost two acres for every one new net developable. As a result, the cost of an acre of land suitable for residential development grew from less than $50,000 in the late 1990s to more than $150,000 in 2002 and more than $300,000 by 2005. After 2005, sales declined to fewer than 100 acres per year even though average prices reached $400,000 an acre in 2006 and exceeded $500,000 an acre in 2007.[76]

Part of the problem is that the federal government acted as a monopoly seller, limiting the size of most individual sale parcels to 2.5 acres or fewer and designing auctions in order to command the maximum possible bid. From a taxpayers' view it might be appropriate to maximize revenue, but from a social view the result is suboptimally high housing prices. In addition, in authorizing the sale of only 75,000 acres, Congress encouraged speculators to bid up land prices.[77]

Rapidly growing land prices pushed Las Vegas housing into unaffordable ranges for the first time in the 2000s. Although price-to-income ratios were just 2.6 in 1999, by 2006 they were 5.3. Much of this growth was evidently due to speculation as California investors, seeing the rise in prices of homes that were still, by California standards, relatively affordable, bought Las Vegas homes in anticipation of flipping them. The federal government also owns a high percentage of lands in Washoe County, where Reno is located, which, combined with speculation, contributed to high housing prices in Reno and Carson City.

Arizona

Like Nevada, most of the land in Arizona is government owned: about 42 percent is federal; 27 percent is in Indian reservations; and 13 percent is state, leaving less than 18 percent in private hands.[78] Additionally, Arizona passed "growing smarter" laws in 1998 and 2000. Under these laws, Arizona's major urban areas have imposed urban-service boundaries limiting development on unincorporated land outside the cities. As a result, the 2008 Wharton Residential Land Use Regulatory Index ranked Phoenix as the 11th most regulated of the nation's 47 largest metropolitan areas.

An indicator of the effect of these boundaries on land and housing prices can be seen in the prices paid by developers for land sold by the state for urban development, mainly in the Phoenix metropolitan area. In 2002, developers paid an average of $33,600 an acre for such land.[79] By 2006, they were paying more than $190,000 an acre.[80] Prices fell to under $21,000 an acre in 2010.[81] The rise and fall in land prices are reflected in housing prices that doubled between 2000 and 2006 and then fell by half from 2006 to 2011.

Other State Growth-Management Laws

A few other states have passed growth-management laws. Georgia passed a law in 1989, and Delaware in 1995, but they do not require cities to use urban-growth boundaries.[82] Minnesota in 1997 and Wisconsin in 2000 passed laws that create a framework for, but do not mandate, growth-management planning. Tennessee passed a law in 1998, but cities drew such large urban-growth boundaries that they did not constrain growth in the 2000s. None of these states saw housing become unaffordable in the 2000s, although some metropolitan areas that practiced growth management did see minor bubbles.

Metropolitan Growth-Management Planning

Denver, Minneapolis-St. Paul, and Northern Virginia are among regions that have engaged in some form of growth-management planning without a state mandate. Denver and Minneapolis-St. Paul have established urban-growth or urban-service boundaries. Several Northern Virginia counties have imposed large-lot zoning, effectively creating urban-growth boundaries around the cities that circle the southern part of the District of Columbia.

146

Four Different Planning Systems

American cities and states have developed four distinctly different land-use planning systems. First is *private planning*, in which government makes little effort to determine land uses. The best example is Houston, which is the largest American city with no zoning. But many counties in Texas and several other states also lack zoning; thus all development is privately planned.

The second planning system is *traditional zoning*, in which existing developments are zoned to maintain their current uses. Undeveloped areas either are unzoned or are placed in a low-density "holding zone" that cities or counties readily change when landowners propose some new development. Traditional zoning codes include a wide range of densities and uses, including one zone often called "planned unit developments" that allows mixed uses, thus allowing developers to easily meet the demand for whatever kind of development people want.

The third major planning system is *slow growth*, which tends to appear whenever all developable land is in one of a number of cities or towns. Individual city plans tend to emphasize low-density uses that are thought to enhance the city's property values, thus minimizing the opportunity for growth. The lack of developable land may be because no unincorporated lands are in the region (as in Massachusetts), or vacant, unincorporated lands are located outside urban-growth boundaries (as in the San Francisco Bay Area).

Finally there is *smart growth*. If slow growth is NIMBYism gone wild, then smart growth is a slightly enlightened form of NIMBYism. Where slow-growth communities say, "You can only move here if you are wealthy," smart-growth communities say, "You are welcome to move here, but unless you are wealthy you will probably be stuck in high-density, multifamily housing."

To increase densities, smart-growth communities encourage the construction of smaller homes on smaller lots and often rezone single-family neighborhoods to allow "accessory units," meaning separate apartments attached to individual homes. Thus, planning has come full circle: where planners once tried to ban working-class practices, such as living in tiny homes and taking in boarders, they now are practically mandating such practices. Many smart-growth cities are even considering allowing backyard chickens.

As shown in Table 9.1, these four different planning systems have significantly different effects on housing affordability. Houston is one of the most affordable housing markets in the nation, while zoned

147

Table 9.1
PLANNING REGIMES AND 2009 HOUSING PRICES

	Median Home Price	Price-to-Income Ratio	Coldwell Banker Home
Houston (private)	$134,400	2.3	$187,211
Atlanta (zoned)	193,600	2.9	255,448
Portland (smart growth)	284,200	4.3	356,769
San Francisco-Oakland (slow growth)	621,100	7.1	807,691
National average	185,200	3.0	293,291

SOURCE: 2009 American Community Survey, tables B19113 and B25077; Coldwell Banker, "Home Listing Report," 2011, tinyurl.com/3dhksrr, for a "middle-manager's" four-bedroom, 2½-bath, 2,200-square-foot home.

regions such as Atlanta are more expensive but still affordable. Slow-growth regions are the least affordable, while smart growth's emphasis on (and, often, subsidies to) multifamily housing makes it more affordable than slow growth but less than traditional zoning.

Upper-Middle-Class Values

Growth management, whether smart growth or slow growth, makes housing expensive. In 2006, at the height of the housing bubble, 12 states had price-to-income ratios greater than 4.0, and all of them except New York had some form of growth-management planning. As previously noted, most metropolitan areas in New York had price-to-income ratios below 4.0, but the state's overall price-to-income ratio was skewed by the New York City-northern New Jersey metropolitan area's price-to-income ratio of 8.2, which in turn was influenced by New Jersey's and Connecticut's growth-management laws.

At the same time, 25 states had price-to-income ratios of less than 3.0, and only one of these states, Tennessee, has a mandatory growth-management law. Two other states in this range, Georgia and Wisconsin, have passed growth management–enabling legislation, but they did not require urban-growth boundaries, and few cities in those states have written comprehensive growth-management plans.

Thirteen more states have price-to-income ratios of between 3.0 and 4.0. Most of these states either have statewide growth-management planning (Connecticut, Delaware, Maine, New Hampshire, and Vermont) or individual metropolitan area planning for major urban areas (Colorado, Minnesota, Montana, New Mexico, Utah, and Virginia). The two exceptions are Alaska, where housing is expensive because of high transport costs, and Illinois, where housing is expensive mainly in Chicago.

Not only is there a strong correlation between growth management and unaffordable housing, there is also a correlation in timing: In almost every state that has imposed some form of growth management, housing was affordable before implementation of growth management and became unaffordable after that implementation. California housing was affordable in 1969, but implementation of the California Environmental Quality Act for every proposed annexation or adjustment in urban-growth boundaries made it unaffordable by 1979. Oregon passed its growth-management law in 1973, and its housing first became unaffordable in 1979. Seattle's King County drew an urban-growth boundary in 1985, and its housing became unaffordable in 1989, while housing in the rest of Washington remained affordable until after implementation of that state's 1991 growth-management law.

Although local slow-growth planning has the greatest effect on housing prices, regional growth-management planning does not completely overcome the exclusionary effects of local zoning. Despite the good intentions of those who have recommended that regional planning be used to keep housing affordable, this result should not be surprising since several studies have shown that "urban areas with few zoning jurisdictions are likely to have higher housing prices than more fragmented urban areas." The reason is "the restrictiveness of zoning laws will vary with the monopoly power of a town."[83]

There are two keys to keeping housing affordable: first, allowing local governments to compete with one another; and second, maintaining unincorporated lands at the urban fringe that are relatively unregulated, allowing developers to meet the needs for whatever kind of housing or other uses the market demands. Growth management both removes the competition and, through urban-growth boundaries, puts unregulated lands out of reach of developers. Massachusetts has competition but is unusual if not unique in having no unincorporated lands at the urban fringes of Boston or other urban areas. No other state without growth-management planning has given up the county level of government.

Growth-management planning suffers from multiple conflicting goals, the main ones being preservation of open space, enhancement of municipal revenues, and affordable housing. In California, where municipal revenues are the paramount concern—partly from passage of the Proposition 13 property tax limitation in 1978—cities have played a "beggar-thy-neighbor" game of trying to keep out low- and even moderate-priced housing, which are perceived to cost more in urban services than they pay in property taxes, while they furiously try to attract retailers and the sales tax revenues they generate. In states with true smart-growth planning, such as Oregon, the planners' drive to increase densities creates a surplus of multi-family housing and a shortage of single-family housing.

Ironically, the cities and regions that have made housing least affordable through their efforts to protect open space and other amenities tend to be the most politically progressive. As sociologist Herbert Gans notes, the values of the urban planners who come up with these ideas "are those of the professional upper-middle class."[84] Thus, they focused more on anti-auto and anti-sprawl policies and less on affordable housing. Whether deliberately or not, their plans ended up being anti–working class. It didn't hurt that, by increasing housing prices, slow-growth and smart-growth policies increased the wealth of existing residents (and voters) at the expense of potential new residents (who are not yet voters).

"Liberal cities issue fewer new housing permits," one analyst notes, adding that "the desire to protect open space and to preempt sprawl may motivate" such limits.[85] Although progressives profess to care about low-income families, they seem to care more about preserving their own lifestyles, whether that means keeping densities low (as in some San Francisco Bay Area communities), maintaining a greenbelt around the city (as in Boulder, Colorado), or preserving scenic but marginal farms around the city (as in San Jose and Portland, Oregon). All these practices create barriers for homeownership.

10. The Urban-Renewal Dream

In 1974, when Congress repealed Title I of the 1949 Housing Act, some cities effectively shut down their urban-renewal agencies for lack of funding. But in 1952, California had developed a local source of funding for urban renewal called *tax-increment financing*, or TIF. Under TIF, cities can sell bonds and repay those bonds from the increased property taxes collected from the new development and enhanced property values.

Although California invented TIF in 1952, most states continued to rely on federal funding as long as that funding was available. At the time Congress halted the public housing program, only eight other states—Rhode Island, Nevada, Oregon, Utah, Florida, Iowa, Connecticut, and North Dakota—had passed laws allowing cities to use TIF. But within five years after Congress repealed the law, 15 more states passed TIF laws, and by 2004 all states but Arizona had legalized TIF.[1]

From Slum Clearance to Social Engineering

TIF was originally used to do the kind of projects funded by the 1949 law—clearing slums so that developers could build hotels, offices, housing, and other high-value structures on vacant land. But true slums were increasingly rare, having been either privately gentrified or replaced by the federal program. For elected officials in many cities, TIF became, and remains, a powerful tool for generating campaign contributions and consolidating political power. But over the last two decades, cities have increasingly used TIF to support a new kind of social engineering program that, ironically, is based on some of the ideas in Jacobs's *Death and Life of Great American Cities.*

Jacobs had chastised planners for wanting to replace high-density mid-rise neighborhoods, which typically had businesses at street level and housing above that level, with high-rise housing and business complexes. As if converted to a new religion, planners after 1990 sought to replace the low-rise developments that characterized many streetcar and automobile suburbs with Jacobs's high-density, mixed-use mid-rise developments. Although their "old urban" predecessors in the 1950s and 1960s had called such neighborhoods "slums," modern planners called them *new-urban* developments. In promoting such developments, planners were consciously attacking the American dream of single-family homeownership, which they thought wasted land and led people to drive too much.

The problem planners faced throughout the country was that most Americans outside of New York City didn't want to live the bohemian lifestyle that so appealed to Jacobs. Knowing that, and considering that many cities already had surpluses of multifamily housing, developers were reluctant to build Greenwich Villages in the suburbs of cities such as Denver, Portland, and San Jose. TIF offered a *Field of Dreams* solution: if cities subsidized it enough, planners hoped people would come and learn to enjoy their idea of utopian developments.

The 2005 Supreme Court decision in *Kelo v. New London*, in which a Connecticut city proposed to demolish a working-class neighborhood so a developer could replace it with middle-class homes, raised public awareness of how cities abuse eminent domain to benefit wealthy developers. But TIF is eminent domain's little-known partner: without TIF, few cities could afford to use eminent domain to take people's land for so-called economic development projects.

How TIF Works

To obtain TIF funds, a city (or, in most states, a county) must draw a line around an area it wants to redevelop. This area may be called an urban renewal district, redevelopment district, or simply a TIF district. At the time the TIF district is created, the property taxes generated by that area become the *base taxes*, and those taxes will continue to fund schools and other services for the lifetime of the district. But from that day forward, any increases (or *increment*) in taxes— whether from new development or from the increased value of existing land and developments—are retained by the urban-renewal agency for redevelopment.

Although 31 states require the municipality to find that the area within the district is "blighted," as anyone familiar with the eminent domain issue knows, the determination of what is "blighted" is often contentious. Not only do 18 states not require a blight determination, at least 16 other states weakened their blight requirements in the decade before the *Kelo* decision.[2]

In Missouri, neighborhoods have been declared blighted simply because the homes were older than 35 years.[3] When homeowners in a Michigan city argued that their neighborhood was not blighted, the city planner responded that "'blighted' does not mean shabby or marked for demolition. It simply means the area has revitalization potential."[4] That definition effectively eliminates the blight requirement for any city whose only goal is to increase tax revenues.

Some states allow cities to create TIF districts for reasons other than blight. Idaho, for example, allows cities near state borders to create TIF districts if they are at a competitive disadvantage with cities in neighboring states. The City of Post Falls used this justification to put 40 percent of the land area of the city in a TIF district. Yet according to the Idaho State Tax Commission, Idaho's overall tax burden is significantly less than Washington's.[5] It seems likely that Post Falls' TIF districts attracted more business away from nearby Idaho cities, such as Coeur d'Alene, than from Washington State. Significantly, Coeur d'Alene created two urban-renewal districts five years after Post Falls created its first district, and two other nearby towns also recently created TIF districts.

Some states require little more than a public hearing to create a TIF district; others may require a study to determine if redevelopment is feasible. Only one state, Georgia, requires cities to ask voter approval to create a TIF district. Georgia also requires cities to obtain the consent of other taxing entities that overlap with the district.[6]

Though 13 states have no limit, most states limit the life of the district to between 20 and 50 years. Planners typically estimate what the tax increment will be over that period. The city then sells bonds that can be repaid by that increment and spends the revenue from the bonds to purchase properties and to clear existing structures. All but eight states and the District of Columbia allow cities to use eminent domain to compel landowners to sell property within TIF districts.[7]

Once existing structures have been cleared, most cities also use TIF funds to make improvements within the district. Cities often build such infrastructure as streets, sidewalks, parks, sewers, water, and parking garages—infrastructure that developers would normally pay for themselves. The city then sells the land to developers, typically for far less than the city has invested.

In lieu of providing infrastructure, cities sometimes give some of the bond proceeds directly to the developers. In other cases, particularly transit facilities, sports stadiums, and convention centers, the city builds the actual structures and then manages, leases, or sells them.

TIF districts have many variations. In addition to property taxes, 17 states allow municipalities to dedicate incremental sales taxes to redevelopment, and three states allow them to dedicate incremental income or payroll taxes to redevelopment.[8] Most states allow cities to create *pay-as-you-go* TIF districts, spending the incremental taxes (or any surplus tax revenues after making bond payments) on district improvements each year. In many such cases, the developer pays for the infrastructure, and then the city rebates the incremental property tax, sales tax, or both until the developer's costs have been covered.

Some states limit the amount of land a municipality can put in a TIF district. Oregon, for example, allows cities to put no more than 25 percent of their land area in a TIF district. Other states have no limit, and cities such as Mission Viejo, California, Port Richey, Florida, and Wheaton, Illinois, have either placed or proposed to place all land within their city limits in a TIF district—effectively claiming (since those states all have blight requirements) that 100 percent of the city is blighted.[9]

In addition to providing funds for redevelopment, TIF districts generally insulate cities from failure. Although most redevelopment agencies are run by boards of directors whose members are identical to the city councils, they are considered separate entities. If a TIF district fails to collect enough incremental taxes to repay its bonds, it can default on the bonds without jeopardizing the city's bond rating. This separation allows cities to take on high-risk projects that developers might avoid even if they were guaranteed no increases in property taxes.

In 1991, the Englewood, Colorado, Urban Renewal Authority defaulted on $27 million worth of bonds sold in 1985 to support a retail development that failed and was eventually bulldozed.[10] Bondholders, not taxpayers, paid the price. But the ability of TIF agencies to default without reducing city credit ratings does not mean that TIF is a good deal for taxpayers. In fact, such defaults are rare because cities have many ways of capturing taxpayer funds to pay for TIF.

First, in many states, TIF agencies get rewarded for inflation. As property values increase because of inflation, TIF revenues rise even if the district does nothing to improve the area. Normally, such increased revenues would be used by schools and other tax entities to offset increased costs, but since the TIF districts are capturing those revenues, other tax districts must either raise taxes or cut back on services.

In some states, property taxes are indexed to government budgets, not to inflation, so increased property values do not automatically boost TIF revenues. But TIF agencies have other ways of using fluctuating property values to capture revenues. For example, in Idaho, when property values decline (as they did in the recent recession), the base value of the property (the portion whose taxes go to schools and other traditional tax entities) also declines. When property values recover, the base value remains at its lowest level, so TIF districts capture "incremental" tax revenues that, before the recession, had gone to other tax districts.

Second, in most states, TIF districts gain when other tax entities persuade voters to increase taxes. Say a school or library district convinces voters to pass a bond levy that increases taxes by $1 for every $1,000 of property value. Taxes are increased both inside and outside the TIF districts, but the increased revenues inside the TIF districts go to TIF, not to the school or library district. For example, in 2006, voters in a fire district in Northglenn, Colorado, agreed to increase the local fire district's tax rates, an increase that the fire district admitted was needed mainly because local TIF districts had taken so much money from the fire district. Yet the increase also increased TIF revenues, effectively rewarding the urban-renewal agency for taking money from the fire district.[11]

Third, TIF districts get credit for development that would have occurred in the district anyway. If a city creates a TIF district out of a neighborhood that is already being gentrified by private developers, all the taxes on new development in the neighborhood go to the TIF district even though that development would have happened without the TIF district.

Fourth, TIF districts get credit for development within their boundaries that would have taken place somewhere nearby anyway. In a growing region, new homes, shops, offices, and other developments will be built somewhere. TIF subsidies may attract such development to the district at the expense of having less development elsewhere in the region. The result is no net increase to the region's total tax base, but a net decrease to the tax revenues for schools and other entities that must compete with the TIF agencies for funds.

Free Money or Stolen Money?

City officials often argue that TIF is "free money" because without the TIF subsidy, the new development would not have been built. After the TIF bonds are paid off, the new tax revenues go back to schools and other traditional programs, supposedly resulting in a net gain for those programs.

This free-money claim is almost always untrue; instead, TIF is, at best, a zero-sum game. As previously noted, the developments stimulated by TIF-supported urban-renewal projects would probably have happened somewhere in the urban area.[12] At most, all TIF does is relocate those projects to the redevelopment district. Thus, TIF does not increase the level of economic growth or the taxes generated by that growth; all it does is direct some of those taxes to the city that creates the redevelopment district rather than to schools, other cities in the urban area, or other tax districts.

At least one study has concluded that TIF is a negative-sum game; that is, that the extra tax burden imposed by TIF causes cities to grow slower than cities that do not use TIF, particularly if TIF is used to support retail and other commercial uses.[13] Although the urban-renewal district itself may grow, "commercial TIF districts reduce commercial property value growth in the non-TIF part of the same municipality."[14] There are two reasons why TIF might actually reduce a region's economic growth. One is that the increased tax burden (or reduced level of funding for schools or other public services) makes the region less attractive to new businesses. The other is that TIF creates what economists call a "moral hazard" for developers: once one hotel, office building, or housing complex is built with TIF subsidies, developers are unlikely to want to build competing projects that are not supported by similar subsidies.

If TIF is a zero- or negative-sum game, then schools and other taxing entities would receive greater revenues without the TIF district than with it. Any new residences in the TIF district that have children will impose higher costs on schools. Any new developments in the district will impose higher costs on fire, police, and other services that rely on tax revenues. Thus, the costs of these government agencies will increase, but for the life of the TIF district, their revenues will not. Consequently, as in the case of inflation, other taxpayers will have to pay higher taxes to support the district or accept a lower level of urban services in their own neighborhoods.

Even if a TIF-supported development did result in a genuine increase in tax revenues, it might not be worth it. As Martin Anderson pointed out in his critique of 1950s-style urban renewal, redevelopment requires taking land out of the tax base for several years while cities acquire, demolish, and build infrastructure in the district and before developers start paying taxes on the redeveloped property. After discounting future tax revenues at whatever interest rate is paid to bond buyers, the increase in revenues in the distant future can easily be smaller than the lost revenues in the near term.[15]

Of course, this outcome assumes anything is built at all. In deciding that cities did not even have to consider a neighborhood blighted before taking it from existing owners and giving it to a developer, the Supreme Court's *Kelo* decision relied on city plans that purported to show that the tax revenues would be greater than the costs. Justice Stevens's majority opinion specifically approved of the taking because New London had "carefully formulated an economic development plan that it believes will provide appreciable benefits to the community."[16] Justice Kennedy concurred, saying, "The taking occurred in the context of a comprehensive development plan."[17] After the Supreme Court's ruling, the city evicted the homeowners and demolished the homes. The land now sits vacant because, despite the plans, the city failed to foresee that there was no demand for new homes in the area.[18]

Subsidizing Pent-Up Demand

Despite the lack of net economic benefits from TIF, TIF has been increasingly used to support new-urban developments based on the supposed environmental benefits from encouraging people to walk and ride transit more and drive less. Many urban planners believe that New Urbanism is the lifestyle of the future: either because of high gasoline prices or because people will be fed up with the onerous chores of yard and home maintenance, Americans will soon abandon single-family homes by the millions.

Many urban planners believe there is a pent-up demand for living in new-urban developments: high-density, mixed-use developments served by transit lines. They observe that most of the households in the high-density housing projects favored by smart-growth plans have no children and that an increasing share of American households is childless. They therefore reason that the share of households that want single-family homes is about to drastically decline, and the recent drop in housing prices is a symptom of that decline.[19] According to these planners, the only reason developers have failed to meet the demand for mixed-use density developments is because existing zoning codes require separation of residential from commercial uses.

Arthur Nelson, an urban planning professor at the University of Utah, projects a "surplus" of 22 million suburban homes by 2025. Nelson made this projection in an article in the *Journal of the American Planning Association* in which he argued that urban planners should "champion the financial incentives and institutional changes" needed to produce the new-urban housing he thinks most people will want in 2025. The projection itself is based on a claim that 38 percent of Americans today prefer to live in multifamily housing, and most of the remainder want homes on small lots. Nelson expects these numbers to increase as the share of families with children declines.[20]

However, Nelson's reasoning has some major flaws. First, his assumption that a decline in the share of families with children translates to an increase in preferences for multifamily housing is based on faulty logic. Most households that live in high-density housing lack children, so Nelson assumes that most households that lack children want to live in high-density housing. That error equates to assuming that, because most dogs have four legs, most animals with four legs must be dogs.

A second problem is Nelson's claim that 38 percent of Americans prefer multifamily housing, which he says "is based on interpretations of surveys by Myers and Gearin."[21] However, by no stretch of imagination does Myers and Gearin's article, which reviews surveys of housing preferences, support Nelson's number. They report that "83 percent of respondents in the 1999 National Association of Home Builders Smart Growth Survey prefer a single-family detached home in the suburbs"; "74 percent of respondents in the 1998 Vermonters Attitudes on Sprawl Survey preferred a home in an outlying area with a larger lot"; and "73 percent of the 1995 American Lives New Urbanism Study respondents prefer suburban developments with large lots."[22]

Indeed, Myers and Gearin's main point is not that most Americans want to live on small lots or in multifamily homes but that many Americans actually prefer such housing. "Some housing consumers actually prefer higher density," they report.[23] They also speculate that people are more likely to join that group as they get older. However, their evidence for this supposition is sketchy: surveys showing that older people are "receptive to decreased auto dependence."[24] Being "receptive" is far from choosing to live in higher densities; the same Vermont survey that reported 74 percent of people want to live on a large lot found that 48 percent want to be within walking distance of stores and services.[25] These two preferences are incompatible on a broad scale, and most Americans have picked the large lot over walking distance to stores.

The information used by Nelson "may not be terribly reliable," comments Emil Malizia, a planning professor at the University of

North Carolina. "The samples are self selected," "the responses may be heavily influenced by the data collection method," and "people often do not behave in ways that are consistent with the preferences or opinions they express."[26]

One of Nelson's predictions is that large numbers of baby boomers will want to move to city centers to "recapture their youth" when they retire or become empty nesters.[27] In fact, a recent survey of affluent baby boomers found that 65 percent don't plan to move at all when they retire, while only 4 percent aspire to move downtown and another 3 percent hope to move into a condominium in the suburbs. Another 14 percent hope to move to a resort location, suggesting that twice as many desire to move to lower densities than to higher.[28]

Should Nelson turn out to be right about future housing desires, taxpayers don't need to subsidize such housing today, as developers will respond to market demand by building New Urbanist-style neighborhoods. Contrary to planner claims, most zoning codes allow such developments, which the codes usually call "planned-unit developments." If Nelson is wrong, then planners who provide "financial incentives" for such developments, as Nelson advocates, are wasting taxpayers' money.

Confusing Cost with Demand

A report titled "Walking the Walk" by economist Joe Cortright found that higher housing prices in "walkable" New Urbanist neighborhoods "command a price premium over otherwise similar homes in less walkable areas." This finding proves, Cortright argues, that "consumers and housing markets attach a positive value to living within easy walking distance of shopping, services, schools and parks."[29] In fact, Cortright confuses cost with demand and presumes that correlation equals causation.

Cortright measured "walkability" by the number of businesses and other destinations—groceries, restaurants, drugstores, schools, libraries, parks, and so forth—located near residences. Scores were highest if destinations were within a quarter mile, and zero if they were more than a mile away. In general, then, the most walkable neighborhoods were the ones with the highest commercial densities.

To understand the flaw in Cortright's reasoning, start with a simple demand curve for housing (Figure 10.1). The curve says that at a high price, the quantity demanded is low, while at a low price, the quantity demanded is high.

Figure 10.1
HOUSING DEMAND

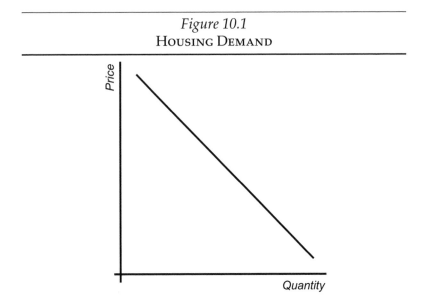

Quantity

Now add a supply curve showing how much housing will be supplied in a walkable neighborhood at different prices (Figure 10.2). The cost of land in areas with high commercial densities is going to be high, typically in the hundreds of thousands of dollars per acre. People wanting housing must compete for this expensive land with other uses, such as shops and offices. One response to high land costs is to build high-rise buildings, but such buildings are also more costly than are low-rise. For all these reasons, the supply curve for housing in walkable neighborhoods will be high, leading to a high price, shown as P1 in Figure 10.2.

By comparison, the cost of land in low-density "drivable" neighborhoods is much lower. At the urban fringe of a city without growth boundaries, the cost will be no more than the cost of farmland or forestland, perhaps around $1,000 an acre. Since such land is plentiful, the supply curve for housing will be much lower, leading to a low price shown as P2 in Figure 10.3.

Figures 10.1–10.4 assume only one demand curve for housing. But most people probably put a different price on what they are willing to pay for housing in dense urban neighborhoods versus housing in low-density suburbs. Cortright claims that the demand curve for housing in a walkable neighborhood is higher than for housing in a

Figure 10.2
SUPPLY OF PEDESTRIAN-FRIENDLY HOUSING

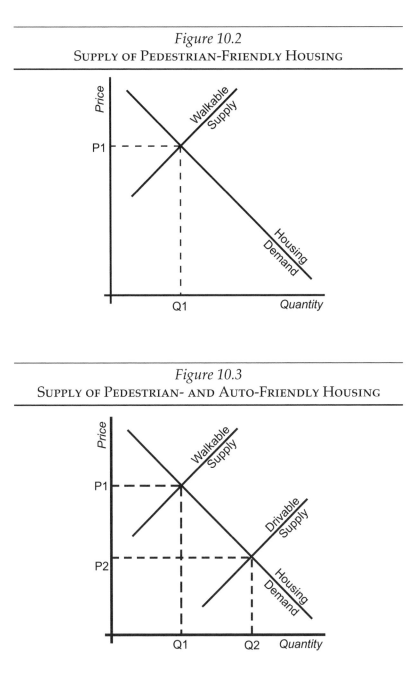

Figure 10.3
SUPPLY OF PEDESTRIAN- AND AUTO-FRIENDLY HOUSING

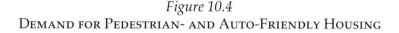

Figure 10.4
DEMAND FOR PEDESTRIAN- AND AUTO-FRIENDLY HOUSING

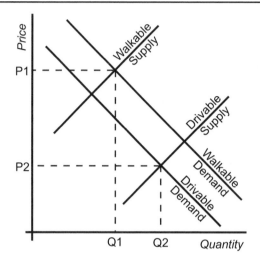

low-density neighborhood, ensuring that P1 is still more than P2, as shown in Figure 10.4.

But what if the reverse is true? What if the demand for housing in drivable suburban neighborhoods is greater than housing in walkable urban neighborhoods? Even if the reverse is true, Figure 10.5 shows that the difference in the supply curves can swamp the difference in demand, so that housing in walkable neighborhoods would still cost more than in drivable neighborhoods.

In other words, the fact that housing in walkable neighborhoods costs more than in drivable neighborhoods says nothing at all about whether people are paying a premium for walkability. All it says is that land in dense commercial and retail areas costs more than land in residential areas, something that people knew more than 100 years ago. Downward-sloping demand curves mean that someone, somewhere, will likely pay that price, but they don't mean that overall demand for walkable housing is greater than for drivable housing.

The Drawbacks of Walkability

New-urban advocates argue that people can save money by driving less, which allows them to pay more for housing. But other costs

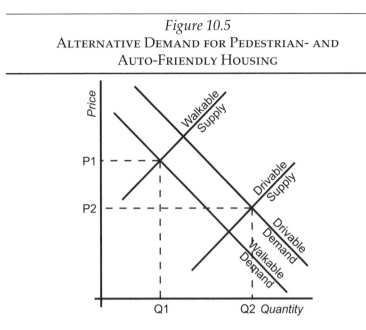

Figure 10.5
ALTERNATIVE DEMAND FOR PEDESTRIAN- AND
AUTO-FRIENDLY HOUSING

of living in dense urban areas make up for any savings from driving less. For one thing, retail costs are going to be higher just because the retailers, like the residents, must pay higher land costs. Moreover, people with cars have access to numerous competing stores, while people on foot typically can reach a limited number of stores. A major supermarket typically needs a customer base of at least 10,000 people. A low-density community of 50,000 people might have five major supermarkets within easy driving distance of most people in that community, and many residents will regularly shop at more than one of those stores. A University of Washington study, for example, found that 85 percent of Seattle-area residents seek either lower prices or higher quality by shopping primarily at grocery stores that average more than twice the distance of the stores closest to their homes.[30]

A walkable neighborhood would need densities of well over 10,000 people per square mile to have even one full-sized supermarket within easy walking distance of those people. Except at extraordinarily high densities, few people will be within walking distance of two or more stores, which means they will be captive to one store that can then charge higher prices. One way stores respond to lower densities is to reduce their product selection. But how many people are satisfied with doing all their shopping at a Trader Joe's (which typically has fewer than 3,000 products on its shelves, compared with more than 30,000 at a Kroger or Safeway) or, worse, an Aldi (which typically has only about 1,400 products on its shelves)?

Higher housing costs, higher consumer costs, and more traffic congestion whenever residents resort to driving to find shops or services outside their neighborhoods all mitigate the supposed benefits of walkability. But in the end, it doesn't matter whether the demand curve for suburban housing is higher or lower than the one for walkable housing. The fact that housing prices in walkable city centers are higher than in suburbs only proves that a few people are willing to pay a premium to live in walkable neighborhoods, not that Americans as a whole are willing to do so.

The New-Urban Experience

Regardless of future housing demand, it is apparent from the experiences of many cities that Americans today do not particularly favor New Urbanist lifestyles. A few such developments have been successful, but many others have failed: either their developers have gone bankrupt, vacancy rates are high, or both. Moreover, behind most of the supposedly successful developments can be found TIF and other subsidies.

Peter Calthorpe, one of the architects who first conceived of New Urbanism, designed such a development outside Sacramento in the early 1990s. The plan called for a transit center surrounded by apartments and condominiums, which were surrounded by single-family homes on relatively small lots. A variety of stores and businesses would be scattered throughout the area within walking distance of the residents.

Although the plan was highly praised by planners, they rarely mention that the developer couldn't sell the high-density condominiums at the center and went bankrupt. A new developer turned the condos into a senior center and replaced the other planned high-density developments with ordinary suburban homes. Residents of those suburban homes were annoyed by the traffic generated by the transit center and successfully lobbied to move the transit stop outside the development. The only businesses in the development are gas stations and a quick lube, and residents drive to a nearby shopping center to get their groceries.

When Portland, Oregon, opened its first light-rail line in 1986, the city zoned much of the land near light-rail stations for high-density development. Ten years later, city planners sadly reported to the Portland City Council that "we have not seen any of the kind of development—of a mid-rise, higher-density, mixed-use, mixed-income type—that we would've liked to have seen" along the light-rail line. City Commissioner Charles Hales noted, "We are in the hottest real estate market in the country," yet city planning maps revealed that "most of those sites [along the light-rail line] are still vacant."[31]

To correct this situation, Hales persuaded the city council to use TIF and other subsidies to encourage developers to build transit-oriented developments. Today, Portland routinely creates urban-renewal districts along all its light-rail and streetcar lines so it can use TIF funds to promote so-called transit-oriented developments along the lines. Portland planners often claim that these developments were stimulated by the opening of new light-rail and streetcar lines.[32] In reality, all the rail lines did was create an excuse for the city to use TIF to subsidize the developments. Portland's famous Pearl District alone received more than $170 million in subsidies, mostly financed by TIF.[33]

Before the recent recession, the Denver metro area had "the highest housing prices of any state without a coastline," observed Denver Chamber of Commerce CEO Tom Clark. So when the city replaced Stapleton Airport with Denver International Airport in 1995, developers would have been ecstatic to build conventional low-density housing in the 4,700 acres vacated by Stapleton.[34] However, the city wanted a new-urban community, so it offered developers $294 million in subsidies to build at higher densities.[35] Though "affordably priced," the higher-density units in the development were "slow to sell."[36]

Albuquerque is another western city that has been rapidly growing in recent decades. In the 1980s, the State of New Mexico decided to make nearly 13,000 acres of vacant state land adjacent to the city available for development. Rather than allow developers to build for the market, the state hired Peter Calthorpe, a leading New Urbanist planner, to design a high-density community called Mesa Del Sol. The developer expects to spend more than $600 million on roads, water, sewer, and other infrastructure. Instead of passing these costs onto home and other property buyers, as would be done in a normal suburban development, the developer will cover most of these costs out of 67 percent of city property and gross receipts taxes (similar to sales taxes) and 75 percent of state gross receipts taxes collected from the development over the next 25 years.[37]

When a Houston developer considered the idea of building a high-density, mixed-use development in that city, he reviewed such developments in other cities and "discovered the ones that were economically successful [that is, that profited developers] were the ones that had government help." Since no such help was coming from the City of Houston, the developer decided not to build one there.[38]

Where existing multifamily housing already saturates the demand for high-density developments, there is little evidence for the environmental benefits claimed for transit-oriented developments. John Charles of Portland, Oregon's Cascade Policy Institute has conducted numerous surveys of how people living in TIF-subsidized developments along Portland's light-rail lines actually get to work, and he has found that the vast majority continue to drive.[39] This result has been confirmed by other researchers.[40] To the extent that New Urbanists report lower rates of driving by residents of such developments, they are likely the result of self-selection: people who prefer to drive less choose to live in such developments.

TIF is a rapidly growing form of municipal finance, and much of that money is being used to support the kind of social engineering represented by so-called transit-oriented developments. From 1990 through 1995, American cities sold $10.2 billion worth of bonds backed by TIF, more than 80 percent of which were for California.[41] During the same period in the late 2000s, cities sold nearly $20 billion worth of TIF bonds, and California's share had declined to less than 64 percent.[42] Although California TIF bonds grew by 55 percent, TIF bonds in other states grew by 260 percent.

Fortunately, the era of TIF may be coming to a close. When Jerry Brown took office for the second time as governor of California in 2011, the first thing he did was propose to eliminate the state's 400 urban redevelopment agencies.[43] Run by the cities and (in a few cases) counties, these agencies siphoned $5.7 billion away from schools and other tax entities into municipal coffers in 2009.[44] Brown suggested that eliminating the agencies would be a major step toward helping the state close its $28 billion deficit.

Brown was intimately familiar with redevelopment agencies: as the mayor of Oakland from 1999 to 2007, he had doubled the size of the city's redevelopment districts.[45] Redevelopment "seemed kind of magical," he said then. "It was the way that you could spend on stuff that they wouldn't otherwise let you."[46] Although redevelopment funds are legally dedicated to fighting blight and promoting economic development, the *Los Angeles Times* noted that cities often used them "as emergency ATMs to pay for core services, including police, fire and code enforcement, and sometimes the mayor's salary." Indeed, 15 percent of Brown's salary when he was Oakland's mayor came from the city's redevelopment agency.[47]

In June 2011, the California legislature approved Brown's proposal to eliminate TIF in the state.[48] Although the redevelopment agencies themselves are fighting this proposal in court, the end seems likely in the state that pioneered TIF and, until recently, did more than half the TIF in the country.[49]

When combined with urban-growth boundaries and other policies that make single-family housing expensive, the use of TIF to subsidize multifamily housing is a major weapon in the war on homeownership. Samuel Adams, the mayor of Portland, Oregon, has gone so far as to advocate that no new single-family homes be built in his city, and that all new residents in the city—which planners expect will grow from about 580,000 people today to more than 800,000 by 2040—should be housed in multifamily projects built within a quarter mile of the city's rail transit lines.[50] For officials such as Adams and the planners who work for them, the actual desires of those future residents are irrelevant.

11. The Housing Market

The San Francisco Bay Area and Houston represent two extremes in housing-market regulation and housing affordability. The San Francisco-Oakland-San Jose urbanized areas have about 4.9 million people, just a little more than the 4.4 million in the Houston urbanized area. But the Houston urbanized area (as the Census Bureau delineated it in 2000) has almost two-thirds more land than the Bay Area does, which means the Bay Area has almost twice the population density.[1]

Incomes in the Bay Area are much higher than in Houston. The Census Bureau estimated that 2009 median family incomes in the Bay Area were close to $90,000 a year, compared with less than $60,000 a year in the Houston urbanized area. Despite lower incomes, Houston has higher rates of homeownership: the 2010 census found 62.3 percent homeownership in the eight-county Houston metro area but only 56.2 percent in the nine-county Bay Area.

The reason for Houston's higher homeownership rates, of course, is that the Bay Area's higher incomes are absorbed by the region's much higher housing costs: the median value of an owner-occupied home in Houston was less than $135,000 in 2009, compared with more than $620,000 in the Bay Area.[2] Part of this difference in costs could be because Bay Area homes are bigger or more luxurious than Houston's. But in 2007, Coldwell Banker estimated that a four-bedroom, 2½-bath, 2,200-square-foot home with a family room and garage in Houston would cost about $170,000, compared with $955,000 in Oakland, $1.1 million in San Jose, and more than $1.4 million in San Francisco. (By 2011, Bay Area prices had fallen to $500,000 to $800,000, while Houston prices had increased to $187,000.)[3] "Starter homes" in Houston are readily available for $30,000 to $50,000; the lowest-priced homes in the Bay Area cost close to $100,000.[4]

Some Bay Area promoters argue that their region has higher median incomes because their planning has made it a nicer place to live and so it has attracted a more productive, "creative class" of people.

As Table 11.1 shows, the Bay Area has gained some high-income households in the last two decades—but not as many as Houston. On the other hand, the Bay Area lost low- and moderate-income households, but Houston gained in every major income category. This finding suggests that the Bay Area's unaffordable housing has pushed low- and even middle-income people out, many of them locating in Modesto, Merced, and other Central Valley cities that are about an 80- to 90-mile commute to the Bay Area yet had median home values of around $350,000 at the peak of the California housing bubble (and much lower before the peak).

Is It Demand or Supply?

Apologists for growth management argue that changes in housing prices are entirely driven by demand, not by land-use regulation. "Market demand, not land constraints, is the primary determinant of housing prices," claim smart-growth advocates Arthur C. Nelson and several of his colleagues.[5] That conclusion is difficult to accept when comparing housing prices and population growth in Houston and San Francisco.

Table 11.1
CHANGE IN NUMBER OF HOUSEHOLDS BY INCOME CLASS
FROM 1989 TO 2009

Quintile	Houston	San Francisco
<$20,000 ($12,500)	90,680	−7,828
$20,000–$40,000 ($12,500–$22,500)	184,840	30,474
$40,000–$60,000 ($22,500–$32,500)	122,329	−12,425
$60,000–$100,000 ($32,500–$60,000)	45,986	−245,948
>$100,000 ($60,000)	219,970	156,477

SOURCES: Census Bureau, 1990 Census, table P080; and 2009 American Community Survey, table B19001.

NOTE: "Houston" includes the Houston metropolitan area, including Chambers County (which is in the 2009 but not the 1990 Houston metro area). "San Francisco" includes the San Francisco-Oakland-San Jose-Santa Cruz metropolitan areas (which are one area in 1990 but the sum of three different areas in the 2009 survey). The quintiles are based on U.S. household incomes in 2009; the quintiles in parentheses are the inflation-adjusted quintiles for 1989.

Housing prices have had much to do with overall changes in the populations of these two iconic metropolitan areas. Between 2000 and 2006, the six-county Houston primary metropolitan area grew from 4.2 million to 4.9 million people, absorbing the equivalent of one Boulder, Colorado, every year.[6] This increase included an influx of people from New Orleans after Hurricane Katrina, as many as 150,000 of whom decided to settle permanently in Houston.[7] Houston was one of the nation's fastest-growth metropolitan areas, yet its housing prices, after adjusting for inflation, grew by just 14 percent. This relatively small increase in housing prices was possible because the number of housing permits issued in the Houston area doubled from 35,900 in 2000 to 71,700 in 2006.[8]

Meanwhile, the six primary counties in the San Francisco-Oakland-San Jose metropolitan area grew from 5.82 million people to 5.89 million people, gaining barely 10,000 people per year, between 2000 and 2006.[9] This relative stagnation in population growth was accompanied by a fierce rise in housing prices: after adjusting for inflation, San Francisco and San Jose prices grew around 60 percent, while Oakland prices grew by more than 90 percent.[10] Despite the increase in prices, Bay Area housing permits issued during this period actually declined from 21,750 in 2000 to 20,630 in 2006.[11]

Economists refer to market responses to changes in demand as *supply elasticity*. A market such as Houston, where price changes are minimal despite large changes in demand, is said to be *elastic*. A market such as San Francisco, where price changes can be large in response to changes in demand, is said to be *inelastic*. The difference is illustrated in Figures 11.1 and 11.2.

Figure 11.1 shows a perfectly elastic supply curve: no matter what happens to demand, the price stays the same. No housing market is perfectly elastic, but Houston probably comes closest in the United States. At any given time, developers of master-planned communities in the Houston metro area have thousands of lots available for sale. Someone can purchase a lot, get all the necessary building permits, contract to have a house built, and move in less than 120 days. Such rapid response times means builders can quickly respond to changes in demand by stepping up or reducing home production.

Figure 11.2 shows a highly inelastic supply curve: a small change in demand can result in a large change in price. The San Francisco Bay Area may not be the most inelastic housing market in the nation, but it is close. The first step in turning an elastic housing supply into an inelastic one is drawing urban-growth boundaries. Once growth

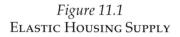

Figure 11.1
ELASTIC HOUSING SUPPLY

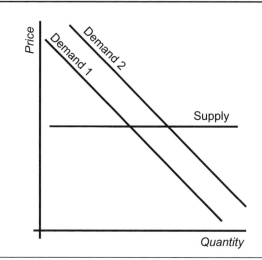

When supply is perfectly elastic, changes in demand have no influence on price.

boundaries are in place, cities no longer need to fear that developers will simply build somewhere else. Establishing growth boundaries gives the cities carte blanche to pass increasingly restrictive rules on new construction. In places like Houston, such rules would drive developers to unregulated land in the suburbs. In the San Francisco Bay Area, the nearest relatively (with emphasis on "relatively") unregulated land is in the Central Valley, 60 to 80 miles away.

An onerous permitting process can significantly delay construction of new homes. Scott Adams, the creator of the *Dilbert* comic strip, reports that it took him more than four years to gain approval to build one home in the San Francisco Bay Area.[12] Approval of larger developments can take even longer and is highly uncertain, as the developers who sought to build in San Jose's Coyote Valley learned.

A lengthy permitting process obviously makes it impossible for developers and homebuilders to quickly respond to changes in demand. California developers responding to the increase in housing

Figure 11.2
INELASTIC HOUSING SUPPLY

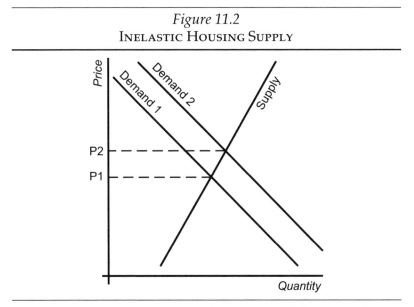

Demand is inelastic, and when supply is also inelastic, small changes in either supply or demand result in large changes in price.

demand in 2000 would have been unlikely to have any product to bring to market before prices collapsed in 2006. Empty homes in states with growth-management planning are symptoms of planning delays, not of any actual housing surplus.

The Cost of Public Involvement

Legal challenges can add to both delays and uncertainties in home construction. Growth-management planners believe almost anyone should have the right to challenge development of private land on the grounds that property is really a "collective institution," says Eric Freyfogle in his book *The Land We Share*. "When property rights trump conservation laws, they curtail the positive liberties of the majority."[13] In other words, if the majority of people decide your land should be preserved as their scenic viewshed, you can effectively lose the right to use it yourself.

In Oregon, for example, the state land-use commission's number one goal is "to provide the opportunity for citizens to be involved in all phases of the planning process," including "implementation measures."[14] That process gives any citizen of the state several opportunities to object to and delay or stop any land-use activity anywhere in the state. Since state and local land-use regulations are both lengthy and complex, citizens can often easily find something wrong with a land-use application that is required for anything from building a giant housing development to fencing a backyard.

No doubt to the distress of James Fenimore Cooper's ghost, the Supreme Court has affirmed the idea that a majority of people can have a say in how landowners use their land. In the *Euclid* zoning case, the Court decided that industrial uses or multifamily housing were nuisances if located in a neighborhood of single-family homes, so zoning was an appropriate exercise of the state's police power.[15] But in 1978, the Court decided that cities did not need to justify regulation based on the need to prevent nuisances.

In *Penn Central v. New York City*, the railroad wanted to build an office tower on top of—without otherwise modifying—Grand Central Terminal, but the city refused to approve the tower, saying the train station was "historic." No one argued that another tower in a city of office towers was a nuisance; it was merely an aesthetic preference. The Court's majority opinion argued that, since the railroad at least retained some value in its use of the terminal, no compensation was required for this regulatory taking.[16] That argument was pretty hollow in view of the fact that, by the time the Supreme Court got around to ruling on the case, the railroad had gone bankrupt partly because it was losing money on passenger services. In any case, this decision set a precedent for allowing planners to downzone anyone's property for almost any reason.

In states that have created public involvement programs for planning of private land uses, residents gain a sense of ownership over other people's land. "I feel that my view is being literally stolen from me, and I resent it," says an environmentalist concerned about suburban home construction. "I take pleasure in driving down a road and being able to participate in what's pretty, and I have to tell you, a great big, brand new house, ugly in most cases, right near the road, that cuts off my view—I feel as if something has been taken from me."[17] The implicit assumption is that people driving on the road own the right to a scenic view, while the people who own the property by the road have an obligation to provide that view even if it means forgoing profitable land uses that might block that view.

Citizen challenges can have a major effect on the type and cost of housing built in a region. Homeowners are more likely to object to new homes that cost less than their own homes, which are perceived as "bringing down the neighborhood," than ones that cost more. They also tend to oppose higher-density developments because of the potential effects on traffic and other issues. At lower densities, homes must cost more to cover the costs of land and permitting. For example, a developer once proposed building 2,200 homes on 685 acres in Oakland, California. After eight years, the developer finally received a permit to build 150 homes, each of which ended up selling for six times as much as the homes in the original plans.[18]

Impact Fees

Regions that use growth management are also more likely to charge stiff developer fees to cover infrastructure costs. Where Houston developers allow homebuyers to pay off infrastructure costs over 30 years, impact fees or development charges require up-front payments often totaling tens of thousands of dollars. The difference is crucial for housing affordability: since development charges increase the cost of new housing, sellers of existing homes can get a windfall by raising the price of their houses.

Increasing land and housing costs make other things more expensive as well. When housing is more expensive, for example, businesses must pay their employees more so that workers can afford to live in the region.

A 2002 study broke down the difference in the costs of a new home in San Jose, which is far from the most expensive part of the Bay Area, and one in Dallas, which has zoning but whose suburbs remain, like Houston's, unzoned and minimally regulated.

- The biggest difference was in land costs: A 7,000-square-foot lot in Dallas cost only $29,000, while a 2,400-square-foot lot in San Jose cost $232,000.
- San Jose's lengthy permitting process (and the high risk that a permit will never be issued) added $100,000 to the cost of a home in San Jose, while permitting cost less than $10,000 per home in Dallas.
- To help pay for roads, schools, and other services, San Jose charged impact fees of $29,000 per new residence, while Dallas charged $5,000.

- Owing mainly to high housing prices, San Jose labor costs are higher: $143,000 for a three-bedroom house compared with $100,000 in Dallas.[19]

Many Bay Area residents believe housing is expensive because the region has run out of land. That is hardly the case. Urban-growth boundaries have excluded 63 percent of the nine-county region from development. Regional and local park districts have purchased more than half the land inside the boundaries for open-space purposes. Virtually all the remaining 17 percent has been urbanized, making it nearly impossible for developers to assemble more than a few small parcels of land for new housing or other purposes. Ironically, environmental groups fret that the land outside the growth boundaries is "at risk" of being developed, when the real risk is to the region's economy due to overregulation of land uses.[20]

Land-use regulation can affect prices in other ways as well. A wide range of homebuilders compete for business in relatively unregulated markets, ranging from small companies that produce only a few homes each year to medium-sized companies that produce a few hundred homes per year to giant national companies that build thousands of homes in many different states. Excessive regulation tends to put the small companies out of business and discourage the national companies as well. The resulting loss of competition helps keep home prices high. Portland, Oregon's "urban-growth boundary has really been our friend," says one mid-sized Portland homebuilder. "It has kept the major builders out of the market."[21]

Given that both demand and supply in regulated regions are inelastic, small changes in either one can result in large changes in price. If lower interest rates increase demand for housing, Houston-area homebuilders respond by building more homes; San Francisco-area builders respond by filing more applications, which may wait several years for approval. If a government purchase of a large block of land for a park or open space restricts supply, Houston-area builders can simply go somewhere else nearby; in the San Francisco area, the nearest alternative building location is more than 80 miles away.

Numerous studies support the idea that land-use regulation makes housing unaffordable. "Government regulation is responsible for high housing costs where they exist," say Harvard economist Edward Glaeser and Wharton economist Joseph Gyourko. In particular, they add, "difficult zoning seems to be ubiquitous in high-cost areas."[22] University of North Carolina real-estate economists have found that rapid growth in housing prices is strongly "correlated with restrictive growth management policies and limitations on land availability."[23]

"When new construction is more constrained, as measured either by a lower supply elasticity or [by] the presence of certain regulations, affordable units are more likely to filter up and become unaffordable," say real-estate analysts Tsuriel Somerville and Christopher Mayer.[24] "Metropolitan areas with more extensive regulation can have up to 45 percent fewer [housing] starts and price elasticities that are more than 20 percent lower than those in less-regulated markets," they estimated in a 2000 article.[25] The difference in the 2000s was probably much greater than 20 percent.

"In places with relatively few barriers to construction, an increase in housing demand leads to a large number of new housing units and only a moderate increase in housing prices," Harvard economist Raven Saks (who is now a researcher with the Federal Reserve) found in 2004. "In contrast, for an equal demand shock, places with more regulation experience a 17 percent smaller expansion of the housing stock and almost double the increase in housing prices." Saks also found that regions with supply restrictions have higher unemployment because employers locate in regions where housing is more affordable.[26]

"Land-use regulations raise housing and developed land prices," conclude economists Henry Pollakowsi and Susan Wachter.[27] "Regulatory stringency is consistently associated with higher costs for construction, longer delays in completing projects, and greater uncertainty about the elapsed time to completion of residential developments," found economists from the University of California (Berkeley).[28]

Economists at the Wharton Real Estate Center developed a database of 70 different land-use regulations in more than 2,700 different municipalities. An economist at the University of Washington used this database to show "a tight association between land use regulations and housing price growth."[29] He further found that high housing prices are "associated with cost-increasing land use regulations (approval delays) and statewide growth management."[30]

When planners make housing unaffordable, their first response is to impose "affordability mandates" on builders. Typically, such regulations require builders to sell 15 to 20 percent of their homes below cost to low-income buyers. Far from making housing more affordable, such mandates make it less affordable since builders build fewer homes and pass the costs onto the buyers of the other 80 to 85 percent of homes. This builder response in turn raises the general price of housing in the region. One econometric analysis found that such affordability mandates in the San Francisco Bay Area increased housing prices by 20 percent.[31]

To ensure that people don't profit by buying "affordable housing" and then selling it at market rates, most such rules prevent people from selling affordable units for more than they paid for them plus some amount of inflation. This type of rule, in effect, turns such homeowners into second-class citizens, unable to take advantage of market changes in housing prices that could add to their wealth.

The high housing prices caused by growth management affect homeownership. Homeownership rates in both California and Oregon peaked in 1960. Since then, Oregon's rate has dropped by more than 7 percent, while California's has dropped by 2.5 percent. A major reason for this decline is the high cost of housing in those states. The economies of these and other growth-management states have also been destabilized by the repeated housing bubbles and crashes that they have suffered.

Homeownership and Minorities

Low-income and first-time homebuyers rarely purchase new homes, but new home construction makes preowned homes available to lower-income buyers. As real-estate economists Stephen Malpezzi and Richard Green note, "To the extent that a city makes it easy for any type of housing to be built, it will also enhance the available stock of low-cost housing."[32] Conversely, observe University of California economists John Quigley and Steven Raphael, "to the extent that cities make it difficult to build new housing, *any type of new housing*, the availability of low-cost housing will be reduced and the affordability of *all* housing will decline." They add, "The most extreme barriers to new housing come in the form of explicit growth controls."[33]

After scrutinizing housing data, economist Matthew Kahn discovered that minority homeownership benefits from urban sprawl. "In sprawled areas," says Kahn, "black households consume larger units and are more likely to own their homes than black households living in less sprawled areas."[34] It is likely that Kahn was really measuring the effect of land-use restrictions on housing affordability and black homeownership. As Kahn measured sprawl, areas with fewer restrictions are more likely to be "sprawled."

Chronic low black homeownership rates are due partly to the high percentage of single-parent families: 47 percent of black households were led by a single female, and 10 percent were led by a single male, compared with 14 percent single female and 6 percent single male for white, non-Hispanic households.[35] Although black families led by married couples enjoyed a 69 percent homeownership rate in 2010, black households led by a single female had just 35 percent homeownership, and those led by a single male had 44 percent homeownership. However, a homeownership gap still exists: non-Hispanic white married couples have an 88 percent homeownership rate, and the gaps for other family types are also about 20 percentage points.[36]

Asian and Hispanic homeownership rates tend to be lower than white non-Hispanic rates, but that is mainly because of large numbers of recent immigrants. Second- and third-generation immigrant families tend to have rates approaching those of whites. Asian rates in Florida and Hawaii, two states with large, settled Asian populations, are both around 70 percent, while Hispanic rates in New Mexico are above 75 percent.[37]

Homeownership has always been a steppingstone for immigrant and low-income families. The home provides opportunities for income and an eventual source of equity for starting small businesses and helping children through college. Policies that restrict single-family homes will impose proportionately greater costs on low-income families who are trying to get out of poverty.

The Land of Declining Opportunity

Artificially high housing prices also create problems of intergeneration equity. The generation that owns homes collects a windfall profit from price increases, but that generation tends to be wealthier than the generation of first-time homebuyers who have to pay the high prices. Growth management is not the primary cause of growing wealth disparities in the United States, but it is a contributor.

The Occupy Wall Street movement focused on concerns about increasing income inequality. Even more worrisome, social scientists have measured a decline in America's income and social mobility. Not only are incomes less equal today than in the late 1960s, but young people entering the workforce today are much less likely to surpass their parents' living standards than they were in the 1960s and early 1970s.[38]

Moreover, despite claiming to be "the land of opportunity," the United States has one of the lowest levels of income mobility in the developed world. A 2007 report published by the Organization for Economic Cooperation and Development found that American children are twice as likely to be stuck in the same income class as their parents as children in Australia, Canada, Denmark, Finland, and Norway. Children in France, Germany, Spain, and Sweden are also more likely to be better off than their parents than are children in the United States. Of the countries studied, only Italy and Britain had lower economic mobility than the United States.[39]

Within the United States, opportunity is not equally accessible to all. Researchers have found that immigrants rapidly become homeowners and immigrant children are highly likely to have higher incomes than their parents.[40] The children of low-income white families have a reasonable chance of moving up the economic ladder, but the children of low-income black families are twice as likely as white children to remain poor.[41]

Probably the main reason for increasing income inequality is the premium employers pay for "knowledge workers" over unskilled and even skilled laborers, who are viewed as more interchangeable. This premium existed before World War II, and the postwar period when working-class incomes approached those of the middle class may have been just a historic anomaly. Today, the best path to upward economic mobility is for children to get a better education than their parents.

One way parents can give their children a better future is to save money that can, among other things, be used to help put children through college.[42] "One of the keys to economic mobility is saving and creating wealth that can be used during one's working life to advance up the economic ladder or can be given to children to improve their economic prospects," says a report from the Economic Mobility Project.

One of the best ways for parents to save money is to buy a home, which not only provides an asset that can be borrowed against and a legacy for their heirs but also provides a stable home life so that children do better in school.[43] "Owning a home is the most significant way Americans build net worth, especially for lower-income Americans," says the same report. "At all income levels, median net worth of homeowners is greater than that of renters."[44]

"Housing is probably the most important bulwark against rising inequality in the United States," says Brookings Institution economist Ron Haskins. "However," he adds, "recent difficulties in housing credit are creating serious problems with home ownership in the bottom of the distribution."[45] Haskins doesn't say so, but the real source of those problems is land-use regulation that has made housing so expensive that low-income and, in some places, even middle-income families had to stretch their budgets and go deeply into debt to buy homes. The increased volatility of housing prices in restricted areas also threatens family balance sheets.

Homeownership rates are high across all income levels. In 2007, 41 percent of households in the lowest income quintile owned their homes, while 93 percent in the highest quintile owned homes.[46] Still, the difference between these two extremes seems large when one considers that, on an international scale, income has little relevance to homeownership rates. Differences in auto ownership in the United States are much narrower: 94 percent of wealthy families and 79 percent of poor families own at least one car.[47]

Houses are more costly than cars, but people who don't have cars can save money by walking, cycling, and using various (often heavily subsidized) public conveyances. Most people who don't own their own homes rent, and in an unfettered market, they could apply that rent to a mortgage for a similar size and quality home. Therefore, the main obstacle to homeownership should be a down payment—and such down payments are often provided by family members.

Fairly decent three-bedroom, two-bath homes are available in the Houston area—the nation's least regulated and fastest-growing housing market—for under $50,000, which means a down payment of $5,000 plus a monthly payment of under $250 is all that is needed to become a homeowner. There is little reason, other than government regulation, why most other housing markets in the United States are not this affordable. If they were, the gap between high-income and low-income homeownership rates would be much smaller.

Homeownership and Urban Form

Economists and planners endlessly debate the effects of government programs on homeownership and the nature of cities and suburbs. In this vein, Harvard economist Edward Glaeser and *Economist* writer Ryan Avent have both recently argued that federal housing and highway programs contributed to suburbanization; that local

181

planning programs are dominated by not-in-my-backyard (NIMBY) politics that keep suburban densities low; and that ending those federal and local programs would lead people to return to the cities or to rebuild the suburbs to higher densities.

Glaeser's and Avent's arguments contain several major flaws. First, the claim that federal subsidies reduced urban densities is unconvincing. Second, their focus on the planning processes of the Boston area (in Glaeser's case) and the San Jose area (in Avent's case) betrays an unfamiliarity with the broad range of planning processes that can be found in the United States. Finally, they overestimate the value of dense cities in several ways.

Glaeser writes that he grew up in a Manhattan apartment, but he currently lives on a 6.5-acre lot in suburban Boston. He blames his decision to move to the suburbs partly on the government, saying that "thanks to the interstate highway system, which was generously subsidized by the federal government," his 15-mile commute takes fewer than 25 minutes.[48] In fact, he admits, he actually drives on the Massachusetts Turnpike, a road funded entirely out of tolls. But, as noted in Chapter 7, even the interstate highways were entirely funded by gas taxes and other highway user fees. These highways did not in any way subsidize suburban commuters, especially the many suburbs built before the interstates.

Glaeser further argues "that the federal government heavily subsidizes home ownership by allowing me to deduct interest on my home mortgage. That subsidy makes owning cheaper than renting, and being pro-home-ownership means being anticity," suggesting that Glaeser thinks that most people who live in cities rent.[49] In fact, the 2000 census found that more than half of all households in the central cities of America's urbanized areas own their homes. Renters outnumber homeowners in just a dozen of the nation's 50 largest central cities. Programs that support homeownership are only "anticity" if "city" is defined as "high-rise apartment buildings." Glaeser's own research shows that the mortgage-interest deduction is largely "irrelevant" to people's decisions to buy or rent homes.[50]

Glaeser's final example of a government program that encourages low-density suburbanization is education. When relatively wealthy people moved to the suburbs, the poor people who remained in cities did not have enough money to fund decent schools, promoting ever-faster flight to the suburbs.[51] Yet many if not most states have school equalization programs that ensure that schools in every district, regardless of the wealth of that district, get equal amounts of support per student. These programs have not slowed the decentralization of urban areas in those states.

Glaeser and Avent both argue that NIMBY politics have made housing in dense cities unaffordable, and without those politics more people would return to those cities. Yet their focus on NIMBYs reveals their limited experience with American urban planning. Glaeser has studied the Massachusetts system in detail and has shown that towns throughout the state have passed low-density zoning ordinances that have kept housing unaffordable. But, as shown in Chapter 9, Massachusetts and several other New England states are unusual in practically giving up the county level of government. As a result, all land-use decisions in Massachusetts are made by towns, leaving no vacant, unregulated land that this book has shown to be essential for affordable housing.

Similarly, Avent's main example of NIMBYs comes from San Jose, whose slow-growth plans were adopted in the 1970s. Both Glaeser and Avent, however, confuse the San Jose urbanized area with the San Jose metropolitan area, which consists of Santa Clara County. "Car-based living goes together with low density levels," says Glaeser. "There are only about 2.14 people per acre living in Santa Clara County."[52] But the density of Santa Clara County is irrelevant considering that (as of the 2000 census) 91 percent of the people in that county live in the San Jose urbanized area, which covers just 20 percent of the county. The density of the urbanized area is almost five times greater than Glaeser's number, and it is 11 percent greater than the New York City urbanized area. If density alone were sufficient to reduce driving, as Glaeser implies, then residents of the San Jose urban area would drive less than those in the New York urban area; in fact, they drive about 30 percent more per capita.

Avent also seems to think that San Jose's density is low, when in fact it is the third-densest urbanized area in the United States (after Los Angeles and San Francisco-Oakland). Avent measures density using a weighted average of census tract densities. Thus, the very high densities in Manhattan are weighted more heavily than the densest areas of San Jose, which are not nearly as dense as Manhattan.[53] But none of the policies that either Glaeser or Avent propose are going to create another Manhattan.

In any case, the slow-growth policies that afflict both Boston and San Jose are the exception rather than the rule in the United States. Even without such policies, most American urbanites choose to live in much lower densities than are found in San Jose, thus showing that the NIMBYs did not cause densities to be low. Glaeser estimates that, without the high building costs imposed by land-use restrictions, a 1,200-square-foot condo in a New York City high-rise would cost only $500,000 compared with "the $1 million or more that such an apartment now costs in New York." But Glaeser also admits that a 2,500-square-foot single-family home on a large lot in Houston costs only $200,000; given that difference, just how many more people does Glaeser think are going to move to the dense, inner cities?[54]

In support of the benefits of density, both writers stress the value of face-to-face communications. Glaeser cites studies showing that such face-to-face contacts will likely never be replaced by electronic communications.[55] Avent offers studies showing that worker productivities and incomes are higher in dense cities than in lower-density suburbs and cities. One study cited by Avent, for example, estimated that doubling the density of urban areas would increase incomes by 6 percent. "Distance is not dead," Avent concludes, referring to an earlier book, *The Death of Distance*, written by Frances Cairncross, who ironically was one of his colleagues at the *Economist*.[56]

Both Glaeser and Avent seem to miss the fact that, for the economic productivities they seek, what counts is not population densities but job densities. The study cited by Avent that found higher productivity with higher densities measured employment densities, not population densities. Job densities do not require that people live in high-rise or even mid-rise dense environments; they only require transportation systems that can move people from residential areas of any density to the job centers. Moreover, the studies cited by Avent did not directly measure productivity; they measured incomes, and much if not all of the higher incomes that were measured were likely due to the higher cost of living that typifies denser areas that, in turn, either pushes low-paying jobs out or forces employers to pay more to be able to attract workers from other, lower-cost regions.[57]

Even if valid, 6 percent is a tiny increase in incomes from such a drastic change as a doubling of population density. Even to find 6 percent, the study had to disregard certain occupations, such as mining, whose incomes are not dependent on job densities.[58] Moreover, the point of Cairncross's book was not that distance is "dead" today but that it is dying; that is, that the cost of distance and, by implication, low densities is steadily declining.[59] To use one example, a study of American labor productivity found that density explained 41 percent of the differences in productivity in 1940, but only 7 percent in 1980.[60]

Another advocate of urban density is Richard Florida, whose series of books on "the creative class" argues that cities should focus on attracting high-tech workers, artists, gays and lesbians, and what he calls "high bohemians." Part of his prescription for attracting such creative people is to build or rebuild dense, mixed-use neighborhoods similar to those promoted by Jane Jacobs.[61]

Ironically, the most devastating critique of Florida's work comes from Edward Glaeser, who analyzed Florida's data and discovered that Florida's "Bohemianism effect is driven entirely by two metropolitan areas: Las Vegas, Nevada, and Sarasota, Florida." Glaeser concludes that "skilled people," not "creative" people, "are the key to urban success."[62]

Glaeser makes a valid point that, for many purposes, there is no substitute for face-to-face communications. But how often do such face-to-face meetings need to take place? Hourly? Daily? Weekly? Given air travel and automobiles, people can manage such face-to-face communications as often as they need without having to live in Manhattan-like densities, which is why telecommuting is one of the fastest-growing forms of commuting.[63]

Unlike urban planners such as Peter Calthorpe, Glaeser and Avent each profess to oppose coercive policies aimed at forcing people to live in higher densities than they wish. Yet their often-erroneous arguments lend credence to those who do support such policies. In the course of 16 years of research on urban issues, I have met with thousands of people who live in cities, suburbs, and exurbs, nearly all of whom enjoy the places they live in. Many of the city dwellers I've met think their lives are so ideal that they unhesitatingly support coercive government aimed at forcing everyone to live that way, but I've never met a suburban or exurban resident who wants to force their lifestyle on anyone else.

Few suburbanites, for example, would have any objection if Glaeser and Avent were correct and it turned out that eliminating government subsidies and coercive land-use policies led to more people living in higher-density cities. Actual trends, however, indicate otherwise. The 2010 census revealed that suburbs continue to grow much faster than central cities: in the nation's 63 metropolitan areas with more than a million people, more than 90 percent of population growth since 2000 took place in the suburbs.[64] Despite the supposed advantages of face-to-face contacts, jobs are growing faster in the suburbs and in lower-density urban areas as well.

Regardless of national or local urban policies, urban densities are declining all over the developed world; the United States is just ahead of the curve.[65] The Internet, the automobile, and the jetliner give more people the opportunity to work where they want and still have the face-to-face meetings they need, which is why the number of people working at home grew by more than 40 percent between 2000 and 2010.[66] Such continuing decentralization is likely to be accompanied by increased homeownership because land tends to be more affordable in low-density areas.

12. The Housing Bubble

In 1995, after remaining flat for nearly a decade, average housing prices in the United States began growing at 4 percent per year (after adjusting for inflation), accelerating to 7 percent per year in 2004. By the end of 2006, they had increased by an unprecedented 61 percent (again, after adjusting for inflation), whereupon they collapsed by (as of the second quarter of 2011) nearly 40 percent, returning them to their 2001 levels.[1]

This housing bubble took many experts by surprise. In June 2005, Federal Reserve Bank Chairman Alan Greenspan told Congress that "a 'bubble' in home prices for the nation as a whole does not appear likely." He added that there were "signs of froth in some local markets where home prices seem to have risen to unsustainable levels," but if housing prices were to decline in those markets, those declines "likely would not have substantial macroeconomic implications."[2] Four months later, soon-to-be Federal Reserve Bank Chairman Ben Bernanke testified before Congress that high housing prices "reflect strong economic fundamentals," not a bubble about to burst, and that "a moderate cooling in the housing market" would not cause the economy to stop growing.[3]

In retrospect, Greenspan was right: there was no national housing bubble. There were instead many local bubbles. However, both he and Bernanke were wrong about the effects of the collapse of those bubbles on the national economy. Bernanke was especially wrong in crediting high housing prices to "strong economic fundamentals," such as growth in jobs, incomes, and new households. These fundamentals, combined with low interest rates and looser lending practices, did push up prices but played less of a role in price increases than growth-management planning.

Flatland and the Zoned Zone

How could they have gone so wrong? "Bubble deniers point to average prices for the country as a whole, which look worrisome but not totally crazy," Paul Krugman responded in 2005. "When it comes to housing, however, the United States is really two countries, Flatland and the Zoned Zone." Flatland, he said, had little land-use regulation and no bubble, while the Zoned Zone was heavily regulated and was "prone to housing bubbles."[4]

Krugman's choice of terms is unfortunate because most of "Flatland" is in fact zoned. What makes the Zoned Zone different is not zoning but growth-management planning. In the absence of such planning, it is reasonable to think that housing prices throughout the country would have followed a similar pattern to those in Houston, not those in the Bay Area.

Across the nation, housing markets followed one of the two patterns illustrated in Figure 12.1: either rising sharply after 1995, peaking in 2005 or 2006, and then crashing, like California, Florida, and Nevada prices; or rising gently, generally peaking in 2007 or 2008, and then declining slightly, like Georgia, North Carolina, and Texas prices. In short, housing markets either bubbled or they did not. Bubble markets were driven by supply constraints, speculation, and a mistiming of new product entering the market just as demand began to weaken, exacerbating the collapse that brought down the economy. The nonbubble markets ultimately declined as a reflection, not a driver, of the economy, and they would not have declined at all if the economy had not crashed.

Was It Supply or Demand?

In assessing the causes of the housing bubble, most analysts have focused on factors affecting demand, including low interest rates, zero-down-payment loans and other easy lending terms, and increased lending to subprime borrowers. By 2009, it became "conventional wisdom that Alan Greenspan's Federal Reserve was responsible for the housing crisis," notes Hoover Institution economist David Henderson in a column in the *Wall Street Journal*.[5] Although Henderson disagreed with this view, several other economists writing in the same issue agree. "The Fed owns this crisis," charges Judy Shelton, the author of *Money Meltdown*.[6]

Other people blame the crisis on the Community Reinvestment Act and other federal efforts to extend homeownership to low-income families.[7] These policies, along with unscrupulous lenders, fraudulent homebuyers, and greedy homebuilders—all of whom have also been blamed for the housing crisis—are all national phenomena. They should therefore have had about the same effect on home prices in

Figure 12.1
INFLATION-ADJUSTED STATE HOME PRICE INDICES, 1995–2011

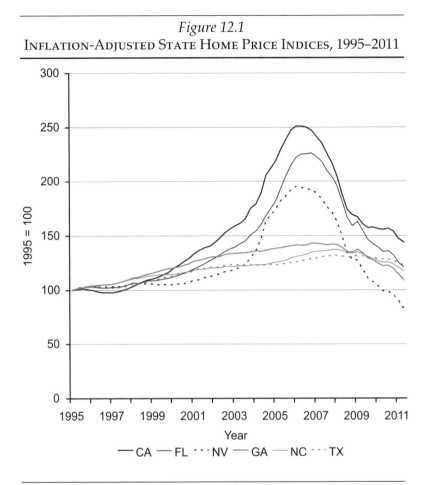

SOURCE: "2nd quarter 2011 Home Price Index Data for States," Federal Housing Finance Agency, 2011.

Houston as in Los Angeles. But they did not. Just as prices rose much more dramatically in Krugman's Zoned Zone than in Flatland, prices fell steeply in most of the Zoned Zone but—except for states where home prices declined due to the collapse of the auto industry—prices hardly fell at all in Flatland. As late as the fourth quarter of 2008, home prices remained stable in many nonbubbling parts of the country.

Demand factors, such as low interest rates, the Community Reinvestment Act, and subprime lending, were equally available in all

50 states, but bubbles occurred in only some of those states. With few exceptions, the one clear difference between the bubble and nonbubble markets was the presence or absence of growth-management planning. With planning or other supply constraints, home prices bubbled; without them, prices did not. Moreover, Chapter 14 will show that in several European countries that have land-use constraints, home prices bubbled even though interest rates were higher and lending terms stricter than in the United States.

Certainly, bubbles are the result of the interaction of both supply and demand. But demand factors alone did not cause the housing bubble. With supply constraints, bubbles can take place with only a small increase in demand; without supply constraints, even a large increase in demand does not lead to a bubble.

In general, the bubble markets were not the fastest-growing markets in the country; high housing prices in California, for example, had already suppressed growth to low levels before the bubble began to grow. The fastest-growing regions, instead, were nonbubble regions where housing was affordable and the costs of land and building new factories, offices, and other employment centers were similarly low.

Chapter 11 showed that growth management makes housing supply inelastic, which means small increases in demand lead to large increases in housing prices. The reverse is also true: small declines in demand lead to large drops in housing prices. This inelasticity is exacerbated by lengthy permitting periods that can put homebuilders out of phase with the market. Thus, land-use restrictions create conditions ripe for housing bubbles.

Several studies have shown that growth management leads to housing bubbles in general and the most recent bubble in particular. Economists Edward Glaeser and Joseph Gyourko have found that land-use rules that restrict "housing supply lead to greater volatility in housing prices." They estimated that "if an area has a $10,000 increase in housing prices during one period, relative to national and regional trends, that area will lose $3,300 in housing value over the next five-year period."[8] Both of these studies were based on data preceding the current housing bubble.

"More restrictive residential land use regulations and geographic land constraints are linked to larger booms and busts in housing prices," two Canadian economists found when comparing land-use regulations and 2000 to 2009 housing prices in more than 300 cities in the United States. "The natural and man-made constraints also amplify price responses to an initial positive mortgage-credit supply shock, leading to greater price increases in the boom and subsequently bigger losses," in other words, a bigger bubble.[9]

Harvard professor Harvey Mansfield criticizes economists for failing to foresee the housing bubble.[10] But, in fact, many economists did see the bubble as it was growing and predicted that its collapse would lead to severe hardships.

For example, as early as 2003, *The Economist* observed, "The stock-market bubble has been replaced by a property-price bubble" and pointed out that "sooner or later it will burst."[11] By 2005, it estimated housing had become "the biggest bubble in history." Because of the effects of the bubble on consumer spending, *The Economist* warned, the inevitable deflation would lead to serious problems. "The whole world economy is at risk," the newspaper pointed out,[12] adding, "It is not going to be pretty."[13] Although *The Economist* did not predict the complete collapse of credit markets, it was correct that the bubble's deflation was not "pretty."

In response to the crisis, some have suggested that the federal government should buy surplus homes and tear them down or rent them to low-income families. This suggestion misreads the crisis, which is not due to a surplus of homes but to an artificial shortage created by land-use regulation. This shortage pushed up home prices to unsustainable levels, but that doesn't mean that no need exists for housing in those regions if it were available at more reasonable prices. Although it might make sense to remove houses in places that have had sustained reductions in population, such as Cleveland, Ohio, or Flint, Michigan, it makes no sense to remove them in places such as Florida that had been growing before the recession.

An Economy Built on Bubbles

Bubbles have characterized recent economic history as institutional and other major investors who control large amounts of money have sought high-income investments. These investments have turned into speculative manias that eventually came crashing down. The last decade alone has seen the telecom bubble, the nearly simultaneous dot-com bubble, the housing bubble, and, most recently, the oil bubble—all of which led to the *Onion* headline, "Nation Demands New Bubble to Invest In."[14]

Of these, the housing bubble is the most significant. On one hand, consumer spending fed by people borrowing against the temporarily increased equity in their homes kept the world economy going after the high-tech and telecom bubbles burst in 2001. On the other hand, the eventual deflation of the housing bubble caused far more severe economic problems than the deflation of the telecom and high-tech bubbles would have caused if the housing bubble had not disguised them.

A *bubble* has been defined as "trade in high volumes at prices that are considerably at variance with intrinsic values."[15] Bubbles are essentially irrational, so they are difficult to describe with a rational economic model. However, the preliminaries to the housing bubble can be explained using simple supply-and-demand curves.

Charles Kindleberger's classic book *Manias, Panics, and Crashes* describes six stages of a typical bubble. First, a *displacement* or outside shock to the economy leads to a change in the value of some good. Second, new *credit instruments* are developed to allow investors to take advantage of that change. This stage leads to a period of *euphoria*, in which investors come to believe that prices will never fall. This euphoria often results in a period of *fraud* in which increasing numbers of people try to take advantage of apparently ever-rising prices. Soon, however, prices do fall, and the market *crashes*. In the final stage, government officials try to impose new regulations to prevent such bubbles from occurring in the future.[16]

All these stages are apparent in the recent housing bubble. The key point of this chapter is that the displacement, or shock, to the economic system that started the bubble was the imposition of land-use regulation, in the form of growth-management planning, in states housing close to half the nation's population.

In a recent attempt to prop up sales, the National Association of Realtors produced a television ad claiming that "on average, home values nearly double every 10 years," or a growth rate of about 7 percent per year.[17] This claim is true only when areas with restrictive land-use regulations are included in the average.

As noted in Chapter 11, before 1970, median home prices in the vast majority of the United States were 1.5 to 2.5 times median family incomes.[18] The main exception was Hawaii, which, not coincidentally, had passed the nation's first growth-management law in 1961.[19] Home value-to-income ratios remain in that range today in most places without growth-management planning. In other words, in the absence of government regulation, median housing prices remain proportional to and average about two times median family incomes.

Without supply restrictions, housing prices grow only if median family incomes grow. Even then, most of the growth in median housing prices arises from people building larger or higher-quality homes, thus increasing the value of the median home. The actual value of any given home will not grow much faster than inflation.

In a "normal" housing market, then, home values keep up with inflation, and median home values keep up with median family incomes. Markets become abnormal when there is some limit on the supply of new homes, and most such limits result from government regulation. The National Association of Realtors' claim that prices increase at 7 percent per year may be correct when regulated housing markets are averaged with unregulated ones, but it is incorrect if applied to unregulated markets alone.

State Bubbles

A careful examination of home price data for the 50 states and 381 metropolitan areas reveals strong correlations between growth-management planning and housing bubbles. On a state level, the biggest housing bubbles—with prices rising by more than 80 percent after 2000 and then dropping by 30 to 60 percent since their peak— were in California, Florida, Maryland, Nevada, and Rhode Island (Table 12.1; all price indexes quoted in this chapter are adjusted for inflation).[20] All these states except Nevada have growth-management laws; as described in Chapter 11, Nevada's housing supply is constrained by the limited amounts of private land available for development. Even though several of these states are located at opposite corners of the country, the price indexes are very similar.

Table 12.1 and Figure 12.2 classify states as having had a bubble if housing prices grew by more than 50 percent after 2000 and then fell by more than 10 percent after reaching a peak in about 2005 or 2006. Prices in all but one of the other states with growth-management laws, including the New England states, also increased by 50 to 100 percent after 2000 and have declined by at least 10 percent since 2006, and in most cases by 20 to 30 percent. The exception is Tennessee, whose price trends are nearly identical to those in Texas. Tennessee housing did not bubble because its law was passed in 1998 and the urban-growth boundaries drawn by the cities were so large that they did not immediately constrain homebuilders.

New York and the District of Columbia had bubbles but did not have growth management. But New York City and Washington, D.C., are both hemmed in by states that used growth management. A few states, such as Minnesota, Montana, and New Mexico, came close to meeting the bubble definition but did not have housing prices rise by the full 50 percent. These states did not have mandatory statewide

Table 12.1
BUBBLE AND NONBUBBLE STATES
(PRICE INDEXES ADJUSTED FOR INFLATION)

	Growth after 2000	Decline since Peak	Housing Bubble?
Alabama	21%	−13%	
Alaska	39%	−7%	
Arizona	80%	−49%	Bubble
Arkansas	19%	−11%	
California	109%	−43%	Bubble
Colorado	18%	−15%	
Connecticut	53%	−22%	Bubble
Delaware	60%	−22%	Bubble
District of Columbia	123%	−15%	Bubble
Florida	102%	−47%	Bubble
Georgia	19%	−24%	
Hawaii	97%	−23%	Bubble
Idaho	45%	−30%	
Illinois	30%	−23%	
Indiana	6%	−14%	
Iowa	12%	−8%	
Kansas	12%	−9%	
Kentucky	11%	−8%	
Louisiana	27%	−7%	
Maine	54%	−17%	Bubble
Maryland	88%	−29%	Bubble
Massachusetts	56%	−24%	Bubble
Michigan	11%	−35%	
Minnesota	41%	−27%	
Mississippi	19%	−12%	
Missouri	21%	−15%	
Montana	50%	−14%	
Nebraska	9%	−10%	
Nevada	86%	−58%	Bubble
New Hampshire	59%	−25%	Bubble
New Jersey	75%	−24%	Bubble
New Mexico	38%	−17%	

(continued)

Table 12.1 (continued)
BUBBLE AND NONBUBBLE STATES
(PRICE INDEXES ADJUSTED FOR INFLATION)

	Growth after 2000	Decline since Peak	Housing Bubble?
New York	63%	−18%	Bubble
North Carolina	20%	−14%	
North Dakota	30%	0%	
Ohio	9%	−20%	
Oklahoma	17%	−5%	
Oregon	53%	−28%	Bubble
Pennsylvania	41%	−13%	
Rhode Island	86%	−31%	Bubble
South Carolina	23%	−15%	
South Dakota	22%	−5%	
Tennessee	17%	−12%	
Texas	17%	−7%	
Utah	34%	−25%	
Vermont	53%	−10%	Bubble
Virginia	71%	−21%	Bubble
Washington	54%	−26%	Bubble
West Virginia	22%	−11%	
Wisconsin	22%	−16%	
Wyoming	53%	−11%	Bubble
United States	39%	−23%	

SOURCE: "2nd quarter 2011 Home Price Index Data for Metropolitan Areas," Federal Housing Finance Agency.

growth management, but some of their major cities practiced growth management. The United States as a whole fits into this category: close to 50 percent growth in prices followed by a decline of more than 20 percent, reflecting the fact that some of the states practiced growth management, while others did not.

Wyoming fits the definition of a bubble state, but it has no growth-management laws. Wyoming housing prices instead were strongly influenced by an oil boom in Casper. Like nonbubble markets, Casper's home prices peaked later than in true bubble markets, and prices fell as a reflection of the economy. Prices in Wyoming's other major housing market, Cheyenne, did not bubble.

Figure 12.2
CHANGES IN HOME PRICES AFTER 1995 AND AFTER PEAK

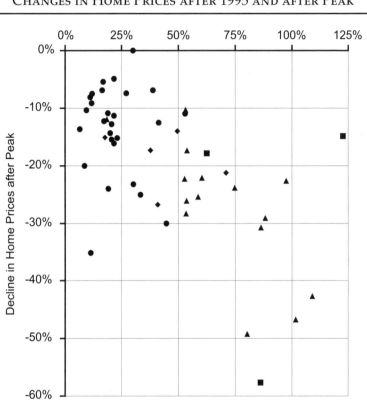

NOTE: Scatter plot of the data in Table 12.1. Triangles represent states with growth-management laws; squares are states whose major cities are land-locked by other states or federal lands (District of Columbia, Nevada, New York); the horizontal line represents Massachusetts, a state where all land is in towns that collectively practice slow-growth management; circles are states with no state growth-management laws; while diamonds are states with no state growth-management laws but where some urban areas practice growth management. Housing prices grew by more than 50 percent in only one state marked by a circle: Wyoming, which had an oil boom. Housing prices grew by less than 50 percent in only one state marked with a triangle, Tennessee, whose cities drew such large urban-growth boundaries that they did not impair growth.

Metropolitan Area Bubbles

There is a clear connection between housing prices in nearby regions. For example, the San Francisco Bay Area is a strong high-tech job center with extraordinarily high housing prices. Many people working but unable to afford housing in the Bay Area bought homes in cities in the Central Valley, such as Merced, Modesto, and Stockton. These three housing markets suffered from the nation's worst bubbles, with prices rising more than 130 percent after 2000 and then falling by more than 60 percent to pre-2000 levels.

Figure 12.3 shows that prices in the Central Valley started rising later, fell faster, and fell further than in the Bay Area. This pattern of

Figure 12.3

METROPOLITAN AREA HOUSING BUBBLES, 1995–2011

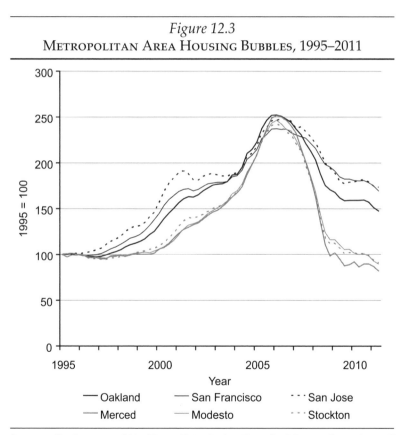

SOURCE: "2nd quarter 2011 Home Price Index Data for Metropolitan Areas," Federal Housing Finance Agency, 2011.

decline illustrates a "last-in, first-out" phenomenon: Since housing in the Central Valley, with its 80-mile one-way commute to jobs in San Francisco and San Jose, was less desirable to begin with, it experienced greater price declines than in the cities where the best jobs were located. In addition, central California counties were less prone to adopt strict growth-management plans. But in 2000, the California legislature amended the local area formation commission law to mandate growth-management planning by all cities and counties. This new mandate combined with the overflow from the Bay Area may have caused central California home prices to bubble with special vigor.

In contrast, Figure 12.4 tracks housing prices in the Atlanta, Dallas, Fort Worth, Houston, Nashville, and Raleigh metropolitan areas. Although a small increase in the growth of housing prices can be discerned in late 1997, prices did not significantly bubble upward, nor did prices begin to fall until after the economic collapse. About 47 percent of America's population lives in metropolitan areas whose prices rose by at least 50 percent after 2000 and then fell by at least 10 percent.

Another way of measuring housing bubbles is to compare residential permits with home prices. Between 1995 and the peak of the housing bubble in 2006, home prices nationwide grew by 61 percent, and cities responded by granting 62 percent more housing permits. Local variations in permits were large relative to housing prices, however. In Texas, the number of permits issued grew three times faster than average housing prices; in Houston, they grew seven times faster. In contrast, states and regions with growth management saw a rapid growth in home prices without much growth in permits. Maryland home prices grew almost seven times faster than permits; Oregon prices grew 4.5 times faster; and prices in Massachusetts, Nevada, Virginia, and Washington all grew about twice as fast as permits.[21] Although California permits kept up with prices on a statewide basis, permits grew far faster than prices in slow-growth regions, such as Los Angeles, San Francisco-Oakland, and Santa Barbara.[22]

The lack of a housing bubble in the metro areas shown in Figure 12.4 is not because they are unpopular places to live. In fact, between 2000 and 2010, the Atlanta, Dallas-Fort Worth, and Houston metro area populations each grew by more than 100,000 people per year. Along with Nashville and Raleigh, these regions are all growing faster than 2 percent per year. By comparison, the San Francisco Bay Area (the combined Oakland, San Francisco, and San Jose metro areas) grew by fewer than 40,000 people (0.5 percent) per year, and central California

Figure 12.4
METROPOLITAN AREAS WITHOUT HOUSING BUBBLES,
1995–2011

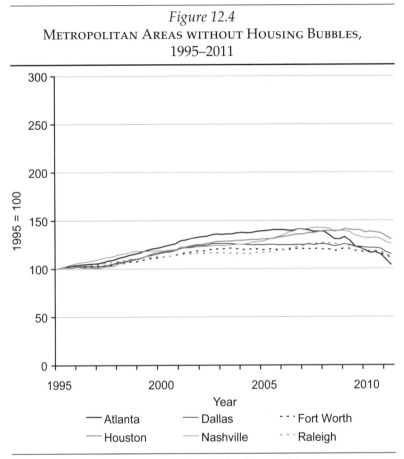

SOURCE: "2nd quarter 2011 Home Price Index Data for Metropolitan Areas,"
Federal Housing Finance Agency, 2011.

(the combined Merced, Modesto, and Stockton metro areas) grew by fewer than 25,000 people (1.8 percent) per year.[23]

Atlanta, Dallas-Fort Worth, and Houston were just as influenced by low interest rates, predatory lenders, and other changes in the credit market as were Merced, Modesto, and Stockton. It may be that changing credit rules are responsible for the slight increase in the growth of housing prices after 1997. The trend lines in Figure 12.4 are likely what would have happened all over the country were it not for government restraints on new home construction.

If metropolitan area bubbles are defined as at least a 50 percent price increase after 2000 and at least a 10 percent decline after the peak (and after adjusting indexes for inflation using gross domestic product deflators), then 118 out of 384 metropolitan areas bubbled. These 118 areas house about 34 percent of the nation's population. More than three-quarters of these bubbly metropolitan areas are either in states with growth-management programs of some kind or are in areas (such as New York City and Washington, D.C.) hemmed in by such states. Many of the remainder have local growth-management programs.

Outside metropolitan areas, housing prices bubbled in 17 states, almost all of which have some form of growth management. The only exceptions are Nevada, which is mostly federal land, and Wyoming, which has no growth management. About 3 percent of Americans live in nonmetropolitan areas whose prices rose by at least 50 percent after 2000 and then fell by at least 10 percent.[24] Adding the 47 percent in metropolitan areas to that 3 percent indicates that the recent housing bubble affected almost exactly half of all American housing.

In short, a very close correlation exists between regions with growth-management planning and regions that have seen a major housing bubble. Without growth management, prices in a few parts of the country, such as Casper, Wyoming, and Midland, Oklahoma, would have grown because of local factors; and prices in other parts, such as Michigan, would have declined because of local factors. In most of the country, however, prices without growth management would have looked like those in Figure 12.4. Some subprime mortgage defaults might have occurred—particularly in Michigan—but there would have been no major housing bubbles, no credit crisis, no need for a bank bailout, and no worldwide recession.

Foreclosure rates and growth-management-induced housing bubbles are strongly correlated. As of January 2009, 1 of every 173 homes in California was in foreclosure. The rate in Arizona was 1 in 182; Florida was 1 in 214; Nevada was 1 in 76; and Oregon was 1 in 357, all of which are worse than Michigan (1 in 400), despite the latter having the nation's highest unemployment rate. By comparison, barely 1 in 1,000 Texas homes was in foreclosure. The rate in Georgia was 1 in 400, North Carolina was 1 in 1,700, and Kentucky was 1 in 2,800. The correlation is not perfect, but the hardest-hit states all have some form of growth-management planning.[25]

Previous Housing Bubbles

Growth management is responsible for most or all of the housing bubbles that American communities have seen in the last decade. Beyond that, growth management also caused several housing bubbles well before 2000. These bubbles took place before the loosening of credit that many claim caused the recent bubble. The difference between earlier bubbles and the recent one is that fewer states were practicing growth management in earlier decades, and so a much smaller share of American housing suffered from such bubbles.

Figure 12.5 shows two earlier bubbles in major California metropolitan areas. The first was when prices grew in the late 1970s in

Figure 12.5
CALIFORNIA HOUSING BUBBLES BEFORE 2000

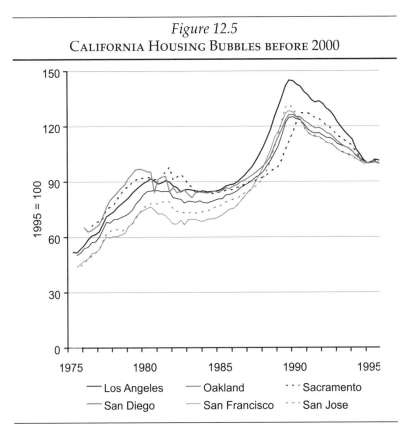

SOURCE: "2nd quarter 2011 Home Price Index Data for States," Federal Housing Finance Agency, 2011.

response to the original imposition of urban-growth boundaries. Prices fell in the early 1980s. Then prices bubbled again, peaking in 1990 and crashing again through 1995. Figure 12.6 shows that Silicon Valley had a small bubble that peaked in 2001, but it was really just a part of the most recent bubble.

Figure 12.6 shows a close correlation between bubbles and growth management. The bubble that peaked in 1980 took place in California, Hawaii, Oregon, and Vermont (not shown in the figure), the only states that were practicing growth management in the 1970s. Massa-

Figure 12.6
STATE HOUSING INDICES BEFORE 2000

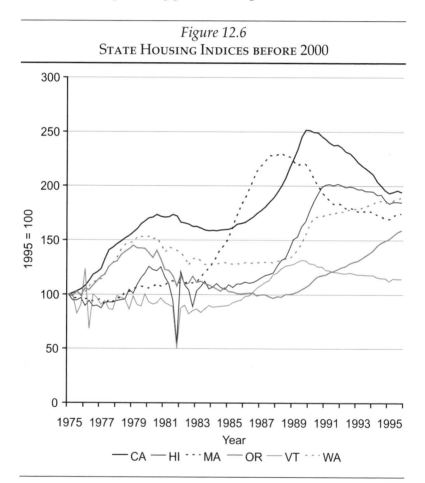

SOURCE: "2nd quarter 2011 Home Price Index Data for States," Federal Housing Finance Agency, 2011.

chusetts prices bubbled in the late 1980s, and declines in those prices were somewhat offset by the California and Hawaii bubble that did not peak until 1990. Oregon did not bubble again until the 2000s. Washington prices rose rapidly after King County (Seattle) imposed an urban-growth boundary in 1985, but this was not a bubble because prices did not decline.

By the 1980s, several New England states and a few urban areas, including Seattle, began practicing growth management, and they joined in the bubble that peaked in 1990. Few if any states or urban areas that were not practicing growth management had bubbles before 2000. For example, Florida, which implemented its growth-management law in the 1990s, did not see prices bubble until the 2000s. Similarly, Arizona and Nevada had no bubbles between 1975 and 2000.

The Canadian researchers who noted the connection between land-use restrictions and the recent housing bubble also noted that prices do not decline as much in crashes as they increase in booms. This trend means successive bubbles can make housing grotesquely unaffordable. In 1969, the nation's least affordable metropolitan area, with a median-home-value-to-median-family-income ratio of 3.2, was Honolulu, mainly because of Hawaii's 1961 growth-management law. As previously noted, most other metropolitan areas had ratios of 1.5 to 2.5.

By 1979, after Oregon and California had implemented growth management plans, the Honolulu value-to-income ratio was 5.5, at which point it became virtually impossible for a median family to get a mortgage on a median home given the terms typical of the day. In much of California, 1979 value-to-income ratios were between 4.0 and 5.0, while they had reached 3.2 (Honolulu's 1969 ratio) in some Oregon communities.

Despite the decline in real California and Hawaii home prices in the early 1980s, the late 1980s bubble pushed California value-to-income ratios to as high as 6.7 in San Francisco, 6.2 in Honolulu, and well above 4.0 in much of the rest of California. This bubble also pushed prices in Boston, New York, and nearby metro areas above 4.0. Oregon, which suffered a greater recession in the early 1980s than most states, did not have a late-1980s bubble.

Prices in California, Hawaii, and the Northeast crashed in the early 1990s, but by 1999 value-to-income ratios had recovered and were poised for another leap. By 2006, price-to-income ratios throughout California and Hawaii ranged from 5.0 to as high as 11.5. In response to growth-management plans written in the mid- to late 1990s, value-to-income ratios in Florida, Maryland, and Washington ranged from 3.0 to 5.5.

The pattern is clear: each successive bubble pushes value-to-income ratios further away from the natural ratio of about 2.0. Even at the bottom of the cycle in 1995, many California value-to-income ratios were well above 5.0, meaning housing was still unaffordable despite the crash of the early 1990s.

Housing bubbles are rare when land is abundant and homebuilders face few obstacles to meeting the demand for new homes. Homebuilders in Houston have shown that they can quickly ramp production up or down in response to changes in demand, so that prices barely change.

Housing can become unaffordable when the amount of land available for development is limited. But lack of available land is rare in the United States; even small states, such as Rhode Island and Connecticut, are more than 60 percent rural open space, while Hawaii is more than 80 percent rural open space. Even if land were limited, it would not necessarily lead to a bubble, because a bubble requires that prices peak and then fall, which would happen only if a housing shortage suddenly became a surplus.

Home prices will rise or fall in response to the growth and decline of a major industry that employs a large share of a region's workers. If the growth is sudden and few expect it to be sustained, builders will probably not construct many new homes. But if the industry is expected to last, then builders should be able to meet the demand for housing. When the industry declines, as the auto industry did in Michigan in the 2000s, then housing prices are likely to fall, but this decline is not a bubble.

Most bubbles take place when government restrictions steepen the supply curve for housing—that is, make it inelastic—so that prices are very sensitive to small increases or decreases in demand. Such government restrictions seem to be the cause of more than three out of four of the metropolitan area housing bubbles of the last decade. When housing becomes very expensive in one region, nearby regions can suffer bubbles even if they don't have as many land-use restrictions. California's Central Valley bubble that peaked in 2006 was worse than the Bay Area bubble because Central Valley housing was less desirable, so people bought it only when Bay Area housing became so expensive that it was worth the tradeoff of an 80-mile commute, and then they fled the market when the decline in Bay Area home prices made that region more affordable.

An important factor in housing bubbles is the time it takes developers and homebuilders to bring their products to market. Builders can be extraordinarily responsive in Houston, where it can take little more than three months to obtain permits and build new homes. In California, where permits can require 4 to 10 years, builders often find they've gained approval to build just as the market is declining.

Speculation plays a role in housing bubbles. It appears that the real demand for housing in California was probably met in late 2004 or 2005, but speculators kept pushing up housing prices through 2006. An overflow of speculation from the California market probably contributed to the housing bubbles in Nevada and Arizona. Without California's land-use regulation, California speculators would not have imagined that prices in Arizona and Nevada would increase fast enough to satisfy their desire for profit from the real-estate market.

This chapter has shown that land-use regulation was the single most important factor in the housing bubble of 2006. The next chapter will show how that regulation and the resulting bubble led to the financial crisis of 2008. Although many people have proposed ways of regulating financial markets to prevent another such collapse, deregulating land and housing markets to prevent any further major property bubbles in the United States would make more sense.

13. The American Nightmare

Most analyses of the financial crisis of 2008 begin with the housing bubble. Economist Joseph Stiglitz, for example, says: "The basic outlines of the story are well known and often told. The United States had a housing bubble. When that bubble broke and housing prices fell from their stratospheric levels, more and more homeowners found themselves 'under water.' They owed more on their mortgages than what their homes were valued. As they lost their homes, many also lost their life savings and their dreams for a future."[1]

But what caused the bubble? Stiglitz does not say, though he suggests it was "fed" by "low interest rates and lax regulation."[2] Other writers, however, blame the bubble on too much regulation.[3] Very few, however, have pointed to growth-management planning as the cause of the bubble.[4] This chapter will show that not only did growth management cause the bubble but once the bubble began, very few things could have been done to prevent the crisis. Most proposals to prevent future crises treat symptoms, not causes; unless future bubbles are prevented, the next crisis is likely to be worse than the last.

Bubbles, Manias, and Frenzies

Prices rise because people think the value of something in the future will be significantly greater than its value today. The famous Dutch tulip bubble did not deal with flowers or flower bulbs but with what amounted to futures contracts on those flower bulbs: buyers paid for bulbs in 1646 that the sellers expected to grow in 1647. Such advance purchases led to a speculative frenzy even though few actually had any bulbs.[5]

Many bubbles, from the South Sea and Mississippi bubbles of 1720 to the dot-com bubble of 2000, have involved corporate stocks. But the real-estate bubbles of recent decades are potentially far worse than stock-market bubbles. For most people, day-to-day swings in the stock market don't matter. Even a large decline in the stock market is relatively unimportant. But when housing prices go up, people spend more, and when housing prices go down, people spend less. Thus, a shift in housing prices can cause a much bigger boom or recession than a similar shift in the stock market. An analysis by economists Karl Case, Robert Shiller, and John Quigley found that "a ten percent increase in housing wealth increases consumption by roughly 1.1 percent . . ., while a ten percent increase in stock market wealth has virtually no effect upon consumption."[6] Thus, a doubling of housing prices leads to 11 percent more consumer spending, which in turn fuels the economy and leads people to pay more for housing.

The 2008 financial crisis has often been described as "complex" because there were so many different participants, including home-buyers, nonbanking mortgage lenders, commercial banks, investment banks, ratings companies, the Federal Reserve Board, the Securities and Exchange Commission, the Commodities Futures Trading Commission, government-sponsored enterprises such as Fannie Mae and Freddie Mac, and various other private and government entities; as well as a variety of confusingly named financial tools, such as collateralized debt obligations and credit default swaps. But the real issues of the crisis boil down to three different factors: state and local growth-management planning, the bond-ratings agencies, and banking reserve requirements.

Growth-Management Planning

The story of the 2008 crisis really began in the 1960s and early 1970s, when Hawaii, California, and Oregon passed growth-management legislation (or, in California's case, legislation that ended up promoting growth management). This legislation led to housing bubbles in those three states that peaked around 1980. Relative to incomes, housing prices nearly doubled between 1969 and 1979, then collapsed by 15 to 25 percent in the early 1980s. California and Hawaii housing prices bubbled again in the late 1980s and were joined by a real-estate bubble in Massachusetts. With the passage of growth-management laws in Florida, Maryland, Washington, and most New England states, the bubble in the 2000s ultimately affected almost half the homes in the United States.

"Most Americans should own their own homes," President Clinton told the National Association of Realtors in 1994, "for reasons that are economic and tangible, and reasons that are emotional and intangible, but go to the heart of what it means to harbor, to nourish, to expand the American Dream."[7] The Clinton administration and its allies in Congress worried that high housing prices were preventing many moderate- to low-income families from becoming homeowners. The Department of Housing and Urban Development had a program that halfheartedly sought to reduce land-use regulation to make housing more affordable, but it was having no effect on state and local policies.

Instead of blaming land-use regulations for unaffordable housing, Congress blamed bankers. In 1977, during the first bubble, Congress passed the Community Reinvestment Act, which encouraged but did not require banks to make loans to low-income families. In 1994, after the second bubble—but when price-to-income ratios were still high in California, Hawaii, New England, and New Jersey—the Clinton administration required that at least 30 percent of the loans purchased by Fannie Mae and Freddie Mac be for homebuyers whose incomes were less than the median income in their area.[8] These borrowers are often described in the media as "low-income" homebuyers, but it obviously includes moderate-income buyers as well.

In 1995, Congress tightened the requirements of the Community Reinvestment Act to make banks more responsible for providing loans to minorities. The next year, the Department of Housing and Urban Development increased Fannie and Freddie's moderate-income target to 42 percent, and increased it again to 50 percent in 2000 and 52 percent in 2005.[9] According to Columbia Business School finance professor Charles Calomiris, the real turning point came in 2004, when Fannie and Freddie reluctantly began to buy no-documentation loans, colloquially known as "liar's loans," in order to meet these targets. This move, Calomiris says, "opened the floodgates of bad credit."[10] Indeed, default rates on loans after 2004 were significantly higher than on loans before that year.

Before blaming the crisis on the Community Reinvestment Act, however, remember that such mandates probably would not have been politically necessary if growth management hadn't made housing expensive in many politically powerful states. In effect, federal policies favoring homeownership for moderate-income families were fighting state and local policies that attempted to discourage construction of single-family homes, the kind that supposedly cause "sprawl" and yet the kind that the vast majority of American homebuyers prefer. Given this fight, the winner was bound to be the state and local policies. In places that did not have growth management, federal policies were likely to lead to increased homeownership—but since housing was already affordable in most of those places, it didn't really matter. In places with growth management, the federal policies ended up making housing more expensive without increasing, and possibly even reducing, homeownership.

Rising housing prices had another effect on the bubble: they brought in speculators even as they deceived banks into believing that mortgage loans, even subprime loans, were safe. Historically, lenders have either required or offered the lowest interest rates to people who made a 20 percent down payment on their home. Several states, including California, allow people to default on their mortgage, returning the home to the bank, with no penalty.[11] Even in states that allow banks to sue people for any difference between the loan and the sold value of the foreclosed house, banks often do not sue because most people who default lack the assets to pay the difference. The low risk from defaulting means people are more likely to default if the value of their home falls to less than what they owe on it. Before growth management, housing prices may have declined during recessions, but they rarely declined as much as 20 percent. People who made a 20 percent down payment will still have equity in their home even if prices fall by 10 or 15 percent, so they are less likely to default on the loan.

For many, a 20 percent down payment on a $50,000 starter home in Houston would not be a formidable obstacle; family members often provide such down payments as gifts or loans. Most non-homeowners trying to buy a $300,000 starter home in San Jose, however, would by stymied by a 20 percent down-payment requirement. High housing prices in growth-managed states led Congress and the Clinton administration to make homeownership more affordable by pressuring Fannie Mae and Freddie Mac to reduce their down-payment requirements. In 1997, Fannie started buying loans that had as low as a 3 percent down payment; Freddie introduced a zero-down-payment loan in 2000, followed by Fannie Mae in 2001.[12]

Moreover, banks might have been willing to accept lower down payments even if Fannie and Freddie had not changed their policies because of rapidly rising home prices. If someone buys a home with a zero down payment and the value of the home increases by 25 percent, the buyer then has 20 percent equity in the home and is less likely to default. The problem with this reasoning that few if any bankers understood was that growth management had greatly increased the chances that housing prices would fall, often by more than 20 percent, thus leaving millions of homebuyers with negative equity. In states and regions with growth management, lenders should have increased, not reduced, the down-payment requirements.

Undermining the Ratings

An even more fateful decision was made in 1975, when the Securities and Exchange Commission issued rules allowing banks to keep lower capital reserves if they held securities that were regarded as especially safe. To determine what was "safe," the SEC designated a number of ratings agencies as "nationally recognized statistical rating organizations." Economist Jeffrey Friedman argues that, by creating an oligopoly of just three accredited ratings companies, the SEC reduced the incentives for those companies to be accurate.[13] In fact, there were originally seven accredited companies, but they were reduced to three—Standard & Poor's, Moody's, and Fitch—by mergers in the 1990s. The real problem was that, by making top ratings a legal requirement, the SEC unexpectedly shifted the balance of power from investors to securities companies.

Before 1975, investors paid the ratings companies for their analyses, leading the various companies to compete based on the reliability of their work. Although the 1975 ruling didn't require securities companies to have their bonds rated, it did make rated bonds more marketable. So the securities companies themselves began paying the ratings companies to evaluate the bonds. "When Lehman took a mortgage pool to Moody's, it paid the fee *only* if it was pleased with the rating," noted *Wall Street Journal* writer Roger Lowenstein. "Otherwise, it could try its luck with S&P or Fitch."[14] This shift in who paid for ratings greatly reduced the incentive for ratings companies to be accurate.

The ratings ranged from AAA to D, with 22 separate ratings or "notches" in all. Anything above BBB-minus or above was considered "investment grade," while anything below was considered junk bonds. The ratings affected both the capital reserve requirements and the amount of collateral someone would have to put up for a particular bond.

In 1991, the United States adopted the Basel Accord, which was an international agreement on how much reserve banks and other financial institutions were required to maintain. The rules require banks to keep 8 percent of their assets in a capital reserve. But mortgage bonds, which were considered particularly safe, required only a 4 percent reserve. Moreover, bonds sold by government-sponsored enterprises—such as mortgage bonds sold by Fannie Mae and Freddie Mac—required only a 1.6 percent reserve. This low reserve for mortgage bonds meant a bank could make a loan, sell the loan to Fannie Mae, then buy it back in the form of a bond, and maintain only a 1.6 percent reserve. Moreover, federal regulators went beyond the Basel Accord to apply the 1.6 percent reserve requirement to any asset-backed security, such as a mortgage bond, that had an AAA or AA rating.[15]

Investment banks quickly learned to "game" the system by packaging bonds so as to guarantee that the ratings companies would give them a coveted AAA rating. To do so, they used a special bond, invented in 1987 by Michael Milken's junk bond department at Drexel Burnham, known as a collateralized debt obligation (CDO). A CDO was a bond that consisted of other bonds. The first mortgage-backed CDO was issued in 2000 by Credit Suisse.[16] Since some of the bonds in the CDO are statistically likely to default and others are not—but no one knows which ones—the bond was divided into pieces called "tranches."

A ratings company would evaluate the CDO and decide that a certain percentage was AAA, another chunk was AA, and so forth. This evaluation would give investors a choice: the AAA portion paid the lowest interest rate but would be the last to lose if some of the bonds that made up the CDO defaulted. The lowest-rated portions of the CDO paid the highest interest rate but would be the first to default if any of the bonds in the CDO defaulted.

To maximize the share of a CDO that was rated AAA, the FICO (Fair Isaac Corporation) scores of the borrowers whose mortgages made up the bonds had to average 615. Homebuyers with such a score rarely defaulted. But the 615 average could also be achieved if half the loans were to people who scored 680 and half to those who scored 550. The people scoring 550 would be highly likely to default, but the bond would be rated the same as if all borrowers scored 615.[17] "So it is that a CDO consisting of BBB-rated and BBB-minus-rated mortgage material can be blessed with ratings roughly as follows: AAA, 75%; AA, 12%; A, 4%; BBB, 4%; equity, 5%," commented bond analyst James Grant in 2006, adding that a small decline in housing prices could destroy most of the value of such a CDO.[18]

In rating CDOs, the ratings companies rarely had access to the credit records of the borrowers of the underlying mortgages. Instead, they relied on their own previous ratings of CDOs and the fact that so few CDOs had ever defaulted. Using their criteria, a mortgage-backed bond that was rated AA+ would, if repackaged as a CDO, automatically be rated AAA. "Analysis of CDOs came to rely almost completely on automated models, with very little human intervention and little incentive to check the accuracy of the underlying collateral ratings," observes one analyst who scrutinized 735 mortgage-backed CDOs. As a result, "there was a striking uniformity in the initial proportion of AAA given to all CDO deals, despite the wide variety in the characteristics of their collateral and the quality of their underwriters."[19]

The lowest-ranked tranches of CDOs were hard to sell, so banks repackaged them into more CDOs. Amazingly, the ratings companies might give 84 percent of a CDO made up of the BBB-rated tranches of other CDOs an AA rating or better, particularly if the bonds consisted of mortgages from all parts of the country.[20] The companies justified their high ratings based on the fact that American housing prices had never seriously declined since the Depression. According to economist Mark Zandi, nationwide prices fell by less than 1 percent in 1963, and by somewhat more in 1941, but otherwise had increased in every year since the mid-1930s.[21]

The ratings companies reasoned that even if home prices in one part of the country declined, any increase in defaults in that part of the country would be offset by increased prices (and lower defaults) elsewhere. They never imagined that home prices might fall in many parts of the country simultaneously, and they had no idea that growth management, which now affected nearly half the homes in the country, had made home prices far more volatile and would produce much larger drops in housing prices than ever before.

Credit analysts noted that default rates tended to be highest in states where home prices were not rapidly increasing. This trend deceived the ratings companies into favoring bonds that emphasized states where prices were increasing. But those tended to be the states with the biggest housing bubbles and where prices were most likely to collapse. Even if prices just stopped increasing, defaults in those states would likely rise. If prices fell, large portions of the CDOs would default.[22]

Naturally, many people could see that a crash was coming well before it happened. Normally, the bulls and bears in a financial market can bet against each other so that, when a market changes direction, the winners and losers offset one another with minimal damage to society as a whole. But unlike a stock or commodity, it was not easy to "short" a mortgage bond—that is, bet that its value would decline. A few enterprising investors found that one way to do so was through something called a credit default swap (CDS).

CDSs were developed by J. P. Morgan Bank in 1994 to insure the CDOs it had created that consisted of corporate bonds. Although there was little chance that a large share of the corporate bonds would default, investors wanted a hedge against that small chance, so J. P. Morgan offered the CDSs as insurance against such defaults. The buyer of the CDS would pay the seller—who was effectively, if not in fact, an insurance company—a small percentage of the value of the bond each year. If the bond defaulted, the insurance company would pay the buyer the value of the bond.[23]

In 2005, a few investors realized that they could buy CDSs on mortgage bonds even if they didn't own the bonds themselves, effectively taking out insurance on someone else's bonds. This practice allowed them to bet against the bond market. But the bet was asymmetrical. Whereas the buyer of a bond paid one fee and then sat back and let the dividends roll in, the buyer of a CDS had to pay an annual fee, just like an insurance premium. In the investment industry, this practice is known as a "negative-carry trade." "Investment pros detest [negative carry] almost as much as high taxes and coach class seating," observes *Wall Street Journal* writer Gregory Zuckerman. When a trader at Deutsche Bank, convinced the housing market was about to collapse, started buying CDSs, others at the bank resented him because, so long as the market held, he was reducing the firm's bonus pool.[24]

One hedge fund manager bought enough credit-default swaps to make $20 billion for his investors (and nearly $4 billion for himself).[25] But other fund managers were forced by impatient investors to get out of the market before the collapse.

The highest-rated bonds are supposed to have negligible rates of default. Only 0.008 percent of AAA asset-backed bonds, for example, are expected to default within three years, while for AA bonds the rate is 0.042 percent; 0.088 percent for A-rated bonds; and 0.488 percent for BBB bonds.[26] By July 2009, the actual three-year default rates for mortgage-backed CDOs turned out to be 13 times greater than expected for AAA-rated tranches and 120 to 340 times greater for most other tranches.[27] "In 2008," reports former trader Michael

Lewis, "the ratings agencies would claim that they never intended for their ratings to be taken as such precise measurements. Ratings were merely the agencies' best guess at a rank ordering of risk."[28] Of course, if the ratings agencies had been working for investors instead of security sellers, such an admission would have put them out of business.

A Crisis of Reserves

By January 2008, mortgage-backed CDOs had lost their investors $542 billion.[29] If it were only a problem of inept bond ratings, then some people would have lost money, but there would not have been a major financial crisis. The crisis came when the bond ratings interacted with the banks' reserve requirements and collateral obligations. In June 2007, the ratings companies finally realized that mortgage bonds weren't as safe as they thought, and over the next few months they downgraded increasing numbers of bonds.[30] CDOs issued in 2002 through 2004 were downgraded an average of three to four notches (for example, from AAA to AA or AA−). CDOs issued in 2005 were downgraded an average of nine notches, while CDOs issued in 2006 and 2007 were downgraded 10 to 16 notches, turning investment-grade bonds into junk bonds overnight.[31] Suddenly, banks that had retained 1.6 percent of liquid reserves for bonds that had been graded AA or better found themselves scrambling to come up with 8 percent liquid reserves when the bonds were regraded to well below AA.

This scrambling is what created the panic on Wall Street. It wasn't so much investors' taking their money out of Bear Stearns, Lehman Brothers, and other financial institutions as it was those companies' having to increase reserves. Ratings also affected contractual obligations that companies had with other banks; if a bank's ratings declined, it would have to put up more liquid collateral to cover its loans.

The first mortgage company to go under was not a subprime lender but one that dealt exclusively with mortgages to wealthy people who wanted to borrow more than $417,000, then the limit for loans insured by the Federal Housing Administration. Although these loans were not risky, they were classified Alt-A mortgages, meaning just below prime. Thornburg Mortgage in Santa Fe specialized in such mortgages, and as of February 2008, 99.56 percent of its borrowers were paying on time. But on February 14, the Swiss bank UBS reported a fourth-quarter 2007 loss of $11.3 billion, part of which was due to a write-off of $2 billion on Alt-A loans. Under mark-to-market accounting standards, Thornburg was required to write down the value of its loans, which it had used as collateral for its short-term borrowings, and the company's creditors demanded that it put up more than $300 million in additional collateral. It was unable to do so, so it went out of business.[32]

As Thornburg was going broke, Standard & Poor's downgraded Bear Stearns by three levels. As a result, the company had to pay 20 percent more to insure its bonds through CDSs. This and other demands for collateral forced it nearly into bankruptcy, a step that was avoided only when J. P. Morgan took over the company for a fraction of what it had been worth a few months before.[33]

The company hit hardest by changes in ratings was American International Group (AIG), which had sold CDSs on more than 400 high-risk CDOs. At first, selling the CDSs made sense—they brought in a stream of revenue and, if the bonds were rated correctly, AIG would never have to pay out on more than one or two of the bonds. What the ratings companies had failed to see was that if the economy went bad enough for one subprime mortgage bond to default, then most if not all of them would default.

"We were doing every single [CDS] deal with every single Wall Street firm, except Citigroup," one AIG trader told writer Michael Lewis. "Citigroup decided it liked the risk, and kept it on their books. We took all the rest." If those CDOs defaulted, AIG would owe $80 billion to the buyers of the insurance policies.[34]

AIG realized its mistake in 2005 and stopped selling CDSs. But as late as 2007, Joseph Cassano, the head of the AIG division that had sold the CDSs, said, "It is hard for us, without being flippant, to even see a scenario within any kind of realm of reason that would see us losing $1 on any of these transactions."[35] Cassano, who had been paid $35 million a year over the previous eight years, was fired by AIG in early 2008 but received another $35 million bonus and a $1 million per month consulting contract.[36]

Up until September 2008, AIG was one of the few companies in the world to have a AAA credit rating. AIG's CDS contracts required it to maintain that rating or put up collateral to show it could pay off the contracts if the bonds defaulted. As the largest insurance company in the world, AIG had a net worth of $78 billion, but most of its assets were backing up its conventional insurance policies and could not be sold without approval from state insurance regulators. While the New York Federal Reserve Bank, the Treasury Department, and various bankers frantically worked to keep Lehman Brothers out of bankruptcy during the weekend of September 14, AIG was quietly facing a downgrading of that rating. If either Standard & Poor's or Moody's reduced the rating to AAA−, AIG would have to post $10.5 billion in collateral; if both reduced the rating, it would owe $13.3 billion.[37]

Eventually, the federal government loaned AIG $180 billion to keep it from going bankrupt, loans that will likely never be repaid in full.[38] These loans reduced the costs of the housing collapse to banks that had insured their CDOs with AIG. As noted by the AIG trader, Citigroup was not one of those banks, and it apparently lost about $60 billion on uninsured CDOs that it had been unable to sell to investors before the market crashed.[39] Rescuing Citigroup was one of the main reasons the Federal Reserve used TARP (Troubled Asset Relief Program) funds to make loans to banks—$45 billion in the case of Citi. Other banks, such as Wells Fargo and J. P. Morgan, didn't really need the loans but were virtually ordered to accept them anyway, apparently to disguise which banks were really in trouble.[40]

Whether the government should have made these loans in 2008, or just let AIG and other companies go bankrupt, as it did Lehman, is a question beyond the scope of this book. But clearly, the situation would never have reached that point in September 2008 if either the ratings companies had properly rated the bonds or growth management hadn't caused the housing bubbles.

It all comes down to growth management.

- If land-use regulation had not made housing unaffordable to moderate-income buyers, it is likely that Congress and the Clinton administration would not have ordered Fannie Mae and Freddie Mac to start buying large amounts of loans to low- and moderate-income buyers.
- If regulation-induced inelastic housing supplies had not caused prices to rapidly increase when the Fed reduced interest rates in 2001, speculators disappointed with the stock market would not have been induced to invest in real estate in growth-managed states.
- If housing prices did not collapse with a small contraction of demand, as they did in growth-management states but not in most other states, then large numbers of people would not have defaulted on their mortgages and Wall Street's mortgage bond market would not have collapse.

- If the passage of growth-management laws in so many states in the 1980s had not completely changed the rules of the housing market, then the ratings companies would not have erred in so many of their bond ratings.

What the Crisis Wasn't

Other factors that have often been cited as the "cause" of the collapse may have contributed to the bubble. But they were not the cause, and preventing them would not have prevented the bubble or much of the pain that resulted when it collapsed.

It wasn't low-income borrowers. In April 2007, a reporter with the *San Francisco Chronicle* reported on a Mexican immigrant who earned $14,000 a year picking strawberries who managed to buy (with three other families) a $720,000 home in California's Central Valley. This farm worker's story has been repeated over and over (often without mentioning the three other families) as evidence that subprime loans led to the mortgage crisis.[41] In fact, the financial crisis wasn't caused by poor people buying houses they couldn't afford. It resulted from middle-class people buying homes made unaffordable by growth-management plans.

If defaults were a result of loans to people who could not afford them, then defaults would have started soon after the subprime industry began to grow in 1998. Interest rates on mortgages with teaser rates typically adjusted after about two years, so defaults should have started growing around 2000. Instead, default rates did not significantly rise until 2005, when housing prices were leveling off and starting to decline in some markets.

The default rates on loans made in 2005 and 2006 were the highest in history.[42] Although CDOs created in 2004 and 2005 had about the same percentage of subprime mortgages as CDOs created in 2006 and 2007, the 2006 and 2007 CDOs were three to four times more likely to default.[43] An analysis by University of Texas economist Stan Liebowitz revealed that most foreclosures after the bubble were prime loans and the biggest reason for such foreclosures was that the value of the house had fallen below the amount due on the loan.[44]

Economists with the Federal Reserve Bank agree. Claims that "a wave of subprime resets set off the crisis is hard to square with the facts," they say; "Most borrowers who defaulted on subprime adjustable-rate mortgages did so well in advance of their reset dates." Nor is there a "case that large numbers of subprime borrowers were inappropriately steered into their mortgages." Instead, a rise in the average credit scores of subprime borrowers as the bubble grew suggests that people with good credit were taking subprime loans—loans with little or no down payment or high debt-to-income ratios. The main reason people defaulted, the economists found, was falling prices.[45]

Another Federal Reserve study found that the average credit scores of people taking out interest-only mortgages was 720, which is generally considered excellent. A much higher share of the people taking out these mortgages are delinquent or have defaulted than people taking fixed-rate mortgages, whose credit scores averaged just 710. Such mortgages "were chosen by prime borrowers" in order "to get more expensive houses within high housing price areas," the study concluded.[46]

These facts suggest that many of those loans were to speculators hoping to flip the houses at a profit, not to people who were too poor to be buying homes. "When we opened a development for sale, bus loads of people from California would come, glance at the homes, and sign the contracts," a developer from Arizona told me in 2010.[47] Raising prices only fed the frenzy, as it confirmed to investors that prices were rising fast enough to make their speculations profitable.

It wasn't greedy bankers or excessive bonuses. The fact that the trader who sent AIG into bankruptcy earned $280 million plus a $35 million firing bonus seems outrageous. But bankers are no greedier than anyone else hoping for a pay raise, and they were no greedier during the 2000s than in any previous decade. Many bank executives received bonuses in the form of shares of their companies that they weren't allowed to immediately sell. The CEO of Lehman Brothers owned stock that at one time was nominally worth $1 billion, but after the company went bankrupt, he ended up selling it for $65,000.[48] Such arrangements should have given bankers incentives to worry about long-term risks; that they did not suggests that they were as deceived by the ratings companies as almost everyone else.

It wasn't deregulation. The most commonly mentioned deregulation that supposedly contributed to the crisis was the 1999 repeal of the Glass-Steagall Act, which had separated deposit banks from investment banks. This repeal supposedly resulted in deposit banks (which are protected by the Federal Deposit Insurance Corporation) spending their depositors money on highly leveraged and risky investments that required taxpayer bailouts to protect the deposits. In fact, all the repeal did was legalize what was happening anyway.

219

To get around the law, banks created offshore corporations known as special-purpose entities that freely invested in securities at virtually unlimited leverage rates, yet the banks were still effectively responsible for any losses the offshore companies sustained.[49]

A lesser-known deregulation was a provision of the Commodity Futures Modernization Act of 2000 that allowed investors to buy credit default swaps for bonds they didn't actually own. This provision opened the door for "synthetic" bonds, which didn't actually represent any mortgages or other assets but merely mirrored the performance of those assets. By 2006, some estimated that half of all mortgage bonds were synthetic, which undoubtedly made the financial crisis worse when the underlying mortgages declined in value.[50] But synthetic bonds or swaps did not cause the crisis itself.

"The banking reform of the late 1990s had little effect on the housing boom and bust," conclude two economists with the Cato Institute. "The many reform ideas currently proposed would have done little or nothing to avert the crisis."[51]

It wasn't low interest rates. After the collapse of the dot-com bubble in 2001, the Fed lowered short-term interest rates, eventually reaching a low of 1 percent in June 2003. It began raising them in mid-2004, but by June 2005 rates were still a low 3 percent. Many analysts have blamed the housing bubble on these low rates. One problem with this explanation is that housing prices began rising in growth-managed states in the late 1990s, before the Fed reduced short-term rates.

More important, fast-growing but non-growth-managed states, such as North Carolina and Texas, experienced no bubbles. This fact suggests that, without growth management, there would have been no bubbles even with the low interest rates. The low interest rates may have made the bubbles a little bigger, but they did not cause the bubbles. This case is confirmed by an analysis by economists Edward Glaeser and Joseph Gyourko, who estimated that "lower real interest rates can explain only one-fifth of the rise in prices from 1996 to 2006"—which is about right considering prices in relatively unregulated markets such as Texas rose only about a fifth as much as growth-managed markets in places such as California and Florida.[52]

Perhaps the biggest negative effect of low interest rates was that they led banks to push people who would have been better off with fixed-rate mortgages into accepting adjustable rate mortgages. But that practice did not cause the bubble, and, for the most part, it did not result in widespread defaults.

Institutions weren't too big or too interconnected to fail. In 2008, Alan Greenspan said the problem with the crisis wasn't that institutions were too big or too interconnected to fail, it was that they were too big or too interconnected to liquidate quickly.[53] Yet such interconnections can be dealt with without government bailouts or takeovers. When Lehman Brothers went bankrupt, the United States allowed Lehman's broker-dealer to remain in business to allow all counterparties to wind down the trades, thus reducing or eliminating the shock to the financial system. In contrast, Lehman's European and Asian offices were forced into immediate bankruptcy, freezing funds and forcing Lehman's counterparties to sell assets to meet reserve requirements, which pushed the market even lower. If all countries had followed the American example, the Lehman bankruptcy would have had little effect on the world economy.[54]

Once the growth-management-induced rise in housing prices began, a bubble and subsequent decline in prices were inevitable. The effects of this bubble could have been minimized if ratings companies had properly rated mortgage-backed bonds. But the companies were unaware that growth management had changed the rules of the housing market and were blinded by the fact that they were now paid by bond sellers who wanted positive ratings rather than by investors who wanted accurate ratings. Accurate ratings would have greatly reduced the effects of the crisis; other changes might have made the crisis less serious. Only a rejection of growth management by state and local officials would have prevented it.

14. The World Dream

In sharp contrast to just a couple of decades ago, when only a small minority of the world's peoples lived in their own homes, homeownership today has become a global phenomenon. Since the years immediately following World War II, Australians have called ownership of a single-family detached home "the Great Australian Dream."[1] New Zealanders call owning a detached home the "New Zealand dream" or "Kiwi dream."[2] Even in Switzerland, which has the lowest homeownership rate in the developed world, more than 80 percent of people say they dream of owning their own home.[3]

Americans like to think their country is number one, but today many other countries have much higher homeownership rates than the United States. Greece, India, Italy, Mexico, and Spain all have rates close to 15 percentage points higher than the United States. Belgium, Ireland, Norway, Britain, and Australia are also higher, though the differences are smaller.[4] Of course, in many of these countries, the homes are smaller and more crowded, sometimes housing three or more generations of families. The average American home, for example, has two rooms per person, while the average Indian home has 2.5 people per room.[5]

As recently as 1990, the vast majority of the world's population still lived in rental, communal, or government-provided housing or squatted on land that they did not own. After 1990, China and many of the former soviet nations privatized most of their housing, and today some of these countries claim almost unbelievably high homeownership rates: 97 percent in Kazakhstan and Lithuania; 96 percent in Bulgaria and Romania; 92 percent in Hungary; and 89 percent in China, compared with 65 percent in the United States. Many of the privately owned residences in these former communist countries are tiny apartments built during the soviet era and often inspired by Le Corbusier's Radiant City.[6]

The high rates reported by some of these countries may be questionable for several reasons. In many developing nations, for example, up to half the people cited as homeowners do not have clear title to their land.[7] Other reports have definitional problems: The government of Taiwan, for example, counts any non-government-owned home as owner occupied even if the home is rented to someone other than the owner. Though Taiwan claims an 88 percent homeownership rate, one analyst estimates that only about 70 percent of homes in Taiwan are occupied by their owners, which is still higher than in the United States.[8]

Privatization in China, and perhaps in some of the former communist countries, did not convey complete title to many of the purchasers. The government retained ownership of the land on which most urban apartments stand. Many low-income families bought only "use rights," including the right to will homes to their children but not the right to sell the homes at market value. If they sell the homes, the government will claim most of any capital gains earned on the sale.[9] The people counted as homeowners may have fewer rights than are usually understood by that term in the United States, but they still have more rights than renters.

Data are not available for every nation, but if the published numbers for China and other countries are accepted, well over half the world's population lives in owner-occupied housing today. India claims 82 percent homeownership, so between China and India alone more than 2.2 billion people live in owner-occupied homes. Adding the published homeownership rates for the other countries in Table 14.1 brings the total to more than 4 billion people, 76 percent of the population of the countries shown and 57 percent of the total world's population. If only 10 percent of households in other countries own their own homes, the worldwide rate is 60 percent. Moving from less than 1 percent to 60 percent homeownership in a couple of centuries represents an extraordinary cultural and economic change.

Why Homeownership Rates Differ

Perhaps surprisingly, per capita income or gross domestic product (GDP) is not a factor in explaining national differences in homeownership rates. In fact, for the countries listed in Table 14.1, a negative correlation exists between per capita GDP and homeownership, mainly because China and other formerly socialist countries with low GDPs recently privatized most of their housing. In 1995, for example, Cambodia had the highest rate of homeownership (95 percent) despite one of the lowest per capita GDPs ($660), whereas

Table 14.1

HOMEOWNERSHIP RATES BY NATION

Country	Rate	Year	Population	GDP/ Capita	Source
Argentina	67%	2010	40.7	15,901	Hofinet
Australia	68%	2008	22.3	29,764	Hofinet
Austria	56%	2009	8.4	39,761	Hypostat
Azerbaijan	71%	2009	8.9	10,063	Hofinet
Belgium	78%	2007	11.0	36,274	Hypostat
Benin	63%	1994	8.8	1,448	UN
Bolivia	60%	1997	10.4	4,604	UN
Brazil	74%	2009	194.9	11,273	Hofinet
Bulgaria	96%	2002	7.4	12,934	Hypostat
Canada	68%	2007	34.2	39,171	Hofinet
Chile	69%	2006	17.1	15,040	Hofinet
China	89%	2010	1,338.3	9,593	Hofinet
Colombia	50%	2009	46.3	9,593	Hofinet
Cyprus	68%	2006	0.8	28,960	Hypostat
Czech Republic	47%	2001	10.5	24,950	Hypostat
Denmark	54%	2009	5.6	36,443	Hypostat
Egypt	32%	2006	84.5	6,417	Hofinet
Estonia	96%	2008	64.9	18,527	Hypostat
Finland	59%	2008	5.4	34,918	Hypostat
France	57%	2007	65.8	33,910	Hypostat
Germany	43%	2004	81.7	36,081	OECD
Greece	80%	2009	10.8	28,496	Hypostat
Haiti	60%	2010	9.9	1,163	Hofinet
Hong Kong	53%	2010	7.0	45,944	Hofinet
Hungary	92%	2003	10.0	18,841	Hypostat
Iceland	80%	2008	0.3	36,730	Hypostat
India	87%	2001	1,210.2	3,408	Census India
Indonesia	67%	2008	232.5	4,347	Hofinet
Iran	81%	1996	75.7	11,883	UN
Ireland	75%	2009	4.6	39,492	Hypostat
Israel	69%	2008	7.8	29,602	ByitinIsrael
Italy	80%	2002	60.0	29,480	Hypostat
Japan	61%	2008	128.0	33,885	JP Stat Yrbk
Kazakhstan	97%	2005	16.3	12,015	Hofinet
Latvia	87%	2007	2.2	14,504	Hypostat
Lithuania	97%	2008	3.2	17,235	Hypostat
Luxembourg	75%	2008	0.5	81,466	Hypostat
Malaysia	67%	2006	27.5	14,744	Hofinet
Malta	75%	2006	0.4	24,833	Hypostat
Mexico	71%	2009	108.5	14,406	Hofinet
Morocco	62%	2001	32.4	4,794	Hofinet
Netherlands	57%	2008	16.6	40,973	Hypostat
New Zealand	67%	2006	4.4	27,130	NZ Census

(continued)

Table 14.1 (continued)
HOMEOWNERSHIP RATES BY NATION

Country	Rate	Year	Population	GDP/ Capita	Source
Niger	93%	1998	15.7	761	UN
Nigeria	10%	2010	158.3	2,437	Hofinet
Norway	77%	2001	4.9	51,959	Hypostat
Philippines	80%	2009	92.0	3,920	Hofinet
Poland	75%	2004	38.2	18,981	Hypostat
Portugal	76%	2006	10.6	23,262	Hypostat
Romania	96%	2009	21.9	11,895	Hypostat
Russia	81%	2009	141.8	15,612	Hofinet
Saudi Arabia	30%	2010	25.4	22,607	Hofinet
Singapore	83%	2010	5.0	56,694	Hofinet
Slovak Republic	88%	2008	5.4	22,195	Hypostat
Slovenia	82%	2006	2.0	28,073	Hypostat
South Africa	76%	2008	50.6	10,518	Statistics SA
South Korea	56%	2005	48.9	29,997	Hofinet
Spain	85%	2008	46.2	29,830	Hypostat
Sweden	66%	2008	9.4	38,204	Hypostat
Switzerland	37%	2007	7.9	41,950	SwissInfo.ch
Thailand	75%	2008	68.1	35,604	Hofinet
Turkey	68%	2000	75.7	13,577	Hypostat
United Kingdom	70%	2007	62.3	35,059	Hypostat
United States	65%	2010	310.0	46,860	Census
Venezuela	83%	2006	28.4	12,048	Hofinet

SOURCES: Populations are in millions and are from the most recent available censuses. Gross domestic products per capita reflect purchasing power parity and are from the International Monetary Fund's World Economic Outlook Database, September 2011, tinyurl.com/6x4btlx.

Sources of homeownership rates include the following: **BuyitinIsrael:** "Rental Prices Rise 15.3% as More Buyers Purchase Property in Israel for Investment," Buy It In Israel website, January 7, 2010, tinyurl.com/3d48ts2; **Census India:** 2001 Census, table S00–013, tinyurl.com/684wjf3; **Hofinet:** "Countries," Housing Finance Information Network, Wharton's Business School, 2011, http://hofinet.org/countries/; **Hypostat:** "Hypostat 2009: A Review of Europe's Mortgage and Housing Markets," European Mortgage Federation, Brussels, 2010, p. 73, tinyurl.com/6fh5gfd; **Stats DE:** "Wohneigentum in Kleinen Gemeinden am Häufigsten" ("Homeownership Highest in Small Communities"), Statistiches Bundesamt Deutschland, 2004, tinyurl.com/6jub6gv; **Stats NZ:** "Housing Indicators 2008," Statistics New Zealand, indicator 8: ownership of dwellings, 2008, tinyurl.com/7xme32x; **Stats Japan:** "Japan Statistical Yearbook," table 18-5, tinyurl.com/3jx8ky4; **Stats SA:** "South Africa and Homeownership, 2009," Business Report, September 2, 2009, tinyurl.com/3dtbluc; **SwissInfo:** Dale Bechtel, "Housing Boom Over for Property Investors," SwissInfo.ch, October 18, 2008, tinyurl.com/3ukdpuu; **U.S. Census:** 2010 American Community Survey,table B25003, Census Bureau, http://factfinder2.census.gov; and **UN:** "Rental Housing: An Essential Option for the Urban Poor in Developing Countries," United Nations Human Settlements Programme, 2003, p. 18, tinyurl.com/3w6ww68.

Switzerland had one of the lowest rates of homeownership (31 percent) despite having one of the highest per capita GDPs ($22,400).[10]

However, growth in income within a given country can increase homeownership rates, suggesting that most people prefer to own their homes if they can afford to do so.[11] Thanks to a healthy economy, Swiss homeownership increased to 36.5 percent by 2005.[12] But it was still the lowest in the developed world, little more than half Britain's 69.5 percent and little more than a third of Bulgaria's 96.5 percent.[13]

Homeownership rates in English-speaking countries have converged toward one another over time.[14] It is likely that, in the absence of government interference in the marketplace, such convergence would take place worldwide; households in lower-income nations would simply live in smaller, lower-quality homes than those in high-income nations. This suggests that government policies that increase or reduce the cost of housing or homeownership are responsible for sustained differences in homeownership rates. Those policies include regulation of the mortgage securities market, public or social housing programs, privatization of such housing, rent controls, and land-use regulation. Other factors that may affect homeownership rates include urbanization and culture.

Urbanization: In most countries—other than places where most rural lands are communally owned—the percentage of ruralites who own homes is greater than urbanites, so homeownership rates tend to decline as nations become more urbanized.[15] Just 30 percent of India's population lives in urban areas, which helps explain why it has an 87 percent homeownership rate.[16]

Mortgage securitization: Homeownership rates tend to be higher in nations where banks legally and actively offload the risk of lending by combining and selling mortgages in the form of asset-backed securities. As political scientists Herman Schwartz and Leonard Seabrooke note, securitization "permits banks to make large, long-term, fixed-interest loans," while banks that can't securitize impose "higher interest rates, variable interest rates, prepayment penalties, and big down payments ."[17]

As of 2003, Britain had "the largest securitization market in Europe," while Italy had virtually none.[18] Whereas British lenders would lend up to 100 percent of the value of a home for up to 25 years, Italian lenders typically lent only half the value of a home for only 10 years, and at substantially higher interest rates.[19] Since 2003, the Italian lending market has become more liberal, with loans up to 30 years, but lenders still require at least a 20 percent, and often as much as a 40 percent, down payment.[20]

Some countries, including Denmark and Germany, allow mortgage securitization, but only as "covered" bonds. These bonds remain on the issuing bank's balance sheet and thus do not completely transfer mortgage risk to other institutions. German banks issue large numbers of covered bonds backed by mortgages whose terms are not as generous as those in Britain; for example, they require larger down payments. Covered bonds are most heavily used in Denmark, Germany, Sweden, France, Spain, and Switzerland, while noncovered mortgage bonds are most heavily used in English-speaking countries.[21]

Public housing: Nations in which the governments provide a high proportion of housing have lower rates of homeownership. The Netherlands, for example, has a homeownership rate that is about 10 percentage points lower than the United States partly because the government provides 36 percent of the nation's housing, compared with less than 3 percent in the United States.[22]

Privatization: During the Margaret Thatcher era, Britain privatized 2 million rental units representing one-third of the nation's public housing. An even greater privatization movement took place in the early 1990s as former Soviet countries in eastern Europe transferred ownership of more than 3 million apartments to residents at "give-away" prices.[23] As a result, homeownership rates in Bulgaria, Estonia, Romania, and Hungary are all above 90 percent.[24] These rates will probably decline over time.

Rent control: Rent controls dating back to 1910 have destroyed Portugal's rental market, making it impossible for landlords to earn a profit and discouraging anyone from building new rental housing.[25] This situation has contributed to Portugal's high homeownership rate of 76 percent.

On the other hand, some countries, particularly Denmark, Germany, Sweden, and Switzerland, have what are known as "second-generation" rent controls that allow landlords to increase rents enough to remain profitable yet preserve tenant rights from exorbitant rent increases and evictions.[26] These controls have kept homeownership rates in these countries lower as many people stay in the same rental houses for years or decades.[27] In Germany, for example, developers can build new rental homes and rent them at market rates, and landlords can increase rates for existing rentals as much as 20 percent every three years. However, landlords cannot evict tenants unless they are causing trouble or the landlord wants to move into the home.[28]

Culture: Southern European nations, including Greece, Italy, and Spain, seem to rely more on families than on government to provide housing. Ireland also appears to fit this cultural system.[29] These nations tend to have very high rates of homeownership and low rates of public housing. Although Italy, for example, has built hundreds of thousands of units of public housing, it has privatized them almost as fast as it built them.[30]

Greeks, Italians, and Spaniards are four to five times as likely to obtain their homes with family assistance—either inheritance or with help in purchase or construction—than, say, Danes or Swedes.[31] Greece's 80 percent homeownership rate, for example, is partly due to a one-time law requiring families to pay a dowry when a young woman married; often the dowry was a house, and often still is despite the 1983 repeal of the law.[32] About 70 percent of Italian homes are owner occupied, but only about 20 percent are rented; the remaining 10 percent are occupied free of charge by relatives of the occupants.[33]

Housing analysts refer to this cultural system as "familialistic" or "Catholic-familial," as these nations tend to be strongly Catholic or Orthodox.[34] One researcher points to the 1891 papal encyclical *De Rerum Novarum* ("Of New Things") that endorses private home-ownership by working-class families as an alternative to socialism's goal of doing away with private property.[35] Debates between capital and labor "cannot be solved save by assuming as a principle that private ownership must be held sacred and inviolable," said the encyclical. Rather than abolish private property, the law "should favor ownership, and its policy should be to induce as many as possible of the people to become owners." One of the benefits, it continues, is that "property will certainly become more equitably divided." "If working people can be encouraged to look forward to obtaining a share in the land, the consequence will be that the gulf between vast wealth and sheer poverty will be bridged over, and the respective classes will be brought nearer to one another."[36]

Geographic mobility: About 2 percent of Americans move from one state to another each year, and another 2 percent move to another county in the same state. Although residents of Britain, France, Ireland, the Netherlands, and Sweden move nearly as frequently as those in the United States, Americans are at least twice as mobile as Europeans as a whole.[37] If it makes sense to buy a home only if someone stays in a location for more than a certain number of years—four is commonly cited—then a more mobile population is likely to have a lower homeownership rate.

Government incentives: The United States offers a variety of incentives designed to increase homeownership, including Federal Housing Administration mortgage insurance, the implicit (or, after 2008, explicit) backing of mortgage securities through Fannie Mae and Freddie Mac, and the mortgage-interest deduction. Very few other countries offer any of these incentives, and none offer all three.[38]

Canada and South Korea insure residential mortgages and issue mortgage-backed securities but do not allow mortgage-interest deductions.[39] The Netherlands has a mortgage insurance program and allows a mortgage-interest deduction but does not issue mortgage securities.[40] The Japan Housing Finance Agency issues mortgage-backed securities but does not guarantee individual mortgages or allow a mortgage-interest deduction.[41] India and Switzerland allow mortgage-interest deductions, and a few other countries, including Belgium, Ireland, and Sweden, allow deductions of part of the mortgage interest. Sweden, for example, allows taxpayers to deduct 30 percent of their mortgage interest.[42]

On a per capita basis, Britain has one of the largest residential mortgage securities markets in the world without the support of government-sponsored enterprises like Fannie and Freddie.[43] British lenders provide loans on terms even more liberal than those in the United States, allowing not just zero down payments but offering 30-year loans of up to 110 percent of the value of the home—effectively a negative 10 percent down payment.[44] Britain and Australia both have homeownership rates that are comparable to or slightly higher than the United States despite lacking any of these incentives.

Taxation of imputed rent: Many economists believe that, since the income renters earn to pay their rent is taxed, homeowners should also be taxed the imputed rent that they would have to pay if they did not own their homes.[45] However, few countries actually impose such a tax, mainly because of the difficulty in estimating how much the imputed rent would be. Switzerland is one that does, and one analysis concluded that this tax is partly responsible for Switzerland's low homeownership rate.[46] Other countries that tax imputed income include Iceland, Italy, Luxembourg, the Netherlands, and Slovenia, four of which have 75 to 82 percent homeownership rates.[47]

Land-use regulation: Differences in land-use regulation account for differences in both homeownership rates and whether or not nations suffered housing bubbles in the 2000s. At least one analysis has concluded that Switzerland's low homeownership rates are attributable primarily to such regulation. "Switzerland's low rate of home ownership is attributable to the fact that prices are very high," said the analysis. "House prices are high in Switzerland mainly because land prices are high," while "land prices are high because there is relatively little developable land, both for topographical reasons and because the Swiss attach considerable importance to conservation of both agricultural landscapes and urban heritage." This situation has led to "tight restrictions on development of agricultural land and redevelopment of urban land."[48]

Switzerland's neighbor Italy has a quite different history of land-use regulation. Italy had few planning constraints on home construction in the 1950s and 1960s, leading to a rapid rise in homeownership. In the 1970s, planning became more restrictive in larger cities, so home construction shifted to smaller cities. "Unauthorized building was common," report two Italian sociologists, who estimate "that about 30 percent of the housing built between 1971 and 1984 was illegal." From the 1980s on, planning restrictions and actions against unauthorized construction became stronger. This constraint predictably led to a steep price increase in housing. Yet during the less regulatory era, Italian homeownership rates grew from about 40 percent at the end of World War II to 70 percent in about 1990 and remain above 70 percent today.[49]

Town-and-Country Planning

The land-use regulation that seems pervasive throughout Europe today was pioneered in Britain after World War II following an anti-suburban campaign that closely resembled the one in the United States. As early as 1932, an English urban planner named Thomas Sharp joined Le Corbusier in challenging the suburbs, which had been first popularized in Britain as "garden cities." Sharp's book *Town and Countryside* urged that city and country should be kept distinct and the suburban attempts to be half one and half the other should be outlawed.[50]

Another English planner, C. E. M. Joad, complained of "hordes of hikers cackling insanely in the woods" and "people, wherever there is water, upon sea shores or upon river banks, lying in every attitude of undress and inelegant squalor." Joad's complaints against people playing "radio sets in the woods" and "gramophones in boats on rivers" and his proposal to close certain roads to automobiles so that people who don't want to drive "can be assured of peace and quiet" foreshadow the attitudes of Sierra Club baby boomers in the United States.[51]

Planning historian Peter Hall observes that Sharp, Joad, and others who "derided and condemned" the suburbs in the 1930s were "all upper-middle class and the offenders were mostly lower-middle class in a typical such suburb." The "chief fault" of the suburbs, Hall continued—echoing John Stilgoe's comments, cited in Chapter 4, about the attitudes of American architects and planners toward the suburbs in the 1920s—was that their residents favored the wrong architectural styles—Neocolonial instead of modern.[52]

"We are at the moment permitting private enterprise to destroy the country," Joad apocalyptically warned. "There is today a real danger that . . . a generation will grow up which knows not the country." To prevent this possibility, "the extension of the towns must be stopped, building must be restricted to sharply defined areas, and such re-housing of the population as may be necessary must be carried out within these areas."[53] That housing, added Sharp, should be in "great new blocks of flats which will house a considerable portion of the population of the future town" in a relatively small area, thus preserving the countryside.[54] Thus, the desire to pack lower-class families in Radiant City-like high-rises was first expressed by English urban planners offended by working-class people moving into the suburbs.

Such policies are exactly what took place in Britain after World War II. In homage to Sharp's book, Parliament passed the Town and Country Planning Act in 1947, effectively setting aside most of the British countryside from development while building large high-rises for housing. In contrast to Le Corbusier's original proposal, however, these high-rises were not for the elite, who continued to live in rural manors, or for the middle class, who lived in low-density suburbs of single-family homes, duplexes, or row houses, but for the working class.

Given Britain's bombed-out cities, people were happy to move into any new housing. But by 1965, both high-density high-rise and high-density low-rise developments "became 'hard-to-let,' i.e., lettable only to the poorest and most disorderly families," says urban historian Peter Hall. The problem, argues Hall, was that "middle-class designers had no real feeling for the way a working-class family lived." Unlike the middle class, the working class didn't have nannies, go for frequent holidays in the country, or send their children to prep schools. "From first to last, Corbusier had no understanding of people who were un-like himself," partly because "he was both middle-class and child-less."[55] Britain gave up on high-rise public housing after about 1970.

Countries throughout Europe followed the same pattern, and Corbusian towers—a few of them designed by Le Corbusier him-self—sprang up in almost every major city on the continent. It became the norm for northern European countries to house 20 to 40 percent of their people in government-owned or "social" housing. Not all of it was high-rises, but all of it had much higher densities than would be found in middle-class suburbs. Today, even after massive privatization, 22 percent of British housing is government owned.

High-rise housing was embraced with particular enthusiasm by central planners in the Soviet Union. *The Ideal Communist City*, a 1965 book written by urban planners at the University of Moscow (and translated into English in 1971), echoes Le Corbusier in calling American suburbs "a chaotic and depressing agglomeration of buildings covering enormous stretches of land." For efficiency's sake, the book argues, "the search for a future kind of residential building leads logically to high-rise structures." To provide urban transit within walking distance of every building, the book called for population densities of 60,000 to 74,000 people per square mile—not quite the densities of Radiant City, but far greater than would be found in "monotonous stretches of individual low-rise houses."[56]

After World War II, Soviet governments built 90 percent of new housing in Russia and well over half of new housing in Eastern Europe.[57] Much of it was in high-rises. Indeed, as former World Bank urban planner Alain Bertaud's graphical representations of major urban areas shows, Moscow comes closest to the town-and-country ideal of a high-density city surrounded by a nearly unpopulated countryside.[58]

In 1998, planners from the University of Stockholm described one Soviet new town, Halle-Neustadt in eastern Germany, as one of "the most sustainable cities" in the developed world because it was designed for mass transit and not automobiles. The planners' rating ignored the fact that, since reunification, more than a third of Halle-Neustadt's residents had moved out while those that stayed purchased thousands of automobiles and parked them "every-where—on pavements, bike-ways, yards and lawn" in the city.[59]

Social democratic governments in western Europe also favored Radiant City–style high-rises. In the 1950s and 1960s, the Swedish government built more than a million units of new housing as the share of Swedes living in cities grew from 55 percent in 1940 to more than 80 percent in 1970. Most of the public housing was in high-rises, as the government was also building a subway system in Stockholm whose fares were supposed to cover all its operating costs and much of its construction costs, and to do so planners calculated that 10,000 to 15,000 people would need to live within walking distance of each subway station.[60]

The government's philosophy was that housing was not an asset to be owned by families but a "social right" for everyone to share. Public housing was open to everyone, regardless of income—though many of the nation's elite no doubt continued to live in the privately owned single-family homes that made up just 10 percent of Stockholm's housing stock in 1970. As long as rapid urbanization contributed to an acute housing shortage, people were grateful to accept whatever apartments the government offered them. But after 1970, the housing shortage turned into an apartment surplus, leading to a revolt against high-density housing in particular and government planning in general.

"In quality terms the results were often disastrous," says Peter Hall. Around 90 percent of new apartments had three rooms or fewer. Le Corbusier's favorite construction material, concrete, gave the buildings an "industrialized, highly monotonous" flavor. The buildings "had high vacancy rates and a very high turnover." In 1971, people protested in the streets against some of the planned new developments, leading the government to dramatically shift its policy in 1972 toward more private housing construction and more single-family homes. Although 70 percent of new construction had been apartments in 1970, new apartments construction declined to 30 percent of the total by 1980.[61] Homeownership increased from 30 percent in the 1960s to 66 percent today.[62] Meanwhile, the high-rises that had been built for everyone became stigmatized as "low-income housing," and "most long-stay residents were immigrants and problem families."[63]

Unlike Britain, Sweden was virtually undamaged by World War II. The country has nearly twice the land area of Britain with less than a sixth of Britain's population in 2009. Eighty percent of the people live in urban areas covering just 3 percent of the country, while farms and forests cover more than 60 percent of the country.[64] So why cram such a large share of the nation's people into high-rise developments? "Influential architects favored high-density development, and they dominated the planning profession in Sweden," answers

Hall. "Public preferences, it seems, carried little weight," except to the extent that the public kept Social Democrats—a party that favored government planning—in power as a virtual "one-party system of government" from 1932 to 1976.[65]

Just as in the United States, where high-rise public housing had fallen out of favor by the time Pruitt-Igoe was imploded in 1972, "the great Corbusian rebuild was over" in western Europe, says Hall, in about 1970. Eastern Europe took a couple of decades longer.[66] But since national town-and-country plans forbade development of the rural countryside, the result was rapidly rising home prices.

With or without high rises, most western European nations adopted town-and-country-like planning laws, though often much later than Britain. Germany passed a law in 1960 requiring local governments to plan.[67] Italy, as previously noted, passed restrictive land-use laws in the 1970s but did not seriously enforce them for another decade.

Housing Affordability

It is probably no coincidence that Britain has both Europe's oldest national growth-management legislation and also some of the least affordable housing markets in Europe. Median-home-price-to-median-family-income ratios are greater than 7.0 in London, and range from 4.6 to 6.1 in other major English and Scottish cities. Thanks to urban-growth boundaries and similar policies, housing is similarly unaffordable in major cities of both Australia and New Zealand. "House prices have skyrocketed principally because of more restrictive land use regulations that have virtually prohibited new house construction on or beyond the urban fringe," says demographer Wendell Cox, who tracks such data for English-speaking countries.[68]

Vancouver, British Columbia, has practiced strict growth-management planning since the late 1960s. By 1980, Vancouver's price-to-income ratio was 5.7, and it has been Canada's least affordable housing market ever since.[69] By 2010, Vancouver's price-to-income ratio had reached 9.5, making it one of the three least affordable urban areas in the English-speaking world.[70]

Unfortunately, comparable data regarding median housing prices are not available for most other countries. The European Union measures housing affordability using the percentage of people who pay more than 40 percent of their incomes on housing. By this definition, Europe's least affordable housing markets are Denmark,

Germany, and Greece, where 22 to 24 percent of people spend this much on housing. Britain, where one out of six people spend more than this much on housing, comes in a distant fourth. Most other countries are around 10 percent or less; France, for example, is only 3 percent.[71]

According to French economist Vincent Benard, however, French housing is far less affordable than would be indicated by this measure. Comparing median home prices with median gross disposable income, Benard calculates that, from 1965 to 2000, French home price-to-income ratios consistently ranged between 2.2 and 2.7. But ratios started growing in 1998, and by 2007 (when British price-to-income ratios averaged 5.5), ratios soared close to 5.0. In analyzing these price changes, Benard initially assumed "land-use regulations would be one factor among others," including "monetary phenomenon, or issues relative to credit practices." Instead, he concluded that land-use regulations were "by far, the main factor explaining our bubble."[72]

Benard noted that Paris, which has had strong land-use laws for longer than the rest of France, experienced a bubble in 1990, when prices briefly reached 4.7 times median disposable incomes. Paris price-to-income ratios then fell to 2.8 in 1998, then bubbled again to more than 5.5 in 2007. Although a 1967 law required French cities to effectively draw urban-growth boundaries, those cities could easily expand their boundaries in the 1980s. By the 2000s, however, expanding the boundaries required a minimum of three years and can sometimes take as long as seven years to overcome environmental litigation. As Benard describes in detail in a book whose title translates to *Housing: Public Crisis, Private Remedies*, these delays set the stage for France's rapid increase in housing prices after 1998.[73]

Other data also suggest that the European Union's affordability ranking is incorrect. Global Property Guide, an online information source for property investors, tracks the ratio of the cost of a "typical upscale housing unit of 100 square meters" to per capita GDP. This measure's focus on "upscale housing" produces very high numbers in undeveloped countries. Global Property Guide's data also come solely from major urban areas, leading to a bias against countries that have a steep rent gradient away from major urban centers. Such bias would be most apparent where major cities practiced growth management while smaller ones did not. In the United States, for example, Global Property Guide tracks prices only in New York and Miami, thus producing a much higher ratio than if it also tracked, say, Atlanta, Dallas, and Houston. Among developed nations with national land-use planning systems (which include most developed countries other than the United States and Canada), however, the results should be roughly proportional to median-value-to-median-income ratios.

Table 14.2 shows Global Property Guide's numbers along with Wendell Cox's calculations of price-to-income ratios for English-speaking countries and Hong Kong. The table suggests that British housing is twice as expensive, relative to incomes, as housing in Italy and Greece, and three to four times as expensive as in most other European countries other than France.

Table 14.2

RATIOS OF HOUSING PRICE TO PER CAPITA GDP

	Price/Per Capita GDP	Price/Median Income
Hong Kong	63	11.4
Britain	50	5.1
France	42	
Japan	36	
United States	29	3.3
Italy	26	
Greece	25	
Switzerland	17	
Portugal	17	
Spain	17	
Finland	15	
Australia	15	7.1
Canada	14	4.6
New Zealand	12	6.4
Germany	12	
Netherlands	11	
Sweden	11	
Austria	11	
Denmark	9	
Ireland	9	4.8
Luxembourg	7	

SOURCES: Price/per capita GDP from http://www.globalpropertyguide.com; price/median income from "Demographia International Housing Affordability Survey," http://demographia.com.

Outside Europe, Australia and New Zealand also saw a huge increase in prices after 2000. After 1998, New Zealand prices more than doubled, and Australian prices nearly tripled. New Zealand prices appear to have peaked in 2007 and have declined slightly since then, while Australian prices continued to climb through 2010.[74] Economist Alan Moran blames Australia's price increases on "the tragedy of planning," specifically the "government-induced land shortage" resulting from urban-growth limits in place around most Australian cities.[75] Similarly, New Zealand's high prices can be traced to that country's 1991 Resource Management Act.[76]

Housing Bubbles

Town-and-country planning not only made housing unaffordable, it made prices more volatile. Not surprisingly, this volatility was first observed in Britain. "By ignoring the role of supply in determining house prices," a 2005 economic analysis of the British housing market found that "planners have created a system that has led not only to higher house prices but also to a highly volatile housing market."[77] Britain has, in fact, had at least four housing bubbles, with real home prices falling by 25 percent after a 1973 bubble, 8 percent after a 1979 bubble, 35 percent after a 1989 bubble, and 15 percent—so far—after the 2007 bubble (Figure 14.1). Prices also fell in the early 1950s, but data do not extend back far enough to determine if this was a bubble.[78]

Due to strict land-use regulation in much of Europe, the 2006 American housing bubble that was supposedly caused by such uniquely American institutions as the Community Reinvestment Act and Fannie Mae was almost perfectly replicated in Britain as well as many other European countries. Between 1998 and 2008, when American housing prices grew by 50 percent, housing prices more than doubled in Belgium, Britain, Denmark, France, Greece, Ireland, Luxembourg, the Netherlands, Norway, Spain, and Sweden (Figure 14.2). Prices peaked in 2006 in Ireland; in 2007 in Britain, Denmark, France, and Spain; and in 2008 in Greece, Italy, Luxembourg, and the Netherlands. Several countries have seen falls of 10 to 30 percent since their peaks, and prices in those countries are continuing to decline. However, prices in Belgium, Norway, and Sweden haven't yet declined.[79]

Italy and Switzerland both experienced a run-up in prices, but to less than double 1998 levels, and neither has yet seen prices fall.[80] Prices also rapidly grew in most eastern European countries, but

Figure 14.1
INFLATION-ADJUSTED BRITISH HOME PRICE INDEX, 1952–2008

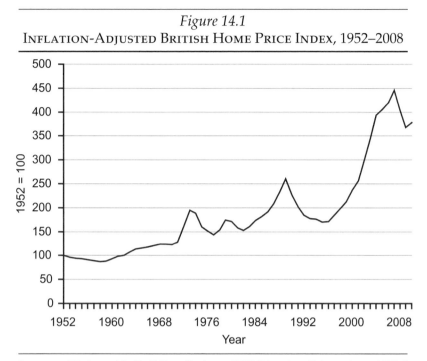

SOURCES: Nationwide Building Society, "UK Housing Prices since 1952," 2011, tinyurl.com/3dxqax; adjusted for inflation using UK GDP deflator from measuringworth.com/ukcompare.
NOTE: Subsequent to passage of the Town and Country Planning Act in 1947, Britain may have had a housing bubble around 1950, and did have bubbles that peaked in 1973, 1979, 1989, and 2007.

increases in some of them were due to housing being underpriced in the 1990s as a result of government giveaways of formerly public housing.[81] Prices in Austria were flat until 2005, but since then they have increased by more than 50 percent.[82]

Although many of these bubbles have not yet fully collapsed, many of these countries have had bubbles before. A Swedish bubble peaked in 1989.[83] The Netherlands had a bubble that peaked in 1978.[84] Denmark had bubbles in both 1979 and 1987. Outside Europe, Australia had four bubbles between 1974 and 1993, and New Zealand has a history of bubbles as well.[85]

Figure 14.2
EUROPEAN HOME PRICE INDEXES, 1998–2009

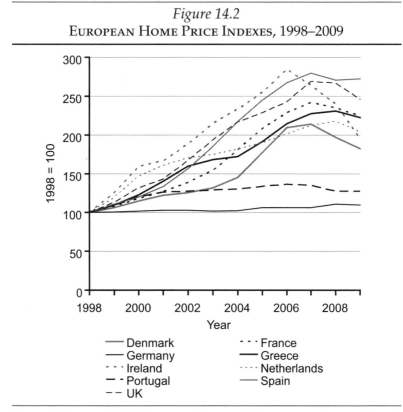

SOURCE: "Hypostat 2009," European Mortgage Federation, p. 79, tinyurl.com/ 6fh5gfd.
NOTE: Price indexes are not adjusted for inflation. Seven European countries with housing bubbles and two—Germany and Portugal—without. Complete data are not available for Austria and Italy, but Italy also had a bubble while Austria probably did not. Prices in Belgium, Norway, and Sweden all more than doubled in this time period but had not fallen as of 2009, the last year for which data are available.

The only major European nations that managed to avoid significant home price increases during the 2000s were Germany and Portugal. Analysts say that Portugal missed the bubble because of a sluggish economy and an abundance of rent-controlled multifamily housing.[86] However, other European countries have sluggish economies and still suffered bubbles. It seems more likely that Portugal's land-use regulation has been laxer than in other countries. A 2005 review of Portugal's planning found that it lagged behind other European countries.[87] A 2006 review of Europe's land-use planning processes also reported "much illegal activity in Portugal, designated as *clandestinos*. *Clandestinos* are basically housing activities either of low-income strata or of private developers wanting to avoid complicated legal procedures."[88]

Germany doubled production of new apartments after reunification by offering tax write-offs for construction, leading to a huge oversupply of multifamily housing. This oversupply, combined with the fact that Germany's population has been shrinking by 50,000 people a year since 2002, has taken pressure off the housing market.[89] Germany has even more rent-controlled housing than Portugal, leading renters to stay in their residences for much longer than renters in other countries.[90]

Most important, German homebuilders face few of the obstacles that commonly confront builders in Britain or the United States. The German constitution actually includes a "right-to-build" clause that allows anyone to build on his property as long as there is no explicit rule against it. Where Californian and English homebuilders might have to spend years getting permits even for uses that are permitted in a zone, German landowners and builders can immediately build anything that is permitted. Local governments also have an incentive to permit new housing as they receive grants from the federal government based on the number of inhabitants. As a result, when low interest rates stimulated demand in new housing, German builders could step up production, whereas British builders could not.[91]

As previously noted, Benard traces France's housing bubble directly to land-use restrictions, and other economists blame Italy's and Switzerland's high housing prices on such restrictions as well. Although it isn't precisely clear why Germany and Portugal did not experience rapid price inflation in the 2000s, the price increases in other countries can no doubt be traced to supply constraints as well.

Japan's property bubble, whose collapse in 1991 led to that nation's near-permanent recession since that time, can also be traced to land-use rules. In 1990, Japan's property prices had reached levels that were obviously unsustainable. At that time, property in Japan was supposed to be worth four times as much as all property in the entire United States, while the 842 acres in the Imperial Palace in Tokyo were supposed to be worth more than all of Canada. Housing prices became so expensive that homebuyers were forced to take out 100-year mortgages.[92]

Few actual land sales took place at these prices, but companies that owned land were able to finance their activities by borrowing against the value of that land. The government-owned Japanese National Railways was forced by politicians to invest in money-losing high-speed rail lines, "a primary purpose of which was the provision of election finance by grateful construction companies," says economist James Doherty.[93] The company financed these lines by borrowing ¥25 trillion (almost $400 billion in 2012 dollars), using its land as collateral.[94] By 1987, the company was unable to make interest payments on the debt, so the government sold it to private operators for a tiny fraction of the cost, hoping to make up the difference by selling the company's surplus land. That hope proved forlorn when the property bubble collapsed—which may have happened because of government plans to put so much land on the market at once—and the government has had to absorb the debt.[95]

Unlike California or other American states, Japan did not regulate its land using growth-management planning. But to preserve farmlands, it placed a 150 percent capital gains tax on short-term property sales, which effectively prevented those lands from being developed. "By discouraging the sale of land and creating an illiquid property market, the fiscal system actually stimulated land speculation," says financial historian Edward Chancellor.[96] That speculation greatly contributed to the bubbles that have plagued nations, states, and urban regions that have used some form of growth-management planning.

Unemployment

In the late 1990s, English economist Andrew Oswald noted that both homeownership and unemployment rates in European nations had significantly increased between 1960 and 1990. He argued that, because "selling a home and moving is expensive," homeowners who became unemployed often decided to remain unemployed rather than move to a new location where they could get a job.[97] Oswald estimated that increasing homeownership by 10 percentage points would increase unemployment by 2 percent. Subsequently, researchers in the United States used 1988 through 1991 data to find "some evidence" that homeownership impaired the ability of unemployed Americans to find work, but "the impact is only an eighth of that reported by Oswald."[98]

The Oswald effect can be tested for the United States by comparing homeownership data from recent censuses with unemployment data from the Bureau of Labor Statistics. Oswald would predict a strong correlation between unemployment rates and homeowner-ship rates in states and metropolitan areas, and that the correlation would be positive, that is, that higher unemployment would go with higher homeownership. Yet there is virtually no correlation between state homeownership and unemployment rates in the 1980 census ($r = 0.03$ where 1.0 is perfectly correlated and 0.0 is zero correlation). The correlation in 1990 is weak (0.11). Although the correlation in 2000 is stronger, it is also negative (-0.35), meaning higher homeownership correlates with lower unemployment, the opposite of Oswald's findings in Europe. The correlation in 2010 is also negative (-0.23). When compared for metropolitan areas in 2000 and 2010, there is virtually no correlation (0.01 in 2000; 0.04 in 2010).

This result suggests that whatever causes European unemploy-ment to increase with increases in homeownership does not apply in the United States. It is possible that even in Europe, increased home-ownership does not lead to increased unemployment, and instead some other factors in Europe cause both homeownership and unem-ployment to increase. Americans have historically been about twice as mobile as Europeans—that is, twice as likely to move to another region of the country.[99]

One possible factor is housing affordability. In 1960, few European nations other than Britain had passed strict growth-management plan-ning laws (and Britain had the second-highest unemployment of any European nation in Oswald's data set for that period), so housing remained affordable. By 1990, such laws were pervasive throughout Europe, and as a result homes had become far less affordable relative to incomes, meaning that the cost of selling a home in 1990 was far greater than the cost in 1960. In addition, the increased volatility of housing prices in growth-management areas would mean that, during recessions when more people are likely to be unemployed, more peo-ple are also likely to be reluctant to sell their homes because of major declines in home values.

If volatile housing prices are more responsible for unemployment than homeownership itself, then the Oswald effect would be lower in the United States, where housing in many states, including Arizona and Florida, has only recently become volatile. American mobility has declined since the 1960s, and one reason for the decline may be the drop in housing affordability in some states. Homeownership rates in California and Oregon have declined since 1960, largely because of the increased costs of housing in those states. Most other growth-management states have only seen housing become unaffordable in the last decade, and so homeownership rates have barely begun to adjust. Today, the correlation between unemployment and growth management appears stronger than the correlation between unemployment and homeownership: of the 15 states that have the strongest growth-management programs, 5 are among the 10 states with the highest unemployment rates in 2010.[100]

Throughout the developed world, land-use restrictions have made housing expensive and property prices prone to bubbles. This circumstance has generally depressed homeownership rates and in many countries has confined homeownership only to the wealthy and middle class. Whether that was the intended goal or an unintended consequence is less relevant than the fact that these exclusionary policies both actively deny homeownership opportunities to many people and make economies more vulnerable to economic shocks.

Homeownership is not just an American dream; it is a dream of people all over the world. Regardless of whether homeownership produces any social benefits, most people who intend to live in an area for four or five years or more would prefer to own their house. Government planners who stand in their way are doing considerable harm to their economies and to the people whom they supposedly serve.

15. The Future of the American Dream

Despite the recent collapse in housing prices, 70 percent of Americans still prefer to own their own homes.[1] Nearly half of all renters, as well as almost all homeowners, think they would be or are better off owning rather than renting their homes.[2] Still, many people deride the notion that "universal homeownership" is an appropriate or worthwhile goal.

Except in media hype, no one believes all households or families should own their own homes. Most college students and other people who expect to stay in a given location for only a short time will prefer renting over the costs and responsibilities of homeownership. What should be universal is the opportunity to own a home at a price affordable to just about any income level. Without even counting the formerly socialist countries that recently privatized much of their public housing, many nations with substantially lower per capita incomes than the United States' still have substantially higher homeownership rates, including Brazil, Greece, and the Philippines. This comparison suggests that the United States remains far short of this goal.

Fundamentals of Homeownership

In the absence of constraints on housing supply, median home prices will normally average about twice median family incomes. That was the typical price-to-income ratio throughout the United States in 1969, with the exception of Hawaii, which already had severe supply constraints in the 1960s. Wealthier families will tend to have larger and better homes, so wealthier communities will tend to have higher median housing prices. Median home prices will rise as incomes rise, but at least part of this increase is due to the construction of larger, more luxurious homes. This fact suggests that, in the absence of supply constraints, people cannot count on the value of their homes rising much faster than the rate of inflation. Homeownership, therefore, is not an investment so much as it is a savings bank, with the interest on mortgages effectively paying for occupancy while the principal is available in the future for retirement or loan equity or to pass along to younger generations.

Supply constraints are almost always the result of government policies. The one exception identified in this book is Hawaii before 1961, when a handful of landowners held oligopolistic control over most of the islands. Elsewhere—in Britain after 1947; much of Europe after the 1960s; Vancouver, British Columbia, California, and Oregon in the 1970s; New England in the 1980s; Florida and Washington in the 1990s; and Nevada and Arizona in the 2000s—government land-use restrictions and time-consuming permitting processes made it difficult for developers and homebuilders to respond to changes in demand for housing.

Given such supply constraints, a small change in demand can lead to large changes in home prices, thus leading to bubbles.

- California, Florida, and other growth-management states showed in the 2000s that bubbles take place when factors stimulating demand, such as lower interest rates or easier mortgage terms, combine with supply constraints, such as urban-growth boundaries or lengthy permitting processes.
- Texas and North Carolina, among many other states with relatively little land-use regulation, show that bubbles do not take place when those same demand-stimulating factors are applied to areas without supply constraints.
- Bubbles in the 1970s (in California, Oregon, and Hawaii) and 1980s (California and New England) show that bubbles take place only after supply constraints are introduced.
- Italy and other European nations where interest rates declined but otherwise mortgage lending remained strict show bubbles do occur where there are supply constraints but far fewer factors stimulating demand.

Interest rates and other demand factors change all the time. If the United States decides to live with growth-management planning, then the nation is going to experience serious problems with housing affordability, repeated housing bubbles, long periods in which millions of homeowners are *underwater*, and unemployment problems as employers flee to places with relative economic stability. The only way to prevent such problems is for states to repeal growth-management laws and regional and local governments to abandon growth-management plans.

Supply constraints have the curious effect of undermining government efforts to promote homeownership. Given that developers cannot easily respond to changes in demand, efforts to promote homeownership mostly increase housing prices, which in turn can actually reduce homeownership. Federal policies and programs, such as Federal Housing Administration insurance and the mortgage-interest deduction, may slightly increase homeownership in places with no supply constraints but may reduce it in places that have them. Since close to half of all homes in America are in areas with supply constraints, such government programs are practically a wash.

The high housing prices caused by government supply constraints also create problems of intergenerational equity. People who are selling their homes tend to be older and financially better off than first-time homebuyers. The windfall gains for home sellers that result from supply constraints translate into huge costs for homebuyers. Homeownership is put further and further out of the reach of young people in nations, states, and regions that restrict single-family home construction and, in effect, homeownership.

Numerous studies show that homeownership benefits the people living in those homes by providing better living conditions for the owners and their children. Homeownership may also benefit society as a whole by increasing community involvement, providing small-business start-ups with a source of equity, and giving homeowners a form of social insurance, thus reducing the need for government social spending. However, these social benefits are widely debated among economists and other social scientists. Given the economic success of countries with low levels of homeownership, such as Germany and Switzerland, the case for subsidizing homeownership is weak.

On the other hand, the case made by smart-growth advocates for discouraging single-family homeownership is weaker still. The supposed environmental benefits of putting more people in mixed-use developments are as illusory as the supposed financial benefits of packing people into higher densities to reduce infrastructure costs.

Although the specific motives of growth-management advocates may vary, both slow growth and smart growth are in effect a continuation of middle-class efforts to keep people with different cultures and attitudes out of their neighborhoods, cities, and regions. Slow-growth advocates say, "Only the wealthy can move to our city." Smart-growth advocates say, "Less-wealthy people can move into our city as long as they are willing to live in one of the high-density enclaves we have prepared for them."

No matter how their plans are prettified with terms like "sustainability" and "collaboration," the fact is that both slow growth and smart growth are anti-single-family homeownership. The effects of these plans on housing costs, the increased volatility of housing prices, and the resulting effects on the local and national economies have far greater consequences than any environmental benefits of these policies—which themselves are negligible.

The negative effects of growth management on housing affordability are far greater than the positive effects of federal housing programs. Although eliminating the mortgage-interest deduction and other federal homeownership programs might reduce homeownership rates by a small amount, at least in states without supply constraints, eliminating state and local growth-management programs is likely to more than offset this reduction.

Many federal housing programs are holdovers from the Great Depression that are no longer needed, if they ever were. Some government programs, such as Fannie Mae and Freddie Mac, did more harm than good during the recent financial crisis by encouraging banks and other lenders to take on overly risky loans, fueling the speculative housing bubble.

Reforming Housing and Land-Use Policies

This book has shown that the 2008 financial crisis was not caused by deregulation, low interest rates, or other federal actions alone, but by the conflict between federal efforts to stimulate homeownership and state and local efforts to discourage single-family housing. The inelastic housing supplies created by the state and local programs led to wild swings in housing prices in those states. The following 10-point plan would change both the federal efforts to promote homeownership and the state and local efforts to discourage it.

1. *Phase out the mortgage-interest deduction:* If the mortgage-interest deduction is meant to promote homeownership, it is poorly targeted. The deduction is largest for those who buy the most expensive homes and have the highest incomes, so it mostly goes to wealthy people who would buy homes anyway. About half of all American workers pay no income tax at all, which means the people who have the most difficult time affording housing cannot benefit from the deduction.

   A 2010 analysis by the congressional Joint Committee on Taxation found that 57 percent of all tax returns are filed by people whose total incomes are less than $50,000 a year, but these returns claim only 3 percent of the dollars deducted due to mortgage-interest. A 2011 analysis from the National Association of Home Builders compared adjusted gross incomes, rather than total incomes, and found that 27 percent of returns reported less than $50,000 in adjusted gross incomes and claimed only 10 percent of mortgage-interest dollars deducted.[3]

Those who do pay taxes have to itemize, rather than take the standard deduction, to make use of the mortgage-interest deduction. Thus, the interest and other itemizations would have to total more than $11,400 (the standard deduction for a married couple) for the interest to affect their taxes. In effect, the first $11,400 worth of interest and property taxes are not truly deductible, so a home costing less than about $200,000 (depending on local property taxes and the interest rate of the loan) has little effect on people's taxes. This lack of effect is why marginal homebuyers who buy more modestly priced homes get little benefit from the deduction.

To better target the mortgage-interest deduction, some have proposed limiting the deduction to only the first $500,000 of home value. But an arbitrary limit is unfair in a country where median home prices range from less than $80,000 in McAllen and Beaumont, Texas, to more than $800,000 in Santa Barbara, California.[4]

A better plan is to phase out the mortgage-interest deduction over 10 years and replace it with a revenue-neutral, across-the-board tax reduction. The deduction saves taxpayers about $100 billion per year, and total personal income tax revenues are about $1 trillion per year, so phasing out the deduction by 10 percent per year would be balanced by a tax reduction of about 1 percent per year. Replacing the regressive mortgage-interest deduction with a flat tax reduction would do more to help low- and middle-income homebuyers. An analysis by real-estate economists from the University of Wisconsin concluded that such a change would result in a net 3 percent *increase* in homeownership rates and as much as a 13 percent increase among lower-income households.[5]

2. *Privatize or Abolish Fannie and Freddie:* Congress originally created Fannie Mae to increase mortgage lending by creating a mortgage securities market. But a government-sponsored mortgage securities entity is unnecessary. American banks had already created mortgage-backed securities several decades

before Congress created Fannie Mae. Though such securities were originally limited to commercial mortgages, there is no doubt that banks would have expanded into private residential mortgages.

Opponents of privatization argue that Fannie Mae "worked beautifully until it was privatized" in 1968.[6] But it was never really privatized. Congress created Fannie as a government-owned corporation in 1937, but turned it into publicly held (i.e., private stockholder-owned) corporation in 1968, primarily to take it off the federal balance sheet so as to make the federal budget appear smaller than it really was. But Congress maintained a federal charter for Fannie and Freddie, allowing investors to believe that the government would bail out the company if its investments went sour—a belief that proved valid in 2008. What caused Fannie to fail in 2008 was the fact that this implicit federal backing allowed it (and Freddie Mac) to take on too much risk, partly in response to political pressure to make housing more affordable and partly because risky bonds provided short-term profits at little risk to the companies' stockholders and managers.

"Fannie Mae and Freddie Mac did little to make housing more affordable," conclude economists Edward Glaeser and Joseph Gyourko. "The prime beneficiaries of these institutions were their management and shareholders until just before their collapse, not the taxpayers or even middle-income homebuyers."[7]

In contrast to Fannie and Freddie, Congress completely privatized Sallie Mae, the student loan corporation, terminating its federal charter in 2004. Privatizing Fannie and Freddie would effectively turn them into investment banks or bank holding companies competing with Goldman Sachs, Morgan Stanley, Bank of America (which owns Merrill Lynch), and JPMorgan Chase (which took over Bear Stearns). Fannie and Freddie could also be simply eliminated by selling their assets to existing banks.

3. *Eliminate or privatize FHA insurance:* Congress created the Federal Housing Administration in 1934 to stabilize the banking industry and mortgage-lending market by providing federal insurance for home loans in the same way that the Federal Deposit Insurance Corporation insures bank deposits. Supporters claim that FHA insurance is a critical part of the nation's homeownership programs. However, of the more than 50 mil-

lion owner-occupied homes that have a mortgage of some kind, the FHA insures just 4.8 million, or less than 10 percent.[8]

4. *Repeal the mandatory investment ratings system:* In 1975, the Securities and Exchange Commission required that bonds and other investments be rated by one of the ratings agencies to be considered safe for banks to hold. This requirement had the perverse consequence of turning ratings from a buyers market, in which investors paid the ratings companies for the most accurate appraisals of a bond's risk, to a sellers market, in which banks creating securities paid the ratings companies that would give the security the safest rating. The misrating of hundreds of billions of dollars worth of mortgage-backed securities was partly if not mainly due to this change.

5. *Increase down-payment requirements in states with growth-management laws:* Lenders and ratings agencies should be aware that slow-growth and smart-growth plans increase the volatility of housing prices. To reduce the risk of this volatility, lenders should increase down-payment requirements for homes in states with growth-management laws. Ratings agencies should downgrade mortgage-backed securities that are based on mortgages in states with growth-management laws that do not have large down payments or excess equity in the loans. This change will greatly reduce defaults and may serve to limit future housing bubbles.

6. *Minimally regulate the mortgage securities market:* An active mortgage securities market is an important part of a home-owner economy, and those making efforts to regulate that market should take care that they do not do more harm than good.

University of Chicago economist Raghuram Rajan has suggested that regulators require banks to replace permanent capital reserves with "contingent capital," such as debt that would automatically convert to equities during a financial crisis. Thus, capital would be available when the bank needs it but would not limit the bank from making investments when the economy is booming. Rajan also suggested that, instead of trying to keep financial institutions from becoming "too big to fail," regulators should require such institutions to maintain a "shelf-bankruptcy plan" that would allow them to quickly resolve debts and other obligations in the event of a failure (as Lehman Brothers was able to do in the United States when it went bankrupt in September 2008).[9]

7. *Restore property rights:* The Fifth Amendment to the Constitution states, "nor shall private property be taken for public use, without just compensation." This clause was once interpreted to mean that the government cannot take private property for private use under any circumstances and that it can only take private property for public use if it pays just compensation.

Today, however, the Supreme Court interprets this amendment very differently. It now says the government can take private property for private use with compensation if it has written a land-use or economic development plan that finds that transferring the property to another private owner would produce greater social benefits (such as increasing the tax revenues to the city). The Court also says that the government can take, through regulation, most of the value of private property for public use without compensation so long as it leaves the owner with some of the value of the property. These reinterpretations of the Constitution have led to the sorts of abuses described in this book.

Restoring property rights would, in most places, make housing supplies more elastic by making a large supply of unregulated land available for developers and homebuyers. Property rights could be restored by the Supreme Court, by Congress, or by the states.

The Supreme Court has made most of its recent decisions regarding property rights, such as the *Kelo* decision, by 5-4 majorities. One swing vote by an existing or new Supreme Court justice is all that would be needed to return to the traditional interpretation of the Fifth Amendment. Such a turnabout would mean overturning several major precedents, including *Penn Central v. City of New York*, *Kelo v. City of New London*, and *Tahoe-Sierra Preservation Council Inc. v. Tahoe Regional Planning Agency*.

Congress could take some steps to discourage states from intruding on people's property rights. Economists Edward Glaeser and Joseph Gyourko propose that Congress "provide incentives that will induce overly restrictive (and only overly restrictive) communities to build" by giving "aid to localities in proportion to the amount of new construction they permit; if a supply-constrained community doubles the number of new units it builds, it doubles the amount of aid it receives."[10] Congress could take more direct action by passing a national property rights act specifying that no federal agency could violate the traditional interpretation of the property rights clause of the Constitution.

States that have passed laws requiring or authorizing cities and counties to write growth-management plans—including California, Connecticut, Georgia, Hawaii, Maine, Maryland, Minnesota, New Hampshire, New Jersey, Oregon, Rhode Island, Tennessee, Washington, Wisconsin, and Vermont—should repeal those laws. Florida has already repealed its growth-management mandate, though it still authorizes local governments to write growth-management plans.[11] Perhaps the best time to repeal such laws is during an economic downturn when housing prices are already low and politicians won't be blamed for making them low.

8. *Privatize zoning:* Zoning of existing developments became popular as an alternative to protective covenants because no one could conceive of an easy way to apply covenants to an existing neighborhood. Zoning created problems when it was applied to vacant lands, thereby limiting the ability of developers to meet the demand for housing and other land uses. Houston, however, has shown that covenants can be applied to existing neighborhoods through a petitioning process that requires a supermajority vote of the owners of property in the neighborhood.

To transition from a zoning system to a system of deed restrictions and covenants, states should allow anyone to petition to opt out of zoning, as has been proposed by University of Maryland public policy professor Robert Nelson.[12] Neighborhoods that opt out should be defined by regular boundaries so that they aren't gerrymandered to include property owners who may not support the covenants. As in Houston, creation of a property owners association and the writing of protective covenants should require the support of the owners of a supermajority of property.

9. *End local policies that make housing less affordable:* Other than public health requirements, including fire and sanitation-codes, state legislatures should forbid or discourage any local ordinance or regulation that increases housing prices. Such action would include impact fees, exclusionary zoning, inclusionary zoning, concurrency requirements, greenbelts, tradable development rights, and other practices that cities use that make housing unaffordable.

There are alternatives that can accomplish the goals of each of these practices without making housing less affordable. People who want to save energy by reducing per capita driving, for example, should recognize that it is far more cost-effective to improve the fuel economy of new cars than to reduce people's mobility. Similarly, making homes more energy efficient is more cost-effective than trying to change people's lifestyles. Moreover, the Department of Energy says single-family detached homes use 30 percent less energy per square foot than multifamily and 4 percent less than attached homes, so the only way cities can save energy through multifamily housing is by persuading people to live in much smaller housing units.[13]

10. *Privatize public housing:* Public housing represents only 3 percent of American homes, but even that amount is unnecessary if local barriers to affordable housing are removed. Although most public housing projects that remain today are not failures on the scale of Pruitt-Igoe, they have failed to meet the housers' original goal of providing decent housing for all low-income people. Instead, they exist mainly to assuage the consciences of liberals who feel guilty for supporting policies that drive up housing prices.

The Optimal Homeownership Rate

After peaking at 69 percent in 2004, homeownership in the United States declined to 65 percent in 2010. Estimating how homeownership rates would respond to these policy changes is difficult, as some changes would increase homeownership and others would reduce it. Comparison with Europe is difficult because Americans are historically more mobile, and people who expect to live in an area for only a short time are less likely to buy homes. Yet there are several reasons to think that implementing these proposals would lead American homeownership to rise from its current 65 percent to somewhere between 70 and 75 percent.

First, the Census Bureau reports that the 2010 homeownership rate for white non-Hispanic families was nearly 73 percent, and the rate was above 75 percent in 14 states, including Alabama, Mississippi, Louisiana, and South Carolina—states with median family incomes well below the national average but which also have few constraints on home construction.[14] Black homeownership rates in these four states are also well above the national average.[15]

A second reason to think that American rates could be higher is the high homeownership rates found in many western European countries, including Greece, Iceland, Ireland, Italy, Norway, and Spain, all of which have between 75 and 85 percent homeownership. Americans' geographic mobility and relatively high immigration rates will tend to depress homeownership rates here a bit below those in European countries, but they should still be over 70 percent.

Homeownership rates in 2010 are above 70 percent in 11 states (and were above 70 percent in 17 states in 2000). They include both states whose populations are mainly rural, such as Maine, Vermont, and West Virginia, and states whose populations are mainly urban, such as Delaware, Michigan, and Minnesota.

A final reason to think that homeownership rates can be significantly increased is that the rates in several states with growth-management laws, including California, Oregon, and Washington, have declined since those laws were put into effect. All three Pacific Coast states had higher homeownership rates in 1960 than they do today. California's 1960 homeownership rate was just 3 percentage points below the national average, while Oregon's and Washington's were 7 to 8 points above the national average. Today, California's is 9 points below and Oregon's and Washington's are 1 to 3 points below the national average.

The urban homeownership rate in California, the nation's most populous state with some of the most restrictive land-use laws, was just 54 percent in 2010. There is little reason, other than growth management, why it should not be as high as the 68 percent found in Michigan and Utah. If the national rate of urban homeownership could be increased to 68 percent, the full national rate (including rural homes) would be 71 percent. Whatever the rate ends up being, the United States in general and homeownership in particular would do very well by trading the negative consequences of growth management for any positive benefits provided by federal homeowner programs.

Preserving the Real American Dream

All American families should have the opportunity to own their own homes when they deem it appropriate and desirable. The main obstacle to this opportunity is not low incomes but government laws and regulations that make housing expensive. While rules that protect public safety, such as fire and sanitation codes, are appropriate, most of the other laws and rules are based largely on aesthetics and serve mainly to keep working-class and lower-middle-class families out of the housing market.

This book has argued that much of the government regulation that has made housing expensive was instigated by upper- and middle-class homeowners to preserve their status and privileges by shutting working-class families out of single-family neighborhoods. This argument is, of course, something of an oversimplification; people had many reasons to support first zoning and later the war on sprawl, and few of them consciously wanted to discriminate against families whose incomes were lower than their own. Yet they happily accepted the windfalls gained when the policies they supported drove up their home values, and many bragged about how the policies that excluded low-income people from their cities had increased "livability."

In fact, the benefits of such land-use regulation are minimal. America's abundant farms, forests, and open space are hardly threatened by urbanization that currently covers only about 3 percent of the countryside. Americans can save more energy and reduce air and water pollution at a far lower cost by making the homes and cars that people want to use cleaner and more efficient than by trying to force people to live in multifamily housing and take transit rather than drive.

If the benefits are negligible, the costs of government land-use regulation go far beyond reduced housing affordability. It made housing prices far more sensitive to changes in demand, attracting speculators to heavily regulated markets during economic upswings and putting more homeowners under water during downswings. High housing prices made it more difficult for homeowners to move when job opportunities arose in other regions and increased local unemployment rates because employers shunned high-cost regions. When nearly half the homes in America were subject to such regulation, the resulting housing bubble and subsequent crash—which would not have happened without government restrictions on housing supply—led to one of the worst worldwide recessions in history.

Owning a home is an important part of the American dream. To keep it from again becoming a nightmare, government should neither promote homeownership by subsidizing risky loans nor restrict homeownership in an absurd attempt to reduce whatever it is that people mean by "urban sprawl." If government gets out of the way, as described in the 10-point plan above, American homeownership rates are likely to rise along with whatever personal and social benefits result from such high rates. More important, people will be able to choose between owning and renting based on their own needs and personal finances and not on the whims of politicians and the arrogance of central planners. Such opportunity and freedom of choice are the real American dream.

Notes

Introduction

1. My colleagues include Sam Staley of the Reason Foundation, Ron Utt of the Heritage Foundation, and independent consultant Wendell Cox, among others.

2. Randal O'Toole, *The Best-Laid Plans: How Government Planning Harms Your Quality of Life, Your Pocketbook, and Your Future* (Washington, D. C.: Cato Institute, 2007), p. 130.

3. "Region 2040 Recommended Alternative Technical Appendix," Metro, Portland, OR, September 15, 1994, table 11.

4. Barbara Kiviat, "The Case against Homeownership," *Time*, September 6, 2010, tinyurl.com/22ppmus.

5. Ryan McMaken, "The Homeownership Rate Is Still Too High," Mises Economics Blog, October 7, 2011, tinyurl.com/633ywr7.

6. Eugene N. White, "The Poor Are Better Off Renting," *Wall Street Journal*, February 10, 2010, tinyurl.com/6yjgezy.

7. Richard Florida, "Homeownership Is Overrated," *Wall Street Journal*, June 7, 2010, tinyurl.com/6npfzoh.

8. Suze Orman, *The Money Class: Learn to Create Your New American Dream* (New York: Random House, 2011), pp. 4, 6.

9. James Truslow Adams, *The Epic of America* (New York: Little, Brown, 1931), p. 198.

10. Jim Cullen, *The American Dream: A Short History of an Idea That Shaped a Nation* (New York: Oxford University Press, 2003), pp. 3, 5.

Definitions and Data

1. *Historical Statistics of the United States: Colonial Times to 1970* (Washington: Census Bureau, 1975), Series A 57–72.

2. Dolores Hayden, *Redesigning the American Dream: The Future of Housing, Work, and Family Life* (New York: Norton, 1984), pp. 36–37.

3. Bennett M. Berger, *Working Class Suburb: A Study of Auto Workers in Suburbia* (Berkeley: University of California Press, 1960), p. 23.

4. Ibid., p. 94.

5. Peter Hellman, "Co-Op Board Hell," *New York Magazine*, November 6, 1995, pp. 26–31; and Jeff Jacoby, "The Spurned Millionaire's Vendetta," *Townhall.com*, August 11, 2011, tinyurl.com/44pud4t.

6. Stephan Thernstrom, *Poverty and Progress: Social Mobility in a Nineteenth-Century City* (Cambridge, MA: Harvard University Press, 1964), p. 110.

7. Stephan Thernstrom, *The Other Bostonians: Poverty and Progress in the American Metropolis, 1880–1970* (Cambridge, MA: Harvard University Press, 1973).

8. Incomes and homeownership rates from 2000 census factfinder.census.gov, Summary File 1, Table H4. Housing Tenure, and Summary File 3, Table P53. Median Household Income in 1999, for cities and urbanized areas.

9. "The Dark Side of the American Dream," Sierra Club, San Francisco, 1998, tinyurl.com/5rlk3vu.

10. All densities are from the 2000 census factfinder.census.gov, Summary File 1, Table P1. Total Population, for cities and urbanized areas, with geographic identifiers for land area.

11. 2000 census factfinder.census.com, Summary File 3, Table H32. Tenure by Units in Structure for United States.

12. 2010 American Community Survey, factfinder2.census.gov, table DP04; and Wendell Cox, "More Americans Move to Detached Homes," Newgeography.com, November 11, 2011, tinyurl.com/6g2tllw.

13. Arthur C. Nelson, "Leadership in a New Era," *Journal of the American Planning Association* 72, no. 4 (Autumn 2006): 393–407.

14. Matt Hudgins, "Residential Condo Glut to Worsen," *National Real Estate Investor*, March 27, 2008, tinyurl.com/5uyqxgr.

15. Lawrence H. Officer, "Annual Wages in the United States Unskilled Labor and Manufacturing Workers, 1774-Present," MeasuringWorth, 2011, tinyurl.com/3bs7sma.

Chapter 1

1. Hernando de Soto, *The Mystery of Capital: Why Capitalism Triumphs in the West and Fails Everywhere Else* (New York: Basic Books, 2000), p. 109.

2. Herbert Hoover, address to the White House Conference on Home Building and Home Ownership, Washington, D. C., December 2, 1931, tinyurl.com/65nbb5c.

3. Opening statement of Senator Elizabeth Dole, Hearing on the Administration's Proposed Fiscal Year 2004 Budget for the Department of Housing and Urban Development, March 4, 2003, tinyurl.com/5vppanz.

4. Donald R. Haurin, "The Private and Social Benefits of Homeownership," Habitat for Humanity Lecture, December 11, 2003, pp. 8–12, ti.org/haurinshow.pdf.

5. William M. Rohe, Shannon Van Zandt, and George McCarthy, "Social Benefits and Costs of Homeownership," in *Low-Income Homeowneship: Examining the Unexamined Goal*, eds. Nicolas P. Retsinas and Eric S. Belsky (Washington, D. C.: Brookings Institution, 2002), p. 395.

6. Dalton Conley and Brian Gifford, "Home Ownership, Social Insurance, and the Welfare State," *Sociological Forum* 21, no. 1 (March 2006): 55.

7. Eduardo Porter, "Buy a Home, and Drag Society Down," *New York Times*, November 13, 2005, tinyurl.com/67h5xrb.

8. See, for example, Daniel Aaronson, "A Note on the Benefits of Homeownership," Federal Reserve Bank of Chicago, June 1999, p. 12, tinyurl.com/3nu7hxp.

9. Dalton Conley, "A Room with a View or a Room of One's Own? Housing and Social Stratification," *Sociological Forum* 16, no. 2 (June 2001): 263.

10. Joseph M. Harkness and Sandra J. Newman, "Effects of Homeownership on Children: The Role of Neighborhood Characteristics and Family Income," *FRBNY Economic Policy Review*, June 2003, pp. 98–99.

11. Haurin, "The Private and Social Benefits of Homeownership," p. 13.

12. De Soto, *The Mystery of Capital*, p. 6.

13. Quoted in Elaine Tyler May, *Homeward Bound: American Families in the Cold War Era* (New York: Basic Books, 1988), p. 143.

14. John L. Gilderbloom and John P. Markham, "The Impact of Homeownership on Political Beliefs," *Social Forces* 73, no. 4 (June 1995): 1589.

15. Herman M. Schwartz and Leonard Seabrooke, "Varieties of Residential Capitalism in the International Political Economy: Old Welfare States and the New Politics of Housing," in *The Politics of Housing Booms and Busts*, eds. Herman M. Schwartz and Leonard Seabrooke (New York: Palgrave MacMillan, 2009), pp. 8–10.

16. "Allodial Title in Nevada," Nevada Corporate Planners, 2006, tinyurl.com/6z9br3v.

17. Robert K. Fleck and F. Andrew Hanssen, "The Origins of Democracy: A Model with Application to Ancient Greece," *Journal of Law and Economics* 49, no. 1 (April 2006): 115–46.

18. Victor Davis Hanson, *The Other Greeks: The Family Farm and the Agrarian Roots of Western Civilization* (New York: Simon & Schuster, 1995), p. 484.

19. C. Wren Hoskyns, "The Land Laws of England," in *System of Land Tenure in Various Countries*, ed. J. W. Probyn (London: Cassell, Petter, Galpin, 1881), pp. 175–76.

20. William Cronon, *Changes in the Land: Indians, Colonists, and the Ecology of New England* (New York: MacMillan, 1983), p. 71.

21. Michael J. Doucet and John C. Weaver, *Housing the North American City* (Kingston, ON: McGill-Queens University Press, 1991), pp. 185, 188.

22. Amelia Clewley Ford, "Colonial Precedents of Our National Land System as It Existed in 1800," *Bulletin of the University of Wisconsin*, no. 352, 1908, pp. 96, 97.

23. Lee J. Aston and Morton Owen Schapiro, "Inheritance Laws across Colonies: Causes and Consequences," *Journal of Economic History* 44, no. 2 (June 1984): 278.

24. Richard B. Morris, "Primogeniture and Entailed Estates in America," *Columbia Law Review* 27, no. 1 (January 1927): 25.

25. Ibid., p. 33.

26. Aston and Schapiro, "Inheritance Laws across Colonies," p. 279.

27. Ford, "Colonial Precedents of Our National Land System as It Existed in 1800," p. 114.

28. Bruce Wilkenfield, "The Social and Economic Structure of New York City, 1695–1795" (Ph.D. diss., Columbia University, 1973).

Chapter 2

1. Thomas Jefferson, October 28, 1785, letter to James Madison, in *The Papers of Thomas Jefferson*, eds. Julian P. Boyd et al. (Princeton, NJ: Princeton University Press, 1950), vol. 8, p. 682.

2. Thomas Jefferson, August 23, 1785, letter to John Jay, *The Papers of Thomas Jefferson*, vol. 8, p. 426

3. Thomas Jefferson, December 20, 1787, letter to James Madison, *The Papers of Thomas Jefferson*, vol. 12, p. 442.

4. Thomas Jefferson, "Notes on Virginia," in *The Complete Jefferson*, ed. Saul K. Padover (New York: Duell, Sloan and Pearch, 1943), p. 678.

5. Donald Worster, *The Wealth of Nature* (New York: Oxford University Press, 1993), p. 100.

6. A. Whitney Griswold, "The Agrarian Democracy of Thomas Jefferson," *American Political Science Review* 40, no. 4 (August 1946): 658.

7. Paul V. Murphy, *The Rebuke of History: The Southern Agrarians and American Conservative Thought* (Chapel Hill: University of North Carolina, 2000), p. 72.

8. "The First American Factories," *U.S. History Online Textbook*, 2011, www.ushistory.org/us/25d.asp.

9. Gwendolyn Wright, *Building the Dream: A Social History of Housing in America* (Cambridge, MA: MIT Press, 1988), p. 66.

10. Thomas Jefferson, 1809 letter to Thomas Leiper, quoted in *The Jefferson Cyclopedia*, ed. John P. Foley (New York: Funk & Wagnalls, 1900), p. 25.

11. Thomas Jefferson, January 9, 1816, letter to Benjamin Austin, in *Thomas Jefferson Writings*, ed. Merrill Peterson (New York: Library of America, 1984), pp. 1370–72.

12. Campbell Gibson, "Population of the 100 Largest Cities and Other Urban Places in the United States: 1790 to 1990," Working Paper no. 27, Population Division, Census Bureau, Washington, D. C., 1998, table 2, tinyurl.com/3h7gtkt.

13. Claire Priest, "Creating American Property Law: Alienability and Its Limits in American History," *Harvard Law Review* 120, no. 2 (December 2006): 440–41.

14. C. Ray Keim, "Primogeniture and Entail in Colonial Virginia," *The William and Mary Quarterly* 25, no. 4 (October 1968): 549.

15. Cyrus Adler, "Jefferson as a Man of Science," in *The Writings of Thomas Jefferson*, ed. Albert Ellery Bergh (Washington, D. C.: Jefferson Memorial Association, 1905), vol. 19, p. vii.

16. Keim, "Primogeniture and Entail in Colonial Virginia," p. 550.

17. Lee J. Alston and Morton Owen Schapiro, "Inheritance Laws across Colonies: Causes and Consequences," *Journal of Economic History* 44, no. 2 (June 1984): 278.

18. Alexis de Tocqueville, *Democracy in America* (New York: Edward Walker, 1847), pp. 396–97.

19. Michael J. Doucet and John C. Weaver, *Housing the North American City* (Kingston, ON: McGill-Queens University Press, 1991), p. 183.

20. Norman Wilkinson, *Land Policy and Speculation in Pennsylvania* (New York: Arno Press, 1958), p. 1.

21. Eric Ford, "New York's Anti-Rent War 1845–1846," *Contemporary Review*, June 2002, tinyurl.com/3g2r7ge.

22. John M. Murrin et al., *Liberty, Equality, Power: A History of the American People* (Boston: Thomson, 2008), p. 408.

23. Brent Tarter, "Disenfrachisement," *Encyclopedia Virginia*, 2011, tinyurl.com/42fggbl.

24. Lee Soltow, *Distribution of Wealth and Income in the United States in 1790* (Pittsburgh: University of Pittsburgh, 1989), p. 3.

25. "George Washington to His Brother Charles," *Mississippi Valley Historical Review* 1, no. 1 (June 1914): 100.

26. Reginald Horsman, "Thomas Jefferson and the Ordinance of 1784," *Illinois Historical Journal* 79, no. 2 (Summer 1986): 99.

27. Archer Butler Hulbert, *Washington and the West* (Cleveland, OH: Arthur H. Clark, 1911), pp. 147–58.

28. Amelia Clewley Ford, "Colonial Precedents of Our National Land System as It Existed in 1800," *Bulletin of the University of Wisconsin*, no. 352, 1908, pp. 102–3.

29. Ibid., pp. 87–88.

30. Payson Jackson Treat, *The National Land System: 1785–1820* (New York: E. B. Treat, 1910), p. 65.

31. Terry L. Anderson and Peter J. Hill, "The Race for Property Rights," *Journal of Law and Economics* 33, no. 1 (April 1990): 196.

32. Measuring Worth calculator, tinyurl.com/2t64sk.

33. *Historical Statistics of the United States: Colonial Times to 1970* (Washington, D.C.: Census Bureau, 1975), Series J20.

34. William E. Bartelt, "The Land Dealings of Spencer County, Indiana, Pioneer Thomas Lincoln," *Indiana Magazine of History* 87, no. 3 (September 1991): 212–13.

35. R. Gerald McMurtry, "The Lincoln Migration from Kentucky to Indiana," *Indiana Magazine of History* 33, no. 4 (December 1937): 387.

36. William E. Bartelt, " The Land Dealings of Spencer County, Indiana, Pioneer Thomas Lincoln," pp. 212–13, 218, 222–23.

37. Anderson and Hill, "The Race for Property Rights," p. 178.

38. Roy M. Robbins, "Preemption: A Frontier Triumph," *Mississippi Valley Historical Review* 18, no. 3 (December 1931): 334.

39. Ford, "Colonial Precedents of Our National Land System," pp. 134–36.

40. Eric Kades, "History and Interpretation of the Great Case of Johnson v. M'Intosh," *Law and History Review* 19, no. 1 (Spring 2001): 77, tinyurl.com/3atuulq.

41. Ford, "Colonial Precedents of Our National Land System," p. 133.

42. Peter W. Culp, Diane B. Conradi, and Cynthia C. Tuell, "Trust Lands in the American West: A Legal Overview and Policy Assessment," Lincoln Institute of Land Policy, Cambridge, MA, 2005, p. 10.

43. *Historical Statistics of the United States: Colonial Times to 1970* (Washington, D. C.: Census Bureau, 1975), Series J21–J25.

44. Culp, Conradi, and Tuell, "Trust Lands in the American West," p. 54.

45. Distributive Preemption Act (27 Cong. Ch. 16; 5 Stat. 453).

46. James M. Bergquist, "The Oregon Donation Act and National Land Policy," *Oregon Historical Quarterly* 58, no. 1 (March 1957): 30.

47. Lee Ann Potter and Wynell Schamel, "The Homestead Act of 1862," *Social Education* 6, no. 6 (October 1997): 359–64.

48. Hernando de Soto, *The Mystery of Capital: Why Capitalism Triumphs in the West and Fails Everywhere Else* (New York: Basic Books, 2000), p. 53.

49. Eric H. Monkkonen, *America Becomes Urban: The Development of U.S. Cities and Towns 1780–1980* (Berkeley: University of California Press, 1988), p. 295.

Chapter 3

1. Robert Owen, *A New View of Society* (New York: AMS Press, 1816, reprint), pp. 67–69.

2. Ivan Reid, *Social Class Differences in Britain: A Sourcebook* (London: Open Books, 1977), p. 34.

3. Louis James, "The View from Brick Lane: Contrasting Perspectives in Working-Class and Middle-Class Fiction of the Early Victorian Period," *Yearbook of English Studies* 11 (1981): 87–101.

4. *Historical Statistics of the United States: Colonial Times to 1970* (Washington, D. C.: Census Bureau, 1975), Series C 89–119.

5. Margaret Garb, *City of American Dreams: A History of Homeownership and Housing Reform in Chicago, 1871–1919* (Chicago: University of Chicago, 2005), p. 7.

6. J. C. Kennedy et al., "A Study of Chicago's Stockyards Community: III. Wages and Family Budgets in the Chicago Stock Yards District," University of Chicago, 1913, p. 64.

7. Garb, *City of American Dreams*, pp. 46–47.

8. Elaine Lewinnek, "Better than a Bank for a Poor Man? Home Financing Strategies in Early Chicago," *Journal of Urban History* 32, no. 2 (January 2006): 274.

9. William S. Worley, *J. C. Nichols and the Shaping of Kansas City: Innovation in Planned Residential Communities* (Columbia: University of Missouri Press, 1990), p. 1.

10. Louise Montgomery, "A Study of Chicago's Stockyards Community: II. An American Girl in the Stockyards District," University of Chicago, 1913, p. 4.

11. Garb, *City of American Dreams*, p. 122.

12. Ibid., p. 20.

13. Ibid., p. 18.

14. Kennedy et al., "III. Wages and Family Budgets in the Chicago Stock Yards District," pp. 11, 57.

15. Montgomery, "II. An American Girl in the Stockyards District," p. 4.

16. Garb, *City of American Dreams*, pp. 14–15.

17. Everett Chamberlin, *Chicago and Its Suburbs* (Chicago: Hungerford, 1878), p. 204.

18. Garb, *City of American Dreams*, p. 118.

19. Michael R. Haines, "Homeownership and Housing Demand in Late Nineteenth Century America: Evidence from State Labor Reports," working paper, Colgate University, Hamilton, NY, 2011, p. 1.

20. Garb, *City of American Dreams*, p. 17.

21. Donald L. Miller, *City of the Century: The Epic of Chicago and the Making of America* (New York: Simon & Schuster, 1996), p. 279.

22. For a photo of some relatively unmodified, low-cost Gross houses, see tinyurl.com/segrosshouses.

23. William S. Worley, *J. C. Nichols and the Shaping of Kansas City*, pp. 18–19.

24. Garb, *City of American Dreams*, p. 132.

25. *Contemporary American Biography: Biographical Sketches of Representative Men of the Day* (New York: Atlantic, 1895), pp. 248–49.

26. Martin Filler, "Review of Gwendolyn Wright, *Moralism and the Modern Home*," *Journal of the Society of Architectural Historians* 40, no. 3 (October 1981): 254.

27. *Contemporary American Biography*, pp. 248–49.

28. "Building and Loan Associations," Commissioner of Labor, Washington, D. C., 1894, p. 15.

29. Sam B. Warner Jr., *Streetcar Suburbs: The Process of Growth in Boston 1870–1900* (Cambridge, MA: Harvard University Press, 1962), p. 104.

30. David Mason, "Savings and Loan Industry (U.S.)," Economic History Association, Santa Clara, CA, 2003, tinyurl.com/2lftl7.

31. Martin V. Melosi, *The Sanitary City: Environmental Services in Urban America from Colonial Times to the Present* (Pittsburgh: University of Pittsburgh Press, 2008), pp. 20–21.

32. Charles E. Rosenberg, *The Cholera Years: The United States in 1832, 1849, and 1866* (Chicago: University of Chicago, 1987), p. 1.

33. Edwin Chadwick, *Report on the Sanitary Condition of the Labouring Classes of Great Britain* (London: Chadwick, 1842).

34. Joel A. Tarr et al., "Water and Wastes: A Retrospective Assessment of Wastewater Technology in the United States, 1800–1932," *Technology and Culture* 25, no. 2 (April 1984): 233.

35. John Snow, "Cholera, and the Water Supply in the South Districts of London," *British Medical Journal* 2, no. 42 (October 17, 1857): 864–65.

36. Tarr et al., "Water and Wastes," p. 237.

37. Garb, *City of American Dreams*, p. 97.

38. Ibid., p. 95.

39. Ibid., p. 152.

40. Ibid., p. 137.

41. Warner, *Streetcar Suburbs*, pp. 30–31.

42. Tarr et al., "Water and Wastes," p. 252.

43. Oliver Zunz, *The Changing Face of Inequality: Urbanization, Industrial Development, and Immigrants in Detroit, 1880–1920* (Chicago: University of Chicago Press, 1982), p. 32.

44. Patrick O'Brien, "Factory Size, Economies of Scale, and the Great Merger Wave of 1898–1902," *Journal of Economic History* 48, no. 3 (September 1988): 646.

45. *Historical Statistics of the United States: Millennial Edition, Volume 2* (New York: Cambridge University Press, 2006), tables Ba4703–Ba4705.

46. Jacob A. Riis, *How the Other Half Lives: Studies among the Tenements of New York* (New York: Scribner's, 1890).

47. For an aerial photo of dumbbell tenements, see tinyurl.com/bayard dumbbell.

48. Robert G. Barrows, "Beyond the Tenement: Patterns of American Urban Housing, 1870–1930," *Journal of Urban History* 9, no. 4 (August 1983): 396–97.

49. Lawrence Veiller, "Housing Needs," *Proceedings of the Academy of Political Science in the City of New York* 2, no. 4 (July 1912): 188.

50. *Fourth Annual Report, New York Association for Improving the Condition of the Poor* (New York: Leavitt, Trow, 1847), p. 23.

51. Edith Elmer Wood, "A Century of the Housing Problem," *Law and Contemporary Problems* 1, no. 2 (March 1934): 138.

52. Gwendolyn Wright, *Building the Dream: A Social History of Housing in America* (Cambridge, MA: MIT Press, 1988), p. 129.

53. Ibid., pp. 127, 129, 134.

54. Edward Everett Hale, *Workingmen's Homes: Essays and Stories on the Homes of Men Who Work in Large Towns* (Boston: James B. Osgood, 1875), pp. 55, 75.

55. "Shape of the City Causes Congestion," *New York Times*, January 7, 1912, tinyurl.com/3bokuqr.

56. Peter Geoffrey Hall, *Cities of Tomorrow: An Intellectual History of Urban Planning and Design in the Twentieth Century*, 3rd ed. (Cambridge, MA: Blackwell, 2002), p. 8.

57. For a photo of some typical two flats, see tinyurl.com/twoflats.

58. Garb, *City of American Dreams*, p. 42.

59. Thomas C. Hubka and Judith T. Kenny, "Examining the American Dream: Housing Standards and the Emergence of a National Housing Culture, 1900–1930," *Perspectives in Vernacular Architecture* 13, no. 1 (2006): 53.

60. Joseph C. Bigott, *From Cottage to Bungalow: Houses and the Working Class in Metropolitan Chicago, 1869–1929* (Chicago: University of Chicago Press, 2001), pp. 3–4.

61. Hubka and Kenny, "Examining the American Dream," pp. 55–57.

Chapter 4

1. Jeffrey M. Hornstein, *A Nation of Realtors: A Cultural History of the Twentieth-Century American Middle Class* (Durham, NC: Duke University Press, 2005), pp. 120–28.

2. Alyssa Katz, *Our Lot: How Real Estate Came to Own Us* (New York: Bloomsbury, 2009), p. 3.

3. *Fifteenth Census of the United States: 1930, Population—Volume 6. Families, United States Summary* (Washington, D. C.: Census Bureau, 1933), table 19.

4. *Fourteenth Census of the United States Taken in the Year 1920—Volume 2. Population: General Report and Analytical Tables* (Washington, D. C.: Census Bureau, 1922), p. 1302.

5. Marc A. Weiss, *The Rise of the Community Builder: The American Real Estate Industry and Urban Land Planning* (New York: Columbia University Press, 1987), p. 33.

6. Gwendolyn Wright, *Building the Dream: A Social History of Housing in America* (Cambridge, MA: MIT Press, 1988), p. 195.

7. Oliver Zunz, *The Changing Face of Inequality: Urbanization, Industrial Development, and Immigrants in Detroit, 1880–1920* (Chicago: University of Chicago Press, 1982), p. 38; and Margaret Garb, *City of American Dreams: A History of Homeownership and Housing Reform in Chicago, 1871–1919* (Chicago: University of Chicago, 2005), pp. 8–9.

8. Ulysses S. Grant, *Personal Memoirs of U. S. Grant* (New York: Webster, 1885).

9. Sam B. Warner Jr., *Streetcar Suburbs: The Process of Growth in Boston 1870–1900* (Cambridge, MA: Harvard University Press, 1962), pp. 60, 73–74.

10. Ibid., p. 55.

11. Ibid., pp. 55–57.

12. Ibid., p. 120.

13. Robert Bradley, *Oil, Gas, and Government: The U.S. Experience* (Lanham, MD: Rowman & Littlefield, 1996), vol. 2, p. 1370.

14. *Facts and Figures of the Automobile Industry* (New York: National Automobile Chamber of Commerce, 1927), p. 39.

15. William S. Worley, *J. C. Nichols and the Shaping of Kansas City: Innovation in Planned Residential Communities* (Columbia: University of Missouri Press, 1990), pp. 103–4.

16. Cynthia Mines, "Nichols' Folly," *Retail Traffic*, May 1, 1999, tinyurl.com/3l9cyyu.

17. Carolyn S. Loeb, *Entrepreneurial Vernacular: Developers' Subdivisions in the 1920s* (Baltimore: Johns Hopkins University Press, 2001), pp. 26, 32, 184.

18. Ibid., pp. 40–41.

19. Ibid., p. 28.

20. Ibid., pp. 28, 53–54.

21. Worley, J. C. *Nichols and the Shaping of Kansas City*, pp. 61, 68, 291.

22. Helen C. Monchow, *The Use of Deed Restrictions in Subdivision Development* (Chicago: Institute for Research in Land Economics and Public Utilities, 1928), p. 2.

23. John R. Stilgoe, *Borderland: Origins of the American Suburb, 1820–1939* (New Haven, CT: Yale University Press, 1988), p. 224.

24. Samuel Swift, "Llewellyn Park: The First American Suburban Community," *House & Garden*, June 1903, pp. 328–30.

25. Worley, J. C. *Nichols and the Shaping of Kansas City*, p. 24.

26. Ibid., pp. 43–44, 293.

27. Ibid., pp. 26–34.

28. Ibid., p. 127.

29. Ibid., pp. 128–29.

30. Ibid., pp. 133–34.

31. Ibid., p. 126.

32. Ibid., pp. 113–14.

33. Ibid., p. 24.

34. See, for example, Robert M. Fogelson, *Bourgeois Nightmares: Suburbia, 1870–1930* (New Haven, CT: Yale University Press, 2005), pp. 123–26.

35. *Yick Wo v. Hopkins*, 118 U.S. 356 (1886).

36. Christopher Silver, "The Racial Origins of Zoning in America," in *Urban Planning and the African-American Community: In the Shadows*, eds. June Manning Thomas and Marsha Ritzdorf (Thousand Oaks, CA: Sage Publications, 1997), pp. 23–25.

37. *Buchanan v. Warley*, 245 U.S. 60 (1917).

38. Monchow, *Use of Deed Restrictions in Subdivision*, pp. 47–54.

39. *Shelley v. Kraemer*, 334 U.S. 1 (1948).

40. *Hadacheck v. Sebastian*, 239 U.S. 394 (1915).

41. Ernest M. Fisher, "Economic Aspects of Zoning, Blighted Areas, and Rehabilitation Laws," *American Economic Review* 32, no. 1 (March 1942): 333–34.

42. Robert E. Alexander (interviewed by Marlene L. Laskey), *Architecture, Planning, and Social Responsibility* (Los Angeles: UCLA Oral History Program, 1989), pp. 163–64.

43. E. Kimbark MacColl, *The Growth of a City: Power and Politics in Portland, Oregon 1915 to 1950* (Portland, OR: Georgian Press, 1979), pp. 300–301.

44. Jerry Johnson, "Task 3 Working Paper: Residential Market Evaluation," 2040 Means Business Committee, Metro, Portland, OR, November 22, 1996.

45. Stephen Sussna, "Residential Densities or a Fool's Paradise," *Land Economics* 49, no. 1 (February 1973): 3.

46. Alexander, *Architecture, Planning, and Social Responsibility*, p. 168.

47. Alfred Balk, "Invitation to Bribery," *Harper's Magazine*, October 1966, p. 19.

48. Monchow, *Use of Deed Restrictions in Subdivision*, pp. 28–31.

49. Fogelson, *Bourgeois Nightmares*, p. 80.

50. Wright, *Building the Dream*, p. 213.

51. Frank Popper, *The Politics of Land-Use Reform* (Madison: University of Wisconsin Press, 1981), p. 54.

52. Daniel P. McMillen and John F. McDonald, "Land Values in a Newly Zoned City," *Review of Economics and Statistics* 84, no. 1 (February 2002): 62.

53. Helena Flam, "Democracy in Debt: Credit and Politics in Paterson, N.J., 1890–1930," *Journal of Social History* 18, no. 3 (Spring 1985): 449.

54. *Village of Euclid, Ohio v. Ambler Realty Co.*, 272 U.S. 365 (1926).

55. Kenneth Baar, "The National Movement to Halt the Spread of Multifamily Housing, 1890–1926," *Journal of the American Planning Association* 58, no. 1 (January 1992): 39.

56. Coleman Woodbury, "Apartment-House Increases and Attitudes toward Home Ownership," *Journal of Land & Public Utility Economics* 7, no. 3 (August 1931): 294.

57. Ibid., p. 325.

58. Coleman Woodbury, "Transit and the Trend of Multi-Family Housing," *Journal of Land & Public Utility Economics* 7, no. 1 (February 1931): 44.

59. Woodbury, "Apartment-House Increases," p. 315.

60. Coleman Woodbury, "Taxation and the Trend of Multi-Family Housing," *Journal of Land & Public Utility Economics* 7, no. 2 (May 1931): 198.

61. Coleman Woodbury, "II. The Trend of Multi-Family Housing in Cities in the United States," *Journal of Land & Public Utility Economics* 6, no. 4 (November 1930): 403–404.

62. Woodbury, "Apartment-House Increases," p. 315.

63. Gail Radford, "New Building and Investment Patterns in 1920s Chicago," *Social Science History* 16, no. 1 (Spring 1992): 14.

64. J. W. Brabner Smith, "The Financing of Large-Scale Rental Housing," *Law and Contemporary Problems* 5, no. 4 (Autumn 1938): 608.

65. Edward M. Bassett, "Zoning for Humanitarian Institutions," *Annals of the American Academy of Political & Social Science* 155, no. 2 (May 1931): 35–36.

66. Charles H. Cheney, "Architectural Control in Relation to Zoning," *Annals of the American Academy of Political & Social Science* 155, no. 2 (May 1931): 160.

67. Becky M. Nicolaides, *My Blue Heaven: Life and Politics in the Working-Class Suburbs of Los Angeles, 1920–1965* (Chicago: University of Chicago Press, 2002), pp. 13, 21, 33.

68. Stilgoe, *Borderland*, pp. 4–5.

69. Anthony Jackson, *A Place Called Home: The History of Low-Cost Housing in Manhattan* (Cambridge, MA: MIT Press, 1976), p. 157.

Chapter 5

1. Herbert Hoover, address to the White House Conference on Home Building and Home Ownership, Washington, D. C., December 2, 1931, tinyurl.com/3srazhm.

2. Ibid.

3. John Fahey, "Beating a Depression: The Portland Home Loan Bank," *Pacific Northwest Quarterly* 75, no. 1 (January 1984): 35.

4. Ibid., pp. 34–36.

5. Marc A. Weiss, "Marketing and Financing Home Ownership: Mortgage Lending and Public Policy in the United States, 1918–1989," *Business and Economic History* 18 (1989): 111–12.

6. C. Lowell Harriss, *History and Policies of the Home Owners' Loan Corporation* (Washington: National Bureau of Economic Research, 1951), p. 1.

7. Ibid., p. 24.

8. Ibid., pp. 1, 3, 75.

9. *Historical Statistics of the United States: Colonial Times to 1970* (Washington, D. C.: Census Bureau, 1975), Series N 301.

10. Heather A. Haveman, "The Winds of Change: The Progressive Movement and the Bureaucratization of Thrift," *American Sociological Review* 72, no. 1 (February 2007): 117; and Fahey, "Beating a Depression," p. 37.

11. Kenneth T. Jackson, "Federal Subsidy and the Suburban Dream: The First Quarter-Century of Government Intervention in the Housing Market," *Records of the Columbia Historical Society*, (Washington, D. C.: Columbia Historical Society, 1980), vol. 50, p. 422.

12. Catherine Bauer, *Modern Housing* (New York: Houghton Mifflin, 1934), pp. 3–62.

13. Joseph C. Bigott, *From Cottage to Bungalow: Houses and the Working Class in Metropolitan Chicago, 1869–1929* (Chicago: University of Chicago Press, 2001), p. 208.

14. Quoted in John P. Dean, "The Ghosts of Home Ownership," *Journal of Social Issues* 7, no. 1–2 (Spring 1951): 59.

15. Harry C. Bredemeier, *The Federal Public Housing Movement: A Case Study of Social Change* (New York: Arno Press, 1980), pp. 43–44, tinyurl.com/436hs8r.

16. Gail Radford, *Modern Housing for America: Policy Struggles in the New Deal Era* (Chicago: University of Chicago Press, 1996), p. 17.

17. Frederick Law Olmsted, "Lessons from Housing Developments of the United States Housing Corporation," *Monthly Labor Review* 8, no. 5 (May 1919): 27–38.

18. Richard Plunz, *A History of Housing in New York City* (New York: Columbia University Press, 1990), pp. 207, 210.

19. Dennis R. Judd and Todd Swanstrom, *City Politics: The Political Economy of Urban America* (White Plains, NY: Pearson Longman, 2005), pp. 120–21.

20. Calculated by dividing the value of new housing units by the number of housing starts from *Historical Statistics of the United States: Colonial Times to 1970* (Washington, D. C.: Census Bureau, 1975), Series N 4 and N 157.

21. Radford, *Modern Housing for America*, pp. 93, 100–1.

22. Bauer, *Modern Housing*, pp. 231–36.

23. Radford, *Modern Housing for America*, pp. 93, 101–2.

24. Gilbert Cam, "United States Government Activity in Low-Cost Housing, 1932–1938," *Journal of Political Economy* 47, no. 3 (June 1939): 365.

25. Ibid., p. 363.

26. Diane Ghirardo, *Building New Communities: New Deal America and Fascist Italy* (Princeton, NJ: Princeton University Press, 1989), p. 179.

27. Marion Clawson, "Resettlement Experience on Nine Selected Resettlement Projects," *Agricultural History* 52, no. 1 (January 1978): 18.

28. Ghirardo, *Building New Communities*, pp. 176–77.

29. Cam, "Government Activity in Low-Cost Housing," p. 372; and "A Brief History of Greendale," Greendale Historical Society, Greendale, WI, 2011, tinyurl.com/3nauh73.

30. "The Greenbelt Mystery," *Time Magazine*, May 10, 1954, tinyurl.com/ybxyees.

31. "Greenbelt," Housing, *Time Magazine*, September 13, 1937, tinyurl.com/3f7uewo.

32. Cam, "Government Activity in Low-Cost Housing," p. 372.

33. Clawson, "Resettlement Experience," pp. 2–3.

34. Ibid., pp. 17, 27, 60, 62.

35. Ghirardo, *Building New Communities*, p. 187.

36. "Greenbelt," Housing, *Time Magazine.*

37. Roger Biles, "New Towns for the Great Society: A Case Study in Politics and Planning," *Planning Perspectives* 13 (1998): 115.

38. Radford, *Modern Housing for America*, pp. 186–89.

39. Cam, "Government Activity in Low-Cost Housing," pp. 374–76.

40. Ruth G. Weintraub and Rosalind Tough, "Federal Housing and World War II," *Journal of Land & Public Utility Economics* 18, no. 2 (May 1942): 156.

41. Radford, *Modern Housing for America*, p. 190.

42. Ibid., p. 192.

43. Gwendolyn Wright, *Building the Dream: A Social History of Housing in America* (Cambridge, MA: MIT Press, 1988), pp. 228–29.

44. Weintraub and Tough, "Federal Housing and World War II," p. 158.

45. "Dayton's Socialist Suburb," *Daytonology*, March 11, 2008, tinyurl.com/3v3ahja.

46. "Two Scandals," Business, *Time Magazine*, November 30, 1942, tinyurl.com/ybffucz.

47. "Truman Committee Exposes Housing Mess," *Life Magazine*, November 30, 1942, p. 45.

48. Manly Maben, *Vanport* (Portland: Oregon Historical Society Press, 1987), pp. 22–31.

49. Trevor M. Kollman and Price V. Fishback, "The New Deal, Race, and Home Ownership in the 1920s and 1930s," *American Economic Review* 101, no. 3 (May 2011): 366–70.

Chapter 6

1. Lee Tire, "These Are Fundamental," *Fortune Magazine*, August 1944, p. 30.
2. *Census of Population: 1950—Volume 2. Characteristics of the Population; Part 1. United States Summary* (Washington, D. C.: Census Bureau, 1953), p. 22.
3. *2000 Census* (Washington, D. C.: Census Bureau, 2003), table P1 for urbanized areas with geographic identifiers.
4. Rémy Prud'homme and Chang-Woon Lee, "Size, Sprawl, Speed and the Efficiency of Cities," *Urban Studies* 36, no. 11 (October 1999): 1849–58.
5. Henry Ford and Samuel Crowther, *My Life and Work* (Garden City, NY: Garden City Publishing, 1922), p. 147.
6. *Earnings by Occupation and Education: 1970 Census of Population* (Washington, D. C.: Census Bureau, 1973), table 1.
7. Edward Glaeser, *The Triumph of the City: How Our Greatest Invention Makes Us Richer, Smarter, Greener, Healthier, and Happier* (New York: Penguin, 2011), p. 28.
8. *1970 Census of Housing—Volume 1. Housing Characteristics for States, Cities, and Counties, Part 1. United States Summary* (Washington, D. C.: Census Bureau, 1972), pp. 1–81, 1–88.
9. "Historical Census of Housing Tables: Homeownership," Census Bureau, Washington, D. C., 2004, tinyurl.com/2m5j5j.
10. "Gini Ratios of Families by Race and Hispanic Origin of Householder," Census Bureau, Washington, D. C., 2011, tinyurl.com/686l4fb.
11. Kevin Star, *Golden Dreams: California in an Age of Abundance, 1950–1963* (New York: Oxford University Press, 2009), pp. 10–11.
12. Cecilia Rasmussen, "He Turned a Dream into Reality: 'If You Build It, They Will Come,'" *Los Angeles Times*, December 16, 2001, tinyurl.com/3d7qn2p.
13. James Thomas Keane, *Fritz B. Burns and the Development of Los Angeles: The Biography of a Community Developer and Philanthropist* (Los Angeles: Historical Society of Southern California, 2001), p. 124.
14. Mark S. Foster, "Henry J. Kaiser and the Consumer/Suburban Culture: 1930–1950," *Western Historical Quarterly* 17, no. 2 (April 1986): 167–68, 178–80.
15. David Colker, "Building a 'Future' in 1948: A Riddle and a Single House Launched 'American Way of Life' in Panorama City," *Los Angeles Times*, September 4, 1999, tinyurl.com/3rdulp6.
16. Greg Hise, *Magnetic Los Angeles: Planning the Twentieth-Century Metropolis* (Baltimore: Johns Hopkins University Press, 1999), pp. 163–208.
17. Alexander Garvin, *The American City: What Works, What Doesn't* (New York: McGraw-Hill, 2002), p. 397.

18. Peter Geoffrey Hall, *Cities of Tomorrow: An Intellectual History of Urban Planning and Design in the Twentieth Century* (Cambridge, MA: Blackwell, 1988; updated to 1996), p. 296.

19. "100 Influences That Have Shaped the Buildings Market," *Buildings*, January 9, 2006, tinyurl.com/3ve6r2g.

20. "Ol' Swimmin' Hole Built-In Here," *Coshocton Tribune*, October 18, 1950, tinyurl.com/3dyqgu4; and Isadore Barmash, *The Self-Made Man: Success and Stress American Style* (Washington: Beard Books, 2003 reprint of 1969 book), p. 112.

21. "Houses for Sale," The Press, *Time Magazine*, September 9, 1957, tinyurl.com/4x6gsbs.

22. Herbert J. Gans, *The Levittowners: Ways of Life and Politics in a New Suburban Community* (New York: Pantheon, 1967), pp. 372–80.

23. Ibid., p. 406.

24. Clarence S. Stein, *Toward New Towns for America* (Cambridge, MA: MIT Press, 1957), p. 39; and Ann Forsyth, *Reforming Suburbia: The Planned Communities of Irvine, Columbia, and the Woodlands* (Berkeley: University of California Press, 2005), p. 30.

25. Forsyth, *Reforming Suburbia*, pp. 107–8, 116–17, 142–45.

26. "Reston, Virginia Master Plan," Simon Enterprises, New York, 1962, pp. 1–8.

27. Forsyth, *Reforming Suburbia*, pp. 53–59.

28. Helene V. Smookler, "Administration Hara-Kiri: Implementation of the Urban Growth and New Community Development Act," *Annals of the American Academy of Political & Social Science* 422 (November 1975): 132, 136.

29. Ibid., pp. 134–35.

30. "New Town Blues," Environment, *Time Magazine*, October 16, 1978, tinyurl.com/3n4t7j8.

31. Michael Pacione, *Urban Geography: A Global Perspective*, 2nd ed. (New York: Routledge, 2005), p. 199.

32. *United States vs. Cedar-Riverside Land Company*, 592 F.2d 470 (8th Cir. 1979), tinyurl.com/3dzuym6.

33. Raymond Gavins, "Soul City," in *Encyclopedia of North Carolina*, ed. William S. Powell (Chapel Hill: University of North Carolina Press, 2006), tinyurl.com/3u4fltt.

34. Sidney Plotkin, *Keep Out: The Struggle for Land Use Control* (Berkeley: University of California Press, 1987), pp. 130–31.

35. "Wellington Mews," Concert Properties, Vancouver, BC, accessed August 23, 2011.

36. William S. Worley, *J. C. Nichols and the Shaping of Kansas City: Innovation in Planned Residential Communities* (Columbia: University of Missouri Press, 1990), pp. xvii, 106–8.

37. "What You Need to Know about Municipal Utility Districts," J. B. Goodwin Realtors, Austin, TX, accessed August 23, 2011, tinyurl.com/43w4mek.

38. Jennifer Dawson, "Closing Credits Roll on Sugar Land Town Square," *Houston Business Journal*, November 18, 2008, tinyurl.com/3ekouog.

39. "Planned Communities in Fort Bend County as of November 2010," Fort Bend Economic Development Council, Sugar Land, TX, 2010, tinyurl.com/3kfkdsw.

40. Jonathon M. Seidl, "Idaho HOA Apologizes for Flag Controversy: 'It Was a Misunderstanding,'" *The Blaze*, November 15, 2010, tinyurl.com/26yn4av; and Valerie Wigglesworth, "HOA Foreclosed on Home of Frisco Soldier while He Was Serving in Iraq," *Dallas Morning News*, June 28, 2010, tinyurl.com/3pao23x.

41. "Industry Data: National Statistics," Community Associations Institute, Falls Church, VA, 2011, tinyurl.com/3lhdmxj.

42. "Texas Property Code Chapter 204: Creating a Property Owners' Association and Extending, Adding to, or Modifying Existing Restrictions," City of Houston, accessed September 30, 2011, tinyurl.com/3rhbyeu.

Chapter 7

1. "Sprawl: The Dark Side of the American Dream," Sierra Club, San Francisco, 1998, tinyurl.com/3o24bw7.

2. Wendell Cox, "Selected Current and Historic City Densities Compared to Sierra Club Classification," Demographia.com, 2001, tinyurl.com/3lbbsjm.

3. Robert Bruegmann, *Sprawl: A Compact History* (Chicago: University of Chicago Press, 2005), pp. 116, 251, n.9.

4. Le Corbusier, "A Noted Architect Dissects Our Cities," *New York Times*, January 3, 1932, tinyurl.com/3uk8khy.

5. Frank Lloyd Wright, *The Disappearing City* (New York: W. F. Payson, 1932), p. 20.

6. Ibid., p. 17.

7. Le Corbusier, *The Radiant City: Elements of a Doctrine of Urbanism to Be Used as the Basis of Our Machine-Age Civilization* (London: Faber and Faber, 1967), p. 128.

8. Frank Lloyd Wright, "'Broadacre City': An Architect's Vision," *New York Times Magazine*, March 20, 1932, tinyurl.com/3wrke3x.

9. Le Corbusier, *The Radiant City*, p. 128.

10. Katherine Don, "Frank Lloyd Wright's Utopian Dystopia," *Next American City*, April 8, 2010, tinyurl.com/2db6fqb.

11. The Netherlands has about 7 million households and more than 10.3 million acres of land. "Netherlands," *The World Factbook* (Washington: Central Intelligence Agency, 2011), tinyurl.com/2w6whd.

12. John Keats, *The Crack in the Picture Window* (New York: Houghton, 1956), p. xii.

13. Herbert Gans, *The Levittowners: Ways of Life and Politics in a New Suburban Community* (New York: Pantheon Books, 1967), p. 144.

14. Keats, *The Crack in the Picture Window*, p. xvii.

15. William Hollingsworth White, *The Organization Man* (New York: Simon & Schuster, 1956), p. 280.

16. Real Estate Research Corporation, *The Costs of Sprawl* (Washington: Council on Environmental Quality, 1973).

17. Helen Ladd, "Population Growth, Density and the Costs of Providing Public Services," *Urban Studies* 29, no. 2 (1992): 273–95.

18. Robert Burchell et al., *The Costs of Sprawl 2000* (Washington: National Academies Press, 2002), p. 13.

19. Wendell Cox and Joshua Utt, *The Costs of Sprawl Reconsidered: What the Data Really Show* (Washington: Heritage Foundation, 2004), p. 10.

20. Kenneth T. Jackson, "Federal Subsidy and the Suburban Dream: The First Quarter-Century of Government Intervention in the Housing Market," *Records of the Columbia Historical Society* (Washington, D. C.: Columbia Historical Society, 1980), vol. 50, p. 427.

21. David L. Ames and Linda Flint McClelland, "Historic Residential Suburbs: Guidelines for Evaluation and Documentation for the National Register of Historic Places," National Park Service, Washington, D. C., 2002, p. 30.

22. "Born of Controversy: The GI Bill of Rights," Department of Veterans Affairs, Washington, D. C., 2009, www.va.gov/opa/publications/celebrate/gi-bill.pdf.

23. Ames and McClelland, "Historic Residential Suburbs," p. 30.

24. Jackson, "Federal Subsidy and the Suburban Dream," p. 427.

25. Benjamin J. Klebaner, *American Commercial Banking: A History* (Boston: G. K. Hall, 1990), pp. 118–22.

26. Edwin S. Mills, "Truly Smart 'Smart Growth,'" *Illinois Real Estate Letter*, Summer 1999, p. 3 (emphasis in the original).

27. Christian A. L. Hilber and Tracy M. Turner, "The Mortgage Interest Deduction and Its Impact on the Homeownership Decision," Spatial Economics Research Center Discussion Paper no. 55, London School of Economics, 2010, p. 2.

28. "Fiscal Year 2012 Analytical Perspectives: Budget of the U.S. Government," Office of Management and Budget, Washington, D. C., 2011, p. 242.

29. "Estimates of Federal Tax Expenditures for Fiscal Years 2009–2013," Joint Committee on Taxation, Washington, D. C., 2011, pp. 28–45, tinyurl.com/5rhyaet.

30. Harvey S. Rosen and Kenneth T. Rosen, "Taxes and Homeownership: Evidence from Time Series," *Journal of Political Economy* 88, no. 1 (February 1980): 69–70.

31. Hilber and Turner, "The Mortgage Interest Deduction," p. 5.

32. Edward L. Glaeser and Jesse M. Shapiro, "The Benefits of the Home Mortgage Interest Deduction," *Tax Policy and the Economy* 17 (2003): 37, 39, 81.

33. Martin Gervais and Manish Pundey, "Who Cares about Mortgage Deductibility," *Canadian Public Policy* 34, no. 1 (March 2008): 1–2, 4.

34. Hilber and Turner, "The Mortgage Interest Deduction," pp. 21–22.

35. Henry Richmond, "From Sea to Shining Sea: Manifest Destiny and the National Land Use Dilemma," *Pace Law Review* 13, no. 2 (Spring 1993): 329.

36. Robert Bradley, *Oil, Gas, and Government: The U.S. Experience* (Lanham, MD: Rowman & Littlefield, 1996), vol. 2, p. 1370.

37. *Highway Statistics Summary to 1995* (Washington, D. C.: Federal Highway Administration, 1996), table HF-210; and annual issues of *Highway Statistics* since 1995, table HF-10.

38. *Highway Statistics Summary to 1995*, table HF-210.

39. Robert Putnam, *Bowling Alone: The Collapse and Revival of American Community* (New York: Simon & Schuster, 2000), p. 215.

40. Ibid., pp. 206–7, 408.

41. "Sprawl: The Dark Side of the American Dream."

42. Bruegmann, *Sprawl: A Compact History*, pp. 60, 69.

43. A. Q. Mowbry, *Road to Ruin* (Philadelphia: J. B. Lippincott, 1969), p. 229.

44. John Jerome, *The Death of the Automobile: The Fatal Effect of the Golden Era, 1955–1970* (New York: W. W. Norton, 1972); Kenneth R. Schneider, *Autokind vs. Mankind: An Analysis of Tyranny, A Proposal for Rebellion, A Plan for Reconstruction* (New York: W. W. Norton, 1971); and Richard Hébert, *Highways to Nowhere: The Politics of City Transportation* (Indianapolis, IN: Bobbs-Merrill, 1972), p. 188.

45. Melvin Webber, "The Marriage of Autos and Transit: How to Make Transit Popular Again," *Access* 5 (Fall 1994): 26–31.

46. Calculated by dividing passenger car and light truck vehicle-miles by total automobile expenditures. Vehicle-miles are from *Highway Statistics 2008* (Washington, D. C.: Federal Highway Administration, 2009), table VM-1; expenditures are from "National Income and Personal Accounts Tables," Bureau of Economic Analysis, Washington, D. C., 2011, table 2.5.5, "Personal Consumption Expenditures by Function," lines 54, "Motor Vehicles," and 57, "Motor Vehicle Operation."

47. Average urban auto occupancy of 1.6 is from A. Santos et al., "Summary of Travel Trends: 2009 National Household Travel Survey," Federal Highway Administration, Washington, D. C., 2011, p. 34; average intercity occupancy of 2.4 is from *California High-Speed Rail Final Program EIR/EIS* (Sacramento: California High-Speed Rail Authority, 2005), appendix 2-F, p. 2-F-1.

48. Total highway subsidies in 2008 were $37.6 billion calculated from line 32, "Other Taxes and Fees," plus lines 16 and 17, diversions of highway user fees for nonhighway purposes and mass transportation, from *Highway Statistics 2008*, table HF-10.

49. Calculated from "2011 Public Transportation Fact Book," American Public Transportation Association, Washington, D. C., 2011, appendix A, tables 2, 35, 38, and 42.

50. Stacy C. Davis, Susan W. Diegel, and Robert G. Boundy, *Transportation Energy Data Book: Edition 30* (Oak Ridge, TN: Department of Energy, 2011), pp. 2–15.

51. Bill Vlasic, "Carmakers Back Strict New Rules for Gas Mileage," *New York Times*, July 28, 2011, tinyurl.com/3f2mg8h.

52. Calculated assuming today's average auto gets 21 miles per gallon and new cars get 27; the auto fleet turns over every 18 years; improvements in new car energy efficiency follow a straight line to Obama's 2025 target; and no improvements are made after the target date.

53. "The Plain English Guide to the Clean Air Act: Cars, Trucks, Buses, and 'Nonroad' Equipment," Environmental Protection Agency, Washington, D. C., 2008, tinyurl.com/3eoosmx.

54. *National Air Quality and Emissions Trends Report, 2003* (Washington, D.C.: Environmental Protection Agency, 2003), appendix A.

55. "Early Estimate of Motor Vehicle Traffic Fatalities in 2010," National Highway Traffic Safety Administration, Washington, D. C., 2011, p. 1; *Highway Statistics 2008*, table FI-200.

56. Randal O'Toole, "Does Rail Transit Save Energy or Reduce Greenhouse Gas Emissions?" Cato Institute Policy Analysis no. 615, Washington, D. C., April 14, 2008.

57. "Making the Connections: A Summary of the LUTRAQ Project," 1000 Friends of Oregon, Portland, 1997, p. v.

58. Genevieve Giuliano, "The Weakening Transportation-Land Use Connection," *Access* 6 (Spring 1995): 7–8.

59. Susan Handy, "Smart Growth and the Transportation-Land Use Connection: What Does the Research Tell Us?" (paper presented at "New Urbanism and Smart Growth: A Research Symposium," University of Maryland, College Park, 2002), p. 16, tinyurl.com/3efr6lt.

60. Reid Ewing et al., "Relationship between Urban Sprawl and Physical Activity, Obesity, and Morbidity," *American Journal of Health Promotion* 18, no. 1 (September–October 2003): 47–57.

61. Smart Growth America, "Research Links Sprawl and Health," press release, August 28, 2003, tinyurl.com/2qudlc.

62. Jean Eid et al., *Fat City: Questioning the Relationship between Urban Sprawl and Obesity* (Toronto, ON: University of Toronto, 2006), p. 1.

63. Andrew J. Plantinga and Stephanie Bernell, "The Association between Urban Sprawl and Obesity: Is It a Two-Way Street?" *Journal of Regional Science* 47, no. 5 (December 2007): 857.

64. Eid et al., *Fat City*, p. 1.

65. Reid Ewing et al., *Growing Cooler: The Evidence on Urban Development and Climate Change* (Washington, D. C.: Urban Land Institute, 2008), p. 1.

66. *Reducing U.S. Greenhouse Gas Emissions: How Much at What Cost?* (Washington, D. C.: McKinsey, 2008), p. xiii.

67. Randal O'Toole, "The Myth of the Compact City: Why Compact Development Is Not the Way to Reduce Carbon Dioxide Emissions," Cato Institute Policy Analysis no. 653, November 18, 2009, p. 17.

68. Edward L. Glaeser and Matthew E. Kahn, "The Greenness of Cities: Carbon Dioxide Emissions and Urban Development," Working Paper

no. 14238, National Bureau of Economic Research, Washington, D. C., August 2008, p. 1.

69. Ibid., pp. 2, 41; and *Highway Statistics 2008*, table HM-72.

70. Glaeser and Kahn, "The Greenness of Cities,", pp. 17–18.

71. "State Electricity Profiles 2008," Energy Information Administration, Washington, D.C., March 2010, pp. 32, 284.

72. David Brownstone, "Key Relationships between the Built Environment and VMT," Transportation Research Board, Washington, D. C., 2008, p. 7, tinyurl.com/y9mro58.

73. Kara Kockelman et al., "GHG Emissions Control Options: Opportunities for Conservation," Transportation Research Board, Washington, D. C., 2008, pp. 57–58, tinyurl.com/yczl8oc.

74. *Driving and the Built Environment: The Effects of Compact Development on Motorized Travel, Energy Use, and Carbon Dioxide Emissions* (Washington, D. C.: National Research Council, 2009), p. 2.

75. *Moving Cooler: An Analysis of Transportation Strategies for Reducing Greenhouse Gas Emissions* (Washington, D. C.: Urban Land Institute, 2009), p. 12, says 28 percent of greenhouse gas emissions in the United States come from transportation. Some 57 percent of those emissions come from autos and light trucks—see Marilyn Brown, Frank Southworth, and Andrea Sarzynski, "Shrinking the Carbon Footprint of Metropolitan America," Brookings Institution, Washington, D. C., 2008, p. 8—and 67 percent of auto and light-truck travel takes place in urban areas—see *Highway Statistics 2007* (Washington, D. C.: Federal Highway Administration, 2008), table VM-1. Multiplying 28 percent by 57 percent by 67 percent is 10.7 percent.

76. John Modell, "Review of *Crabgrass Frontier*," *Journal of Social History* 20, no. 3 (Spring 1987): 605.

77. Joseph C. Bigott, *From Cottage to Bungalow: Houses and the Working Class in Metropolitan Chicago, 1869–1929* (Chicago: University of Chicago Press, 2001), p. 6.

78. James L. Wunsch, "The Suburban Cliche," *Journal of Social History* 28, no. 3 (Spring 1995): 647, 648.

79. See, for example, Jackson, "Federal Subsidy and the Suburban Dream," pp. 421–51.

80. Aaron Antonovsky, "Social Class, Life Expectancy and Overall Mortality," *Milbank Memorial Fund Quarterly* 45, no. 2, part 1 (April 1967): 36.

81. Leonard Beeghley, "Social Class and Political Participation: A Review and an Explanation," *Sociological Forum* 1, no. 3 (Summer 1986): 496.

82. Howard W. Kilbride, David L. Johnson, and Ann Pytkowicz Streissguth, "Social Class, Birth Order, and Newborn Experience," *Child Development* 48, no. 4 (December 1977): 1686.

83. C. Langenberg et al., "Central and Total Obesity in Middle-Aged Men and Women in Relation to Lifetime Socioeconomic Status: Evidence from a National Birth Cohort," *Journal of Epidemiology and Community Health* 57, no. 10 (October 2003): 816.

84. Ronald King, "Sex and Social Class Inequalities in Education: A Re-Examination," *British Journal of Sociology of Education* 8, no. 3 (1987): 287.

85. Martin S. Weinberg and Colin J. Williams, "Sexual Embourgeoisment? Social Class and Sexual Activity: 1938–1970," *American Sociological Review* 45, no. 1 (February 1980): 33.

86. Lisa A. Barnett and Michael Patrick Allen, "Social Class, Cultural Repertoires, and Popular Culture: The Case of Film," *Sociological Forum* 15, no. 1 (March 2000): 156.

87. Mary Nell Trautner, "Doing Gender, Doing Class: The Performance of Sexuality in Exotic Dance Clubs," *Gender and Society* 19, no. 6 (December 2005): 771–78.

88. Stacy J. Silveira, "The American Environmental Movement: Surviving through Diversity," *Boston College Environmental Law Review* 28 (2001): 502.

89. Bennett M. Berger, *Working Class Suburb: A Study of Auto Workers in Suburbia* (Berkeley: University of California Press, 1960), pp. 23–24.

90. Peter Geoffrey Hall, *Cities of Tomorrow: An Intellectual History of Urban Planning and Design in the Twentieth Century*, 3rd ed. (Cambridge, MA: Blackwell, 2002), p. 253.

Chapter 8

1. Housing Act of 1949, Public Law 81–171.

2. Eugene J. Meehan, *The Quality of Federal Policymaking: Programmed Failure in Public Housing* (Columbia: University of Missouri Press, 1979), p. 31.

3. Jane Jacobs, *The Death and Life of Great American Cities* (New York: Random House, 1961), pp. 150–51.

4. Alexander Garvin, *The American City: What Works, What Doesn't* (New York: McGraw-Hill, 2002), p. 175;

5. William J. Collins and Katharine L. Shester, "Slum Clearance and Urban Renewal in the United States, 1949–1974" (paper presented at Economic History Workshop, Cambridge, MA, October 2009), p. 3, tinyurl.com/32baovk.

6. Charlotte Allen, "A Wreck of a Plan," *Washington Post*, July 17, 2005, tinyurl.com/cl7rp.

7. *Berman v. Parker*, 348 U.S. 26 (1954).

8. Peter Geoffrey Hall, *Cities of Tomorrow: An Intellectual History of Urban Planning and Design in the Twentieth Century*, 3rd ed. (Cambridge, MA: Blackwell, 2002), p. 246.

9. Kenneth B. Clark, "A Conversation with James Baldwin," *Freedomways*, Summer 1963, pp. 361–68, reprinted in *Conversations with James Baldwin* (Jackson: University Press of Mississippi, 1989), p. 42.

10. Jacobs, *Death and Life of Great American Cities*, p. 13.

11. Hillel Italie, "Author Jacobs Sets City Standard," *Wilmington Morning Star*, November 24, 2000, tinyurl.com/cewz8jm.

12. Herbert J. Gans, "City Planning and Urban Realities: A Review of *The Death and Life of Great American Cities*," *Books in Review* (1961): 170–73.

13. Ibid.

14. Ibid.

15. Michael A. Rossetti and Barbara S. Eversole, *Journey to Work Trends in the United States and Its Major Metropolitan Areas, 1960–1990* (Washington, D. C.: Federal Highway Administration, 1993), p. 2–2.

16. William Tucker, "Building Codes, Housing Prices, and the Poor," in *Housing America: Building Out of a Crisis*, eds. Randall Holcombe and Benjamin Powell (Oakland, CA: Independent Institute, 2009), p. 66.

17. Collins and Shester, "Slum Clearance and Urban Renewal," p. 2.

18. "Large USA Urban Areas: 1950 to 2000," Demographia.com, http://demographia.com/db-uza2000.htm; and "Core Cities with 1950 Boundaries: Population Trends from 1950," Demographia.com, demographia.com/db-corecities1950.htm (compiled from census data by Wendell Cox, demographia.com).

19. Harlan Paul Douglass, *The Suburban Trend* (New York: Century Co., 1925), p. 18.

20. Robert Bruegmann, *Sprawl: A Compact History* (Chicago: University of Chicago Press, 2005), p. 43.

21. Alexander von Hoffman, "Why They Built Pruitt-Igoe," in *From Tenements to the Taylor Homes: In Search of an Urban Housing Policy in Twentieth-Century America*, ed. John F. Bauman (University Park: Pennsylvania State University Press, 2000).

22. Hall, *Cities of Tomorrow*, p. 256.

23. Oscar Newman, *Defensible Space: Crime Prevention through Urban Design* (New York: Collier, 1973).

24. Meehan, *The Quality of Federal Policymaking*, pp. 28, 197.

25. Hall, *Cities of Tomorrow*, pp. 258–59.

26. Ibid., p. 5.

27. Theodore Dalrymple, "The Architect as Totalitarian," *City Journal*, Autumn 2009, tinyurl.com/yhyfqyf.

28. Catherine Bauer, "The Social Front of Modern Architecture in the 1930s," *Journal of the Society of Architectural Historians* 24, no. 1 (March 1965): 50–52.

29. Debbie Cenziper and Jonathan Mummolo, "A Trail of Stalled or Abandoned HUD Projects," *Washington Post*, May 14, 2011, tinyurl.com/ 3b9vhbk.

30. Jane Jacobs, *Death and Life of Great American Cities*, p. 4.

31. Martin Anderson, *The Federal Bulldozer: A Critical Analysis of Urban Renewal, 1949–1962* (Cambridge, MA: MIT Press, 1964).

32. Jon C. Teaford, "Urban Renewal and Its Aftermath," *Housing Policy Debate* 11, no. 2 (2000): 448–50, tinyurl.com/2wfjrt9.

33. Amy R. Kaufman, "Tours Recapture Long-Lost Old South Portland," *Jewish Review*, 2006, tinyurl.com/3ehazsh (posted August 2009).

34. Barry Johnson, "The Histories of a City: Portland and the Halprin Plazas," *Oregonian*, December 14, 2009, tinyurl.com/3vr8x9t.

35. John T. Reuter, "Razed and Confused: Boise's Turbulent History of Urban Renewal," *Boise Weekly*, August 4, 2010, tinyurl.com/36qkfxd.

36. Teaford, "Urban Renewal and Its Aftermath," pp. 457–59.

37. Anderson, *The Federal Bulldozer*, p. 75.

38. D. Bradford Hunt, "What Went Wrong with Public Housing in Chicago? A History of the Robert Taylor Homes," *Journal of the Illinois State Historical Society* 94, no. 1 (Spring 2001): 96.

39. Howard Husock, *America's Trillion-Dollar Housing Mistake: The Failure of American Housing Policy* (Chicago: Ivan R. Dee, 2003), p. 14.

40. Bauer, "The Social Front of Modern Architecture in the 1930s," pp. 48, 52.

41. Dowell Myers and Seong Woo Lee, "Immigrant Trajectories into Homeownership: A Temporal Analysis of Residential Assimilation," *International Migration Review* 32, no. 3 (Autumn 1998): 593.

42. 2010 Census, tables H16B, H16H, and H16I, available at factfinder2.census.gov.

43. 2000 Census, tables H11 and H12, available at factfinder2.census.gov.

44. William J. Collins and Robert A. Margo, "Race and Home Ownership from the End of the Civil War to the Present," *American Economic Review* 101, no. 3 (May 2011): 355–57.

45. Eric H. Monkkonen, *America Becomes Urban: The Development of U.S. Cities and Towns 1780–1980* (Berkeley: University of California Press, 1988), p. 203.

46. John F. Kain, "What Should Housing Policies Be?" *Journal of Finance* 29, no. 2 (May 1974): 687–88.

47. Kristen B. Crossney and David W. Bartelt, "Residential Security, Risk, and Race: The Home Owners' Loan Corporation and Mortgage Access in Two Cities," *Urban Geography* 26, no. 8 (November 16, 2006): 707.

48. Beth J. Leif and Susan Goering, "The Implementation of the Federal Mandate for Fair Housing," in *Divided Neighborhoods: Changing Patterns of Racial Segregation*, ed. Gary A. Tobin (Thousand Oaks, CA: Sage Publications, 1987), pp. 227, 229.

49. Ronald Bayer, "Racism as Public Policy in America's Cities," in *Crossing Boundaries: The Exclusion and Inclusion of Minorities in Germany*, ed. Larry Eugene Jones (New York: Berghan Books, 2001), p. 72.

50. John Kimble, "Insuring Inequality: The Role of the Federal Housing Administration in the Urban Ghettoization of African Americans," *Law and Social Inquiry* 32, no. 2 (May 2007): 399.

51. Douglas S. Massey and Nancy A. Denton, *American Apartheid: Segregation and the Making of the Underclass* (Cambridge, MA: Harvard University Press, 1993), p. 99.

52. "Federal Compensation for Victims of the 'Homeownership for the Poor' Program," *Yale Law Journal* 84, no. 2 (December 1974): 295–99.

53. Scott J. South and Kyle D. Crowder, "Housing Discrimination and Residential Mobility: Impacts for Blacks and Whites," *Population Research and Policy Review* 17, no. 4 (August 1998): 369.

54. Christian A. L. Hilber and Yingchun Liu, "Explaining the Black-White Homeownership Gap: The Role of Own Wealth, Parental Externalities and

Locational Preferences," London School of Economics Research Papers in Environmental and Spatial Analysis no. 124, 2007, p. 25, tinyurl.com/6levlq8.

55. David M. P. Freund, *Colored Property: State Policy and White Racial Politics in Suburban America* (Chicago: University of Chicago Press, 2007), pp. 6–7.

Chapter 9

1. Dionne Peeples-Salah, "Rezoning for Transit Traps Downtown Homeowners," *Oregonian*, January 18, 1996, East Portland section, p. 1.

2. Ibid.

3. Gwendolyn Wright, *Building the Dream: A Social History of Housing in America* (Cambridge, MA: MIT Press, 1988), pp. 8–9.

4. James Fenimore Cooper, *Home as Found* (New York: D. Appleton, 1880 ed.), pp. 23–24 (emphasis in original).

5. Susan Fenimore Cooper, *Pages and Pictures from the Writings of James Fenimore Cooper, with Notes by Susan Fenimore Cooper* (New York: W. A. Townsend, 1861), p. 299.

6. J. F. Cooper, *Home as Found*, p. 271.

7. Eric Freyfogle, *The Land We Share: Private Property and the Common Good* (Washington, D. C.: Island Press, 2003), p. 271.

8. Eric J. Sundquist, "Incest and Imitation in Cooper's *Home as Found*," *Nineteenth-Century Fiction* 32, no. 3 (December, 1977): 268.

9. Fred Bosselman and David Callies, *The Quiet Revolution in Land Use Control* (Washington, D. C.: Council on Environmental Quality, 1971), p. 1.

10. Quoted in Geoffrey Sheilds and L. Sanford Spector, "Opening Up the Suburbs: Notes on a Movement for Social Change," *Yale Review of Law & Social Action* 2 (Summer 1972): 305.

11. Paul E. King, "Exclusionary Zoning and Open Housing: A Brief Judicial History," *Geographical Review* 68, no. 4 (October 1978): 462–64.

12. Adam Rome, *The Bulldozer in the Countryside: Suburban Sprawl and the Rise of American Environment* (New York: Cambridge University Press, 2001), p. 7.

13. John R. Nolon, "Golden and Its Emanations: The Surprising Origins of Smart Growth," Pace Law Faculty Publications, Paper no. 173, Pace Law School, White Plains, NY, 2003, pp. 18–19.

14. *Draft Petaluma General Plan 2025* (Petaluma, CA: City of Petaluma, 2004), p. 57.

15. Peter Pollack, "Controlling Sprawl in Boulder: Benefits and Pitfalls," *Proceedings of the 1998 National Planning Conference* (Chicago: American Institute of Certified Planners, 1999), tinyurl.com/7q2rglf.

16. Julienne Marshall, "Whatever Happened to Ramapo?" *Planning*, December 2003, p. 7.

17. Bernard J. Frieden, "The Exclusionary Effect of Growth Controls," *Annals of the American Academy of Political and Social Science* 465 (January 1983): 123.

18. "Open Space and Mountain Parks Real Estate Acquisition Program," City of Boulder, CO, 2011, tinyurl.com/3fw4ku3.

19. "Economic Trends: Employees, Wages and Unemployment," Boulder Valley Comprehensive Plan, City of Boulder, CO, 2011, tinyurl.com/3qncbsx.

20. Stephan Schmidt and Kurt Paulsen, "Is Open-Space Preservation a Form of Exclusionary Zoning?" *Urban Affairs Review* 45, no. 1 (September 2009): 92.

21. Edward L. Glaeser, "Do Regional Economies Need Regional Coordination?" Harvard Institute of Economic Research Discussion Paper no. 2131, 2007, p. 1.

22. Nolon, "Golden and Its Emanations," pp. 66–69.

23. John W. Frece, "Lessons from Maryland's Smart Growth Initiative," *Vermont Journal of Environmental Law* 6 (2004–2005), tinyurl.com/8sj28.

24. Sam B. Warner Jr., *Streetcar Suburbs: The Process of Growth in Boston 1870–1900* (Cambridge, MA: Harvard University Press, 1962), p. 163.

25. 2000 Census, tables P77 and H76.

26. American Community Survey, Census Bureau, Washington, D. C., tables B19113 and B25077 for years 2004–2009; tables P101 and H074 for years 2001–2003.

27. "Income Limits," Department of Housing and Urban Development, 2011, tinyurl.com/3os8n7h.

28. "House Price Indexes," Federal Housing Finance Agency, 2011, tinyurl.com/3ch7oue.

29. Bosselman and Callies, *The Quiet Revolution*, p. 7.

30. George Cooper and Gavan Daws, *Land and Power in Hawaii* (Honolulu: University of Hawaii Press, 1990), p. 87.

31. *1960 Census of Housing—Volume 1. States and Small Areas, Part 1. United States Summary* (Washington, D. C.: Census Bureau, 1963), table 20.

32. Sumner La Croix, "Economic History of Hawai'i," *EH.Net Encyclopedia*, 2010, tinyurl.com/3qhxxhk; and Michael N. Marcus, "1527?: First Pineapples in Hawaii," *For the First Time (or the Last Time)*, a blog by Michael Marcus, August 15, 2007, tinyurl.com/3qqrkzr.

33. Cooper and Daws, *Land and Power in Hawaii*, pp. 39, 45–46.

34. Helen Altonn, "Growth of His Project Might Surprise Kaiser," *Honolulu Star-Bulletin*, September 28, 2003, tinyurl.com/7er67xj.

35. "Hawaii Kai Demographics," Zillow, 2011, tinyurl.com/7v33lno.

36. David L. Callies, *Regulating Paradise: Land Use Controls in Hawaii*, 2nd ed. (Honolulu: University of Hawaii Press, 2010), pp. 1, 4, 5.

37. For example, Jerry Anthony lists Florida, Hawaii, Oregon, and Vermont as "pioneers" that passed growth-management laws before 1986. "Do State Growth Management Regulations Reduce Sprawl?" *Urban Affairs Review* 39, no. 3 (January 2004): 378.

38. *Census of the Population 1950—Volume 2. Characteristics of the Population* (Washington, D. C.: Census Bureau, 1953), table 24.

39. Paul Rogers, "Hamann: San Jose's Growth Guru," SiliconValley.com, February 28, 2002, tinyurl.com/2yqyrh.

40. Sharon Simonson, "Influential Board Showing Its Mettle in Coyote Valley Annexation," *San Jose Business Journal*, June 9, 2006, tinyurl.com/3xu5g4.

41. *Bozung et al. vs. Ventura LAFCo*, cited in *25-Year Activity Survey 1963–1988* (Sacramento: California Association of Local Agency Formation Commissions, 1989), p. 52, tinyurl.com/34kgzd.

42. *1994 General Plan* (San Jose, CA: City of San Jose, 1994), p. 163.

43. Santa Clara Valley Audubon Society, "Former South Bay Public Officials Criticize Cisco's Expansion Plan; Unite with Environmentalists in Call for Major Revisions," press release, 2001.

44. "Coyote Valley Planning Effort Is Underway," *Coyote Valley Vision*, May 2004, tinyurl.com/2kb7e4.

45. Sharon Simonson, "Sierra Club Will Seek $100 Million Mitigation," *San Jose Business Journal*, December 30, 2005, tinyurl.com/38czvz.

46. Sharon Simonson, "Developers Drop Coyote Valley Housing Plans," *San Jose Business Journal*, March 18, 2008, tinyurl.com/44dw6ss.

47. Joseph Perkins, keynote speech before the Preserving the American Dream conference, San Jose, CA, November 11, 2007.

48. John Ritter, "San Francisco Hopes to Reverse Black Flight," *USA Today*, August 28, 2007, tinyurl.com/2qmync.

49. James Temple, "Exodus of S.F.'s Middle Class," *San Francisco Chronicle*, June 22, 2008, tinyurl.com/3b6j7hk.

50. "Land-Use Ballot Measure Results for November 2000," *California Planning and Development Report*, December 1, 2000, tinyurl.com/43uzseq.

51. Tom Means, Edward Stringham, and Edward Lopez, "Below-Market Housing Mandates as Takings: Measuring the Impact," policy report, Independent Institute, Oakland, CA, November 2007, p. 1, tinyurl.com/ctzrgnj.

52. "Zoning Acres by County—1986," Department of Land Conservation and Development, Salem, OR, 1986, tinyurl.com/ctzrgnj.

53. "Using Income Criteria to Protect Commercial Farmland in the State of Oregon," Oregon Department of Land Conservation and Development, Salem, 1998, p. 2, tinyurl.com/3bv2ge6.

54. R. Gregory Nokes, "Backers Pitch Zero Option to Metro," *Oregonian*, November 30, 1995, p. C2.

55. Eric Mortenson, "Land Plan: Anger on West Side, Amity East," *Oregonian*, September 20, 2009, Local News, p. 1.

56. "Region 2040 Recommended Alternative Technical Appendix," Metro, Portland, OR, September 15, 1994, table 11.

57. Gordon Oliver, "Once a Solution, Row Houses Fall out of City Favor," *Oregonian*, August 11, 1999, p. C2.

58. Dana Tims, "Road to Bigger, Better Damascus Leads to Dead End," *Oregonian*, January 16, 2009, tinyurl.com/ahwwfa.

59. R. Gregory Nokes, "Portland Housing Ranks as 2nd Least Affordable in U.S.," *Oregonian*, July 19, 1997, p. A1.

60. "Statewide Planning and Growth Management Programs in the United States," New Jersey Office of State Planning, Trenton, 1997, pp. 64–65.

61. Ibid., pp. 32, 58.

62. Ibid., pp. 12, 40.

63. Amy Dain, "Housing and Land Use Policy in Massachusetts," Pioneer Institute, Boston, 2007, pp. 8–10.

64. Edward L. Glaeser, Jenny Schuetz, and Bryce Ward, "Regulation and the Rise of Housing Prices in Greater Boston," Policy Brief no. 2006-1, Rappaport Institute, Boston, 2006, pp. 1–4.

65. "Statewide Planning and Growth Management Programs," pp. 15–17.

66. Zac Anderson, "Growth Rules Rollback Goes to Scott," *Miami Herald-Tribune*, May 6, 2011, tinyurl.com/3rvlfjb.

67. Edward L. Glaeser, Joseph Gyourko, and Raven Saks, "Why Is Manhattan So Expensive? Regulation and Rise in Housing Prices," *Journal of Law and Economics* 48, no. 2 (October 2005): 352, tinyurl.com/6hjq9qo.

68. Roderick J. Hills Jr. and David Schleicher, "Balancing the 'Zoning Budget,'" *Regulation* 34, no. 3 (Fall 2001): 24, tinyurl.com/5rf3zz9.

69. "Statewide Planning and Growth Management Programs," pp. 69–70.

70. Kit Oldman, "County Council Unanimously Approves New King County Comprehensive Plan on April 8, 1985," HistoryLink.org, 2006, tinyurl.com/3zm9fw8.

71. "Statewide Planning and Growth Management Programs," pp. 35–36.

72. "Federal Land Ownership in Nevada Counties," Nevada State Library, 2000, tinyurl.com/3r4cxhc.

73. Doug French, "Feds Drive Up Nevada Home Prices," Nevada Policy Research Institute, Las Vegas, August 12, 2002, tinyurl.com/43ps2qj.

74. Southern Nevada Public Land Management Act, Public Law 105-263, Section 2(b).

75. "Winning Bidder Reports," Bureau of Land Management, Las Vegas, NV, 2011, tinyurl.com/3hw9rmt.

76. French, "Feds Drive Up Nevada Home Prices"; and "Winning Bidder Reports."

77. John Ritter, "Las Vegas Closing In on Full House," *USA Today*, November 13, 2006, tinyurl.com/y9maeo.

78. "Annual Report 2002–2003," Arizona State Land Department, Phoenix, 2003, p. 1, tinyurl.com/3rol2ld.

79. "Annual Report 2001–2002," Arizona State Land Department, Phoenix, 2003, p. 16.

80. "Annual Report 2005–2006," Arizona State Land Department, Phoenix, 2006.

81. "Annual Report 2009–2010," Arizona State Land Department, Phoenix, 2011, p. 7, tinyurl.com/3o5dx5t.

82. "Statewide Planning and Growth Management Programs," pp. 10–11, 20.

83. James A. Thorson, "An Examination of the Monopoly Zoning Hypothesis," *Land Economics* 72, no. 1 (February 1996): 43.

84. Herbert J. Gans, *The Urban Villagers: Group and Class in the Life of Italian Americans*, updated ed. (New York: Free Press, 1982), p. 300.

85. Matthew E. Kahn, "Do Liberal Cities Limit New Housing Development? Evidence from California," *Journal of Urban Economics* 69 (2011): 227.

Chapter 10

1. "2008 TIF State-by-State Report," Council of Development Finance Agencies, Washington, 2008. This report errs in claiming that Tennessee authorized TIF in 1945. In fact, Tennessee's law was passed in 1978. See Rose Naccarato, "Tax Increment Financing: Opportunities and Concerns," Tennessee Advisory Commission on Intergovernmental Relations, Nashville, March 2007, p. 4.

2. Alyssa Talanker and Kate Davis, "Straying from Good Intentions: How States are Weakening Enterprise Zone and Tax Increment Financing Programs," Good Jobs First, Washington, D. C., 2003, p. 1, tinyurl.com/37nq9xy.

3. Greg LeRoy and Sara Hinkley, "No More Secret Candy Story: A Grassroots Guide to Investigating Development Subsidies," Good Jobs First, Washington, D. C., 2002, p. 77.

4. Jane Ford-Stewart, "Homeowners Oppose 'Blighted' Designation," *MuskegoNow*, June 29, 2010, tinyurl.com/2dlcfcq.

5. "State and Local Tax Burden Analysis, FY 2008," Idaho State Tax Commission, Boise, 2009, p. 13.

6. "2008 TIF State-by-State Report."

7. Ibid.

8. Ibid. New Mexico's gross receipts tax is counted as a sales tax.

9. James Bovard, "Political Plundering of Property Owners," Future of Freedom Foundation, Fairfax, VA, 2002, tinyurl.com/235ao; and Matthew Waite, "'Blighted' Isn't All Bad, City Says," *St. Petersburg Times*, January 10, 2002, tinyurl.com/2dn9ug8.

10. "Englewood Urban Renewal Office Defaults on June Bond," *Rocky Mountain News*, June 13, 1991; and John Rebchook, "King Soopers Aims to Demolish Trolley Square," *Rocky Mountain News*, March 4, 1995.

11. Monte Whaley, "Growth Fanning Fire District Needs," *Denver Post*, September 9, 2006.

12. David Swenson and Liesl Eathington, "Do Tax Increment Finance Districts in Iowa Spur Regional Economic and Demographic Growth?" economics working paper, Iowa State University, Ames, 2002, p. 1, tinyurl.com/3463tow.

13. Richard Dye and David Merriman, "The Effects of Tax Increment Financing on Economic Development," *Journal of Urban Economics* 47, no. 2 (March 2000): 306.

14. Richard Dye and David Merriman, "Tax Increment Financing: A Tool for Local Economic Development," *Land Lines* 18, no. 2 (January 2006): 1, tinyurl.com/29uvwaj.

15. Martin Anderson, *The Federal Bulldozer* (New York: McGraw-Hill, 1964), 161–172.

16. *Kelo v. City of New London*, 545 U.S. 469 (2005).

17. Ibid., concurrence.

18. Katie Nelson, "Conn. Land Taken from Homeowners Still Undeveloped," Associated Press, September 25, 2009, tinyurl.com/824dfsq.

19. See, for example, Arthur C. Nelson, "Building the New Damascus" (paper presented at "Building the New Damascus: A Smart Growth Conference for Realtors, Community Leaders, and Citizens," Damascus, OR, May 7, 2009, p. 12, tinyurl.com/3k7upk2.

20. Arthur C. Nelson, "Leadership in a New Era," *Journal of the American Planning Association* 72, no. 4 (2006): 397.

21. Ibid.

22. Dowell Myers and Elizabeth Gearin, "Current Preferences and Future Demand for Denser Residential Environments," *Housing Policy Debate* 12, no. 4 (2001): 635–36.

23. Ibid., p. 638.

24. Ibid., p. 642.

25. Ibid., p. 638.

26. Emil Malizia, "Comment on 'Leadership in a New Era,'" *Journal of the American Planning Association* 72, no. 4 (2006): 407.

27. Arthur C. Nelson, "Building the New Damascus," pp. 17–19.

28. Adam Ducker and Bob Gardner, "Anticipating the Upscale Empty-Nester Condo Market Recovery," *The Advisory*, August, 2011, p. 1, tinyurl.com/3r4u9qg.

29. Joe Cortright, "Walking the Walk: How Walkability Raises Home Values in U.S. Cities," CEOs for Cities, Chicago, 2009, pp. 2–3.

30. Philip M. Hurvitz et al., "Proximity to Food Stores May Not Predict Use," *FASEB Journal* 24, no. 4 (April 2010): 331.

31. Quotes from the October 23, 1996, city council meeting are taken from a videotape of that meeting made by the City of Portland, a synopsis of which is available at tinyurl.com/76u98g6.

32. "Portland Streetcar Development Oriented Transit," Office of Transportation and Portland Streetcar Inc., Portland, OR, 2008, p. 1, tinyurl.com/5tlqfbn.

33. John Charles, "TOD: A Solution in Search of a Problem," Cascade Policy Institute, Portland, OR, July 2003, p. 2, tinyurl.com/yo87vs.

34. Jennifer Lang, "New Urban Renewal in Colorado's Front Range," Issue Paper no. 2-2007, Independence Institute, Golden, CO, 2007, pp. 11–12, tinyurl.com/3uq2w5x.

35. "Stapleton Fact Sheet," Denver Urban Renewal Authority, Denver, CO, 2002, tinyurl.com/26kbv2t.

36. Naomi Zeveloff, "Affordable Housing a Tough Sell in Stapleton," *Denver Westword News*, November 8, 2007, tinyurl.com/324ox8s.

37. Andrew Webb, "Funding for Mesa Del Sol Debated," *Albuquerque Journal*, December 10, 2006; and "Tax Increment Development Districts (TIDDs) Information Memo," City of Albuquerque, 2008, p. 2, tinyurl.com/44lebrh.

38. Nancy Sarnoff and David Kaplan, "High-Density, Mixed-Use Trend Takes Root in Houston," *Houston Chronicle*, March 3, 2007, tinyurl.com/2dbb9yl.

39. John Charles and Michael Barton, *The Mythical World of Transit-Oriented Development: Light Rail and the Orenco Neighborhood* (Portland, OR: Cascade Policy Institute, 2003), tinyurl.com/2kh6s.

40. Bruce Podobnik, *Portland Neighborhood Survey Report on Findings from Zone 2: Orenco* (Portland, OR: Lewis and Clark College, 2002), p. 1.

41. Craig Johnson, "The Use of Debt in Tax Increment Financing," in *Tax Increment Financing and Economic Development: Uses, Structures, and Impact*, eds. Craig Johnson and Joyce Man (Albany, NY: SUNY Press, 2001), p. 74.

42. "TIF Bonds 2005 to 2010," Securities Data Corporation spreadsheet, 2011.

43. Dale Kasler, "Brown's Countdown, Day 1: Plan Takes on Powerful Redevelopment Forces," *Sacramento Bee*, January 10, 2011, p. 1A.

44. John Chiang, "Community Redevelopment Agencies Annual Report," California State Controller, Sacramento, December 31, 2010, p. 1, tinyurl.com/62q7exb.

45. John Diaz, "Jerry Brown's Audacity," *San Francisco Chronicle*, February 13, 2011, tinyurl.com/66bg6cb.

46. Ibid.

47. Jessica Garrison, "Cash to Fight Blight Paying City Salaries in California," *Los Angeles Times*, February 18, 2011, tinyurl.com/6ld7d62.

48. Shane Goldmacher, "Gov. Jerry Brown Signs Laws to Ax Redevelopment Agencies, Collect Taxes from Online Retailers," *Los Angeles Times*, June 29, 2011, tinyurl.com/3mutg8l.

49. Patrick McGreevy, "Suit Asks State Supreme Court to Overturn State Action Targeting Redevelopment Agencies," *Los Angeles Times*, July 19, 2011, tinyurl.com/5uwrywc.

50. Sam Adams, "From Here to Portland's Tomorrow" (speech to Portland City Club, Portland, OR, July 20, 2007).

Chapter 11

1. Note the distinction between *urbanized area*, which includes only developed land, and *metropolitan area*, which includes all the land in the counties of an urban area. When calculating densities, urbanized area data are essential, but when comparing economic trends, the small numbers of people in rural portions of metropolitan areas are not significant. As of this writing, the Census Bureau hasn't defined urbanized area boundaries for the 2010 census, so this discussion will use metropolitan area data for some comparisons.

2. 2009 American Community Survey, table B25077 for urbanized areas.

3. "2011 Home Price Comparison Index," Coldwell Banker, 2011, tinyurl.com/3dhksrr. Coldwell Banker does not keep previous years' data on line, but 2007 data can be downloaded from tinyurl.com/3wln7oh, and 2011 data can be downloaded from tinyurl.com/44xnkpj.

4. A search of realtor.com in November 2011 found more than 500 three-bedroom homes in Houston offered for $30,000 to $50,000 but just 8 two- to three-bedroom homes in the Oakland area—the lowest-cost portion of the San Francisco Bay Area—for less than $100,000.

5. Arthur C. Nelson et al., "The Link between Growth Management and Housing Affordability: The Academic Evidence," Brookings Institution, Washington, 2002, p. i, tinyurl.com/3fn4j92.

6. The six counties in the Houston primary metropolitan area, as defined at the time of the 2000 census, include Chambers, Fort Bend, Harris, Liberty, Montgomery, and Waller.

7. Nicole Gelinas, "Houston's Noble Experiment," *City Journal*, Spring 2006, tinyurl.com/g8pwq.

8. "Housing Units Authorized by Building Permits: Table 3. Metropolitan Areas," Census Bureau, Washington, D. C., 2011, tinyurl.com/79af2bs.

9. The six counties in the San Francisco, Oakland, and San Jose primary metropolitan areas at the time of the 2000 census include Alameda, Contra Costa, Marin, San Francisco, San Mateo, and Santa Clara.

10. "House Price Indexes for Metropolitan Statistical Areas and Divisions through 2011Q2 (Not Seasonally Adjusted)," Federal Housing Finance Agency, Washington, D. C., 2011, tinyurl.com/3ch7oue.

11. "Housing Units Authorized by Building Permits: Table 3. Metropolitan Areas."

12. Scott Adams, "The Economy Again," *The Dilbert Blog*, March 4, 2009, tinyurl.com/cg2rzu.

13. Eric Freyfogle, *The Land We Share: Private Property and the Common Good* (Washington, D. C.: Island Press, 2003), p. 219.

14. "Oregon's Statewide Planning Goals and Guidelines—Goal 1: Citizen Involvement," Department of Land Conservation and Development, Salem, 2010, tinyurl.com/5shpa46.

15. *Village of Euclid, Ohio v. Ambler Realty Co.*, 272 U.S. 365 (1926).

16. *Penn Central Transportation Co. v. New York City*, 438 U.S. 104 (1978).

17. Margot Adler, "Behind the Ever-Expanding American Dream House," NPR, July 4, 2006, tinyurl.com/324x69.

18. David E. Dowall, *The Suburban Squeeze: Land Conservation and Regulation in the San Francisco Bay Area* (Berkeley: University of California Press, 1984), pp. 141–42.

19. Tracey Kaplan and Sue McAllister, "Cost of Land Drives Home Prices," *San Jose Mercury News*, August 4, 2002.

20. Bill Eisenstein and Elizabeth Stampe, *At Risk: The Bay Area Greenbelt* (San Francisco: Greenbelt Alliance, 2006), p. 4.

21. Jonathan Brinckman, "Arbor Homes Dominate as Urban-Growth Limits Keep National Developers at Bay," *Oregonian*, September 1, 2005.

22. Edward L. Glaeser and Joseph Gyourko, *The Impact of Zoning on Housing Affordability* (Cambridge, MA: Harvard Institute of Economic Research, 2002), p. 3.

23. G. Donald Jud and Daniel T. Winkler, "The Dynamics of Metropolitan Housing Prices," *Journal of Real Estate Research* 23 (January–February 2002): 29–45.

24. C. Tsuriel Somerville and Christopher J. Mayer, "Government Regulation and Changes in the Affordable Housing Stock," *FRBNY Economic Policy Review*, June 2003, p. 53.

25. Christopher J. Mayer and C. Tsuriel Somerville, "Land Use Regulation and New Construction," *Regional and Urban Economics* 30, no. 6 (December 2000): 639.

26. Raven E. Saks, "Job Creation and Housing Construction: Constraints on Employment Growth in Metropolitan Areas," Working Paper no. W04-10, Harvard University Joint Center for Housing Studies, Cambridge, MA, December 2004, p. iv.

27. Henry O. Pollakowski and Susan M. Wachter, "The Effects of Land-Use Constraints on Housing Prices," *Land Economics* 66, no. 3 (August 1990): 323.

28. John M. Quigley, Steven Raphael, and Larry A. Rosenthal, "Measuring Land-Use Regulations and Their Effects in the Housing Market," in *Housing Markets and the Economy: Risk, Regulation, and Policy*, eds. Edward L. Glaeser and John M. Quigley (Cambridge, MA: Lincoln Institute, 2009), p. 296.

29. Theo S. Eicher, "Municipal and Statewide Land Use Regulations and Housing Prices across 250 Major US Cities," working paper, University of Washington, Seattle, 2008, tinyurl.com/2fw44e.

30. Theo S. Eicher, "Growth Management, Land Use Regulations, and Housing Prices: Implications for Major Cities in Washington State," working paper, University of Washington, Seattle, 2008, tinyurl.com/3ol4u5k.

31. Tom Means, Edward Stringham, and Edward Lopez, "Below-Market Housing Mandates as Takings: Measuring Their Impact," policy report, Independent Institute, Oakland, CA, November 2007, p. 15, tinyurl.com/6rnugn.

32. Stephen Malpezzi and Richard Green, "What Has Happened to the Bottom of the US Housing Market?" *Urban Studies* 33, no. 10 (December 1996): 1807.

33. John M. Quigley and Steven Raphael, "Why Is Housing Unaffordable? Why Isn't It More Affordable?" *Journal of Economic Perspectives* 18, no. 1 (2004): 205 (emphasis in original).

34. Matthew E. Kahn, "Does Sprawl Reduce the Black/White Housing Consumption Gap?" *Housing Policy Debate* 12, no. 1 (2001): 77, tinyurl.com/3emjwhk.

35. 2010 American Community Survey, Census Bureau, Washington, D. C., 2011, tables B1101B and B2201H.

36. "The Black Alone Population in the United States: 2010," Census Bureau, Washington, D. C., 2011, table 15, tinyurl.com/836eb53.

37. 2010 American Community Survey, Census Bureau, Washington, D. C., 2011, tables B25003D and B25003I.

38. Isabel V. Sawhill and Daniel P. Mcmurrer, "Declining Economic Opportunity in America," Urban Institute, Washington, D. C., 1996, p. 1, tinyurl.com/75lmlaa.

39. Anna Cristina d'Addio, "Intergenerational Transmission of Disadvantage: Mobility or Immobility across Generations? A Review of the Evidence for OECD Countries," Organization for Economic Cooperation and Development, Paris, 2007, p. 33,tinyurl.com/ytest4.

40. Dowell Myers and Seong Woo Lee, "Immigrant Trajectories into Homeownership: A Temporal Analysis of Residential Assimilation," *International Migration Review* 32, no. 3 (Autumn 1998): 593.

41. Tom Hertz, "Understanding Mobility in America," Center for Economic Progress, Chicago, 2006, p. i, tinyurl.com/yccmgxv.

42. Reid Cramer et al., "A Penny Saved Is Mobility Earned: Advancing Economic Mobility through Savings," Economic Mobility Project, Washington, D. C., 2009, p. 4, tinyurl.com/3asggnu.

43. Donald R. Haurin, "The Private and Social Benefits of Homeownership," Habitat for Humanity Lecture, December 11, 2003, pp. 11–13, ti.org/haurinshow.pdf.

44. Stuart M. Butler, William W. Beach, and Paul L. Winfree, "Pathways to Economic Mobility: Key Indicators," Economic Mobility Project, Washington, D. C., 2008, pp. 37–38, tinyurl.com/8945m6a.

45. Ron Haskins, "Wealth and Economic Mobility," in *Getting Ahead or Losing Ground: Economic Mobility in America*, eds. Julia B. Isaacs, Isabel V. Sawhill, and Ron Haskins (Washington, D. C.: Economic Mobility Project, 2008), p. 50, tinyurl.com/6nz2pmx.

46. Brian K. Bucks et al., "Changes in U.S. Family Finances from 2004 to 2007: Evidence from the Survey of Consumer Finances," *Federal Reserve Bulletin*, February 2009, p. A31, tinyurl.com/6d5vlud.

47. Yihua Liao, "Vehicle Ownership Patterns of American Households," Information Brief no. 10B-02, 2002, Urban Transportation Center, University of Illinois at Chicago, p. 3, tinyurl.com/863nq88.

48. Edward Glaeser, *The Triumph of the City: How Our Greatest Invention Makes Us Richer, Smarter, Greener, Healthier, and Happier* (New York: Penguin, 2011), p. 194.

49. Ibid.

50. Edward L. Glaeser and Jesse M. Shapiro, "The Benefits of the Home Mortgage Interest Deduction," *Tax Policy and the Economy* 17 (2003): 37.

51. Glaeser, *The Triumph of the City*, p. 195.

52. Ibid., p. 33.

53. Ryan Avent, *The Gated City: How America Has Made Its Most Productive Places Ever Less Accessible* (Seattle: Amazon, 2011), Kindle location 18.

54. Glaeser, *The Triumph of the City*, p. 150.

55. Ibid., pp. 34–37.

56. Avent, *The Gated City*, Kindle locations 270, 614.

57. Antonio Ciccone and Robert Hall, "Productivity and the Density of Economic Activity," *American Economic Review* 86, no. 1 (March 1996): 54.

58. Ibid., p. 60.

59. Frances Cairncross, *The Death of Distances: How the Communications Revolution is Changing Our Lives* (Cambridge, MA: Harvard Business School, 2001), pp. xiii–xvii.

60. Kris James Mitchener and Ian W. McLean, "The Productivity of US States since 1880," *Journal of Economic Growth* 8, no. 1 (March 2003): 99.

61. Richard Florida, *Who's Your City? How the Creative Economy Is Making Where to Live the Most Important Decision in Your Life* (New York: Basic Books, 2008), pp. 243–44.

62. Edward L. Glaeser, "Review of Richard Florida's *The Rise of the Creative Class*," 2004, p. 4, tinyurl.com/77qxtm5.

63. Wendell Cox, "Surprise: Higher Gas Prices, Data Shows More Solo Auto Commuting," NewGeography.com, October 17, 2011, tinyurl.com/6h63npf.

64. Joel Kotkin and Wendell Cox, "Cities and the Census," *City Journal*, April 6, 2011, tinyurl.com/3qlfds5.

65. See, for example, 1960 through 1990 density data for 46 cities in Asia, Australia, Europe, and North America in Jeffrey R. Kenworthy and Felix B. Laube, *An International Sourcebook of Automobile Dependence in Cities 1960–1990* (Boulder: University of Colorado, 1999).

66. "American Community Survey," Census Bureau, Washington, D. C., table P30 from 2000 and table B08301 from 2010.

Chapter 12

1. All references to home prices for the United States are based on "2nd Quarter 2011 Home Price Index Data for U.S. and Census Divisions (Not Seasonally Adjusted)," Federal Housing Finance Agency, Washington, D. C., 2011, downloadable from tinyurl.com/3ch7oue. Adjustments for inflation made using the "Current-Dollar and 'Real' Gross Domestic Product," Bureau of Economic Analysis, Washington, D. C., 2011, downloadable from tinyurl.com/ad629c.

2. Robert X. Cringely, "Greenspan's 'No Housing Bubble' Prediction, 5 Years Later," *AOL Real Estate*, June 11, 2010, tinyurl.com/5skqy2p.

3. Nell Henderson, "Bernanke: There's No Housing Bubble to Go Bust," *Washington Post*, October 27, 2005, tinyurl.com/85v9s.

4. Paul Krugman, "That Hissing Sound," *New York Times*, August 8, 2005, tinyurl.com/9lwmp.

5. David Henderson, "Don't Blame Greenspan," *Wall Street Journal*, March 26, 2009, tinyurl.com/ddjhvc.

6. Judy Shelton, "Loose Money and the Derivative Bubble," *Wall Street Journal*, March 26, 2009, tinyurl.com/ddjhvc.

7. Peter J. Wallison, "The True Origins of This Financial Crisis," *American Spectator*, February 2009, tinyurl.com/bzh64s.

8. Edward Glaeser, *The Economic Impact of Restricting Housing Supply* (Cambridge, MA: Rappaport Institute, 2006), p. 1, tinyurl.com/6rgnk2k.

9. Haifang Huang and Yao Tang, "Residential Land Use Regulation and the US Housing Price Cycle Between 2000 and 2009," working paper, University of Alberta, Edmonton, 2011, p. 1, tinyurl.com/3nzecs9.

10. Harvey Mansfield, "A Question for the Economists: Is the Overly Predicted Life Worth Living?" *Weekly Standard*, April 13, 2009, tinyurl.com/dkfuhz.

11. Pam Woodall, "House of Cards," *Economist*, May 29, 2003.

12. "The Global Housing Boom," *Economist*, June 16, 2005.

13. "After the Fall," *Economist*, June 16, 2005.

14. "Recession-Plagued Nation Demands New Bubble to Invest In," *Onion*, July 14, 2008, tinyurl.com/5jgfha.

15. Ronald R. King et al., "The Robustness of Bubbles and Crashes in Experimental Stock Markets," in *Nonlinear Dynamics and Evolutionary Economics*, eds. R. H. Day and P. Chen (Oxford: Oxford University Press, 1993).

16. Charles Kindleberger and Robert Aliber, *Manias, Panics, and Crashes: A History of Financial Crises*, 5th ed. (Hoboken, NJ: Wiley, 2005), pp. 25–33.

17. "Home Values," National Association of Realtors, Chicago, 2008.

18. *1970 Census of Housing—Volume 1. Housing Characteristics for States, Cities, and Counties, Part 1: United States Summary*, Table 17, Financial Characteristics for Areas and Places; *1970 Census of the Population—Volume 1. Characteristics of the Population, Part 1. United States Summary, Section 2*, Table 366, Median Income in 1969 of Families by Type of Family and Race of Head for Standard Metropolitan Statistical Areas of 250,000 or More, Census Bureau, Washington, D. C., 1972.

19. Hawaii State Land Use Law (Hawaii Revised Statutes, Chapter 205).

20. All references to home prices by state are based on "Home Price Indexes for States through 2011Q2 (Not Seasonally Adjusted)," Federal Housing Finance Agency, Washington, D. C., 2011, downloadable from tinyurl.com/3ch7oue.

21. "Housing Units Authorized by Building Permits: Table 2. States," Census Bureau, Washington, D. C., 2011, tinyurl.com/79af2bs.

22. "Housing Units Authorized by Building Permits: Table 3. Metropolitan Areas," Census Bureau, Washington, D. C., 2011, tinyurl.com/79af2bs.

23. "Metropolitan and Micropolitan Statistical Area Population and Estimated Components of Change: April 1, 2000 to July 1, 2007," Census Bureau, Washington, D. C., 2008, tinyurl.com/8xc4qr5.

24. References to home prices in nonmetropolitan areas are based on "Home Price Indexes for State Nonmetropolitan Areas through 2011Q2 (Not

Seasonally Adjusted)," Federal Housing Finance Agency, Washington, D. C., 2011, downloadable from tinyurl.com/3ch7oue.

25. "Foreclosure Activity Decreases 10 Percent in January," Realtytrac.com, 2009, tinyurl.com/89fuddq.

Chapter 13

1. Joseph Stiglitz, *Freefall: America, Free Markets, and the Sinking of the World Economy* (New York: Norton, 2010), pp. 1–2.

2. Ibid., p. 2.

3. Jeffrey Friedman, "Capitalism and the Crisis: Bankers, Bonuses, Ideology, and Ignorance," in *What Caused the Financial Crisis?* (Philadelphia: University of Pennsylvania Press, 2011), pp. 16–17.

4. One popular book that has blamed the bubble on growth-management planning is Thomas Sowell, *The Housing Boom and Bust* (New York: Basic Books, 2009).

5. Edward Chancellor, *Devil Take the Hindmost: A History of Financial Speculation* (New York: Penguin, 2000), p. 18.

6. Karl E. Case, Robert J. Shiller, and John M. Quigley, "Comparing Wealth Effects: The Stock Market versus the Housing Market," *Advances in Macroeconomics* 5, no. 1 (January 2005): 27.

7. Quoted in "Homeownership and Its Benefits," Urban Policy Brief no. 2, Department of Housing and Urban Development, Washington, D. C., August, 1995, tinyurl.com/5bta7k.

8. Peter J. Wallison, "Cause and Effect: Government Policies and the Financial Crisis," American Enterprise Institute, Washington, D. C., 2008, p. 5.

9. Anna J. Schwartz, "Origins of the Financial Market Crisis of 2008," *Cato Journal* 29, no. 1 (Winter 2009): 20.

10. Charles Calomiris, "The Mortgage Crisis: Some Inside Views," *Wall Street Journal*, October 27, 2011, tinyurl.com/3w8c8gg.

11. "State Limits on Deficiency Judgments," ForeclosureFish.com, February 25, 2010, tinyurl.com/62nw9nx.

12. Friedman, "Capitalism and the Crisis," p. 4.

13. Ibid., pp. 13–14.

14. Roger Lowenstein, *The End of Wall Street* (New York: Penguin, 2010), pp. 39–40 (emphasis in original).

15. Friedman, "Capitalism and the Crisis," pp. 21–22, 26.

16. Michael Lewis, *The Big Short: Inside the Doomsday Machine* (New York: Norton, 2010), p. 254.

17. Ibid., pp. 99–100.

18. James Grant, *Mr. Market Miscalculates: The Bubble Years and Beyond* (Mt. Jackson, VA: Axios Press, 2008), pp. 182–83.

19. Anna Katherine Barnett-Hart, "The Story of the CDO Market Meltdown: An Empirical Analysis," Harvard Department of Economics, Cambridge, MA, 2009, pp. 4, 17, 21, tinyurl.com/ygspe7o.

20. Donald MacKenzie, "The Credit Crisis as a Problem in the Sociology of Knowledge," *American Journal of Sociology* 116, no. 6 (May 2011): 1813.

21. Lowenstein, *The End of Wall Street*, p. 44.

22. Gregory Zuckerman, *The Greatest Trade Ever: The Behind-the-Scenes Story of How John Paulson Defied Wall Street and Made Financial History* (New York: Broadway Books, 2009), pp. 100–101.

23. Gillian Tett, *Fool's Gold: How the Bold Dream of a Small Tribe at J. P. Morgan Was Corrupted by Wall Street Greed and Unleashed a Catastrophe* (New York: Simon & Schuster, 2009), pp. 53–54.

24. Zuckerman, *The Greatest Trade Ever*, pp. 119, 170.

25. Lewis, *The Big Short*, p. xviii.

26. Mark Adelson, "Bond Rating Confusion," Nomura, New York, 2006, tinyurl.com/6xo4243.

27. Donald MacKenzie shows actual default rates in table 1 of "The Credit Crisis as a Problem in the Sociology of Knowledge," p. 1821. MacKenzie's listing of expected default rates is based on an older version of Adelson, "Bond Rating Confusion."

28. Lewis, *The Big Short*, p. 51.

29. Barnett-Hart, "The Story of the CDO Market Meltdown," pp. 23–24.

30. Tett, *Fool's Gold*, pp. 173, 199–200.

31. Barnett-Hart, "The Story of the CDO Market Meltdown," p. 3.

32. William D. Cohan, *House of Cards: A Tale of Hubris and Wretched Excess on Wall Street* (New York: Doubleday, 2009), pp. 4–7.

33. Ibid., pp. 75–79.

34. Lewis, *The Big Short*, p. 86.

35. Zuckerman, *The Greatest Trade Ever*, p. 233.

36. Lowenstein, *The End of Wall Street*, p. 122.

37. Andrew Ross Sorkin, *Too Big to Fail: The Inside Story of How Wall Street and Washington Fought to Save the Financial System—and Themselves* (New York: Viking, 2009), pp. 226–27.

38. Lewis, *The Big Short*, pp. 237, 259.

39. Ibid., p. 244.

40. Sorkin, *Too Big to Fail*, pp. 525–27.

41. See, for example, Lewis, *The Big Short*, p. 100.

42. "Global Financial Stability Report: Containing Systemic Risks and Restoring Financial Soundness," International Monetary Fund, Washington, D. C., 2008, p. 5.

43. Barnett-Hart, "The Story of the CDO Market Meltdown," pp. 9, 16.

44. Stan Liebowitz, "New Evidence on the Foreclosure Crisis: Zero Money Down, Not Subprime Loans, Led to the Mortgage Meltdown," *Wall Street Journal*, July 3, 2009, tinyurl.com/mvr6mz.

45. Christopher L. Foote et al., "Just the Facts: An Initial Analysis of Subprime's Role in the Housing Crisis," *Journal of Housing Economics* 17 (2008): 292, 303, 305.

46. Gene Amromin et al., "Complex Mortgages," Working Paper no. 2010-17, Federal Reserve Bank of Chicago, November 24, 2010, pp. iii, 4, 34–35, 38, tinyurl.com/3p2x6ha.

47. Interview with developers at the Home Builders Association of Central Arizona, May 5, 2010.

48. Sorkin, *Too Big to Fail*, p. 506.

49. Tett, *Fool's Gold*, pp. 97–98.

50. Zuckerman, *The Greatest Trade Ever*, pp. 175–76.

51. Jagadeesh Gokhale and Peter Van Doren, "Would a Stricter Fed Policy and Financial Regulation Have Averted the Financial Crisis?" Cato Institute Policy Analysis no. 648, Washington, D. C., October 8, 2009, p. 1.

52. Edward L. Glaeser, Joshua D. Gottlieb, and Joseph Gyourko, "Can Cheap Credit Explain the Housing Boom?" Working Paper no. 16230, National Bureau of Economic Research, Washington, D. C., July 2010, p. i, tinyurl.com/3hzywtr.

53. Sorkin, *Too Big to Fail*, p. 176.

54. Ibid., p. 393.

Chapter 14

1. "The Great Australian Dream: Just a Dream?" AMP Financial Services, 2011, p. 2, tinyurl.com/cannxft.

2. Maryan Street, MP, "Home Ownership: Protecting the Kiwi Dream" (speech to Nelson Chamber of Commerce, Nelson, NZ, February 20, 2008), tinyurl.com/65cjz9q.

3. Steven C. Bourassa and Martin Hoesli, "Why Do the Swiss Rent?" Centre de Recherche de Bordeaux Ecole de Management, Bordeaux, 2007, p. 3, tinyurl.com/6kwav5j.

4. Soula Proxenos, "Homeownership Rates: A Global Perspective," *Housing Finance International* 17, no. 3 (December 2002): 3, tinyurl.com/ 67h75r4; and "Hypostat 2009: A Review of Europe's Mortgage and Housing Markets," European Mortgage Federation, Brussels, 2010, p. 73.

5. "Social Indicators: Average Number of Persons per Room," United Nations Statistics Division, New York, 2011, tinyurl.com/ecab9.

6. Christine Hanneman, "Architecture as Ideology: Industrialization of Housing in the GDR," Working Paper no. 2A, Institut für Sozialwissenschaften, Berlin, 2004, p. 6, tinyurl.com/5uvkhdb.

7. Marianne Fay and Anna Wellenstein, "Keeping a Roof over One's Head: Improving Access to Safe and Decent Shelter," in *The Urban Poor in Latin America*, ed. Marianne Fay (Washington, D. C.: World Bank, 2005), p. 98.

8. Hua Chang-i, "Home Ownership Rate Is Misleading," *Taipei Times*, April 14, 2010, tinyurl.com/6cofdan.

9. Mark Duda, Xiulan Zhang, and Mingzhu Dong, "China's Homeownership-Oriented Housing Policy: An Examination of Two Programs Using

Survey Data from Beijing," Working Paper no. W05-7, Harvard University Joint Center for Housing Studies, Cambridge, MA, July 2005, p. 11, tinyurl.com/7d9stsw.

10. Lynn M. Fisher and Austin J. Jaffe, "Determinants of International Home Ownership Rates," *Housing Finance International* 18, no. 1 (September 2003): 39; and "Cambodia" and "Switzerland," *The World Factbook* (Washington, D. C.: Central Intelligence Agency, 1996), tinyurl.com/6fua2yr.

11. Fisher and Jaffe, "Determinants of International Home Ownership Rates," pp. 34–35.

12. Clare O'Dea, "Swiss Home Ownership Increases Steadily," Swiss-Info.ch, August 31, 2005, tinyurl.com/3ls7ldu.

13. "Hypostat 2009," p. 73.

14. Michael Oxley, "Owner Occupation in Various European Countries," in *Land Management: New Directions—Proceedings of the Land Management Research Conference Held at Leicester Polytechnic, 15–17 September 1983*, eds. D. Chiddick and A. Millington (Cambridge: Cambridge University Press, 1984).

15. "Compendium of Human Settlements Statistics 1995," United Nations, New York, 1995, table 17, tinyurl.com/6hwrr95.

16. "Urbanization," *The World Factbook* (Washington, D. C.: Central Intelligence Agency, 2011), tinyurl.com/3uwoxly.

17. Herman M. Schwartz and Leonard Seabrooke, "Varieties of Residential Capitalism in the International Political Economy: Old Welfare States and the New Politics of Housing," in *The Politics of Housing Booms and Busts*, eds. Herman M. Schwartz and Leonard Seabrooke (New York: Palgrave MacMillan, 2009), p. 19.

18. *Mortgage Banks and the Mortgage Bond in Europe*, 4th ed. (Brussels: European Mortgage Federation, 2003), pp. 15, 131.

19. Fabrizio Bernardi and Teresio Poggio, "Home-Ownership and Social Inequality in Italy," in *Home Ownership and Social Inequality in Comparative Perspective*, eds. Karin Kurz and Hans Peter Blossfeld (Palo Alto, CA: Stanford University Press, 2004), p. 192.

20. "Italian Mortgage Information," LiguriaGuide.com, 2011, tinyurl.com/3uk25ay.

21. Schwartz and Seabrooke, "Varieties of Residential Capitalism in the International Political Economy," pp. 16–17.

22. Ibid., pp. 8, 16–17.

23. Ivan Tosics, "The Mass Give-Away: Lessons Learnt from the Privatization of Housing in Central and Eastern Europe," *Eurocities Magazine*, no. 14 (Autumn 2001): 15, tinyurl.com/63j4n8o.

24. Jósef Hegedüs and Nóra Teller, "Security and Insecurity Aspects of Home Ownership in Hungary: Interaction of Preconditions and Motivations" (paper presented at "Home Ownership in Europe: Policy and Research Issues" conference, Delft, the Netherlands, November 23–24, 2006), p. 2, tinyurl.com/6f2noto.

25. Sharon Smyth and Jim Silver, "Portugal's Towns Crumble and Century-Old Rent Controls Strangle Investment," Bloomberg, February 2, 2011, tinyurl.com/4jjcxoq.

26. Richard Arnott, "Time for Revisionism on Rent Control?" *Journal of Economic Perspectives* 9, no. 1 (Winter 1995): 102.

27. Jon Palmer, "Brits Buy Homes, the Germans Rent—Which of Us Has Got It Right?" *Guardian*, March 18, 2011, tinyurl.com/6x4mtql; and Julia Kollewe and Larry Elliott, "Home Sweet Home Is a Rented Property for Many Germans," *Guardian*, March 16, 2011, tinyurl.com/6frslsf.

28. Marietta Haffner, Maria Elsiga, and Joris Hoekstra, "Balance between Landlord and Tenant? A Comparison of the Rent Regulation in the Private Rental Sector of Five Countries" (paper presented at the Sustainable Urban Areas International Conference, Rotterdam, June 26, 2007), p. 11, tinyurl.com/3uxbjz6.

29. Schwartz and Seabrooke, "Varieties of Residential Capitalism in the International Political Economy," p. 9.

30. Teresio Poggio, "Different Patterns of Home Ownership in Europe" (paper presented at "Home Ownership in Europe: Policy and Research Issues" conference, Delft, the Netherlands, November 23–24, 2006), p. 7, tinyurl.com/66mf7bo.

31. Ibid., p. 9.

32. Fionnuala Earley, "What Explains the Differences in Homeownership Rates in Europe?" *Housing Finance International* 19, no. 1 (September 2004): 27, tinyurl.com/38xpyzq.

33. Bernardi and Poggio, "Home-Ownership and Social Inequality in Italy," p. 189.

34. Poggio, "Different Patterns of Home Ownership in Europe," p. 2; and Schwartz and Seabrooke, "Varieties of Residential Capitalism in the International Political Economy," p. 9.

35. Poggio, "Different Patterns of Home Ownership in Europe," pp. 7–8.

36. *Rerum Novarum* on Capital and Labor, Encyclical of Pope Leo XIII, May 15, 1891, tinyurl.com/4xs74y.

37. Holger Bonin et al., "Geographic Mobility in the European Union: Optimising Its Economic and Social Benefits," Research Report no. 19, Institute for the Study of Labor (IZA), Bonn, July 2008, p. 4.

38. Michael Lea, "International Comparison of Mortgage Product Offerings," Research Institute for Housing America, Washington, D. C., 2010, p. 14, tinyurl.com/3eq557j.

39. "About CMHC," Canada Mortgage and Housing Corporation, 2011, tinyurl.com/4x6ugmy; and "Corporate Overview," Korea Housing Finance Corporation, 2011, tinyurl.com/3wpghms.

40. "NHG: The Safest Way to the Most Affordable Mortgage," Nationale Hyptheek Garantie, Zoetermeer, the Netherlands, 2011, tinyurl.com/423kds9.

41. "FAQs about MBS," Japan Housing Finance Agency, Tokyo, 2011, tinyurl.com/3epbnkf.

42. Charlotte West, "Getting a Swedish Mortgage," *The Local*, March 21, 2007, tinyurl.com/3w3dp8r.

43. Michael Lea and Anthony B. Sanders, "The Future of Fannie Mae and Freddie Mac," Working Paper no. 11-06, Mercatus Center, Arlington, VA, March 2011, p. 2.

44. Manuel B. Aalbers, "Residential Capitalism in Italy and the Netherlands," in Schwartz and Seabrooke, *The Politics of Housing Booms and Busts*, pp. 149–150.

45. Richard Goode, "Imputed Rent of Owner-Occupied Dwellings under the Income Tax," *Journal of Finance* 15, no. 4 (December 1960): 504.

46. Bourassa and Hoesli "Why Do the Swiss Rent?" p. 32.

47. Dan Andrews, Aida Caldera Sánchez, and Åsa Johnson, "Housing Markets and Structural Policies in OECD Countries," Working Paper no. 836, OECD Economics Department, Paris, 2011, p. 39, tinyurl.com/6qfuu25; and John F. McDonald, "Tax Treatment of Residences: An International Comparison," *Illinois Real Estate Letter*, Winter–Spring 1994, p. 9, tinyurl.com/5wf4jxk.

48. Bourassa and Hoesli, "Why Do the Swiss Rent?" pp. 5, 23.

49. Bernardi and Poggio, "Home-Ownership and Social Inequality in Italy," pp. 189–90.

50. Thomas Sharp, *Town and Countryside: Some Aspects of Urban and Rural Development* (London: Oxford University Press, 1932), p. 11.

51. C. E. M. Joad, "The People's Claim," in *Britain and the Beast*, ed. Clough Williams-Ellis (London: J. M. Dent, 1937), pp. 72–73.

52. Peter Geoffrey Hall, *Cities of Tomorrow: An Intellectual History of Urban Planning and Design in the Twentieth Century* (Cambridge, MA: Blackwell, 2002 ed.), pp. 79–80.

53. Joad, "The People's Claim," pp. 79–82.

54. Thomas Sharp, *English Panorama* (London: Oxford University Press, 1936), p. 107.

55. Hall, *Cities of Tomorrow*, pp. 246–47.

56. Alexei Gutnov et al., *The Ideal Communist City* (New York: George Braziller, 1971), pp. 69–70, 76.

57. Jose Palacin and Robert C. Shelburne, "The Private Housing Market in Eastern Europe and the CIS," Discussion Paper no. 2005.5, United Nations Economic Commission for Europe, Geneva, 2005, p. 2.

58. Alain Bertaud, "Metropolis: A Measure of the Spatial Organization of 7 Large Cities," April 2001, p. 3, tinyurl.com/3vcycxw.

59. Karin Book and Lena Eskilsson, *Transport, Built Environment and Development Control: A Comparative Urban Study* (Lund, Sweden: Department of Social & Economic Geography, 1998), pp. 109–11.

60. Peter Hall, *Cities in Civilization* (New York: Pantheon Books, 1998), pp. 857, 863.

61. Ibid., pp. 872–75.

62. "Hypostat 2009," p. 73.

63. Hall, *Cities in Civilization*, p. 873.

64. Lars Astrand, "Country Report 2011: Sweden," Royal Institution of Chartered Surveyors, London, p. 1, tinyurl.com/5v6mscj.

65. Hall, *Cities in Civilization*, p. 879.

66. Hall, *Cities of Tomorrow*, p. 246.

67. Gerhard Larsson, *Spatial Planning Systems in Western Europe: An Overview* (Amsterdam: IOS Press, 2006), p. 160.

68. Wendell Cox, "7th Annual Demographia International Housing Affordability Survey: 2011," Demographia.com, 2011, pp. 3–4, demographia.com/dhi.pdf.

69. Randal O'Toole, "Unlivable Strategies: The Greater Vancouver Regional District and the Livable Region Strategic Plan," Public Policy Sources no. 88, Fraser Institute, Vancouver, BC, 2007, p. 11.

70. Cox, "Demographia International Housing Affordability Survey: 2011," p. 3.

71. Anna Rybkowska and Micha Schneider, "Housing Conditions in Europe in 2009," Eurostat, 2011, p. 7, tinyurl.com/4hmntdo.

72. Vincent Benard, "Land Use Regulations: Housing Unaffordability and Other Socially Undesirable Impacts in France" (presentation at the Preserving the American Dream conference, Bellevue, WA, April 18, 2009), tinyurl.com/d7qbsz.

73. Ibid.

74. Leith van Onselen, "Don't Forget New Zealand," *Unconventional Economist*, October 26, 2010, tinyurl.com/3tbt4tz.

75. Alan Moran, *The Tragedy of Planning: Losing the Great Australian Dream* (Melbourne: Institute of Public Affairs, 2006), pp. 4–5.

76. Owen McShane, "The Impact of the Resource Management Act on the 'Housing and Construction' Components of the Consumer Price Index," Reserve Bank of New Zealand, Wellington, 1996, pp. 4–5, tinyurl.com/3kkudhk.

77. Alan W. Evans and Oliver Marc Hartwich, *Unaffordable Housing: Fables and Myths* (London: Policy Exchange, 2005), p. 9, tinyurl.com/4xohme6.

78. "UK House Prices since 1952," Nationwide Building Society, London, 2011, tinyurl.com/3dxqax; prices adjusted for inflation using the UK GDP deflator from measuringworth.com.

79. "Hypostat 2009," p. 79.

80. "House Prices Worldwide: Italy," Global Property Guide, 2011, tinyurl.com/3b3rj8k; and "House Prices Worldwide: Switzerland," Global Property Guide, 2011, tinyurl.com/3uorhnv.

81. "Hypostat 2009," p. 79.

82. "House Prices Worldwide: Austria," Global Property Guide, 2011, tinyurl.com/3ddhvrj.

83. Leith van Onselen, "Sweden's Bubblicious Housing," Macrobusiness.com.au, June 23, 2011, tinyurl.com/3fp7k7a.

84. Leith van Onselen, "Dutch Show How Not to Run Housing Policy," Macrobusiness.com.au, June 30, 2011, tinyurl.com/4yl89by.

85. Jens Ledefoged Mortensen and Leonard Seabrooke, "Egalitarian Politics in Property Booms and Busts: Housing as a Social Right or Means to Wealth in Australia and Denmark," in Schwartz and Seabrooke, *The Politics of Housing Booms and Busts*, pp. 126–127.

86. "Portugal's Housing Market Weakens Further," Global Property Guide, August 27, 2011, tinyurl.com/6hlb4u2.

87. Artur Piers, "The Fragile Foundations of European Spatial Planning in Portugal," *European Planning Studies* 13, no. 2 (March 2005): 237–52.

88. Larsson, *Spatial Planning Systems in Western Europe*, p. 228.

89. "Germany's House Prices Up on Strong Economy, Rising Employment," Global Property Guide, November 4, 2010, tinyurl.com/3qykknu.

90. Palmer, "Brits Buy Homes; and Kollewe and Elliott, "Home Sweet Home."

91. Leith van Onselen, "How Germany Achieved Stable and Affordable Housing," Macrobusiness.com.au, June 22, 2011, tinyurl.com/3tlonf4.

92. Edward Chancellor, *Devil Take the Hindmost: A History of Financial Speculation* (New York: Penguin, 2000), p. 301.

93. James Doherty, "The Railway Policy Debate in Japan and Its Domination by Old Debt," *Journal of Transport Economics & Policy* 33, no. 1 (January 1999): 100.

94. Yoshitaka Fukui, "Twenty Years After," *Japan Railway & Transport Review* 49 (March 2008): 6.

95. Doherty, "The Railway Policy Debate in Japan," p. 103.

96. Chancellor, *Devil Take the Hindmost*, p. 293.

97. Andrew J. Oswald, "The Housing Market and Europe's Unemployment: A Non-Technical Paper," University of Warwick, UK, May 1999, p. 3, tinyurl.com/4xzwba4.

98. Richard K. Green and Patric H. Hendershott, "Home Ownership and the Duration of Unemployment: A Test of the Oswald Hypothesis," Center for Urban and Regional Analysis at Ohio State University, Columbus, August 2, 2001, p. 2, tinyurl.com/89aq4vq.

99. Bonin et al., "Geographic Mobility in the European Union," p. 4.

100. The 15 states are Arizona, California, Connecticut, Delaware, Florida, Hawaii, Maine, Maryland, Massachusetts, Nevada, New Jersey, Oregon, Rhode Island, Tennessee, and Washington.

Chapter 15

1. "Trulia Optimistic about Long-Term Housing Demand as 80 Percent of Homeowners Plan to Buy Again," Trulia.com, September 20, 2011, tinyurl.com/3j8jjlm.

2. "Fannie Mae Own-Rent Analysis: Key Findings," Fannie Mae, Washington, D. C., 2010, p. 2, tinyurl.com/3crt84s.

3. Robert Dietz and Natalia Siniaviskaia, "Who Benefits from the Housing Tax Deduction?" National Association of Home Builders, Washington, D. C., 2011, tinyurl.com/63pvgpt.

4. 2009 American Community Survey, Census Bureau, Washington, D. C., table B25077 for urbanized areas.

5. Richard K. Green and Kerry D. Vandell, "Giving Households Credit: How Changes in the Tax Code Could Promote Homeownership," Working Paper no. 96-10, Center for Urban Land Economic Research, University of Wisconsin, Madison, 1996, pp. 25–26.

6. Robert Kuttner, "Nationalize Fannie Mae? It Worked until It Was Privatized," *Huffington Post*, September 9, 2008, tinyurl.com/3b73x2d.

7. Edward L. Glaeser and Joseph Gyourko, *Rethinking Federal Housing Policy: How to Make Housing Plentiful and Affordable* (Washington, D. C.: American Enterprise Institute, 2008), p. xv.

8. 2009 American Community Survey, Census Bureau, Washington, D. C., 2011, table B25081 for United States; and "The Federal Housing Administration," Department of Housing and Urban Development, Washington, D. C., 2011, tinyurl.com/3d82rxz.

9. Raghuram Rajan, "Cycle-Proof Regulation," *Economist*, April 8, 2009, tinyurl.com/3ps3zku.

10. Glaeser and Gyourko, *Rethinking Federal Housing Policy*, p. 127.

11. Valeir J. Hubbard, "Florida's New 'Community Planning Act,'" Legal Update Extra, August 24, 2011, tinyurl.com/6fe7nhd; and Wendell Cox, "Florida Repeals Smart Growth Law," NewGeography, October 7, 2011, tinyurl.com/43u6f5g.

12. Robert Nelson, "Privatizing the Neighborhood: A Proposal to Replace Zoning with Private Collective Property Rights to Existing Neighborhoods," *George Mason Law Review* 7, no. 4 (Summer 1999): 827–80.

13. "2010 Buildings Energy Data Book," U.S. Department of Energy, Washington, D. C., 2010, p. 2–20, tinyurl.com/5urbnr4.

14. 2010 American Community Survey, Census Bureau, Washington, D. C., 2011, table B25003H.

15. 2010 American Community Survey, Census Bureau, Washington, D. C., 2011, table B25003B.

Index

About the Author

Randal O'Toole is a senior fellow at the Cato Institute who has written four previous books and numerous papers on transportation, urban growth, and public land issues, including his most recent books, *The Best-Laid Plans: How Government Planning Harms Your Quality of Life, Your Pocketbook, and Your Future* and *Gridlock: Why We're Stuck in Traffic and What to Do about It*. Described by *U.S. News and World Report* as a researcher who "has earned a reputation for dogged legwork and sophisticated number crunching," he has been a leader in innovative thinking on environmentalism, natural resources, and urban land use. From 1975 through 1995, O'Toole helped the nation's leading environmental groups eliminate government subsidies that were harmful to the environment. In 1998, Yale University named O'Toole its McCluskey Conservation Fellow. He was the Scaife Visiting Scholar at UC Berkeley in 1999 and 2001 and the Merrill Visiting Professor at Utah State University in 2000. In 2003, he helped form the American Dream Coalition, which is a grassroots group that promotes free-market solutions to urban problems. An Oregon native, O'Toole currently resides in Camp Sherman, Oregon.

Cato Institute

Founded in 1977, the Cato Institute is a public policy research foundation dedicated to broadening the parameters of policy debate to allow consideration of more options that are consistent with the traditional American principles of limited government, individual liberty, and peace. To that end, the Institute strives to achieve greater involvement of the intelligent, concerned lay public in questions of policy and the proper role of government.

The Institute is named for *Cato's Letters*, libertarian pamphlets that were widely read in the American Colonies in the early 18th century and played a major role in laying the philosophical foundation for the American Revolution.

Despite the achievement of the nation's Founders, today virtually no aspect of life is free from government encroachment. A pervasive intolerance for individual rights is shown by government's arbitrary intrusions into private economic transactions and its disregard for civil liberties.

To counter that trend, the Cato Institute undertakes an extensive publications program that addresses the complete spectrum of policy issues. Books, monographs, and shorter studies are commissioned to examine the federal budget, Social Security, regulation, military spending, international trade, and myriad other issues. Major policy conferences are held throughout the year, from which papers are published thrice yearly in the *Cato Journal*. The Institute also publishes the quarterly magazine *Regulation*.

In order to maintain its independence, the Cato Institute accepts no government funding. Contributions are received from foundations, corporations, and individuals, and other revenue is generated from the sale of publications. The Institute is a nonprofit, tax-exempt, educational foundation under Section 501(c)3 of the Internal Revenue Code.

CATO INSTITUTE
1000 Massachusetts Ave., N.W.
Washington, D.C. 20001
www.cato.org